OPERATING SYSTEMS
Communicating with and
Controlling the Computer

In loving memory
of Courtland G. Smith,
my father,
who instilled in me
the confidence to try.

OPERATING SYSTEMS
Communicating with and Controlling the Computer

LAURIE S. KELLER

The Open University, Milton Keynes, UK

PRENTICE HALL

New York • London • Toronto • Sydney • Tokyo

First published 1988 by
Prentice Hall International (UK) Ltd,
66 Wood Lane End, Hemel Hempstead,
Hertfordshire, HP2 4RG
A division of
Simon & Schuster International Group

© **1988 Prentice Hall International (UK) Ltd**

All rights reserved. No part of this publication may be reproduced, stored in a retrieval system, or transmitted, in any form or by any means, electronic, mechanical, photocopying, recording or otherwise, without the prior permission, in writing, from the publisher.
For permission within the United States of America contact Prentice Hall Inc., Englewood Cliffs, NJ 07632.

Printed and bound in Great Britain by
BPCC Wheatons Ltd, Exeter

Library of Congress Cataloging-in-Publication Data

Keller, Laurie S.
 Operating systems: communicating with and controlling the computer / by Laurie S. Keller.

 Includes index.
 ISBN 0-13-638040-9
 1. Operating systems (Computers)   I. Title.
 QA76.76.063K45 1988   005.4'3--dc19   87-25815

British Library Cataloguing in Publication Data

Keller, Laurie S.
 Operating systems: communicating with and controlling the computer.
 1. Operating systems (Computers)
 I. Title
 005.4'3   QA76.76.063

 ISBN 0-13-638040-9
 ISBN 0-13-638032-8 Pbk

4   5   92

ISBN 0-13-638040-9
ISBN 0-13-638032-8 PBK

Contents

Preface ix
Acknowledgements xiii
Trademarks xiv

PART I FUNDAMENTALS OF OPERATING SYSTEMS 1

1 A model of the computer system 3

    1.1   The computer and its operation 7
    1.2   The basic computer 11
    1.3   Early systems software 14
    1.4   Substantial steps forward 16
    1.5   Data in early systems 19

2 Systems software and early operating systems 24

    2.1   Models for sharing work cooperatively 25
    2.2   Simple operating systems 33
    2.3   Improving system utilization 38
    2.4   Basic auxiliary storage management 41
    2.5   File management: organization and access 43

3 Multiprogramming systems 48

    3.1   Changing concepts in operating-systems design 48
    3.2   Cooperative working 52
    3.3   Sharing space 58
    3.4   Concurrency concepts 67
    3.5   Data in multiprogramming systems 76
    3.6   Multiprogramming: contention, conflict and fairness 79
    3.7   Scheduling in multiprogramming systems 85
    3.8   Protection and integrity 88
    3.9   Performance monitoring and accounting 91
    3.10 Summary 93

4 Virtual storage systems 96

- 4.1 Performance and virtual systems 97
- 4.2 Concepts of virtual storage 100
- 4.3 Implementing virtual systems 105
- 4.4 Managing virtual storage 115
- 4.5 System uses 117
- 4.6 Summary 119

5 Multicomputer and multiprocessor systems 122

- 5.1 Definitions and classifications 124
- 5.2 Principles of multiprocessor and multicomputer systems 131
- 5.3 Multiprocessing operating systems 136
- 5.4 Multiprocessing system performance 140
- 5.5 Network and distributed systems 143
- 5.6 Summary 147

6 A brief look into the future 149

PART II CASE STUDIES 155

7 CP/M: a microcomputer operating system (by Gordon Davies) 157

- 7.1 Structure 157
- 7.2 Storage allocation 159
- 7.3 File organization 161
- 7.4 Device mapping 164
- 7.5 Portability 165
- 7.6 MP/M 165
- 7.7 CP/Net 167

8 MS-DOS and PC-DOS 170

- 8.1 Structure 171
- 8.2 Storage allocation 172
- 8.3 File organization 174
- 8.4 Portability 177

9 The p-System (by Mark Woodman) 178

- 9.1 The universal operating system? 178
- 9.2 A brief history 179
- 9.3 Using menu-driven commands 181
- 9.4 The file system 186
- 9.5 Architecture of the p-machine 190
- 9.6 P-code program execution 193

Contents

9.7	The p-machine emulator 196
9.8	Overcoming weaknesses and restrictions 198
9.9	p-System components 200
9.10	Device independence 201
9.11	Networking the p-System 202
9.12	Variations on a theme 208
9.13	Summary 209

10 Unix (by Gordon Davies) 211

10.1	The shell command language 212
10.2	Files on Unix 215
10.3	Implementation of the file system 220
10.4	Shell programming 226
10.5	The Unix kernel 228
10.6	Primary storage 236
10.7	Communication between processes 237
10.8	An evaluation of Unix 238

11 TPF/II: a high-performance system 246

11.1	History of TPF/II 248
11.2	Functional requirements 249
11.3	Meeting system requirements 252
11.4	What about support functions? 269
11.5	Cohabitation and the hypervisor 271
11.6	Case study conclusions 273

12 Virtual Machine/SP: an operating system 276

12.1	Requirements 276
12.2	Overview of VM/SP 278
12.3	The virtual machine 280
12.4	Managing virtual resources 283
12.5	Managing virtual I/O 292
12.6	The user's view 295
12.7	Communication between virtual machines 296
12.8	Case study conclusions 300

13 OS/VS2 MVS 304

13.1	Functional requirements 306
13.2	The computer system MVS controls 310
13.3	The supervisor 312
13.4	The master scheduler 317
13.5	Data management 318
13.6	Interactive system use – TSO 320
13.7	Miscellaneous system elements 321
13.8	Job entry 323

13.9 Error recovery 329
13.10 System integrity 331

14 General conclusions 335

Glossary 338
Index 359

Preface

The material for this book was originally gathered and written in a different form as the operating systems' half of a module, *PMT601: Computer Architectures and Operating Systems*, from the Open University's postgraduate course in the *Industrial Applications of Computers*.

I would like to thank the people who had a hand in producing it: Gordon Davies, who wrote the original versions of the CP/M and Unix case studies (Chapters 7 and 10) and Mark Woodman, who wrote the p-System case study (Chapter 9). Their work remains substantially as they wrote it. I would also like to thank Jonathan Blandon of Geophysical Service International (who is also my husband) for the benefit of his experiences as 'systems man' on the older IBM/360 systems and MS-DOS, Mike Cowlishaw of the IBM (UK) Scientific Centre at Winchester who took the time to read and comment on the material on VM and to demonstrate to me the latest bells and whistles, Geoff Gardiner of PA Technology (Cambridge) who had a hand in the computer architectures side of the original course and taught me a lot about array processors and multiprocessors, and Derrick Robinson of IBM (UK) Ltd who read the material on TPF/II.

Special thanks go to Prof. D.J. Howarth of Imperial College, University of London and Patricia Endacott — former boss and mentor — now friend and at Prime Computers (Europe) who read and commented on the original material.

ORGANIZATION AND ORIENTATION OF THE BOOK

This work is divided into two major parts. The first part describes the nature of and fundamental principles which govern operating systems. Part I answers the questions: what is an operating system and what does it do? Part II contains case studies of specific operating systems, ranging from the simple one-user microcomputer's operating system to the complex mainframe operating system. The range of case studies given is intended to impart a flavor of the variety of computing needs and how those needs are met by the different operating systems.

Though Part I is not a history of computing or of operating systems, I have chosen to approach this subject from an historical point of view for convenience of exposition. When reading the following material you will find that you can obtain the best understanding by keeping a framework, which I shall describe in a moment, in mind, and by using that framework as a kind of tool with which you should evaluate what you read.

I intend to use an historical perspective in viewing the development of computers and their operating systems (particularly the latter) for two reasons. This will show you the requirements which caused operating systems to develop in the first place and show how new computational needs and economic and technological factors then shaped their further development. As operating systems developed, they moved from simple to complex and at the same time increased the distance between the user of the computer and the computer itself. Yet this increased distance made the interface between that user and computer simpler for the user. To make use of an analogy, a pianist, to play the piano, need not learn about the science of acoustics unless, perhaps, he or she wishes to design a piano. (On the other hand, if the pianist wishes to learn acoustics to enhance his or her understanding and appreciation of music on another level, that is always possible!)

An historical perspective allows me to introduce fundamental concepts and then build on them in the same way that a basic concept gave rise to simple systems software upon which increasingly complex operating systems were designed and built.

WHY STUDY OPERATING SYSTEMS AT ALL?

It is the operating system which presents the 'face', the outward manifestation of the computer, to its user. The operating system also interprets the user's commands into actions. Therefore, it is the interface between the user and the hardware that makes up the computer system.

These days so-called *user-friendly* systems are widely available and are popularly supposed to obviate the need for the user to know much about the principles of the operating system. In this model of computer use, the user need know only some commands or recognize a few icons and some responses to error messages and the operating system will take care of the rest of the interface. However ideal this model may seem in the abstract, two things tend to be wrong with it. The first is that software designers have been arguing for over 40 years as to who or what a 'user' is. No set definition exists, so each designer makes assumptions about that 'user' and designs accordingly; thus a user may be someone with lots, little or no experience of computers. The degree of 'friendliness' a system manifests reflects this design decision. Secondly, knowing how a system works, what its functions are, how it is organized and what assumptions drive its design means that the user can make better use of the system's strengths and can avoid its pitfalls and weaknesses. The more the user knows, the more effective his or her use can be.

THE CASE STUDIES

Part I introduces the fundamental principles of operating systems and shows some of the techniques, methods and algorithms used by designers of operating systems to build a system which will meet *general* needs. In Part II, you will meet some popular, general-purpose operating systems in some detail. You will also meet something different − a special-purpose operating system.

First, I shall talk about an operating system which, on the one hand, is general-purpose, but on the other hand is specifically designed for a particular class of users who use a particular class of computer − users requiring general facilities on a microcomputer. This is CP/M. Then I shall compare CP/M to MS-DOS, another popular microcomputer system.

Secondly, I wish to bring up the issue of software portability including that of operating systems. In the past, the diversity of processors and configurations meant that there were severe limitations placed on portability of software. High-level languages exist in numerous dialects, which has meant that software writers have had to translate source programs from one dialect to another and recompile the result. Even languages designed according to national and international standards suffer from problems of portability due to the latitude allowed to manufacturers in many particulars.

The problem of recompiling to obtain a machine-code program suitable for a particular computer system remains. While Unix, discussed in Chapter 10, goes some way to addressing the problems of portability, it does this by requiring the presence of a C compiler which will produce the correct machine code for the computer system to be used. Again, it depends upon portable source code. The UCSD p-System described in Chapter 9 takes a rather different approach to portability. The high-level language used is Pascal, and the Pascal compiler generates 'object' code (called p-code) for a pseudo-machine. The p-System includes an emulator on which any p-code program can run, regardless of the underlying computer. Thus the p-code ('object') program is portable. The p-System is widely available for most popular 8-, 16-, and 32-bit machines.

Lastly, I shall discuss a highly specialized operating system, TPF/II, in order to show how that system modifies what a general-purpose computer can do in order to meet stringent requirements. This is accomplished by sacrificing function to performance. However, the need for certain functions does not vanish simply as a result of the need to meet high-performance criteria. Thus I shall introduce two other operating systems, VM and MVS, which are used in concert with the specialized system, as well as quite separately also, in order to meet all of an organization's needs.

In reading these case studies you should keep two things in mind.

The first is that you should be aware of *how* each of these operating systems meets certain needs and requirements, including economic needs and requirements.

The second is the comparisons and contrasts between these systems. Note how the computer itself and the organizational needs it has been obtained to address interact to *shape* the operating system.

L.S.K.

Acknowledgements

Grateful acknowledgement is made to the following sources for permission to use the material in this book:

Figure 5.9, R. Turn (1974), *Computers in the 1980s,* Columbia University Press
Figure 9.6, adapted from the *Liaison Operating System Reference Manual* (1984), SofTech Microsystems
Figure 9.7, *p-System Adaptable System Installation Manual,* Softech Microsystems
Figures 9.11–9.15, *Internal Architecture Reference Manual, p-System,* Softech Microsystems
Figure 10.4, adapted from P. Silvester (1984) *The UNIX System Guidebook,* Springer-Verlag
Figures 10.7–11 and 10.13, © K. Christian (1983) *The Unix Operating System,* reprinted by permission of John Wiley & Sons, Inc.
Figure 11.1 copyright 1985 International Business Machines Corporation, reprinted with permission from the *IBM Systems Journal,* **16**(2), 1977.

Trademarks

'p-System' and 'Liaison' are trademarks of SofTech Microsystems, Inc.

'UCSD' and 'UCSD Pascal' are trademarks of The Regents of the University of California.

'CP/M', 'MP/M', 'CP/NET' and 'CP/M-86' are trademarks of Digital Research.

'Unix' is a trademark of AT&T Bell Laboratories.

'MVS', 'TPF/II' and 'VM' are trademarks of International Business Machines Corporation.

'MS-DOS' is a trademark of MicroSoft Inc.

'PC-DOS' is a trademark of International Business Machines Corporation.

'CRAY-1' is a registered trademark of Cray Research, Inc.

PART I

FUNDAMENTALS OF OPERATING SYSTEMS

CHAPTER

1
A model of the computer system

Every digital computer system consists of several elements which are common to them all. These elements can be thought of as *resources* to be used to carry out work, such as: the **processor**, **storage** (also called **memory**), and **input** and **output devices**. These last two items enable communication with the operator — who may be the user (for example a clerk in a bank or a scientist using a model) or a specialist in computer operations. Input and output devices can also enable communication between the outside world and the computer system. For example, an input device may be a temperature sensor in a chemical reactor, and an output device may be an escape valve in the same chemical reactor, with the computer responsible for reading temperatures and operating the escape valve in response to excessive temperature buildup.

Data are also a necessary resource. Data come from the outside world, are manipulated within the computer in predefined ways and are, in their altered forms, again communicated to the outside world. They are the most valuable resource of a computing system, in a sense. Were there no data, there would be no need to have the computer system.

Lastly, there is the **process** itself — a task in the act of being accomplished, a **program** executing. The process acts upon data in order to do work.

All these elements must interact in a controlled way according to a predetermined policy about the work to be done. The policy is set by the individual or organization assembling the elements of a computing system together in order to accomplish work which that individual or organization considers important or vital. The **computer system** is, in many senses, the entire collection of the elements mentioned above considered as a whole.

Discussion of computer systems often assumes to some extent that the computer operator, the computer user, the computer manager and

4   Fundamentals of Operating Systems

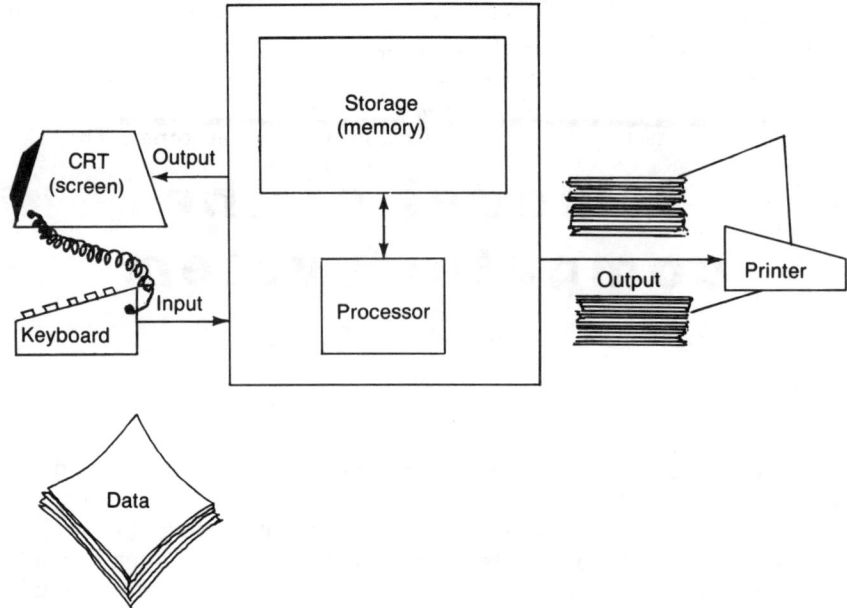

Figure 1.1 Basic resources of a computer

other people more or less directly in contact with a system are actually a part of the system. The **hardware**, which provides the base of the system, is: the processor, storage, and the input and output devices attached. The process (which an operating system treats as an object) is a program in operation. That is, a process is the execution of a series of pre-written instructions (the program) that carries out the task the designer of the program has set for it. This is a matter of solving a problem in the external world, like taking employee data, hours worked and salary data and producing the paperwork for a payroll, or operating an air traffic control simulator, or aiding in the design of integrated circuits, or operating a heat pump in response to readings from a thermostat. To do any task, the computer system requires data.

The operating system, broadly defined, *manages the computer system's hardware, the process itself, the data and the communications with the operator, user or outside world, in accordance with the policy set by the individual or organization controlling the computer system.* In other words, the operating system is a means of controlling the resources and the communications between the elements making up the computer system.

There exists a feedback mechanism between the designs of the hardware and the operating system in which the nature of the available hardware will influence or even dictate the way in which an operating system

A Model of the Computer System

is designed and operates, while the operating system represents a model of what is desired and that model can demand a solution in the technology of the hardware. Thus, while computer architecture is considered a separate subject from the study of operating systems, the two integrate to form a computer system and each influences the other. This has historically been so, as you will see. It continues to be so.

The operating system must take into account the characteristics of the processor which it manages: the instructions available to it, how data are to be located within storage, how the processor is to be controlled and how important parts of the system are to be protected from error. The need for higher performance or additional function, or perhaps the achievement of some economic goal such as lower cost means that some functions of the operating system may be performed by hardware in subsequent versions of a system, or that special hardware may provide boosts or special capabilities for the operating system.

As you read the following material you should ask yourself what resources are involved, and how those resources are being managed. Notice how the elements of a system interact and communicate and how the operating system facilitates their interaction.

You should see that there are many ways of approaching any element of the computer system, and several ways to manage that element — ranging from the very simple to the highly complex.

Historically, of course, the simple precedes the complex, but *simple methods continue in use because they continue to meet the needs of certain communities of users*. Also, some methods have wide applicability at different levels within a system. Thus, methods of scheduling a task's entry into a computer system extend to the scheduling of requests for output to a particular device. Which method is chosen in a particular circumstance depends upon the resolution, quite often through compromise, of a complex problem which must take into account the type of use to which the computer system is to be put, the objectives which the organization hopes to achieve, the costs of achieving them and synergistic factors, since a choice of one method in one area may preclude the choice of other methods in other areas. The point at issue is that of the principle of resources. Expressed in a different fashion than above, resources are: space in storage and time in the processor. Resources must be husbanded even in large, fast systems; methods and algorithms to manage them exist and an operating systems designer can choose among those methods.

The purpose of all this is to achieve the objectives set by the individual or organization controlling the system. Usually the goal is to accomplish the necessary processes as efficiently and cheaply as possible.

Efficiency is difficult to define. Each individual or organization will define it differently in terms of needs. A software house intent on developing commercial data-processing software for sale will want a system which facilitates software development, while an airline accepting reservations from a geographically dispersed network of offices, airport check-in counters and travel agents will want a quite different system. Such different objectives are not necessarily compatible, so that the process of designing a computer system consists of many compromises in order to achieve the best possible system for the given circumstances, at the best possible price.

I cite specific operating systems in this first part as examples, but they are meant only to provide illustrations of the realization of one or more principles or methods. Thus the examples are background material — though they may interest you because you have some personal experience of this or that operating system.

DEFINITIONS AND CAUTIONS

Before I proceed any further, let me impart some basic definitions and cautions.

One reason why computing is sometimes a difficult area to write about is that the jargon is both poorly defined and necessary in order to avoid circumlocution. Thus, a term which may be readily understood among experts without any qualification can have many meanings; the context of any discussion provides the exact meaning. I have tried to be as exact as possible in my use of terms, and have adopted Galland's *Dictionary of Computing* (1982) as my standard.

However, there still remain some problems which you should bear in mind when reading this material. One is that of multiple meanings for the same term depending upon the context. Another is the complementary problem of one thing being called by different names, sometimes in the same context, and sometimes in slightly different contexts. A third problem is that in the different realms of hardware and software, or of operating system and other system software, the distinction between them is often fuzzy, or moves. Many a function can be carried out either by hardware or by software (or a combination of the two!). That which is a function of the operating system in one computer system may not be a part of the operating system, or may not even exist, in another computer system. In some systems a thing will be done in one way and in other systems in another.

Yet another problem concerns theoretical issues such as the nature of computability. I shall use the term *computability* and its verb form *compute* quite a bit in what follows. By *compute* I mean to perform an operation by means of a computer, since computer operations are not limited to the **arithmetic operations** but can include what are called **logical opera-**

A Model of the Computer System

tions. Thus *computability*, in this somewhat informal sense, refers to the ability to operate on data by means of computer operations. Finally, *computing* is the activity or science of using computers. While it may seem obvious what arithmetic operations are (adding, subtracting), logical operations are those which can be expressed as AND, OR, NOT and combinations of these — for example, those operations which compare — based on Boolean algebra.

Figure 1.2 shows a map of a computer system which you might find it helpful to keep in mind.

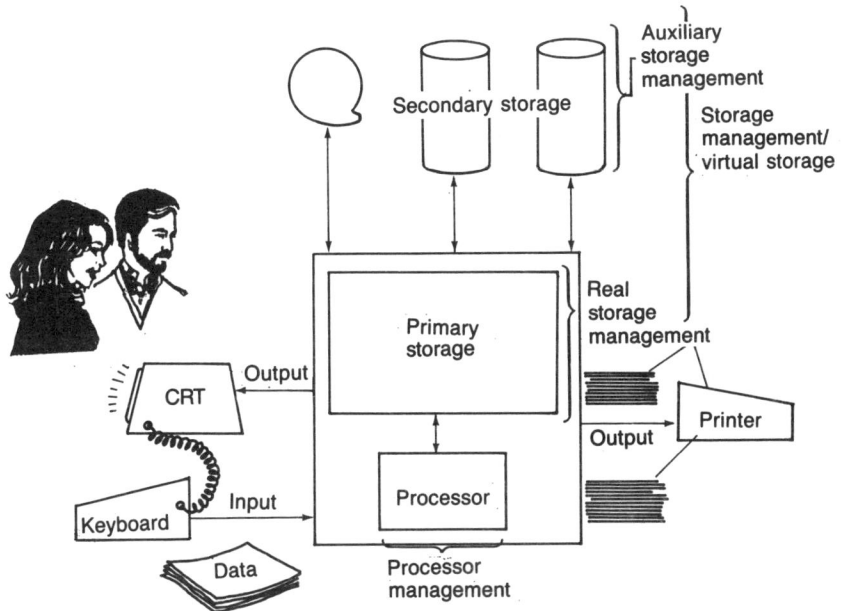

Figure 1.2 A 'map' of a computer system

Questions for review

(i) List the resources that make up a computer system.
(ii) List the major functions of an operating system.

1.1 THE COMPUTER AND ITS OPERATION

Since one of my objectives is to give you some understanding of the economic impetus behind developments in computing technology, I shall begin at the beginning.

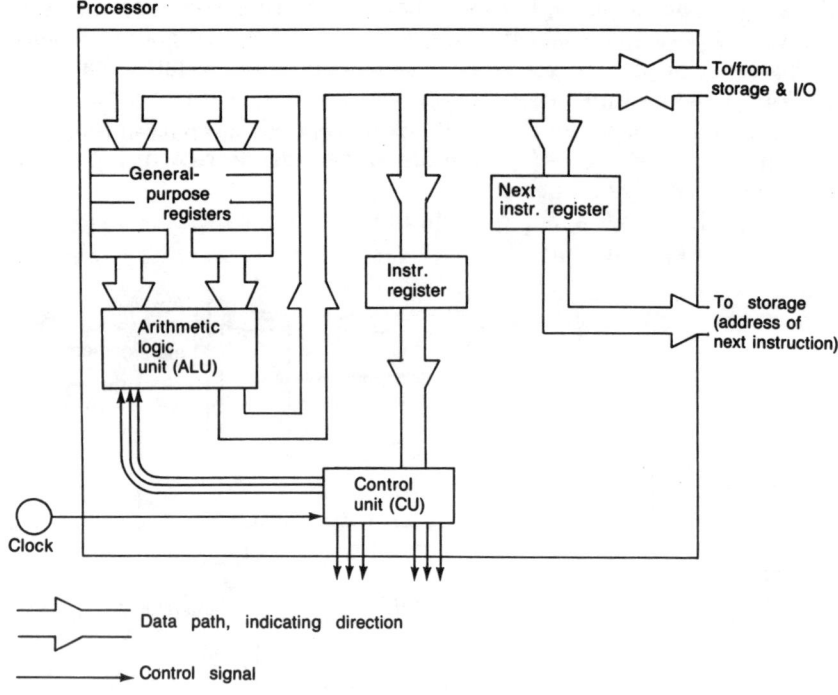

Figure 1.3 A very simplified view of the internal structure of a computer's processor

The hardware underlying any computer system provides only an *inert tool* for computation. The hardware can no more compute on its own than a piano can play music without the external application of power and guidance by a pianist.

The naked computer requires the closest attention from the programmer, who is forced to take into account the detailed action of the computer in designing the solution to any problem. As well as determining a step-by-step method for computing, the programmer must be intimately concerned with loading the program into the computer, with starting the program once it is loaded, with the acquisition of each bit of data, and with the communication of each signal to any output device. It is as though pianists had to concern themselves with the complex assembly and tuning of the piano in order to produce music from it.

(Many microcomputers (of the on-a-chip variety) continue to be sold as 'naked'. This allows their adaptation by a custom-designed and written program for specialist use where no general-purpose features are required. An example is a program to control the actions of an ordinary domestic washing machine, put onto a microcomputer which has no operating system, programming language support, or other general-purpose aids to the programmer.)

John von Neumann and his colleague H.H. Goldstine in 1946 wrote an unpublished paper [1] describing certain computational requirements which had arisen. In certain classes of problem in mathematics, namely in nonlinear problems such as nonlinear partial differential equations in fluid dynamics, the then existing analytical methods were inadequate. Solutions to such problems can, however, be approximated by purely arithmetic finite procedures. This requires very large amounts of simple computation. Such arithmetic approximations become a feasible solution to these problems if a high-speed computing device is available.

A number of computing devices based on electromechanical technologies already existed in 1946. They had been designed and built from the mid-1930s onward in universities and military research establishments and had vastly increased the speed of computation. Von Neumann and Goldstine provide a comparison of estimated times for calculating a ballistic trajectory: from seven hours for hand methods to 15 minutes using a high-speed relay device to 0.5 minutes on ENIAC, the first digital electronic computing machine (it had no memory and hence does not fit my definition of a computer). They foresaw further reduction, to 0.25 seconds for 'advanced' machines then under development.

This millionfold reduction in computing time, however, is uneconomic for solving a single problem because of the time it takes to specify and set up the problem. However, once the specification and setting-up has been carried out, hundreds or thousands of similar computations can be carried out, each computation taking a trivial amount of time.

As well as problems in ballistics and fluid dynamics, other, more complex computational problems were beginning to appear in 1946, for example the computation of astronomical orbits. Whereas a trajectory might have 50 points, each point requiring 15 multiplications, an astronomical orbit might have 600 000 points and require 90 million multiplications.

Thus, speed in computation emerged as a very real requirement in mathematics and the sciences. However, in order to take full advantage of high-speed computational devices, there is a need to allow flexibility in the programming of them. Early devices had programs 'wired' in and changes were difficult and time consuming. Further, there is a need to hold data and instructions in readiness so that they can be transferred to the actual computation device at a speed approaching its operational speed. Data and instructions also must be provided to the computer from the outside world in the first place, and the results of the computation must be made available to the outside world for analysis and action. These requirements were translated by von Neumann, Goldstine and A.W.

Burks in another paper [2] to the following description of a computer architecture.

> Inasmuch as the completed device will be a general-purpose computing machine it should contain certain main organs relating to arithmetic, memory-storage, control and connection with the human operator. It is intended that the machine be fully automatic in character, i.e. independent of the human operator after the computation starts ... It is evident that the machine must be capable of storing in some manner not only the digital information needed in a given computation ... but also the instructions which govern the actual routine to be performed ... it must be possible to instruct the device to carry out any computation ... Hence there must be some organ capable of storing these program orders. There must, moreover, be a unit which can understand these instructions and order their execution ... Lastly, there must exist devices, the input and output organ, whereby the human operator and the machine can communicate with each other ... It must be possible to transfer data from the memory to the arithmetic organ and back again ... one must be able to get numbers from any part of the memory at any time. The treatment in the case of orders can, however, be more methodical since one can at least partially arrange the control instructions in a linear sequence ... The utility of an automatic computer lies in the possibility of using a given sequence of instructions repeatedly, the number of times it is iterated being either preassigned or dependent upon the results of the computation ... We ... recognize the possibility of constructing a hierarchy of memories, each of which has greater capacity than the preceding but which is less quickly accessible.

This describes the classic architecture often called a **von Neumann architecture**. It is a *general-purpose* computational machine designed to accommodate a wide class of computational needs. Since it is a general-purpose computer, the program instructions are what modifies this generality in order to accomplish a specific task. This program nevertheless may itself accept several different sets of data (e.g. data for several different trajectories) and thus to some extent *is itself a general-purpose notional 'computation machine'* for a specific type of computation.

Though computers vary considerably in the power of their instructions, the resources available in a computer are similar throughout the range. The operator/programmer/user can enter data from the external world through an input device. Those data can be manipulated by the arithmetic and logic unit (ALU) according to instructions stored in memory storage, which in turn are accessed, interpreted and executed by the control unit. Results can be conveyed back to the operator/programmer/ user via an output device. Instructions are normally fetched and executed in turn from successive locations in memory, except when a jump or branch instruction alters the program address pointer to point to an alternative instruction in the program. Such branches can be made conditional

A Model of the Computer System

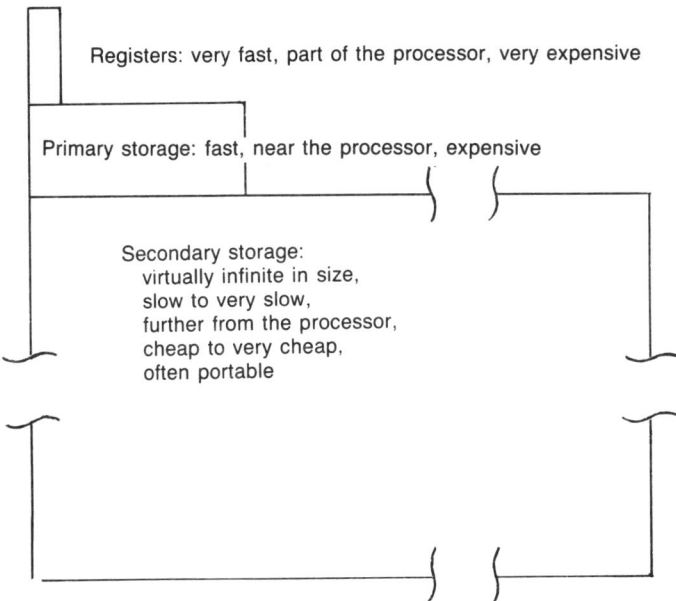

Figure 1.4 A hierarchy of memories

on the current state of the system or data; this allows the program to react to data coming in as it executes or to react to the results of its own actions.

The partial or complete separation of data from any operations to be performed on those data is the fundamental principle which allows this. The program stands to data in the same relation as an algebraic formula stands to specific numeric values.

Questions for review

(i) Explain briefly the economic justification for high-speed computation.
(ii) Describe the basic elements of the von Neumann machine.

1.2 THE BASIC COMPUTER

Initially, all programming was done in **machine language**, the set of bit patterns which represents a set of very low-level instructions to the control unit. The computer itself was a new, rare, very expensive device and its users, mathematicians, were primarily interested in the computation itself and only secondarily in the technique of programming automatic computation. The engineers who designed and built these early computers were interested in the correct functioning of the hardware. Initially the task of programming was thought to be rather uninteresting and even trivial. Thus a very intense interface between programmer and computer was considered reasonable by everyone concerned — except possibly the programmers.

What, then, occurs on such a computer (for 'naked' computers still exist)? The programmer specifies the computation in terms of the arithmetic and logical steps required in order to achieve the desired result, breaks it down into the tiny discrete steps that the computing machinery requires in order to complete the computation, translates that into the necessary code, prepares the data on a medium suitable for the computer's input device, sets up the program by loading it into the computer, and then signals the computer to begin the execution of the programmed instructions. Upon completion of execution (which may mean reaching a point where the program can proceed no further due to an error) it is necessary to return the computer to a usable state for the next program.

Machine code exists on an extremely low level, not simply because it must be in a representation of the necessary bit patterns, but because the discrete instructions are so detailed. An example will demonstrate this, and give you a flavor of what is involved. In order to carry out the following formula

$$F(y) = x \cdot \frac{x^2 - y^2}{x^2 + y^2}$$

one must determine the necessary sub-operations: (1) square x; (2) square y; (3) subtract the square of y from the square of x; (4) add the square of x and the square of y; (5) divide the subtrahend by the sum; (6) multiply the dividend by x. I shall use additional symbols to represent intermediate results. Thus,

1. $q = x \cdot x$
2. $r = y \cdot y$
3. $t = q - r$
4. $n = q + r$
5. $p = t / n$
6. $F(y) = x \cdot p$

Further, in setting up this computation, the value of x and the value of y must be fetched from storage (I shall assume these values are already present there) to where the operations can act upon them, and intermediate results must be held where they will be accessible for subsequent operations. Thus, in machine-language terms I have to do the following. (I have chosen certain instructions, such as those involving a half-word

A Model of the Computer System

(two bytes) of storage, from the list of the computer's available instructions — its **instruction set**.)

1. Square x by the following actions.
   (a) Load the value at the address where x (a half-word of storage) resides into general-purpose register 3.
   (b) Multiply that register by the value x still in storage, result (q) is stored in register 3.
2. (a) Load the value found at the half-word in storage designated as y into register 4.
   (b) Multiply that register by the value y in storage, placing the result (r) in register 4.
3. Since the next arithmetic operation will destroy the contents of one of the registers but I shall need that value for a subsequent step:
   (a) store (i.e. copy) the contents of register 3 (q), which I choose arbitrarily, in storage at an address pointed to by register 6;
   (b) subtract the value in register 4 (r) from the value (q) in register 3; the result (t) is in register 3.
4. I now require the value I stored in step 3(a), so I shall:
   (a) store the value (t) now in register 3 in one half-word of storage at an address two bytes away from the address pointed to by register 6;
   (b) reload the value I stored in step 3(a) (q) into register 3;
   (c) add the contents of registers 4 (r) and 3 (q), storing the result (n) in register 3.
5. (a) Load the value (t) I stored in step 4(a) into register 4.
   (b) Divide contents of register 4 (t) by the contents of register 3 (n) with the result (p) in register 4.
6. (a) Load the value x (found at the half-word pointed to by the address in register 5 plus a displacement of 116 bytes) into register 3.
   (b) Multiply the contents of register 3 (x) by the contents of register 4 (p); result in register 3.
   (c) Load the value of y into register 4 to use this as an index register in the following instruction.
   (d) Store the result (in register 3) in the half-word of storage pointed to by the address in register 5 plus a displacement of 128 bytes and indexed by the value (y) in register 4.

Figure 1.5 illustrates a machine-code program (loosely based on IBM S/370 machine codes) to accomplish this. Note that the programmer must *know* all the addresses she or he uses in advance, must plan register and storage use carefully, and must know the capabilities and limitations of the computer intimately.

Address	Opcode	Operands
003404	48	30 50 7A
003408	4C	30 50 7A
00340C	48	40 50 80
003410	4C	50 50 80
003414	40	30 60 00
003418	1B	34
00341A	40	30 06 02
00341E	48	30 60 00
003422	1A	34
003424	40	40 60 02
003428	1D	43
00342A	48	30 50 7A
00342E	1C	34
003430	48	40 50 80
003434	40	34 50 70

Figure 1.5 A partial machine-language program for an imaginary computer

Question for review

Briefly describe the requirements of the job of a programmer on a 'naked' computer: i.e. one without software.

1.3 EARLY SYSTEMS SOFTWARE

By the early 1950s it became clear to programmers that this intense concentration on the details of the computer's architecture and instruction set had to be reduced in the interests of solving problems which, after all, originated in the world outside the computer. One of the first steps was to make the coding of instructions simpler by replacing operation codes with mnemonic codes and by allowing the use of a symbolic address or data name so that a program (called an **assembler**) could read and process a **source program** so written and translate it into the necessary machine instructions and absolute addresses (called an **object program**) which the computer could then execute. Figure 1.6 shows a partial assembly-language program to solve the problem given above.

Notice that the same number of instructions are required, but that the programmer need not be concerned with absolute addresses. Instead, storage can be defined with symbolic labels, and the assembler itself will resolve these as it translates the program to machine code.

The programs in Figs. 1.5 and 1.6 are, of course, only fragments of complete programs on an imaginary computer! The point is that the assembler automatically translates into machine language what the programmer has written in a more readable, easier-to-write code.

A Model of the Computer System

Label	Opcode mnemonic	Operands	Comments
BEGIN	LH	3,XVAL	LOAD VALUE OF X
	MH	3,XVAL	MULTIPLY BY X GIVING Q
	LH	4,YVAL	LOAD VALUE OF Y
	MH	4,YVAL	MULTIPLY BY Y GIVING R
	STH	3,QVAL	STORE Q TEMPORARILY
	SR	3,4	SUBTRACT FROM Q GIVING T IN REG.3
	STH	3,TVAL	STORE T TEMPORARILY
	LH	3,QVAL	FETCH Q BACK AGAIN
	AR	3,4	ADD Q & R GIVING N (IN REG.3)
	LH	4,TVAL	FETCH T BACK AGAIN TO REG 4.
	DR	4,3	DIVIDE T BY N GIVING P (IN REG.4)
	LH	3,XVAL	FETCH X BACK AGAIN
	MR	3,4	MULTIPLY X BY P; RESULT IN REG. 3
	LH	4,YVAL	LOAD VALUE OF Y INTO INDEX REGISTER
	STH	3,4,FVAL	STORE RESULT AT FVAL INDEXED BY VALUE OF Y
.			
DATADEF	DS	OCL50	DEFINE DATA STORAGE
XVAL	DS	H	X IN FIRST HALFWORD
YVAL	DS	H	Y IN SECOND HALFWORD

Figure 1.6 An assembly-language equivalent to the machine-language program shown in Figure 1.5

The assembler, a program itself, must be loaded into storage by a program called a **loader**, which later loads the object program that results from the assembler. The assembler and loader constitute the earliest systems software. The object of such software is to provide a 'cushion' between the programmer and the computer. This eases the programming task and allows that programmer to concentrate more fully on the real-world problem by making the computer take over some of the more tedious tasks. This automation, in addition, reduces the time required by a programmer to set up a problem and to return the computer to a usable state for the next program to run. This time occupies a significant portion of the total required for most computations; hence, its reduction results directly in both more valuable computer time available for other uses and in more economic use of the programmer's own time.

These tentative steps made it clear that such a cushion of software between programmer and computer is useful both from the aspect of the economic use of an expensive resource (the computer) and from the point of view of the programmer, whose understanding of the workings of the computer can be somewhat less deep and who can profitably spend time otherwise engaged in laborious coding in designing better programs.

Question for review

What are the steps in obtaining an automatically computed solution to a problem and which were themselves automated to form the earliest systems software?

Question for discussion

Based on what you have read above, what would you say were some of the limiting factors in what can be considered computable?

1.4 SUBSTANTIAL STEPS FORWARD

All early computers executed all work serially, one instruction at a time. This meant in terms of an executable program, that it set up the conditions necessary for it to run (called **initialization**), read a unit of input (e.g. a punched card), moved data from the input device into storage, loaded data from there to registers, operated on the data, stored the result in storage and (let us say) printed the result, then read the next card, stored the data in storage, moved it to registers, operated on it, stored the result back in storage, printed the result, *ad nauseam*. With such a computer no action can commence until the preceding action completes. Whatever internal computation speeds are achievable, the speed with which the fully serial computer executes the entire program is constrained by the speed of the input and output devices. The input/output functions are minutely programmed and are executed by the processor which waits, idle, for the input or output operation to complete before proceeding to execute the next instruction. Input and output devices are under the direct control of the computer itself.

Problems of reliability, speed and ease of use

Even as advances in software were taking place, circuit technology and computer design were also improving reliability and speed.

Each improvement in reliability opens up new areas to automatic computation. For example, if a computer's **mean time between failures (MTBF)** is 15 minutes, wise programmers limit their programs' scope to what can be accomplished with a 'reasonable' assurance of completing. If MTBF can be increased to hours or days, then problems requiring long hours of processing time can be tackled.

Computation speed also has a strong influence on what users will consider as problems suitable for automatic computation. Good examples are any time-constrained problems: those which must be completed by a certain time or during a given period of time in order for their results to be of any use. If accurate computer-generated weather forecasting is to be useful, the computations must be completed within a 24-hour period. If computations for a daily forecast take more than 24 hours to complete, however accurate the results, they are available too late to be of more than academic interest. The only possibilities are either to produce forecasts which are less accurate but which can be processed within the time limit, or to forego the use of digital computation in the production of weather forecasts. (I mention daily weather forecasting because only recently have a combination of increased computation speeds and advanced techniques in hardware and software made this practicable.)

The low speed of input and output devices, which have mechanical limitations, is very much a limiting factor of the net speed with which a computation can be performed. This factor was acknowledged from the beginning, when von Neumann and Goldstine [1] noted that '... the most commonplace objection against a very high speed device is that, even if its extreme speed were achievable, it would not be possible to introduce the data or to extract (and print) the results at a corresponding rate ... the ENIAC has the standard IBM punch card recording time [200 milliseconds (msec)], and with it a multiplication time of 3 msec.' They tentatively suggested running several input devices in parallel.

Another perceived bottleneck was the difficulty of programming; even assembler language focuses on the computer and its characteristics rather than allowing the programmer to concentrate on the problem to be solved.

Solutions

Steady, often spectacular improvements in circuit technology such as the invention of the transistor helped improve both the speed of the computer and its inherent reliability. As importantly, the computers resulting from improvements in circuit technology are smaller, consume less power and cost less than their predecessors. It is primarily due to these factors that computers have achieved such widespread use.

There are economic limitations, however, to obtaining more speed merely from improvements in circuit technology. From 1950 to 1977 computer performance increased around 100 000-fold, but circuit switching speeds improved only about 1000-fold. The additional improvements in performance were a result of searching out parts of the computer system that are idle for significant periods of time and devising ways of occupying those parts more fully with useful tasks.

While most such improvements have more to do with the hardware than with the software, they nevertheless are important. One such approach was **pipelining**, also called **lookahead processing**. Here computer designers looked carefully at the components of the control unit which fetched and then executed program instructions. The fetch−execute cycle of a computer consists of a number of sub-operations which require different sub-units of the processor at different times; by overlapping instruction fetch and execute as much as possible, often at the (small) cost of some extra hardware, great improvements in performance are achievable.

Another approach is the interleaving of instruction and data fetch. The extra hardware necessary for pipelining is often a small, specialized storage which can be interposed between two units to reduce the delays in transmitting data between them and thus can improve the utilization of those units.

Another approach was to move some simple functions to a cheaper, smaller satellite computer which can hold programs and input data in readiness for transfer to the main computer when that becomes ready for work; after execution of a program the output can be held and then printed under the control of the satellite while the next lot of work (called a **job**) is acquired from the satellite by the main computer. The satellite works more cheaply, and at the slower speeds dictated by input and output devices and human interface. Yet it is fast enough to feed the main computer at speeds approaching the latter's own.

The satellite is thus a kind of buffer between the slowest parts of a system and the fastest. This technique is still used in some supercomputers. It has two advantages: that of freeing the main computer from the speed limitations set by slower devices and that of removing some of the less specialized or important work from the more costly, faster computer. In so doing, it increases the **availability** of the main computer for work.

Use of satellite arrangements led to the development of simple **job-control languages**, another facet of systems software. These allow the programmer or operator to make statements about how a job is to be run, thus directing the computer at one level higher than that of the program. Such statements may delineate where one job ends and the next begins, or may signal which part of a stream of data is program and which part data, and may specify the conditions necessary for the job to run. Initially, a job was one program and its associated data, but later a job could include several programs to be run one after another, especially in cases where the output of one program becomes the input to a subsequent one. Job-control languages thus provide a kind of 'package' to contain programs and data, and in which to present them to the computer.

The introduction of **high-level languages**, several of which (FORTRAN, COBOL, LISP) appeared in 1959−60, eased the programmer's task. These languages can equally be termed **problem programming languages** since they each focus on a class of problems in the real world which it is the task of the programmer to design a program to solve. FORTRAN, for FORmula TRANSlation, is a language primarily for arithmetic computation, while COBOL − COmmon Business Oriented Language − is best suited for commercial data processing, and LISP, LISt Processing, was designed for logical processing of 'lists'.

A Model of the Computer System

A program called a **compiler**, now added to the available systems software, took over the task of translating statements made in a high-level language into machine language. The problem of:

$$F(y) = x \cdot \frac{x^2 - y^2}{x^2 + y^2}$$

can now be stated by the programmer (in a high-level language) as shown in Fig. 1.7.

F[Y] := X * (X ∧ 2 − Y ∧ 2) / (X ∧ 2 - Y ∧ 2)

Figure 1.7 A Pascal program equivalent to the programs shown in Figures 1.5 and 1.6

The program still must be translated into machine code (compiled) and loaded in order to be run. Once translated and found to be correct it can, of course, be stored in machine code (executable) form and loaded directly.

Increased execution speeds becoming available in the early 1960s meant that the inefficiencies which high-level programming languages create − because the compiler must 'generalize' its machine code − were acceptable because of the attendant advantage of the ease of programming, especially since this increased the likelihood of correctness.

Question for review

List three means of improvement in computer performance. Which of them affected software?

Question for discussion

How did developments in software respond to the requirement to improve computer utilization? To the need to improve programming productivity?

1.5 DATA IN EARLY SYSTEMS

Early computer systems engaged in pure arithmetic computation dealt with input and output data using techniques which were dictated by the medium on which such data could be presented to the computer as well as by the nature of the data themselves. Virtually all data processed in such early computer systems consisted of numbers. These numbers were thought of, and treated by the program, as discrete. Since the programmer would know, as part of the definition of the computational problem to be solved, the size of each number (in terms of the number of digits) and the type (integer, non-integer — real, in computing terms — or scientific (floating point) notation, signed and unsigned), he or she wrote the program to take in a *stream* of digits and then logically to delineate each discrete number. An analogy would be taking a series of digits written continuously on a strip of paper and using a pencil to mark the divisions between five-digit numbers. This method of 'marking off' discrete data from a stream of characters is simple, and is still used, for example in **real-time** monitoring and control applications, among others.

Output likewise consisted of discrete numbers; these could be printed one at a time on continuous sheets of paper. Print a number, advance to next position, print.

However, the computer's logical, as opposed to its strictly arithmetic, capabilities also suited it for work with non-numeric, but nevertheless digital, data which could appear in any form. Such data are usually facts, such as a person's name, or age. Such data present two major problems. Firstly, most such data cannot be depended upon to conform to the same sort of rigid guidelines as numbers in arithmetic computation. Secondly, such data are usually very voluminous, and change.

Anyone collecting data for later use needs a means of:

- grouping those data into manageable and meaningful units (**records**)
- collecting those units together (**files**) in a form that renders the collection useful (its **organization**)
- identifying individual collections
- storing those collections
- retrieving a stored collection in order to refer to it or to work on the data contained within it (**access**).

A means of automated mass storage was provided by the introduction, in the 50s and early 1960s, of magnetic media such as **magnetic tapes**, **drums** and **disks**. Unautomated methods for collection, collation, storage and reference to data had, however, existed for centuries. These methods and the terms associated with them were naturally adapted for their automated counterparts. Thus one speaks of records, files and archives, and of reading and writing.

The magnetic media, such as tapes, disks and drums, are adjuncts to a computer system which have the effect of greatly enlarging its total memory or storage capacity. However, this extension is made up of media which have a much larger capacity than the internal storage of a computer, but which are much slower in terms of access time and which have certain limitations placed on the means of access (data on tape, for instance, can only be accessed serially). They are, however, much cheaper and are mostly portable.

Like input and output devices, these media must be accessed through one of a computer's **I/O ports** because they are not directly addressable in the computer's machine language. However, they are *not* I/O devices, strictly speaking, because they do not facilitate communication to or from the world outside the computer system. Their magnetic patterns can only be interpreted through the agency of a computer system. These media and the devices attached to the computer system through I/O ports which enable the computer system to access data on those media are collectively termed **secondary storage**, or sometimes **auxiliary storage**. They represent one level within the 'hierarchy of memories, each of which has greater capacity than the preceding but which is less quickly accessible' [2], as I mentioned in quoting von Neumann and his colleagues earlier. The next higher level in the hierarchy of memories is called **primary storage** (or sometimes **main storage**, **main memory**, or **core**) and is that memory which is integral with the central processing unit and which *can be directly addressed by machine-code instructions*.

In terms of computing, one speaks of files as those organized collections of records which reside in secondary storage, though the term *file* can be used more loosely, as you will see, to describe collections of data for input, collections of data which have been or are being output, or even for devices which can be treated in programming terms exactly like a file (see the Unix case study in Part II).

In order for a process to deal with a file, that process must be able to request that a file be located, open it to make the data in it available for access, close it to signal that it is no longer required, create one if it did not previously exist, destroy it when its usefulness has ceased, rename it (for convenience), or view its contents by displaying them on a terminal or printer.

A process might need to deal with the individual items (records) which make up the file by reading them, writing them, updating them, inserting a new item within a sequence of items, or by deleting an item which is no longer required. *Reading* means to make a record available to a process. This involves transferring that record from secondary storage or an input device to primary storage. *Writing* involves taking a record which a process has created or manipulated, and transferring it from primary storage to secondary storage or an output device. *Updating* is the modification of an existing record. To be updated, a record in secondary storage must be read, the process must modify it, and must then rewrite it. *Insertion* involves the writing of a newly created record to an existing file. *Deletion* means the erasure of a record. This can be accomplished several ways: by specially marking the record as 'not there' even though it continues to exist physically, or by not copying the record to any new copies of a file, or by making the space it occupied on the file available for other use. (Note that terms like *read* and *write* can have other definitions than those I have used above. You will see this especially in the use of these terms with reference to architectures.)

The amount and type of data with which a computer system deals vary with the work one hopes to do. This variation can be pictured as a spectrum. A **data-processing system**, as the name implies, works primarily with data of several types and processes those data in a flexible way. In such systems most of the computer's power is expended upon the manipulation and storing of *large volumes of data*. This bias places special constraints upon the design of any system. Since the data may be diverse in type and the manipulations performed various, this calls for a general-purpose system in which a great deal of emphasis has been placed on file handling, storage media and their management, input–output operations, and their optimization in terms of the system's total performance. You will see an example of this in the MVS case study in Part II.

At the other extreme of this spectrum might be a real-time control system with small amounts of data which must be acted on as they occur, after which they can be ignored or even destroyed. Such systems tend to be highly specialized and inflexible, with emphasis placed on the reliable, very high-speed performance of a very limited number of carefully defined tasks. A humble example would be a computer controlling a domestic washing machine: it need only respond to water temperature and level sensors, a microswitch indicating door open/shut, the pressing by the user of a few wash-program indicators such as cold/warm/hot wash, gentle/normal agitation, and so on. No data need be stored between one wash and the next, no temperatures recorded for later processing.

Between the two extremes may appear scientific systems, where large amounts of data may be present (which may have been collected in real time, as in acquiring signals from a satellite for later processing). Such data are not very diverse in type, and the emphasis rests on very high-speed performance of mathematical computation. Other systems might be small systems or systems of hybrid function (quite common today) which provide both real-time control and data-processing functions.

Another type now emerging is that which treats data not as data – characters and digits – but as logical entities, carrying out symbolic processing. An example is a knowledge-based system. Where this would fit in the spectrum I describe is not entirely clear; this seems to constitute a new dimension.

Questions for discussion

(i) List some possible effects that the type and amount of data might have on a computer system.
(ii) What parts of a computer system will each type affect?
(iii) How does the volume of data affect the design of a computer system?

REFERENCES

[1] von Neumann, J., and Goldstine, H.H. (1946), 'On the principles of large scale computing machines' (an unpublished paper of 1946), reprinted in von Neumann, J. (1962) *Collected Works, Vol. V*, Pergamon Press, Oxford.
[2] von Neumann, J., Goldstine, H.H. and Burks, A.W. (1946), 'Preliminary discussion of the logical design of an electronic computing instrument, part I, Vol. 1' (1946) in a report prepared for the US Army Ordinance Department and subsequently reprinted in von Neumann, J. (1962) *Collected Works, Vol. V*, Pergamon Press, Oxford.

A general reference I have used here and throughout to resolve problems with technical terminology and jargon is:

Galland, F.J., Editor (1982) *Dictionary of Computing*, John Wiley, New York.

FURTHER READING

Danhof, K.J. and Smith, C.L. (1981) *Computing System Fundamentals*, Addison-Wesley, Reading, Massachusetts. Chapter 1 describes computer architectures and machine-level programming constructs: instruction formats and addressing modes.

Eccles, W.J. (1985) *Microprocessor Systems: a 16-bit approach*, Addison-Wesley, Reading, Massachusetts. The book looks at a microprocessor beginning with its architecture and describes in detail the task of programming at the assembler/machine language level.

Stern, N. (1981) *From ENIAC to UNIVAC: an appraisal of the Eckert—Mauchly computers*, Digital Press, Bedford, Massachussetts. Chapter 4 looks at John von Neumann and the Moore School computers. The book is concerned with the early development of digital computers and the social forces at work in early development teams. Ms Stern also looks at interplay between academic, commercial and governmental forces.

CHAPTER

2

Systems software and early operating systems

From the mid-1940s to the late 1970s when the cheap microprocessor revolutionized computing, the computer remained relatively large and expensive and required highly skilled and highly paid staff to manage, program and run it. Though its power and reliability increased phenomenally and its relative price decreased steeply during that period, its users had every incentive to develop software designed to increase its efficiency and usefulness.

The phenomenal increase in speed, efficiency and therefore in usefulness was made possible by two lines of improvement in computer hardware. The first was increases in speed and improvement in operating characteristics due to changes in circuit technology. The basis of logic elements which make up the processing units and data routing functions of a computer are electronic switches; thus their speeds are crucial to the performance of a computer. Transistors replaced thermionic tubes (also called valves) in the early 1960s. Early bipolar transistors were then replaced by integrated circuits consisting of combinations of resistors, diodes or transistors. More recently, the field-effect transistor (FET) has become the basic switching element for a large class of logic elements, especially in microprocessor-based components. The general thrust has been toward improvements such as increased switching speed, reduced power consumption, reduced capacitance and reduced size.

However, reduced switching speeds have accounted for only about one per cent of the 100 000-fold improvement in computer performance. The biggest improvements have been brought about by changes to the basic computer architecture I have described earlier. In a fully serial machine, each instruction must be fetched and executed before the fetch of the next instruction can begin. Many of the components of a processor must, perforce, remain idle in this case. Pipelining, also called lookahead

Systems Software and Early Operating Systems

processing, is a technique whereby the architecture is altered in a conceptually rather simple way to allow the overlap of instruction fetch from storage of one (or more) instructions and execution of the current instruction so that the processing of the instructions overlaps as much as possible. I shall discuss other, non-pipelining techniques which alter the basic architecture of a computer as they apply to operating systems. They are: peripheral processors, buffers and cache memories.

Two further avenues for possible improvement existed which concerned the way in which the computer was used rather than how it was constructed and organized.

The first was that programmers needed to make the task of programming both simpler and less error-prone. The improvement which resulted from this line of effort is **systems software**: assemblers, compilers and interpreters, linkers and loaders.

The second avenue of interest was to attempt to share the work cooperatively among several processors and to allow the work each did to overlap with the work of the others. The most obvious instance was to allow the overlap of I/O, which is slow, with computation, which is fast. To accomplish this without asking each programmer to design and write complex control functions for each program would require a new kind of software, a program which would have overall control and management of the computer system as its function: the operating system.

In this chapter, I shall discuss simple systems software, how work can be shared cooperatively, how this is applicable to computing, how a simple operating system accomplishes this and how it controls the interfaces between the many parts of a computer system.

Finally, I shall briefly examine the implications these developments had for later developments in operating systems.

2.1 MODELS FOR SHARING WORK COOPERATIVELY

There are several possible ways to divide the work between two (or more) workers in any undertaking. Two workers, both skilled in all aspects of the job, each with a complete set of tools, could each work side by side on two different pieces of work — each, for example, constructing a different chair. But suppose both were set to cooperate on the building of a single chair between them. To avoid getting in each other's way, they might agree on a method of dividing the work yet cooperating and sharing tools in such a way that they could work with a minimum of mutual interference.

Let us look at three ways of organizing cooperative work where some interface between two workers is necessary in order to achieve a goal, but where the amount each must interfere with the other is reduced to a minimum. To simplify comparisons between the various methods, I shall use the same model in each description, that of a librarian and a book borrower, who are working to achieve the same goal: obtaining a book for the borrower through inter-library loan.

The model

A library user needs a particular book which isn't available in the library. The user approaches one of the librarians in order to *interact* with him or her to obtain the required book. The librarian can obtain the book through an inter-library loan scheme. Once the book arrives at the library, the librarian needs to be able to tell the user that the book is available.

In other words, these two people are both working to accomplish a particular task – getting information (the book) to the one who wants it. Neither can take the time simply to stand and wait for the book to arrive from some other library, so each will work largely independently of the other and they will only interact as required to make the request and then to hand over the book.

The interrupt method

Notice how the librarian's regular flow of work is *interrupted* by the borrower; the request prompts an action. While the librarian processes this request, the borrower continues working independently. The librarian also continues to work independently. When the librarian receives the book through the inter-library loan service, it becomes necessary to *interrupt* the borrower by telephoning with the message that the book is available. The borrower, who is in a bit of a hurry to obtain the book, quickly brings any work to a point where it can be laid aside so that it can be resumed later; that is, the borrower suspends normal business temporarily to go to the library to check out the book.

The polling method

Another possible model for the interaction between the librarian and book borrower is that the anxious would-be borrower telephones the librarian on a regular basis (say, hourly) to enquire whether the desired book has arrived. While this works, it requires more of the borrower's time than the interrupt method above. The librarian, however, could simply ignore

Figure 2.1 Cooperating to obtain and transfer information

the ringing telephone until the book has been received (this is a very simple model!); this avoids the problem of wasting his or her time as well.

The mailbox method

A third model for the interaction between the librarian and book borrower can be termed *mailbox*. The borrower fills in a request form and puts it into a pre-designated place, the librarian's 'in tray', for the librarian to find. The librarian checks this tray on a regular basis and processes any requests found there. When the librarian obtains the book, it is shelved in a pre-arranged place for the borrower, who drops into the library from time to time, to find. If the book is there, then the borrower can take it and use it. The two need not communicate directly with each other.

Comparing the three methods

In comparing the three methods, note that each has some advantages.
   The interrupt method is the most efficient in terms of the minimal interference between the two people, yet as soon as the book arrives the borrower is made aware of it. Thus, this method is also usually the fastest.
   By comparison, the polling method may seem to be unnecessary, for it appears neither faster nor more efficient. However, suppose that the borrower had asked a dozen librarians in a dozen libraries to search for a dozen different books and yet is anxious that little time be lost in obtaining any of them. Then the polling method begins to look more rational.
   Obviously, the mailbox approach is a relaxed one. Both people can proceed virtually entirely independently of each other. But the method is also one in which time and efficiency are not of over-riding importance. It may be some time before the librarian notices the request in the tray, and some time after the book appears on the shelf before the borrower finds it there.

How cooperation applies to computing

The satellite computer I mentioned in Section 1.4 represents an attempt to share work between two processors. The division of labor between the two occurs primarily by assigning one processor a subordinate position: the role of supporting the other by dealing with the slowest aspects of processing: input and output. The main computer signals the satellite when it is ready to accept work or ready to transmit output, whereupon

Systems Software and Early Operating Systems

the satellite feeds the main computer with an *entire batch* of work, or accepts an *entire batch* of output. The Cray-1 supercomputer is supplied with a Data General Eclipse minicomputer as such a satellite, but it can use other computers in this fashion.

The next step beyond the practice of using a satellite computer is to set a subordinate processor to work controlling slower devices for the main computer in an *interactive* fashion. Because a program consists of sets of instructions which are repeated (loops) which at each iteration require new data, an interactive exchange between the main processor executing the program and a subordinate processor which has access to the data is fundamental to fully automatic processing. This is especially important, not only with input and output devices, but also with bulk magnetic data storage devices like tapes, drums and disks. Though they are considerably faster than input and output devices, they do not approach the speeds with which a processor or its primary storage operate.

Such a subordinate processor is called a **peripheral processor**, an **I/O processor** or a **data channel**. The data channel is a small processor capable of carrying out I/O programs (small programs which control the transfer of data between devices). These data channels relieve the main processor of the simple task of moving data into and out of primary storage. Where the main processor could typically accomplish this with an instruction fetch, a data fetch and then an output cycle to move data from primary storage to its destination, the intelligent data channel requires only a data fetch cycle and a prior instruction from the main processor. This instruction sets up the data transfers and leaves the data channel to carry out the work.

In large systems, the data channel is attached between the main processor and the various secondary storage and I/O devices (collectively called **peripherals**) which make up the computer system. Few or none of these peripheral devices are connected directly to an I/O port of the main processor. Instead, a data channel is connected to the main processor by an I/O port and is, in turn, connected to a **peripheral controller**. These, in turn, are connected to the actual peripheral devices: disk drives, tape drives, and so on.

Several data channels can be connected to a main computer. Each channel can control several peripheral controllers, each of which in turn can control several peripheral devices. Thus, control fans out toward the periphery of the system. In smaller systems, however, such a high degree of dispersal of control is unnecessary and can be counter-productive.

Given a three-half-byte (24-bit) address for peripheral devices (and using hexadecimal code) a single processor can address up to 16 channels (the first byte of the address indicates the channel number). Each channel can address up to 16 control units (second byte of address), and each control unit can address up to 16 devices (third byte), giving a maximum

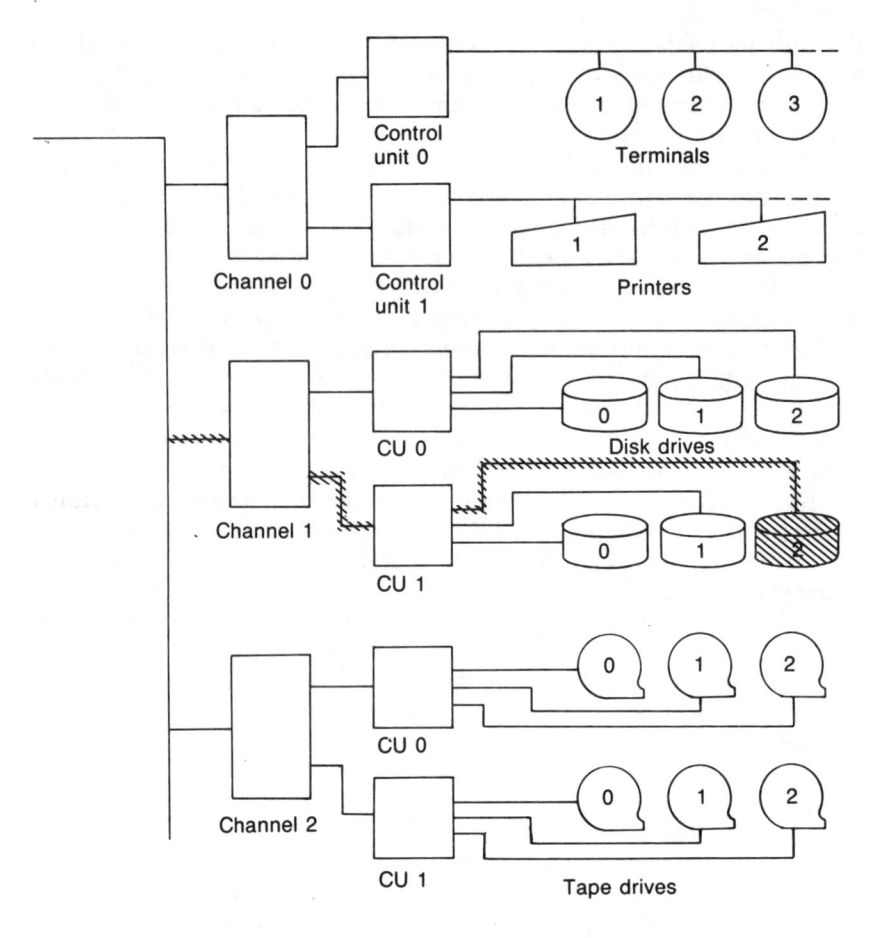

Figure 2.2 An arrangement of channels, control units and secondary storage and I/O devices; device at address 112 and the path to it are shaded

of 4096 addressable devices! Of course, a realist would not load a processor with anything near the addressable maximum — it would be likely to 'constipate' the whole system!

Recall for a moment the three models of cooperation between the librarian and book borrower. The two exchange data and signals in order to work together. The borrower signals the librarian with a request and the librarian signals the borrower that (s)he has received the book.

A data channel can execute an I/O program, transferring data between primary storage and a peripheral device, following the path indicated by the device's address. In requesting data from a device, the main processor sends a request for I/O to the data channel. If the data channel is available (not busy), it executes an I/O program (often called a channel program) to comply with that request. The data channel obtains the data, places it in primary storage and then *signals* the main processor that the request for I/O has been complied with.

I have just described one type of **interrupt** — a signal which requires the main processor to suspend other work and respond with some form of action. Interrupts are signals which require urgent service from the main processor.

Interrupts can be thought of as two types: hardware-generated and software-generated. Hardware-generated interrupts may occur when a fault occurs in the machine itself (machine check), when the operator signals a machine restart, upon expiry of a unit of time as measured by one of the computer's clocks or due to a signal from a data channel or peripheral device. Descriptions of a processor's architecture show which types of interrupt the hardware will recognize. Very simple architectures may recognize only one — the restart — which is what occurs when the power to the device is turned on. More complex architectures may recognize several types of interrupt.

Software interrupts generally are a software version of hardware interrupts. They occur when a process requires some service from the hardware or the operating system: detecting the need for the system to switch to another task, opening or closing a file, requesting I/O, obtaining or releasing space in primary storage. Later, I shall discuss how interrupts are handled by the processor in more detail.

Some systems use **polling**. The main processor is *interrupted* by a periodic time signal. It then checks the status of its attached units, going around each one in turn. For example, when a processor responds to the periodic 'time to poll' signal, it suspends whatever task it is doing and polls its data channels. It checks each data channel in turn to see whether that data channel has anything which the processor needs. If there is a negative (or in some types of polling no) reply, the main processor carries on polling until it has polled each data channel; then it resumes its suspended task and polls again later. If any data channel signals that it has data, the main processor then suspends its polling, prepares for the transfer of that data and then continues its polling.

Polling has a relatively high performance overhead compared to interrupt-driven systems, but finds uses in situations where the overhead does not adversely affect the desired performance of a system or where there are many, many devices. (As you will see in the TPF II case study, *any* device which has sufficient 'intelligence' can poll devices attached to it. Thus a great deal of data can be accumulated and made ready for the main processor on the next polling round.)

Mailbox systems allow maximum independence among processing elements at the sacrifice of some additional time between the time any request originates and the time it is satisfied. Like polling systems, a mailbox system is regularly *interrupted* by a timer, at which time the processor checks the area of primary storage designated as the mailbox to see whether it contains anything. Mailbox systems must be carefully organized so that one processor doesn't over-write data in a mailbox before the other processor has had access to it. Furthermore, the amount of time any request takes is less predictable than is true of the *interrupt-driven* system. However, this can be a quite acceptable way to meet particular processing needs.

Passing data between processors

Recall again the librarian and book borrower. The two exchange data in order to work together. The librarian must have a way of handing the book to the borrower once he or she has it. The librarian could hand it to the borrower directly, but this depends upon their meeting face-to-face. One may have to hold the book and wait for the other to arrive to

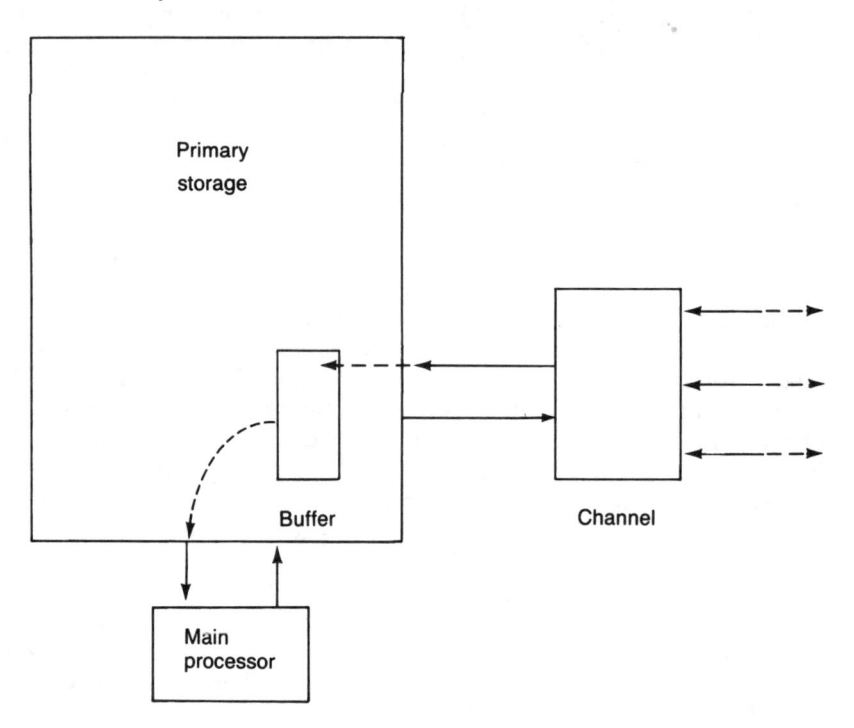

Figure 2.3 Transferring (input) data through the medium of a buffer

take it. Better still, the book can be left in a pre-arranged place for the borrower to find on arrival at the library.

When a main processor and one of its data channels exchange data, they do so through a **buffer**. A buffer is an area of primary storage where data are held temporarily to facilitate their transfer between devices which operate at different speeds or on different time cycles. (The term also has other meanings in computing which do not apply here.) To comply with a request for input, the data channel can obtain the data from a peripheral device and place it into the buffer. Once the buffer is full, the data channel signals the main processor which can then access the data. For output, the process puts data into the buffer. When the buffer is full, the operating system then requests the data channel to deal with it. The data channel accesses the buffer and transfers the data to a storage or output device.

Questions for review

(i) What are the three methods by which processors can organize communication in order to undertake work on a common task? Describe their differences and relative strengths and weaknesses.
(ii) Describe the purpose and nature of a data channel.
(iii) How do the data channel and main processor use a buffer?

2.2 SIMPLE OPERATING SYSTEMS

How an interrupt works

If you were interrupted by the telephone while reading a chapter in a textbook, you might finish the sentence you were reading, then make a pencil mark immediately beside it in the margin so that, when you've finished your telephone conversation you could start reading again where you left off without having to backtrack to the top of the last page or the start of the last chapter you'd read.

The computer's processor alternates between running a process and handling interrupts. In addition, polling systems poll and mailbox systems check the mailbox after each timer interrupt.

When a processor is interrupted, it must complete the current instruction and save the status of whatever task it is executing so that it can resume that task, exactly where it left off, later. Thus, an interrupt causes the processor to save — store — vital information on the status of the task that was executing when the interrupt occurred. It then deals with the interrupt signal. Once it has dealt with the interrupt, the processor restores the interrupted task as it was, and recommences work on it.

Task switching

The shift made by the processor between running a process and handling an interrupt is called **context** or **state switching**.

Any process in the computer system can be said to be in a **state** or **context**. When a process is actively executing, it is running. Running is one possible state. If a process could use the processor but the processor isn't available, the process is in a ready state — ready to run if it could. If it has started running but has been interrupted it is said to be in blocked state.

The instructions which control context switching and which handle interrupts (and conduct polls and mailbox checks) make up the most fundamental level of an operating system, with some functions being handled directly by the hardware. Code which handles an interrupt is called an **interrupt handler**. Each type of interrupt which the system allows will have a special interrupt handler to deal with that type of interrupt. Thus, one can think of an operating system as program code which controls and manages the hardware and the interaction between the hardware and other software (including pieces of itself!). But how does a simple operating system actually work?

Each processor has a hardware feature designed to control the fetch and execution of program instructions. It is a special register which always contains the address of the next instruction to be fetched and executed. It is called the **PSW** (**program status word**, also in smaller, simpler machines called the **program counter [PC]**, the **program address counter [PAC]** or the **instruction pointer [IP]**). It can be thought of in two ways: first as a hardware structure, i.e. a special register, and secondly as the data (an address of an instruction) contained within the register.

At the minimum, this register contains the address of the next instruction (or portion of an instruction) which the control unit of the processor is going to fetch and execute. The size of the register, therefore, depends upon the number of address bits the processor is designed to handle, which in turn determines the maximum amount of primary storage directly addressable. (Architectures sometimes have *separate* instruction and data storage areas and thus have somewhat different means of addressing than architectures which combine instructions and data in a single storage area.)

The PSW of some processors contains information in addition to the address of the next instruction: for example, condition code bits which an instruction can set in order to convey information about its results, modes of operation, **storage protection keys**, and various **masks**. The PSW *controls the fetching and the execution of an instruction*. The operating system uses the *data* in the PSW to control a context switch.

In a context switch, an interrupt occurs and the currently executing process must be suspended in order for the process to deal with the interrupt. The currently executing instruction completes, and the data in the PSW (the next-instruction-address register) is saved. This preserves the address of the next instruction to be executed *when that process is resumed* and the condition codes set by the last instruction in that process to have completed. The address associated with the starting instruction of the appropriate interrupt handler (often called an **interrupt vector**) is moved to the PSW. The processor then fetches the instruction indicated by the address in the PSW and executes it.

The reverse occurs when an interrupted process resumes. The stored PSW (the address of the next instruction of the suspended task) is restored to the PSW register, and the processor fetches the instruction indicated by the address now in the PSW for execution.

Managing a process

However, an operating system must know more about a process under its control than merely the next instruction to be fetched and executed. Thus, when an operating system takes program code and turns that into a process it also creates a small item of data in order to keep track of other aspects of that process in its progress through the system. The operating system creates a **process control block** (**PCB**). This is an entirely software concept: a small, discrete piece of data created by the operating system when it creates the process and which it uses *to control the execution of the process*. Some operating systems keep this information in a table; others keep each datum discrete from all the others.

Such a control block consists of the process's unique identifier, start-time stamp, priority, the address of the first instruction, the status of the process (running, blocked, or ready) and pointers to any other control blocks related to the process. For example, a PCB may contain a pointer to a task I/O table (TIOT), which in turn contains pointers to a file control block (FCB) for each file required by the process, each of which in turn contains a pointer to a unit control block (UCB) for the device containing the file. (A control block contains information necessary for operating-system control of some aspect of the system; a unit control block contains status information about a device attached to the system.)

The operating system updates the PCB to reflect any change in status of the process (first to blocked, then to ready, then to running). For other control blocks, changes in the status of their objects will be noted by the operating system. For example, the operating system will alter a unit control block to show whether the unit is online (accessible) or offline (inaccessible, as it might be if the engineer were maintaining it). In some systems, tables are used in place of control blocks, but the functions are the same. When a process completes, the operating system destroys it by deleting mention of it from the system and by deleting the control block(s) associated with it.

From the point of view of operating systems, all control blocks of a given type are identical *except for their logical connections to the object to be controlled and to related control blocks*. This connection is usually established by means of a pointer; that is, any control block will contain an address within primary storage where a related control block, program code or other object is to be found. Such pointers frequently form chains. This method allows a system to establish temporary links between such ephemeral phenomena as processes and more permanent parts of the system such as the peripheral devices attached to the computer system which are temporarily allocated to a process.

Among the simplest and earliest operating systems are those which contain little more than interrupt handlers and which allow context switching. Such an operating system must be able to treat processes as objects; minimally, it must be able to *create* a process from program code, suspend the process to deal with interrupts (*block* it), wake the process to resume execution (*ready* it), *resume* executing the process, and, finally, *destroy* the process once it has completed.

Processes

While programmers give names to their programs, there is usually nothing to prevent two different programmers from duplicating program names. In fact, it may be useful to have two programs with the same name — for example a test and a live version. To create a process, the operating system must find a unique identifier for it. Then the process must be made known to all parts of the operating system and a means of tracking its progress must be established. Lastly, any resources a process requires must be allocated to it and identified as belonging to it.

Bear in mind that *an operating system is itself a group of processes, and it must switch the attention of the processor among several processes: the user process and various operating system routines*. Let us follow the progress of a process through a system.

The operating system selects an 'inert' program which someone has requested should run, and creates a process from it: creating a PCB, allocating resources and building their necessary control blocks. When the processor is available for work, the operating system dispatches the process (which I shall call a *user process* to distinguish it from processes which are a part of the operating system), which begins to run. It runs (which means it has control of the processor) until it reaches a point where it is interrupted. The user process itself initiates a request for a state transition to *blocked* in the case of I/O. All other interrupts are initiated

Systems Software and Early Operating Systems

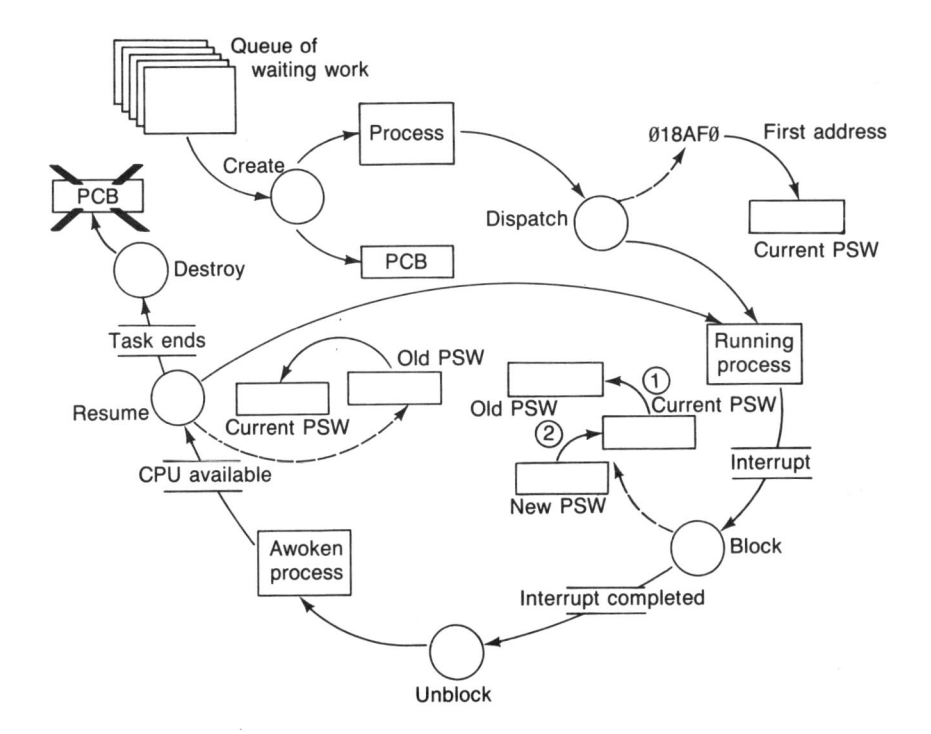

Figure 2.4 The life cycle of a process. Dotted lines show causation

from outside. The process remains blocked until the event it awaits is completed, when the operating system is said to *wake* the process *up*. That is, the operating system changes the process's status from *blocked* to *ready*. As soon as the processor is available, the operating system dispatches the unblocked process to continue execution.

This cycle of blocking, waking up and dispatching to run repeats itself until the user process completes. Then the operating system destroys the process and selects a new program to turn into a process. Whenever a process is blocked, the contents of the PSW are saved, and the appropriate interrupt vector is copied to the PSW. When a process is dispatched for the first time, the address of its first instruction is put into the PSW. On all subsequent dispatches, the saved address is returned to the PSW so that the process resumes where it left off.

Questions for review

(i) What is meant by the term *context switching*? What must happen in a context switch?
(ii) What is the role of the PSW? Interrupt vector? Saved address?

(iii) What must an operating system be able to do to a process?
(iv) What purpose is served by a control block such as the PCB?

2.3 IMPROVING SYSTEM UTILIZATION

By developing the data channel to carry out the work of input and output, three important things occur. First, the main processor's work is less hampered by the slow speeds of peripheral devices. Secondly, as it is doing less of the work of the system it has available time in which to do other work. Thirdly, it can support bulk data storage on a number of different types of device.

Interfacing process, data and storage

Magnetic tape was introduced early. A reel of magnetic tape (called a **volume**) by its nature is a serial access medium, but it can contain a great deal of data. Serial access means that, to read the 549th record on a reel of tape, the system must first have read the first 548.

Two devices which resemble each other in that they permit direct access to any record so long as the position of that record is known are the magnetic drum and the magnetic disk. They differ primarily in the arrangement of **tracks** (analogous to the grooves in the surface of a record) for storage of data: the drum, being a cylinder, is a continuous surface, whereas the disk is composed of one or more platters in a protective covering, each surface of a platter being divided into concentric rings called tracks. If there is more than one platter, they are arranged vertically upon a spindle and this is called a **disk pack**. A disk pack, or single-platter disk, is also referred to as a volume. A diskette or floppy disk uses the same principles but both are smaller, have a much smaller data capacity, and are more portable.

The operating system or user process (or the two together) must have a means to find any record on a **volume** such as a reel of magnetic tape or a disk or disk pack, even if, in the case of tape, access is restricted to serial mode. How does one know when one has reached the 549th record, or the 386th?

Whether the medium is tape or drum or disk, a clearly identifiable point at which a record begins and ends must exist. In what are known as **hard-sectored disks**, areas (**sectors**) of a given size are set at the time the disk is manufactured. These sectors are available to hold a record. That is, each track is divided into equal-sized sections. A record may be smaller than the sector available to hold it, in which case some of the

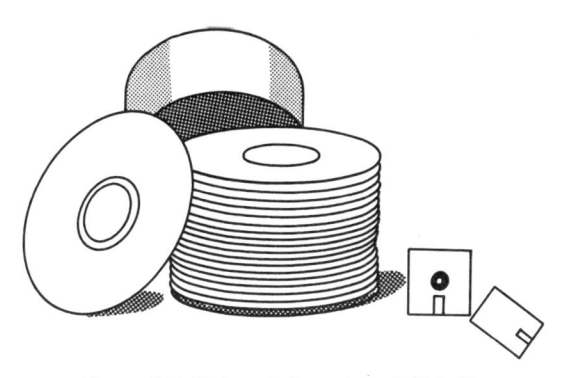

Systems Software and Early Operating Systems 39

Figure 2.5 Disks, disk pack and diskettes

capacity of the sector is wasted, or it may (rarely) be as large as the sector, or may even be larger than one sector and thus spread over two or more. An I/O operation transfers one sector at a time.

In so-called **soft-sectored disks** the sector size is determined by software at the time the disk is initialized. This can be manipulated to more closely match a system's needs. In a few systems, there is no set sector size up to full track size, in which case the unit of transfer is equal to the physical record, which I describe below. In this last case, the unit of data transfer, up to the maximum size, is determined by the programmer.

Tape, consisting as it does of a continuous strip of about 750 meters (2400 feet) in length, can be more flexibly subdivided. Since a **tape drive** passes tape across a stationary read/write head at high speed, the tape cannot stop instantaneously without damage. Hence a gap (called the **interblock gap**), a blank space in which the tape drive can brake the tape or gain speed, exists between one record and the next. The record can be as long or short as need be (subject to some technical limitations) and is thus not constrained by something like sector size, but the need for interblock gaps means that a tape cannot be completely filled with data.

The programmer, however, writes a program which looks at records which are often rather small. Yet with sectored disks, putting one record in each sector where that record does not approach sector size is very wasteful of an expensive resource. On tape, a single inch (2.5 cm) can hold at least 200, and up to 6400 bytes, and there must be approximately 2.5 cm gap between each record. So small records are also wasteful, especially on very large files where the empty space on the tape may exceed the data and force the file to occupy several volumes. In addition, I/O is expensive in terms of the time it takes, since it involves blocking the process, waiting for the I/O to complete, then waking up and resuming the process. Therefore it *pays* to do as little I/O as possible.

To reduce the amount of I/O and wasted space, it is necessary to group records together as efficiently as possible. (Here, as you will see in Part II, different operating systems use different philosophies.)

A record as it is defined in a program and as people commonly think of it is called a **logical record**. For example, a record can be one date-and-time stamp with one temperature reading, or a collection of information about one person: name, address, telephone number. If several logical records can be grouped together, they can be transferred and stored as a unit called a **physical record** or a **block**.

In disks, it is useful to make the best use of a sector by making the size of the block as close as possible to that of a sector. Thus, given a sector which contains 256 bytes and logical records of 25 bytes each, ten logical records grouped as a physical record or block of 250 will waste only six bytes of the total possible space available. In addition, an I/O operation transfers ten logical records at one time. A buffer, then, must be the same size as the unit of transfer, the block.

However, the program as the programmer wrote it still expects one logical record at a time to be presented to it, separately from all other logical records, whether or not that record is a part of a block. This apparent discrepancy is dealt with at the interface between the operating system and the process by updating a pointer which points to the logical record within the buffer which the process is currently concerned with.

A *read* instruction in, say, a COBOL program advances this pointer to the next logical record within a buffer, which contains a block. An I/O operation occurs only when the last logical record in a buffer has been dealt with by the program and the program issues the next *read* or *write* instruction. For example, where a block contains 10 logical records, the first *read* will cause an I/O operation to transfer the first block into a buffer and set the pointer to the first logical record. The subsequent nine *read* instructions only advance the pointer, one logical record at a time, through the buffer's contents. The eleventh *read* instruction causes an I/O operation to transfer the next block, place it in the buffer and update the pointer to point again to the first logical record within the buffer. Such pointers operate on a formula of logical record length multiplied by position number of logical record within buffer.

Improving performance with buffers

The processor can, however, more than keep up with the speed of even blocked, buffered data transfer. It still has time available for more work. What other work? In the case of output the main processor can easily carry on executing instructions in the same process without necessarily waiting for the output to complete. But what if one instruction requires data which are to be transferred by the preceding instruction? Will the processor not still have to wait for the input data to appear in the buffer in order to carry out the next instruction? Yes, but this limitation can be partly overcome by having more than one buffer available. The processor can request I/O transfer with one buffer, then proceed immediately to work with the records contained in a second buffer. The data channel transfers the first buffer then, on the next I/O operation, transfers the second.

Output operations work similarly, with the process filling one buffer, signalling the data channel that the buffer is full and ready to be transferred, then proceeding to fill the second buffer while the data channel transfers the contents of the first. Different pairs of buffers are usually used for each input or output stream, though some operating systems use buffers common to several processes, as you will see when you read the Unix case study in Part II. In some systems, for example IBM's OS/MVS, more than two buffers are used to improve the system's overall performance (multibuffering).

Questions for review

(i) What does an I/O operation do? Make special reference in your answer to the use of blocks.
(ii) How might triple buffering operate? When might it be useful?

2.4 BASIC AUXILIARY STORAGE MANAGEMENT

The problem of files and storage

The management of files is an important function of the operating system. A reel of magnetic tape or a floppy disk can be stored in a vault or moved between computers at widely separated locations. This property is true of *any* removal medium or any collection of data which can be copied onto a removable medium.

However, the volume is not the same as the file(s) which may reside on it; the medium itself is erasable. When a file 'ages' to the point where it no longer serves any purpose, the medium can be re-used for another file — and that file is not necessarily a newer version of the old file. Thus there are two problems: the storage and retrieval of files of data, and the management of the volumes of recording medium.

The volume, whether of tape, diskette, disk or other medium, *must be externally identifiable* since it will be handled by operators and kept together with many similar volumes. The exception is where one person uses a personal microcomputer; even here though, the microcomputer user is likely to have several floppy disks that look identical on the outside unless they are labelled.

Yet what is contained on one volume one day may reside elsewhere the next and a new file of a different name may appear on the first volume. Also, more than one file may reside at one time on any volume. Thus an external label on a volume is insufficient to identify fully what is on it. *There must be a means of cross-checking that the right file is present for the process requesting it.*

Managing files and storage

Externally, volumes carry a label I shall call a **volume identification label**. This may be a combination of letters and numbers. Most computer installations have established standards and control procedures to avoid duplication.

Verification that this external label is correct can only be done if the volume contains an internal **volume label** in computer-readable form which corresponds to the external label. Thus, if a process asks for a file on volume PAY004 and the librarian selects this volume and sends it to the operator who mounts it on a drive, the system can read the internal volume label to see whether the volume is actually PAY004 or has been mismarked.

An internal volume label is of a fixed format and contains fixed information of importance to the operating system in verifying that the volume is the correct one. Many microcomputer users initialize their floppy disks without this volume label; however, there may come a time when it is important to distinguish between two apparently identical copies and the volume label may prove very valuable – saving hours of detective work.

On disks, and sometimes on volumes of magnetic tape, more than one file will be present at a time. This is especially true of disks which, like long-playing records containing several bands, will contain several files which are *individually accessible*. Thus the operating system, in addition to verifying the volume identification, must also be able to determine whether the desired file is present, and where the file is. The operating system also needs to be able to determine whether there exists sufficient free space to begin writing a new file and where the writing of a new file can begin. I shall discuss the problem of file identification and access first.

On disks, there will appear in a fixed place, not only the volume label, but also something known as a **volume table of contents** (**VTOC**) or a **file index**. (I shall use the former term to avoid confusion with other types

Systems Software and Early Operating Systems 43

of index.) This VTOC will contain information regarding each file found on its volume: the file name, its starting location, its protection keys (such as an expiry date), its owner, its organization and some vital accounting information. The VTOC will also contain information about unused space available for either extending existing files if necessary or beginning new files.

On tapes, a file header record identifies the first file and immediately follows the volume label. A file trailer record signals the end of each file. For each file subsequent to the first, a new file header record appears, identifying that file. As there is no single record identifying all the files on a tape volume if more than one exists, the operating system must make a serial forward search to locate any files subsequent to the first.

In checking the data storage resources assigned to a process, then, the operating system verifies that the correct volume is present (microcomputer systems may ignore this step), that the file exists on that volume, and, depending upon the operating system, verifies the organization of the file (for example, whether it is sequential, indexed or random) and, when the process first accesses the file, marks in the appropriate control blocks or tables that the file is open. When processing ends, this control information is deleted by the operating system as a part of destroying the process.

The file location information in a disk's VTOC establishes the base (starting) point from which all addresses within the file can be calculated. This in turn results, through a complex interaction of hardware, operating system and applications software, in the positioning of the read/write head for record access.

Questions for review

(i) What actions does an operating system take to recognize a volume?
(ii) What actions might an operating system take upon recognizing that an incorrect volume has been mounted?

2.5 FILE MANAGEMENT: ORGANIZATION AND ACCESS

All media available on early computing systems were sequential in nature. The only practicable way to access records on such a medium is to pass through them one after another in the order in which the medium presents them. For processing purposes, two 'orders' were possible: ordering by some kind of **key**, or no ordering at all.

A file ordered by key is one in which one or more fields (the key field or fields) act as a key for arranging the records in a logically useful sequence. For example, a common telephone directory is arranged in alphabetic order by, first, surname, and where two or more entries have the same surname, by forename(s) or initials. If this ordering is for any reason inconvenient, such a file must be re-sorted into another sequence. For example, telephone engineers might find that a directory by surname is virtually useless to them; they might need one ordered by telephone number, or one ordered by, first, district, second, street within the district, and third, house number. Punched cards were once a popular medium because a single file of them could easily be re-sorted by an electro-mechanical sorter into a variety of sequences according to need.

Unordered files always have a hidden order: the time in which each record is presented to be written on the medium. Thus, for example, an automatic log of telephone calls might seem to have no order, but would appear in the time order in which these telephone calls are made, an order which might be irrelevant for any purpose other than the initial collection of the data.

An operating system provides the means for reading or writing files. The type of physical access (e.g. read or write) or the type of file access (e.g. sequential) is called the **access mode**. The method by which a record in a file is located is termed the **access method**. (The term can apply to location of any item in any storage.)

Sequential files

Sequential files are dealt with by the **sequential access method**. If a file is blocked, then the access method is called the **queued sequential access method** (because blocked logical records can be thought of as a queue through which the process must work its way). The queued sequential access method provides for reading or writing a block of data and for creating and updating the interface with the process which deals with single logical records (the pointer which points to the current logical record within the buffer).

If a file is not blocked the access method is called the **basic sequential access method**. This access method reads or writes a physical record which it assumes to be the same as a logical record. That is, it provides a physical record to the buffer but does not concern itself with any subdivision which may or may not exist within this record; this then becomes a task for the user process.

Direct access files

Since any record on a disk can be directly accessed (sometimes this is called **random access**, but it is *not* a random process), the operating system

Systems Software and Early Operating Systems

provides an access method for this: **basic direct access method**. Simply stated, it is a means of finding the location of a record within the file by determining its exact storage location (sometimes called a **bucket**) in terms of an address which states which read/write head (if more than one exists) is to be active, over which track it is to be located, and which sector is the correct sector. In response, the read/write head moves to the correct track (this movement is called a **seek**) and waits for the correct sector to rotate under the head. Disk performance can be calculated in terms of **seek time** (the average time it takes for the head to move from its parked position to any correct track) plus **rotational delay** (the maximum time taken for the correct sector to rotate into position under the head).

Organization versus access

Sequentially *organized* files on disk cannot have their records accessed directly. This is because file organization is determined at the time the file is created, and it is at that time the appropriate mechanisms must be in place in order to allow a particular type of access.

However, many systems provide an intermediate form of organization called **indexed sequential**, in which records are in sequential order by key but there is a separate index indicating which keys are in which locations. For example, in an indexed sequential file containing job numbers and their corresponding descriptions, the file is ordered by job number: A0000 is first, A0001 second, and so on. But an index is built as the file is written showing that the first bucket or sector contains records beginning with A0000, the second bucket or sector contains records beginning with A0037, the third bucket contains records beginning with A0074, and so on. This allows both types of access on a single file. This file organization is useful when both types of access are required, such as in applications where the bulk of processing is in sequence by key, but direct access is required in accessing records for random enquiries — for example credit-card processing where billing is done on a sequential basis but enquiries from merchants about credit-worthiness are random.

There are two types of access methods used with this type of file organization. The first is the **indexed sequential access method** (**ISAM**), where records which will not fit into their designated (home) area are stored in special overflow areas which are pointed to by the home area. The second is the **virtual storage access method** (**VSAM**), in which full home areas are simply divided into two with the records distributed between them and with the index changed to show the altered situation. The first (ISAM) has the disadvantage of sometimes creating long overflow chains which slow record retrieval; this in turn necessitates periodic reorganization of the file to eliminate those chains. The second (VSAM) has the disadvantage of processing overhead each time a home area must be divided and the index updated, but the main body of the file will always be in the correct sequence.

Low-level input and output

At a lower level still, if a sequential file is on magnetic tape, the operating system must distinguish this and execute the appropriate I/O instructions for tape. If the same file resides on a disk, the low-level I/O instructions will be different from those for tape because of the need to locate the file, move the disk head to the beginning of it, and keep the head in position to access records in sequence. For direct access files, the instructions are different yet, since the head(s) must move in response to random requests.

These low-level routines are called **device drivers**. They vary for each type, make and model of device and for each computer system, because I/O in each case is unique to that device and system combination.

Questions for review

(i) Why is it necessary to provide different low-level routines for the same file organization on different devices?
(ii) What information must be available to the operating system for a direct access file that is not needed for a sequential access file?

Questions for discussion

(i) Once all programmers wrote their own I/O code; later prewritten and tested code (called IOCS) was included in the source program and assembled with it. Briefly discuss the limitations of these two methods. What could you suggest to overcome them?
(ii) Do you see any possible problems in the easy movement of data between one computer system and any other? What types of problems?

FURTHER READING

Danhof, K.J. and Smith, C.L. (1981) *Computing System Fundamentals*, Addison-Wesley, Reading, Massachussetts. Chapter 11 looks at micro-processor interrupt systems and specifically at interrupt-driven I/O.

Deitel, H.M. (1984) *An Introduction to Operating Systems*, Addison-Wesley, Reading, Massachussetts. Chapter 3 discusses process concepts.

Gorsline, G.W. (1980) *Computer Organization: hardware/software*, Prentice-Hall, Englewood Cliffs, New Jersey. Chapter 4 discusses memories (primary and secondary storage, magnetic media) in some detail. Chapter 5 discusses overlapping I/O and interrupt processing.

Lorin, H. (1972) *Parallelism in Hardware and Software: real and apparent concurrency*, Prentice-Hall, Englewood Cliffs, New Jersey. Chapter 1 introduces a basic analogy to explain the concepts of coexistence in time for computer tasks.

Peterson, J.L. and Silberschatz, A. (1985) *Operating System Concepts*, 2nd edn, Addison-Wesley, Reading, Massachussetts. Chapter 3 covers file systems.

CHAPTER

3
Multiprogramming systems

During the late 1950s and early 1960s computers users developed an appetite for computing. 'The hunger for more ... often stimulated by the new devices themselves, as well as by new marketing techniques associated with them, enabled their rapid spread throughout society and society's increasingly rapid transformation under their influence.' [1]

Large-scale automation became an important factor in maintaining a competitive edge in industry and commerce; in government and other institutions such automation enabled those institutions to keep more information without a commensurate increase in paper work. Programmers had gained sufficient experience to attempt more and to achieve what was attempted more easily. Machines were faster, cheaper and more reliable, thus expanding the type of problems amenable to automated solutions.

However, this expansion resulted in intense pressure to make ever more effective use of the computer: a pressure which drove both hardware and software development in a number of directions. In hardware, continuing improvements in electronics and in the design of secondary storage devices increased speed, reliability and capacity. In software, there were improvements in techniques for managing computing resources and for wringing ever greater performance from the system as a whole. There were also major strides forward in facilitating computer use for the user, including interactive (conversational) and shared modes of use, as I shall describe later in this section.

3.1 CHANGING CONCEPTS IN OPERATING-SYSTEMS DESIGN

An operating-systems revolution occurred in April of 1964 with IBM's announcement of its System/360 series of computers, though the impact of this revolution was not immediate.

Multiprogramming Systems

Until early 1964, each time an organization's computing needs outstripped the capacity of its particular computer system, the organization found itself in the position of having to obtain a newer and more powerful system. Each such change required that organization to convert hundreds of existing programs. Such a process is fraught with problems. The incompatibility of one system with another required enormous inputs of programmer and computer time. Problems of incompatibility do not necessarily show up as programs which don't run at all; they may show up as programs which run *differently* than they did on a previous system. The process can be compared to a person who loses or gains a lot of weight. He or she might buy a new item of clothing or two in celebration (or acceptance) of the fact, but normal economics makes it likely that one has to rip out and restitch all the seams, darts and tucks in one's clothing in order to make it all wearable again.

IBM recognized these problems as a serious hindrance to both computing growth and change. It saw the marketing potential of a solution to them.

The System/360 concept was designed to address those problems. The concept was of a *family* of computers available in a wide range of sizes and speeds for a wide range of applications with 'upward' compatibility guaranteed between members of the family. 'Upward' means that any program which runs on the slowest and smallest member of the family will also run on *any* of the larger and faster members. (Programs which run on the larger, faster members of the family *may* run on slower and smaller members *provided* the programs fit the size criterion of the smaller member; thus 'downward' compatibility is possible but cannot be guaranteed.) A user organization could begin its 'computerization' with the smallest, least powerful and cheapest member of the family commensurate with its needs and then grow into using larger members of the family, all without the need for expensive, time-consuming and frustrating conversions.

The System/360 family members *each had different underlying architectures*. This had been the practice in the past, as one can see by looking at other, earlier IBM 'families' like the 1400 and 70xx series. However, all members of the System/360 family used a common **instruction set**. The *instruction set* is the collection of all the machine-language instructions and their assembly-language equivalents which a given architecture is capable of executing. This commonality of instruction sets was made possible by using **microcode** to make the format and action of each machine or assembler instruction appear identical regardless of which member of the System/360 family executed it.

Microcode consists of instructions held as bit patterns in a read-only memory (ROM) in a control or arithmetic unit. These instructions control logic gates and bits within or between registers and components of the processor like the control unit, the arithmetic—logic unit, and so on; each microinstruction is a *step within a machine instruction*. Thus, a single machine instruction to add the contents of two registers together might consist of a half-dozen or more microinstructions.

IBM also considered the marketing problem of attracting users of existing, incompatible equipment (including earlier IBM architectures like its 1400 and 70xx series) to its new family. Once an organization became a System/360 user, the compatibility factor would be a strong incentive to remain one.

To attract new users and convert existing IBM customers to the new family, IBM decided to provide the potential customer with an incentive to switch to the new family at a time when experience with changing computing equipment was a powerful disincentive. To create this incentive, IBM supplied its customers converting from older IBM equipment with a large assortment of machine **simulators** and **emulators**.

Simulators are primarily software-driven. They are cheap to produce but run rather slowly. They make one computer *simulate* the action of a dissimilar computer. Emulators involve some hardware modifications. They are generally faster than simulators but more expensive. Either allows a user to run a program without making changes to the program code. Organizations moving to the System/360 family were thus enabled to install a System/360 and convert individual programs to the efficient 'native' code at leisure, perhaps changing it only when changing business needs demanded changes in the program's function.

In addition to simulators and emulators, IBM supplied, with its OS/360 operating system, the largest array of **utility programs** (general programs designed to carry out a variety of common tasks like file copying, file maintenance, creation of program test data, etc.) ever provided to facilitate computer use.

Many other computer manufacturers, at about the same time, made offerings of computers with advanced features which IBM had eschewed in its designs. For example, Burroughs introduced a virtual memory system (which I describe in Chapter 4). Though IBM did not offer many of these more advanced features, their marketing strategy was eminently successful. They had concentrated on two of computer users' main problems: growth and compatibility. Solving these problems which the users organizations considered of prime importance to them proved more attractive to new and converting buyers than new concepts and new features, which past experience had shown, for many organizations, were chancy, expensive and often only a marginal improvement on past practice. IBM's design and marketing strategy dominated thinking about computer design and operating systems for the next 15 years. Certainly the concept of offering a 'familial' range of compatible computers has come to be a *de facto* industry standard.

IBM's hopes of offering a single general-purpose operating system which would answer the needs of all types of user organizations were, however, frustrated. The user organizations' different needs and demands could not be met by one all-purpose operating system. Smaller organizations with modest needs found that their systems were much degraded in performance by the high overheads of OS/360. These overheads likewise made this operating system unsuitable for applications requiring very fast response times, such as transaction processing and real-time processing.

As a result, a number of different IBM operating systems ultimately appeared during the 1960s, and their lineal descendants are with us yet. Three varieties of OS/360 appeared; there were some short-lived operating systems like TOS (*Tape Operating System*) and BOS (*Basic Operating System*); there was DOS/360 (*Disk Operating System*), which continues into the present. ACP (described in Part II, Chapter 11) was developed in conjunction with the airlines to provide a transaction-processing operating system with fast response times. There were some operating systems which, though made available commercially, were largely special-purpose or experimental.

In the early 1970s, another revolution, primarily of marketing technique, occurred. Until then, manufacturers sold *hardware*: processors, disks and tape drives, controllers, channels, terminals, card readers and punches and all the other hardware appurtenances of a computer system. The software (operating system, utility programs, compilers and relevant documentation) tended to be viewed by the manufacturer as 'give-away' items 'bundled' in with the cost of the hardware.

Hence manufacturers tended to feel little responsibility for software quality, which was, in any case, difficult to achieve. User organizations, who obtained the software 'for free', found it difficult to justify to their own managements the purchase of software from a third party unless they had special requirements. Because the market for operating systems and much systems software was poor, there was little incentive for software companies to create operating systems and systems software for sale. Instead, they concentrated on providing applications software. Further, there was little incentive for computer user organizations themselves to put time and effort into developing their own systems software. IBM introduced separate charges for all but the most basic software ('unbundling') and changed all that.

The user organization's management now saw separate items on the invoice for much of the software and began to feel much more strongly that they were buying a product which at least had to function properly.

The manufacturer, in charging for (and having to market) such software, felt a greater responsibility for its quality. Seemingly overnight, an industry producing competitive systems software (especially in areas where visible applications and program development performance gains could be made, as in sort/merge utilities and compilers) grew up. It became possible to 'shop around' for software to meet one's requirements. The so-called PCMs (plug-compatible mainframes) received a boost in that their customers could buy a manufacturer's software without having to buy the hardware, or vice versa.

IBM also, unintentionally, provided the computing world an important lesson with its OS/360 operating systems series. Operating systems on the scale of OS/360 and others developed during the 1960s were huge and unwieldy, were often thought out and designed as they were being written, were programmed by teams of dozens, even hundreds, of people who could only be vaguely aware of overall design. The long development time spans and turnover of personnel on projects of that kind of complexity and scope meant that much effort was scrapped and then redone.

When users received the product, it turned out to be riddled with difficult-to-find, expensive-to-repair errors. Its extreme complexity meant that correction of one error might spawn a dozen new ones. The design and development effort that went into the 'third generation' operating systems was simple when compared to the resulting maintenance effort. This experience has since been repeated many times in many ambitious software development projects.

From this experience the realization came to many people both in industry and the academic world that hardware, however complex it may seem, is easier to develop than software, because the former is *engineered* carefully according to known principles and it can be rigorously tested. In future, software would also have to be engineered. The lessons of operating systems development in the early 1960s have given rise to the new and growing discipline of software engineering.

Questions for review

(i) What factor(s) led the designers of the System/360 family to implement certain functions using microcode? Can you think of how this concept could be used in another way, and if so, how?
(ii) What impact did the development of large operating systems have on software development in general?

3.2 COOPERATIVE WORKING

Earlier, I described a simple model for cooperative working and its computing equivalent. This allowed two (or more) agents, the processor and data channel, to cooperate in the transfer of data by sharing buffers and by arranging a means of communication about those buffers.

Multiprogramming Systems

When only one user process can execute at a time, many processor cycles are 'wasted' — that is, the processor is idle. This is because any program has a tendency to execute faster than even buffered, concurrent I/O can take place. One way to obtain yet more performance from a given computer system is to use the structures of the interrupt, either that caused by a clock signal or one caused by completion of an awaited event, to allow *several processes to execute in an apparently concurrent fashion*. It is a small step from interrupting a process in order to do I/O, polling or mailbox checking to deciding to interrupt a process so that *another process can have a slice of the processor's time*.

There are problems in organizing any kind of sharing, as anyone who has tried to teach a young child to share toys with playmates surely knows! Broadly speaking, in computing there are a number of issues which must be resolved in order to make the (apparent) concurrent sharing of the processor among a number of processes possible. I shall discuss these below.

Since any process which is executing must be present in primary storage, there must be a way of either having several processes resident at once, or of having the executing process 'change places' with another on some kind of time-sharing basis.

There must be a means of identifying 'possessions' (resources like data) by 'owner', as several different data files must also be present for those processes which are executing concurrently. Though any process must be given access to its data files in order to accomplish its work, conversely other processes must not be able to interfere, or to gain unauthorized access to those files.

There must be certain 'public' facilities. As I shall explain, it may occasionally be necessary for a process to have exclusive control over such a public facility temporarily. In that case, the system must ensure that no situation will arise in which this control continues indefinitely, thereby denying access to other processes requiring that facility.

There is a need to prevent conflict over resources and to preserve order through management and scheduling.

Volatile but valuable resources like data while they reside in primary storage must be protected from corruption.

There must a means of avoiding the situation where two processes each gains exclusive control of any facility which the other then requires in order to complete, or, if such a situation occurs, there must be a means of identifying that it has occurred and preventing it from continuing indefinitely.

Sharing an expensive resource requires that the sharers pay for their part of the costs. Accounting for use is necessary in order to charge users and is further a valuable tool for understanding the system's workload.

In the subsections which follow, I shall address each of these problems in turn to show how operating systems and computer designers developed mechanisms to allow sharing.

An extended model for cooperative working

In Chapter 2, I discussed models for coordinating work between two agents working cooperatively on a single task. Those models, however, dealt only with the communication between the two (for instance, the interrupt) and the sharing of a resource (the buffer). It seems a simple enough model, but I have purposely ignored the dynamic aspect of what must occur in order to keep the model simple. In order to understand concurrency fully, I must expand the model.

Sharing a resource

As any small child quickly realizes when an adult urges it to share a favorite toy with a playmate, it can no longer hold onto the toy but must relinquish it − graciously or otherwise − in favor of someone else. At a more advanced age the child may realize that this is not, in fact, a necessarily bad thing, since both children can then invent games in which the presence of the other child is a necessary and enjoyable part of the scenario.

Sharing a computer system

Most programs are not wholly computation bound. They do not make continuous use of the processor, but must read or write data from input, output or secondary storage devices on a recurring basis. Each I/O operation leaves at least some processor cyles idle. The use of **asynchronous I/O** using semi-autonomous data channels and buffers eliminated some, but not all, of these idle cycles. The direction taken, then, was to make use of those idle processor cycles in order to advance the execution of more than one process at a time. The idle cycles caused by one process waiting for I/O could be used by another process if there were another one ready to execute. However, there was still but one processor, and its use among different processes was shared on a temporal basis: first one process uses some cycles, then, as it waits for I/O, another process executes and uses some cycles. Figure 3.1 illustrates the division of processor time among three processes.

In order to undertake the temporal sharing of a processor, the system's designers had to decide upon what basis the sharing could be

Multiprogramming Systems

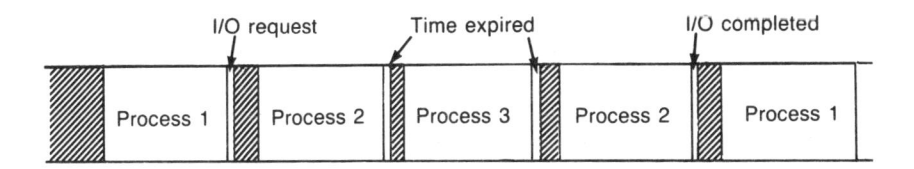

Figure 3.1 Division of a processor's time among three processes

done. For example, each process could be considered of equal importance to every other process — then processor time could be shared on the basis of each process receiving an equal increment of time with every other active process, each in turn. In other words, first I would have the processor for, say, 10 milliseconds, then you would have it for 10 milliseconds, then the third person, then me, then you, then him or her — equal periods of time in regular order. The difficulty with this scenario is that you may not be ready to use your 10 milliseconds when my time is up. Does this mean that your 10 milliseconds are wasted, idle?

A second possible basis is that I keep control of the processor until I need to do some I/O, then I relinquish it in your favor. You may then keep control until you need to do some I/O. By that time the third person may get control. But what if your program requires frequent I/O whereas mine requires little I/O but has long, long sequences of pure computation? What if my task is more important than yours?

The notion that one task may be more important than another is inherent in many systems. If, in a hospital's use of a computer one task is monitoring life-support equipment and one is updating patient records with the day's temperature and blood pressure readings, clearly the life-support equipment monitoring must take place regularly without any unpredictable long delays, and any emergency signalled as a result of such monitoring *must* take priority over any other less important task. This ability to rank tasks by importance and then to allow a more important or urgent task to interrupt a less important task is called **preemption**. In computing terms, any task more urgent than that of the currently running process can preempt that process from the processor in order to claim processing time for itself.

Even if the basis for sharing a processor assumes that all processes are 'equal', if each process is given an equal increment of time, then the process must be interruptable by the clock, and the system must be able to preempt one process to allow the next process to have its time increment.

Recall how a buffer works. One agent fills the buffer with data and the other agent then deals with that data. In the case of input, it is the data channel which fills the buffer and then interrupts the processor, thereby preempting any running process. This causes the processor to switch to the interrupt handler for I/O interrupts. In the case of output, the processor fills the buffer and then wakes up the data channel, which then transfers the buffer's contents to an output or secondary storage device.

Time-sharing computer systems

In early computer systems someone wishing to use a computer could request a block of time, appear at the appointed hour, and have exclusive use of the computer for that period. However, this is not a particularly flexible arrangement and can result in a great deal of wasted time. If one's program had an error, one might leave the computer in order to investigate it, while the computer remained idle because the next user had not yet arrived. Conversely, it was wasteful for someone with a running program which had not quite finished to be 'booted off' the machine simply because he or she hadn't booked sufficient time. What was now proposed was to allot a brief period of time to each user – a **time-slice** – in a round-robin fashion.

A revolution in computer use which occurred early in the 1960s was the development of systems which allowed several different users, none of whom could individually justify the expense of computing equipment, to share one computing system concurrently among themselves with those users restricted to using a series of short tasks rather than allowed to 'batch' large amounts of work together as had been the method before.

Most work can be broken down into a series of discrete steps in this way. A distinct advantage of this mode of working is that a dialogue between the user and the computer system becomes possible. The user can request a small task, see the result of that and base the next request on the outcome of the earlier request. He or she thereby interacts with the computer system in a more dynamic way than is possible with what are called **batch processing systems**.

In batch processing systems, as much work as possible is packaged together in a 'batch', to be done with virtually no intervention from the operator once the process is underway. Time-sharing systems are also called **interactive processing systems** because the operator, programmer or user interacts with the computer system, giving a relatively trivial command which might take a few seconds, obtaining a result from the system, then entering another command perhaps based on the preceding result.

In addition, it seemed reasonable to try to bring computing power to the individuals, especially those with short tasks to run, near where they sat rather than ask them to make the trek to the computer. The computer could, after all, control input/output devices such as especially adapted teletype equipment which would allow the user to type in commands and small amounts of data. When a person sits at a terminal, his or her thinking and keying time will greatly exceed the time the computer requires to process that user's request. It thus becomes possible to divide this otherwise idle time among a number of users, each sitting at a terminal, thinking and keying in.

Because any running process must be present in primary storage, the simplest way to share small time-slices, and one of the earliest methods used, was to allow each user in turn full use of the computer. When any task completed or a time-slice expired the status of the user's entire session at that instant was **swapped out**, that is, saved on a high-speed device such as disk, and the next user in the round-robin had his or her task **swapped in** from disk and was allowed to process for the next time-slice. First proposed in 1959 by Christopher Strachey of the University of Oxford and demonstrated by the Massachusetts Institute of Technology's Computation Center in November of 1961 [2], the facility was not widely available for nearly another decade.

Figure 3.2 shows how a swapping time-sharing system works. The whole of primary storage is allocated to a single process for a short length of time, just as though that user were the only user to have any access to the system. The user's process runs until it finishes or its increment

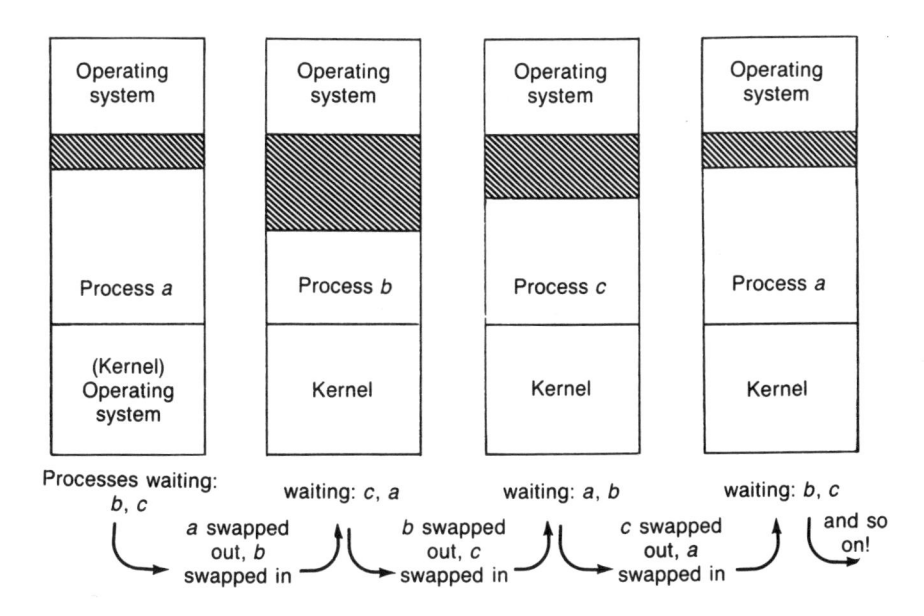

Figure 3.2 A simple swapping time-sharing system

of time expires. Then that process is removed from primary storage — swapped out — and another user's process is swapped in. It is dispatched and runs until it finishes or its time increment expires, then it is swapped out and yet another user's process is swapped in. Any given process will normally be swapped in this way several times before it completes.

So long as there are few users on such a system, each can proceed with work without noticing the presence of any of the others. However, if too many users are present on such a system the time between one turn in the round-robin and the next must increase to the point where the delay between turns becomes noticeable.

These systems provided an important foundation for future developments. I shall discuss them later in this context.

Question for review

Why is the concept of preemption a necessary precursor to time-sharing systems?

3.3 SHARING SPACE

Sharing a computer system by simply dividing up the time available has some disadvantages, as *all updated information must be saved with each swap-out and a complete copy of everything must be returned to primary storage with each swap-in.* This creates a high overhead of input−output. The processor is also idle a great deal: 40 per cent of its time in the 1961 demonstration system at the Massachusetts Institute of Technology.

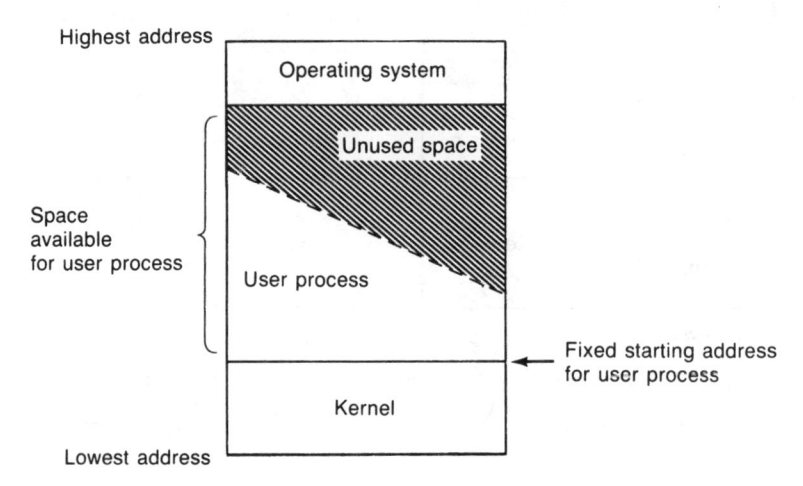

Figure 3.3 The simplest form of space use involving an operating system

Multiprogramming Systems

When a number of processes can be active at once, it also becomes possible for them to share resources. In the simple time-sharing system mentioned earlier, space is *not* shared — only one user process is resident in the computer system at a time and all others are swapped out awaiting a turn.

In the mid 1960s another approach was taken — to allow several processes to be resident in primary storage simultaneously, all of them except one either blocked or ready and waiting to execute.

One resource that such processes must share is primary storage. An analogy might be a group of patients sharing a hospital therapy pool with a physiotherapist helping them do individual exercises. They are all in the pool together, but the physiotherapist's attention can only be given to one patient at a time. In computing, some means must be found of sharing out space in the 'pool' of primary storage.

The monolithic model

Several possible means of allocating primary storage exist; it will be instructive to examine some.

Figure 3.3 shows a system which allows only a single user process to reside in primary storage at one time. An example of such a system was an early version of the IBM operating system OS/360, called OS/360 PCP (for *P*rimary *C*ontrol *P*rogram). The user process begins at an address just above the permanently resident kernel which occupies the lowest possible addresses, and can extend to any address just short of the high-address portions of the operating system — usually the non-kernel portions of an operating system.

Many microcomputer operating systems use this system of storage allocation: one process is allowed and can use all the space not used by the operating system itself, and may, in some circumstances, even use some of the space normally reserved for the operating system. CP/M is an example.

Partitioning space

In such one-process-at-a-time operating systems, it is necessary for one process to finish or to be interrupted (as in the time-sharing system I described earlier) for the next process to begin (or continue). Figure 3.4 represents a departure from this method. It shows an operating system which *divides* primary storage into several fixed-size areas called *partitions*. This is a fairly straightforward extension of a one-process-at-a-time system. The larger primary storages available meant that it was a rare program

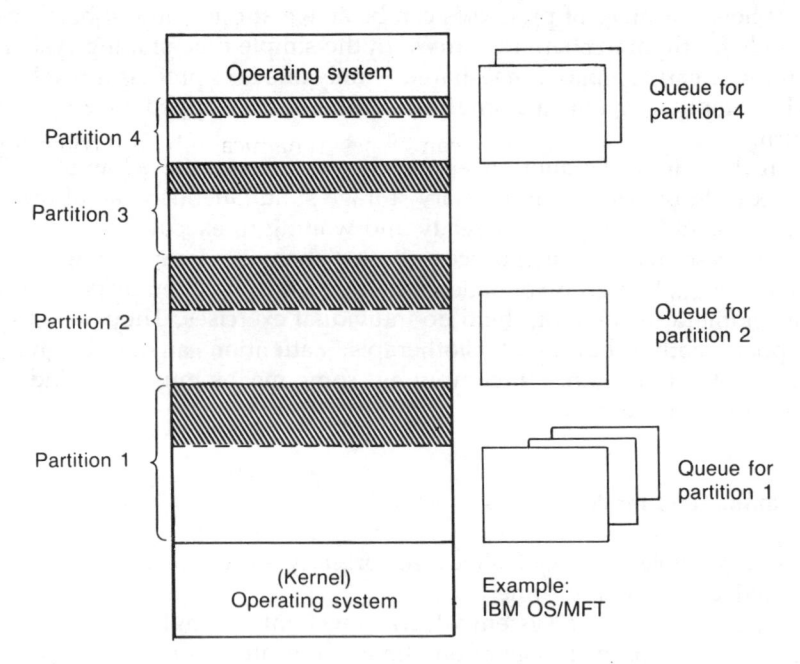

Figure 3.4 Using fixed-boundary partitions to share primary storage among processes in a multiprogramming system

which required more than a small part of the total available primary storage; hence it is logical to divide that storage up so that several processes can be resident in primary storage simultaneously. By fixing the boundaries of these partitions, the problem of allocating storage to a process is simplified. Again, a version of IBM's OS/360 operating system family used this technique; it was called OS/360 MFT (for *M*ulti-programming with a *F*ixed number of *T*asks).

Each partition in such an operating system is a contiguous section of primary storage. Figure 3.4 shows a system with four partitions, but up to 15 were possible in the IBM system. Each program, as it becomes a process, is loaded into primary storage beginning at the lowest storage address in the partition it will occupy. It can extend up to the highest address in that partition. The operating system occupies the lowest addresses in primary storage (kernel), and some of the highest. All the space between these two portions of the operating system can be used for user processes. The sizes of the partitions can be, and usually are, different in order to make as efficient use as possible of the available storage. A program awaiting execution *queues* for the partition appropriate

Multiprogramming Systems

to it. For example, a 32K program cannot queue (successfully, at any rate) for a 16K partition. Though a 32K program might run in a 64K partition, this is highly wasteful and would be unusual except in cases where the 64K partition was free much of the time.

The sizes of the partitions can be set dynamically by the computer operator, who can also control the queues, though the initial queueing usually occurs automatically. The operator sets partition sizes based on a manually determined workload schedule. Very large programs might only be run late at night or over a weekend to avoid having to devote the computer system entirely to one or two such large programs.

While such a strategy improved the amount of work that could be done on a computer system and reduced the amount of idle time for the processor (since several processes were ready and available in storage and the processor does not have to wait on a swap-in), it still presents some problems.

Figure 3.5 illustrates two possible problems. The first can be seen by looking at the 32K partition — the process in it requires only 21K, but 21K is too large for the 10K partition, so it must occupy the next larger partition, at the waste of some 11K. Altogether, the figure shows that enough unused space exists in these empty fragments to accommodate another process. Even though program *e* is only 11K and could run in the empty 11K of the 32K partition, this cannot be done without re-assigning the partitions manually, and it would be unproductive since the partitions would then need to be returned to their original sizes once

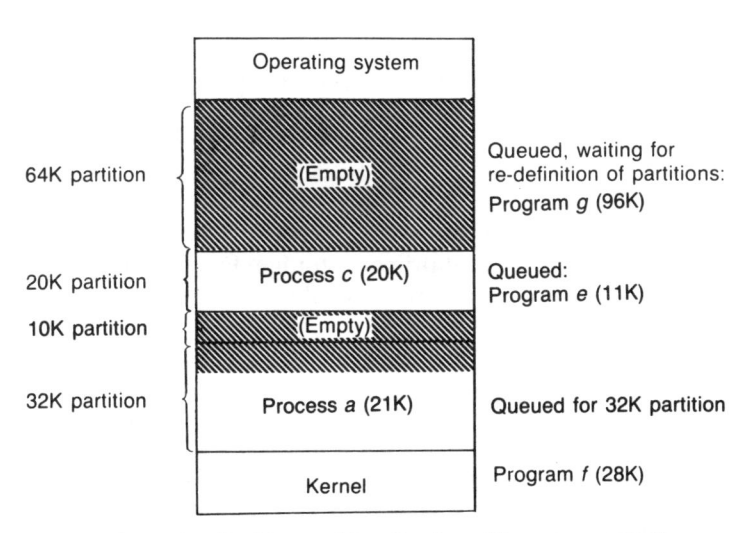

Figure 3.5 Problems with a fixed partition arrangement

all these processes have completed. Also, the 64K partition is empty, but a 28K program is queued for the 32K partition. The operator would have to override the normal operation of the system to queue the 28K program for the 64K partition — and what if a 60K program then entered the system queues? The 96K program will have to wait in a queue until some unpopular hour when the operators can afford to reconfigure the system for one large partition.

Apportioning space

The difficulty with using a strategy of fixed partitions to achieve multiprogramming is that it is relatively inflexible. In order to achieve better flexibility, the operating system needs to provide a space in primary storage which fits the program intended to use it. In other words, it would be better to allocate space in primary storage according to the needs of the programs, in chunks of variable size. Figure 3.6 illustrates such a scheme. Again, an example can be taken from another version of the IBM/360 OS operating system called MVT for *M*ultiprogramming with a *V*ariable number of *T*asks.

In such a scheme, when the computer system starts up, primary storage will be empty except for those low-address and very-high-address portions used by the operating system itself. Any programs queued will be loaded into primary storage from the queue, end-to-end, until no more will fit. The programs remaining in the queue will only be loaded into primary storage when some process finishes, releases its storage and leaves a sufficiently large portion of free space for the next program.

Initially, when programs are loaded into an empty storage, this works well. Precious space is not wasted. However, suppose one process of 48K ends, and the two programs available in the queue are 42K and 52K in length. The 42K program will be loaded and run, and the 52K program will have to wait for free space of at least 52K to become available. In the meantime, 6K of free space, too small to use, exists next to the 42K process. Eventually, many of these small fragments of free space are likely to appear, scattered throughout primary storage. Primary storage is then said to be *fragmented*, and in the interests of improving performance the fragmentation must be dealt with.

Generally, there are two ways in which to deal with fragmentation. One is to 'dry the system up' — that is, to prevent new processes from starting until primary storage is empty and then release the queues again. In other words, the operator periodically 'cleans the slate' so that programs are loaded into an empty user storage area. This was the practice in OS/360 MVT systems. Other systems which use variable-sized regions of storage reshuffle processes around dynamically in order to recover fragmented space; Unix (in many of its versions) is one of these. Doing

Multiprogramming Systems

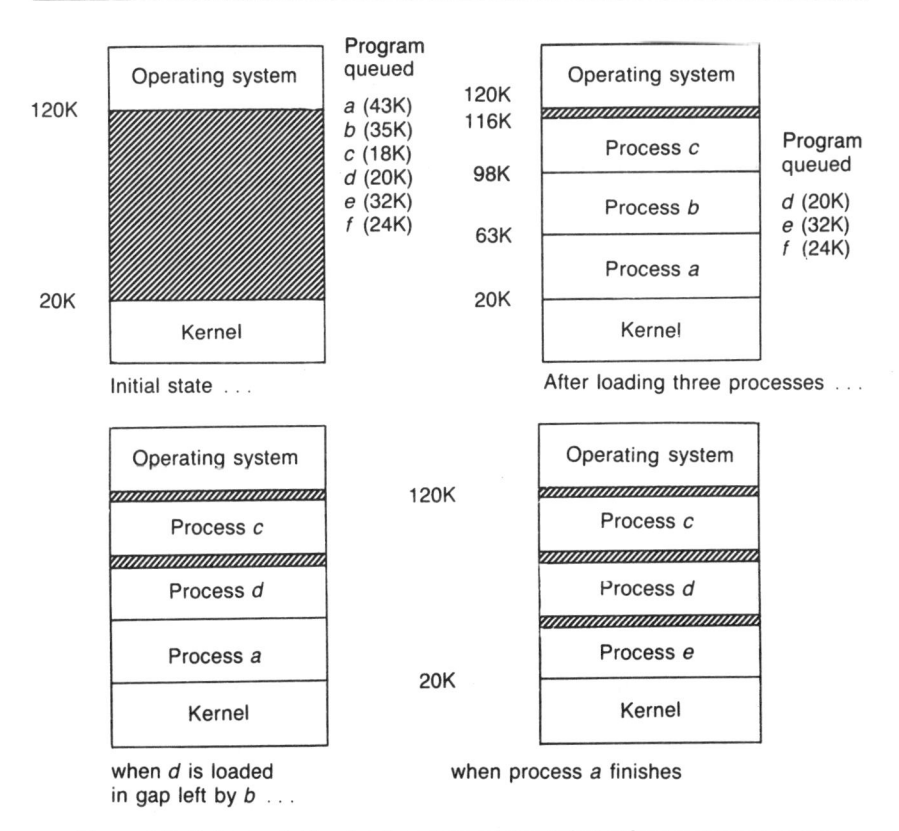

```
                Program
                queued
 Operating system                          Operating system
120K            a (43K)   120K
      Kernel   b (35K)    116K                                    Program
                c (18K)          Process c                        queued
                d (20K)    98K                                    d (20K)
                e (32K)          Process b                        e (32K)
                f (24K)    63K                                    f (24K)
                                 Process a
 20K                       20K
      Kernel                     Kernel

 Initial state ...              After loading three processes ...


 Operating system                          Operating system
                          120K
    Process c                              Process c

    Process d                              Process d

    Process a                              Process e
                          20K
      Kernel                                  Kernel

 when d is loaded           when process a finishes
 in gap left by b ...
```

Figure 3.6 Using variable-sized regions to apportion primary storage space among processes in a multiprogramming system

the shuffle automatically and dynamically takes time, and the operator has little or no control over its occurrence. However, no one has to remember to do it. So the two methods demonstrate the trade-offs between added function (but higher overhead and less control) and less function (but less overhead and more control).

Strategies for apportioning space

I have discussed various specific means of sharing primary storage above. It will be well to describe the general strategies for sharing space in any environment which allows 'variable fit' — such as OS/MVT as shown in Figure 3.6. These strategies provide the basis on which any actual mechanism is designed. Such strategies are collectively termed **placement strategies**, that is, strategies to determine where incoming programs and data are loaded.

Best-fit means that the operating system searches primary storage for an area in which it can place a program with as little waste as possible. If a program requiring 42K of space is waiting and free spaces of 48K, 64K and 128K exist, the operating system will place the program in the 48K area, with a 'waste' of only 6K. As you might guess, this has a relatively high overhead since the operating system must look at *all* available free spaces before making a decision.

First-fit means that the incoming program will be allocated the first available area of free space large enough to contain it. The advantage of this strategy is its speed.

The last strategy is **worst-fit**. Worst-fit means that the incoming program is placed in the largest of all the available areas of free space. If 'maps' of free space can be kept in order by size, the overhead of such a strategy is as low as the first-fit strategy. While worst-fit may seem an odd choice, it means that any area of free space left over may also be quite large and thus able to hold another relatively large program.

Summary

All of the above multiprogramming strategies have in common the philosophy of sharing the resource of primary storage among several simultaneously resident processes. But if one thinks of primary storage as not only a space, but as a space existing within time, it becomes obvious that one can also share this resource by dividing its use by both space and time. Several time-sharing systems use the swapping technique – it combines well with other techniques since a process can be swapped in and out of a partition or region as well.

Questions for review

(i) Can you think of a way in which a swapping time-sharing type system could be combined with the use of fixed-size partitions? What limitation might that place on the user or the task?
(ii) How would the use of variable-sized regions combine with a swapping time-sharing system? What would be necessary with each swap?

Mutual exclusion

To avoid problems caused by two or more processes trying to alter the same resource at the same time it becomes necessary to *serialize* a process's access to a particular resource: to ensure that *only one process at a time can access any resource which cannot be safely used by two or more processes simultaneously*.

Thus, updating ('writer') processes in a shared data environment can institute **mutual exclusion**. That is, whichever updating process gets hold of the data (or other resource) does so in a way that *excludes any other access to that data* (or other resource) *by any other process*. It blocks the possibility of any other process, whether reader or updater, accessing the same data at the same or nearly the same time. The process which has the data must then complete the update and release the data from exclusion so that they can once again be accessed by other processes. I have mentioned that mutual exclusion can apply to 'other resources' lest you be led to believe that it applies only to data in files or databases. There are other resources to which access by a process must be serialized.

It would be very unwise to allow an operation which has a resource held under mutual exclusion to be interrupted. The resource held under mutual exclusion has passed to the control of the process executing. In the case of an interrupt occurring, it would be difficult to save the exact status of the process and resource if the former were interrupted once it got under way. And if a process has exercised mutual exclusion over a resource and then becomes blocked, this effectively *also blocks any other process requiring that resource*. Any process holding a resource in mutual exclusion can be said to be in a **critical section** or **region**. The process is not preemptable for the duration of that section.

The most fundamental operations in mutual exclusion are in *entering that state*, and *leaving it*. These operations are mutual exclusion primitives, being the most fundamental operations inherent in mutual exclusion. This is true of data on files, as in the example of the airline booking system, and of systems data such as information held in the form of a control block.

What the implementation of mutual exclusion requires is a form of synchronization which ensures that *only one process will be in a critical section at one time*. The simplest means of doing this is to *disable* interrupts for the duration of the critical section, and then enable them again upon exit from the critical section. This prevents any state transition from occurring once the critical section of a process is entered. In an operating system's processes, which update system-wide data such as major control blocks, this is a necessary technique. However, it is only suitable for critical sections of very short duration and for specially authorized users such as systems programmers. Otherwise, any system based upon interrupts will quickly become severely impaired.

Setting signals

Another method of providing the necessary synchronization is to institute **semaphores**. These are 'signals' which are set to show that a process has entered a critical section. A simple analogy for this is an airport which can have several planes running on several taxi-ways and parallel runways but which has places where two or more paths cross or feed into a single path. Control over this type of situation was long established in the railroads through using semaphores. The same technique applies to airports, where one plane proceeding onto a single taxi- or runway from a parallel runway first causes a semaphore to be set, thus warning other pilots that the single path is in use. When that plane leaves the single path, the semaphore is reset, allowing any other plane to proceed. Note that it is impossible to 'interrupt' the progress of a plane down this single path and simply 'lift it aside' so that some other aircraft can use the path. The aircraft in the path must be allowed to proceed so as to complete part of its journey. Note also that some outside agent, namely the air traffic ground controller, must mediate among the demands of the other planes to use this resource in order to ensure that everything occurs in an orderly and safe fashion.

The same technique applies in computing. Any process which needs a resource which only one process at a time can use sets a semaphore which effectively says, 'this resource under exclusive, uninterruptable control by a process'. Most semaphores are simple 'on−off' switches, but more complex semaphores can be created by using a counter, so that the semaphore's value can be between zero and n where n is the maximum number of processes which can be in critical section where more than one is allowed.

A queue of waiting processes may develop at a point where one or a limited number of processes can proceed under mutual exclusion. The operating system's designer must then address the question of establishing a queue and of serving, in some fashion, the waiting processes. To return to the analogy of an airport, he or she must do this in the same way that the air traffic ground controller must establish a queue of aircraft and serve each in turn. Yet in processing terms, as you shall see when I discuss multi-user shared systems, keeping these uninterruptable operations to the minimum possible length of time avoids building up too large a queue. As any air traveller who travels at a busy time knows, such queues build up quickly and can seriously impact the working of the entire airport!

Deadlock

A problem may occur when a process gains control under mutual exclusion of that which another process requires in order to complete, if at the same time the other process has gained control under mutual exclusion of that which the first process requires. This situation (shown in Figure 3.7) is termed **deadlock**; neither process can proceed (nor can any

Multiprogramming Systems

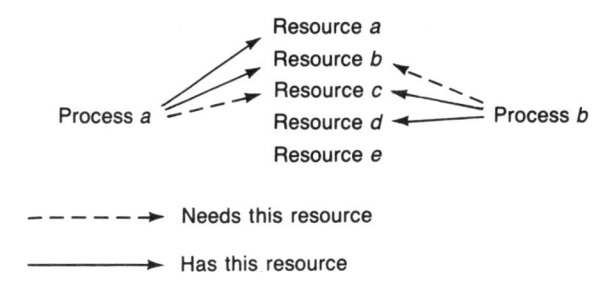

```
              Resource a
            ╱ Resource b ╲
           ╱  Resource c ╲
Process a ╱   Resource d  ╲ Process b
              Resource e
```

– – – – – → Needs this resource

──────→ Has this resource

Figure 3.7 Deadlock

queued behind either of them) until the other gives way.

If there is no means of blocking one process in order to allow the other to claim the contended resource(s), and if any process already allocated resources holds on to them (waits) while waiting to be allocated the additional resource, a genuine deadlock condition exists. Avoidance, prevention, detection of and recovery from deadlock are vital parts of any operating system in which more than one process can share resources with any other process and which I shall discuss later.

Questions for review
  (i) What are the two methods of identifying files in multiprogramming, multi-user systems? Can you think of one reason in each case why one method might be preferable to the other? Give an example for each.
 (ii) What method prevents interference between a 'writer' process and other processes accessing shared data? How does this method work?
(iii) What are some of the characteristics of a critical region?
(iv) Briefly explain the difference between interrupt disablement and use of semaphores.
 (v) What is deadlock? Why is its occurrence to be avoided or prevented?

3.4 CONCURRENCY CONCEPTS

Executions which overlap in time are said to be **concurrent**. This overlap can be at any of a number of levels in a computing system. For example, many processors overlap the execution of microinstructions. This is done at a hardware level, by perhaps double-buffering the program counter so that consecutive fetches of instructions can take place on successive clock cycles. Instead of having parts of the processor idle while first one instruction is fetched, then executed, then the next instruction is fetched,

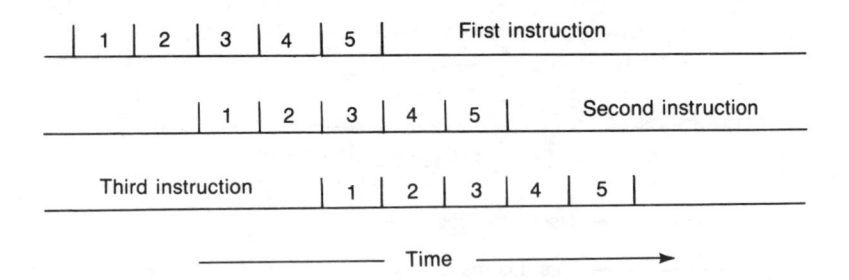

```
| 1 | 2 | 3 | 4 | 5 |    First instruction

            | 1 | 2 | 3 | 4 | 5 |    Second instruction

Third instruction   | 1 | 2 | 3 | 4 | 5 |

                    ———— Time ————→
```

Figure 3.8 The overlapping of the sub-operations of fetching, decoding and executing instructions in a pipelined arrangement

the instruction fetches overlap in time, so that the first fetch has only just begun when the second fetch gets underway, as shown in Figure 3.8.

Concurrency occurs at the higher levels of instructions and processes. Where processes are concurrent but there is a single processor, the concurrency is one where the processes' individual instructions are *interleaved* in time but the processes themselves are concurrent. Here, I shall be concerned with concurrency in processes.

The concept of concurrency cannot be thought of independently of the concept of time. Behavior of processes (or instructions or microinstructions) in time can be of two kinds. The first kind can be termed *time-dependent* behavior. In time-dependent behavior, events must occur in a particular order to achieve correct results: say, *a* must happen before *b*. This compulsory ordering in time can be termed *precedence*. For example, it is not possible to produce a baby unless a woman has first become pregnant. In other words, events *must be serial*, conception and then pregnancy must precede birth, in order to achieve results.

In the computation

$$F(y) = x \cdot \frac{x^2 - y^2}{x^2 + y^2}$$

x and *y* must be squared first in order to achieve correct results. You can prove this principle to yourself with a pocket calculator and the simple problem of

$$3 \times 2 + 1.$$

The answer will be different if you carry out the operations in a different order. Thus the operations must be ordered, must be carried out serially (one after the other), and must be carried out in the *correct* order in order to achieve the correct result.

The second kind of behavior can be termed *time-independent*. Two processes which are completely independent of each other are said to be *disjoint*; disjointedness is sufficient for time-independent behavior. A woman going through a pregnancy and having a baby is disjoint from manufacturing cars: the pregnancy and the manufacturing can be concurrent processes. True disjointedness is simple to deal with due to the complete independence of two or more processes.

All 'good' programs have a *consistency requirement*; one expects a program, given the same input but in different executions, will always produce the same output. This means that the result of a program can be predicted from knowing (1) the input and (2) the functions carried out by the program. It also implies that a consistent program cannot produce output without first having received input, and if the input at time t always results in output at time $t + 1$, then output at time $t + 2$ will always result from input at time $t + 1$.

Improperly managed concurrency may cause a problem in program consistency. For example, suppose two processes refer to a common control block, both read a value from that control block and carry out some action based on that value, and either process may change the value. In this case the two processes are not entirely disjoint; they *interact*, that is, they are concurrent *and* share resources. If they were to be treated as though they were truly disjoint, one process could alter the value in the control block before the other process read it. In this case, consistency would not be maintained and the second process would behave differently depending upon whether the first had or had not changed the value in the common control block. The result of the program can no longer be predicted and different executions of the same program may produce different results.

Yet, there is nothing within the program itself which is 'wrong' and which causes this problem; the problem lies in the management of the concurrency — in other words, in achieving synchrony. One event (e.g. one process reading and perhaps updating the control block) must occur before the other (the second process accessing the control block), but it makes no difference which one. This is akin to two people trying to pass through a narrow door at the same time. The *end* result, that both will be on the other side of the door, is not affected by which one proceeds first and which one goes after. (Performance may be affected by which proceeds first and which comes after, but that is beyond the scope of this discussion.) This type of synchrony can be termed **priority**.

Mutual exclusion revisited

Interacting processes are processes which share resources; in order to do so they must be synchronized. Synchrony means the ordering of events or operations in time. Where processes are fully disjoint, there is no problem. Where processes interact, the parts which interact must *never* be executed at the same time. If both process *a* and process *b* require exclusive use of the same resource, there must exist some means of ensuring that one has priority over the other.

One possibility is to associate a Boolean variable with each resource, the value of which can be either *free* (available for a process to obtain) or *reserved* (in use by a process). Each process wanting the resource could check the Boolean, and if the status is *free*, set it to *reserved* and proceed. When the process completes, its last act is to reset the Boolean to *free*, thus allowing any other process wanting that resource to gain it. However, both processes *a* and *b* could check the Boolean, find its status was *free* and reset it to *reserved* simultaneously! It wouldn't even require that the processes' instructions to check and set the Boolean were concurrent: *a* checks the Boolean and finds it set to *free*; *b* now checks the Boolean and finds it (still) set to *free*; *a* sets the Boolean to *reserved*; *b* sets the Boolean to *reserved*. Results, in this situation, are unpredictable.

A possible solution to this is to let the Boolean associated with the resource be set to *a* or *not a*, depending upon which process had control. Process *a* would have to check that the Boolean was set to *a* before using the resource. The last instruction in process *a* would be to set the Boolean to *not a*. Process *b* can use the resource only when the Boolean is set to *not a*; upon exit its last instruction must be to set the Boolean to *a*. This appears to work, but it forces a strict alternation of *a* and *b*, which, if they are truly independent of each other, is unacceptable.

Using two Booleans will not solve the problem. If one Boolean, *A*, takes the values *a* and *not a* and the second Boolean, *B*, takes the values *b* and *not b*, process *a* can proceed if *not b* and sets *A* to *a*. When process *a* ends, it sets *A* to *not a*. Process *b* can only proceed if *not a* and it first sets *B* to *b*, then as it ends sets *B* to *not b*. But if process *a* sees *not b*, process *b* sees *not a*, process *a* sets *A* to *a* and then process *b* sets *B* to *b*, a deadlock occurs. If it is possible to be certain that *only one concurrent process at a time can reserve a common resource for a finite time*, then all will be well.

The problem is at its most acute when, as you have seen, resources (even those, like data files, held over a fairly long period) are at the point of being allocated to competing processes by the operating system. One possible solution is to define a critical section, which by definition allows only one process at a time to enter it and makes that process uninterruptable for the duration of the section. Imagine using a single measuring cup to measure the amounts of a number of different liquids. The measuring cup can contain only one fluid at a time, but if the person measuring does not allow any one liquid to remain in the measuring cup indefinitely, the measuring of all the liquids can proceed to completion.

If the common variables such as the Boolean which shows whether a resource is free or allocated can only be accessed *from within* the critical

Multiprogramming Systems

section, this means that processes in critical sections referring to the same common variable can exclude each other in time.

Critical sections, as I have noted, impose some constraints on scheduling. Because a process in critical section is uninterruptable, the critical section must be as short in duration as possible; it most certainly cannot be allowed to continue indefinitely! Thus, the rules are:

- one process, at most, can be within a critical section;
- a process will only remain within a critical section for a *short* finite period;
- when a process needs to enter a critical section, it will be allowed to proceed within a finite period (there is no indefinite waiting);
- if a critical section is 'empty' then a process needing to enter it can do so immediately;
- if a critical section is not empty, processes needing to enter it will wait;
- when a critical section for which there are processes waiting becomes empty, one of the waiting processes can proceed to enter it;
- the priority rule for allowing waiting processes to enter a critical section will be 'fair' so as not to delay any process indefinitely and so that more urgent processes can complete;
- all rules must be applied within a finite, short period.

Achieving synchrony

In order for processes to interact, they must be able to exchange data. It is the exchange of data which allows one process to signal to another that an event has occurred; thus the two can achieve synchrony.

People cooperating on a task who cannot or do not see each other usually communicate by means of messages. For example, two people sharing an office job might leave messages such as: 'Terry, I've finished filing all the forms through Menzies; the remaining forms are in the bottom left-hand drawer of the teak cabinet.' 'Jean, the manager of the quality assurance department telephoned and would like you to call back when you're next in.'

When processes communicate by means of messages, one process creates messages, while the receiving process can be said to *consume* messages. If the exchange is direct, process *a* to process *b*, the sending process may be delayed while the sender waits for the receiving process to get ready to receive the message. A *buffer* for messages avoids this delay by providing temporary storage for the message, just as a bulletin board in an office or another agreed 'message storage spot' such as under the telephone avoids the need for one worker to wait for the arrival of the other in a job-sharing arrangement. The sending process, however, cannot be allowed to place more messages in the buffer than there is capacity for. If the buffer is empty, however, the receiving process will be delayed.

Initially, of course, a buffer will be empty. If the sender puts messages into a buffer faster than any receiver can deal with them, the buffer will eventually fill and the sender will be forced to wait. If the receiver accepts messages faster than the sender sends them, then the buffer will frequently be empty and the receiver will be forced to wait. If the *average* rates of the sender's production of messages and of the receiver's consuming of them are nearly the same, the queue of messages in the buffer will fluctuate in length but little or no delay will be forced on either the sender or receiver. Hence the size of such buffers can be critical to cost and performance: it 'costs' more to provide a larger buffer, but performance is better when the buffer is the optimum size for the message traffic it must handle.

Interprocess communication using messages and a buffer will use a send or receive critical section in respect of a particular buffer to serialize input to and output from the buffer. The *send* and *receive* communication primitives both access a common item — the buffer — hence they must be serialized to prevent loss of integrity in the buffer and any deadlock.

Buffers for interprocess communication can be organized on a one-to-one basis (one sender, one buffer, one receiver) or on a many-to-many (several senders, one buffer, several receivers) basis. This, and the size of message to be passed among processes, determines how large the buffer must be. If the message is small, the whole of it can be placed on the buffer by the sender and removed from the buffer by the receiver: this is called **transmit by value**. If communication is on a one-to-one basis, the buffer can then be quite small.

If messages are large, then the overheads of a very large buffer to contain them and of the time required to copy them into and out of the buffer become very detrimental to system performance. Instead, the sending process sends the *address* of the message, which is placed on the buffer, and the receiving process removes the *address* of the message and uses this to access the message itself: this is termed **transmit by reference**. Even if the message is as small as an address, if communication is organized on a many-to-many basis the buffer may need to be quite large.

If the only purpose of interprocess communication is to achieve synchrony and any other sharing of data is unnecessary, then *semaphores* are a more appropriate form of communication. A semaphore is a tool for achieving synchrony. A simple form is that where only a timing signal is required: it says only 'the event with which I am associated has occurred'; it conveys no other information. The white and black smoke used by the conclave of cardinals in Rome to indicate the success or not of an attempt to elect a new Pope are classic semaphores of this type. Black smoke means 'a vote has taken place, but we have not selected a

Multiprogramming Systems

new Pope yet' and white means 'a vote has taken place and a Pope has been selected'. It cannot say *who* has been selected Pope, give a name, age, country of origin, or anything other than that an event has occurred. The number of times smoke appears from the conclave indicates how many votes have been taken. Thus, semaphores also can be used to *count* the occurrences of an event.

Semaphores are basically of two types: on/off (Boolean) and counting. Two primitives are associated with semaphores: *signal* and *wait*, and as signal primitives can change a single semaphore, there is a critical section with respect to a semaphore. Wait primitives, by their very nature, cannot be allowed to occur within a critical section (remember, a critical section *must* take a finite and short period).

The counting type of semaphore has one or, in some cases, two components. If a semaphore has only one component, it is an integer count of events of one type. A two-component semaphore is more complex and counts, for example, signals sent and signals received.

A single-component counting semaphore counts occurrences of an event, but it could also be associated with a list which can contain one to several processes waiting on that semaphore. Instead of processes cycling and constantly checking the semaphore's status (called *busy-waiting*), the processes are blocked and wait in the list/queue.

In the case of two-component counting semaphores, the semaphore indicates that a process can send or receive some signals (or, of course, no signals). The number of signals received cannot, of course, be fewer than none and cannot exceed the number of signals sent (a process may be *capable* of receiving signals faster than they are being sent, but cannot receive what has not been sent). The counting semaphore is itself finite; it can only count to an upper limit set by the word-size of a given architecture. For example, an eight-bit microcomputer can contain eight bits worth: 256. The semaphore thus counts the number of messages received (which is equal to or greater than zero) and the number sent, which is equal to or greater than the number received [3]. Such a semaphore could be used to control a message buffer.

It will be useful to pause here and summarize the concepts I have presented so far in terms of problems to be solved and tools to solve them. I show this in Table 3.1.

Deadly deadlock and its avoidance or prevention

The possibility of an occurrence of deadlock exists when concurrent processes are not fully disjoint, but interact in some way. Under what conditions can a deadlock occur?

One condition that leads to deadlock is the *partial* allocation of

Table 3.1 Problems in concurrent execution and tools to solve them

Problem	Tool
serializing use of resources	mutual exclusion
mutual exclusion	critical sections
exchanging timing signals	semaphores
exchanging data	message buffers
controlling access to critical sections or buffers	semaphores

resources to be held under mutual exclusion: where the operating system allocates resources to a process one resource at a time and that process holds any allocated resource to the exclusion of any other process needing it, yet has not acquired *all* the resources necessary to proceed to completion.

Piecemeal allocation by itself is not a problem; nor is holding resources under mutual exclusion. The two must be combined. A third necessary condition is *non-preemptive scheduling*. Non-preemptive scheduling means that any active process acquiring a resource under mutual exclusion will not be preempted through the normal scheduling mechanisms of the operating system. Thus, a process holding a resource will remain in control of that resource *indefinitely*. Where two or more processes each need a resource that the other holds under these conditions, a condition of *circular waiting* arises: process *a* waits for process *b* which waits for process *a* and neither can continue to completion.

Deadlock can be prevented by ensuring in the operating system design that one or more of the three conditions I have mentioned *never* occurs. However, the choice of how to do this may not be a simple one. For example, mutual exclusion is a necessity in cases where data will be updated, though the amount of time resources are held under mutual exclusion can be reduced. Preemptive scheduling, a 'simple' prevention measure, has a concomitant overhead which may make it unattractive or unacceptable from a system performance standpoint. Non-preemptive scheduling may thus be necessary in order to achieve high performance.

Another possible preventive is to allocate all resources to a process at once rather than allocating them one-by-one. This will force processes competing for the same resource to run at different times.

Yet another way to assure that resource sharing does not lead to deadlock is to consider all resources of one type, for example disk drives of a certain model, as equivalent, and to base allocation of resources on this premise. In other words, the process itself cannot specify a particular disk drive, only a disk drive of a certain type.

The system contains a pool of one or more resources of this certain type and allocates them by assigning a free (not being used at the time) resource from within the pool. The resources available to the system for allocation are the total resources minus those already allocated. If a system has 20 magnetic tape drives capable of reading and writing 6250 bpi (bits per inch) tapes and seven are already allocated to various processes, then 13 remain available.

The algorithm which controls this type of allocation is called the *banker's algorithm* (first proposed by E. Dijkstra), and it will be instructive to look at it in a little detail.

The banker's algorithm says that resources of a particular type constitute a pool of resources from which requests for that type of resource can be satisfied. The number of 'free' (unallocated) resources is the difference between the total number of resources and the number currently allocated. It is 'safe' to allocate a resource to a process if that can be done within a finite period. A process, in turn, has a claim on resources equal to its total need for resources of a particular type minus the number of those resources it currently has allocated to it.

The algorithm looks at the *type* of resource requested, checks whether it is safe to allocate (*safe* is defined as the ability to allow all requesting processes to complete within a finite time), finds a requesting process whose claim on resources does not exceed the available free resources, and allocates. Upon completion of the process, the resources allocated are returned to the pool of free resources. If an unsafe situation occurs, a deadlock *might* follow; while a safe situation will *never* result in a deadlock.

Assume that a system has ten resources of a given type. Suppose that three processes, *a*, *b* and *c* are active and using resources of this type. Table 3.2 shows each process, how many of the ten resources it has allocated and how many more of that type it will need to complete.

Table 3.2 **Allocation of resources**

Process	has allocated	needs
a	3	1
b	5	3
c	0	6
total allocated	8	
total free	2	
grand total	10	

Eight resources of this type are allocated from a total pool of ten; this leaves two free resources to be allocated. Note that, if the operating system's allocation algorithm allocates the two free resources to process b a deadlock will occur. In that case, processes a and c could not proceed because there would be no more free resources available to allocate to them, and process b would be unable to continue for the same reason, so all three would wait on each other. However, if the operating system's allocation algorithm chooses to allocate one of the two free resources to process a, then a can proceed to completion and release its resources, of which it had four. Thus a total of five free resources are available once process a completes. This is then sufficient to allow process b to complete, and once b completes there will be sufficient resources for process c, which needs many.

Questions for review

(i) Define *concurrency*. How is it related to *interleaving*?
(ii) What are the differences between truly disjoint, interacting and time-dependent processes?
(iii) What role do critical sections play in serializing concurrent processes?
(iv) What is meant by the *consistency requirement*?
(v) What conditions lead to deadlock? How can deadlock be avoided?
(vi) What is the purpose of the banker's algorithm and how does it work?

3.5 DATA IN MULTIPROGRAMMING SYSTEMS

In Section 3.2 I described how a system can have all active processes sharing a major resource — space in primary storage. Other resources can be shared, for example data. However, the sharing must be controlled. Data often have great value, and like other things can be used for good or ill, can be stolen and can be altered. The 'owner' needs to be able to control access to them, and yet must also be able to share them with others who need them.

Identifying owners

One constraint that widespread sharing places on any system occurs when some part of the system can be owned by particular programs or persons, for example data files. Recall that data files can often reside on a volume which holds other data files, and that these data files must be identifiable. It is one thing, however, to be able to identify a file by name, and another to know to whom (or what) it belongs and to whom (or what) access is allowed.

Early systems and most microcomputer systems rely upon the user or programmer to indicate at least the name of the file and to make available to the system the volume on which it resides. For example, in a microcomputer system, the user must usually insert the correct volume in one of the disk drives.

In larger systems, the user may also have to provide information about the type of medium and the recording method (is it disk or tape? what model? what density is the recording made at? what type of parity is used? and so on). This dependence on the user or programmer becomes less workable in a large community of users each with many files (especially when the system includes many naive or end users whose jobs and interests are not strictly limited to computing *per se*). Many operating systems quickly developed means of automatically cataloging the file name and its attendant volume identifiers and necessary medium and recording information so that the user need only know the correct file name. Most modern microcomputer systems shield the user and programmer from the details of recording information even when they do not have a multiple-user file cataloging function.

Depending upon the philosophy used, the operating system's file management software can maintain a system-wide catalog or a system of linked catalogs of files in which the name of the file (and perhaps the name of its owner) is stored together with the type of medium, recording information (where these are necessary) and the volume identifier(s). This is done in such a way that the user need only request the file by name. All additional information necessary to the locating and reading or writing

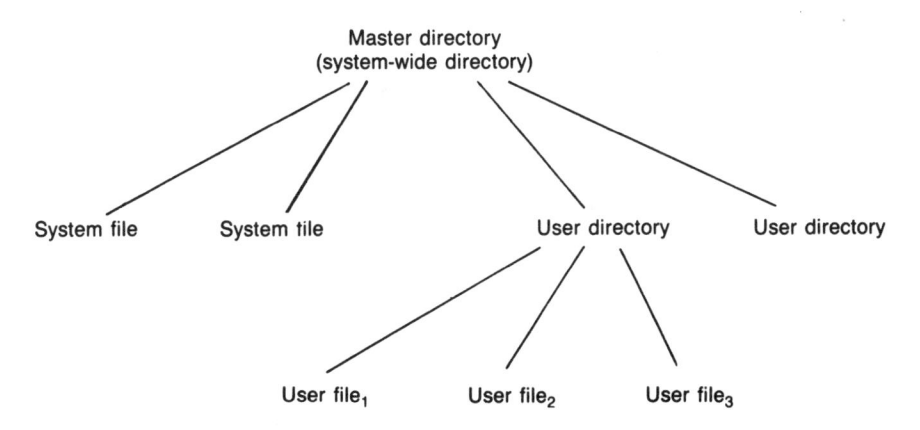

Figure 3.9 An arrangement of directories and files

of that file will be automatically extracted from the information held in the catalog, the VTOC entry, or both.

An alternative scheme is to allow each user of the computer system to have his or her own **user directory** to which he or she (and perhaps a limited number of other people) has access. All files belonging to this person will be listed under this personal directory and the operating system itself will maintain a system directory which points to system files and to all personal directories.

How the file management subsystem functions depends upon what may be put into the catalog or directory, under what circumstances it may be put there, and what information the catalog carries. Some file management subsystems allow both programs and data files to be represented in a catalog or directory; others have special provisions for executable programs, which must be accessed in a different fashion. Some file management software allows for automatic or user requested **archiving** (the making of a copy for secure off-line storage), while others make this a function to be carried out independently of the system.

Readers and writers

In an airline reservation system there is a large database against which a number of enquiries are made of the nature of: 'What is the latest, most direct flight from London to Bombay on Fridays? Are two business-class seats still available? Would it be cheaper if I flew by way of Delhi instead?' All such queries are what could be termed *readers*. They only *read* the database in order to answer a query. Since they only read and do not *update* the data, many readers can access the data, in parallel, without harm.

Avoiding and preventing mutual interference

However, in airline reservation systems it is also possible to update the database, as for example when a customer decides to reserve two business-class seats on Friday's flight from London to Bombay. There is then a double risk: first that readers accessing the same data at the same moment they are being updated will be given incorrect information (for example, they may be told seats are available when the last one has just been sold); secondly, another process may try to update the same data at the same time. In the second case, the double update will result in false data, since whichever of the two simultaneous updates finishes last will over-write whatever the first update wrote.

3.6 MULTIPROGRAMMING: CONTENTION, CONFLICT AND FAIRNESS

The apparent concurrency of several processes is termed **multiprogramming**. Multiprogramming usually implies the *apparent* parallel (concurrent) execution of processes which belong to one or several different users. I say *apparent* because I assume in my discussions so far that there is but one processor capable of executing program instructions. In Chapter 5 I shall discuss the situation which arises when two or more processors are coupled together in some fashion.

Multi-user systems

Pause for a moment to consider some of the implications of several users using a system simultaneously. By the term *multi-user* I mean a system in which several different users can have processes running simultaneously.

Data and secondary storage

The separation of data from the instructions which operate on them is highly desirable since the instructions can operate on any data of the appropriate type and data can easily be altered without having to alter the program. Suppose this concept of separation were carried further: into the realm of where the data reside, how they are organized, and who owns and controls them.

When only one user at a time can use a computer system, the operating system designer can safely assume that the user will be at least partly responsible for any data. This responsibility may be understood to be in the sense of assuring data correctness, and the safety and proper identification of files and the media on which they reside.

In the early days of computing, any files on portable media were often kept by the user in any place of convenience. (Desk drawers and coat pockets were popular.) As data came to be viewed as a valuable resource, and as organizations experienced agonizing and expensive losses of data due to cavalier (or occasionally malicious) attitudes of their employees, these organizations removed care and ownership of data from individuals and centralized all data control. In many senses, the trend toward the increased use of microcomputers represents a return to practices of the past, where the individual user is responsible for the integrity and security of data, usually on diskettes. The implications of central control of data, however, for any operating system are great. You will see in the case studies in Chapters 10, 11, 12 and 13 in Part II how various philosophies of data security result in very different assumptions about the people who use computer systems and about the contrasting needs for control and freedom.

In a multi-user environment, whether or not the philosophy is one of control and security or of freedom:

- files must be *uniquely identifiable by the operating system*;
- the operating system must manage secondary storage to some extent (automatic management normally extends only to magnetic media, not printed output or paper — cards or tape — input);
- the operating system must seek to prevent, or when it does occur, to correct situations of deadlock.

Where the philosophy of central control exists,

- there must be some means of protecting a file against inadvertent or malicious use, damage or destruction.

Policies needed for sharing

Since multiprogramming systems require several processes to reside simultaneously in primary storage, there is a risk that a problem with any one process can cause difficulties for other resident processes. Also, both primary storage and time in the processor become resources to be parcelled out among contending candidate processes.

In simple, single-user, single-process systems (such as a microcomputer) any 'scheduling' is a relatively straightforward matter (almost always done by hand where one system is shared among several users or else left to chance). In multiprogramming multiple-user systems **scheduling** is far more complex and has a large impact on the efficiency of the system.

A policy for scheduling work is required in multi-user systems. The scheduling may be done by hand in systems where the work is primarily *batch* and the workload is relatively light and well-known. An example might be a small office which runs regularly scheduled programs to produce payroll, invoices, accounts payable and receivable, and so on. Here a schedule might be of the nature of: 'start weekly payroll program by 4 p.m. every Thursday, start the invoices program after the orders update has completed, which is after the close of business each working day', and so on.

More often, the scheduling on systems belonging to large organizations is done automatically; this is especially true where much of the system use is *interactive* and the workload is heavy or fluctuates without warning. The scheduling in such a system must be flexible enough to respond to unforeseen demands. It may be based on achieving a balance of types of work in order to achieve near-optimum use of the processor. It should be dynamic — able to respond to changes in workload.

Accounting functions, which are at least partly a mechanism for encouraging adherence to policies of computer use and sharing, must be more complex in multi-user systems. Most large organizations with large computer systems charge departments for computer use so that the costs of acquiring and running a computer system are apportioned among its users. These charges can be designed to encourage or discourage certain ways of using the computer system in order to help achieve goals set by the organization.

When more than one user's process can be active at one time (that is, executing) there must exist a policy for the *resolution of any conflicts* over resources. Some processes, or classes of processes, will be more urgent or important than others. It is natural, however, for each user to consider his or her own use to be of primary importance; thus an organization has to have some means of resolving conflicts so as to maximize the benefits to the organization itself or at least to appear fair in providing a service to all users.

In addition to any questions of urgency for particular processes or classes of processes, there is a question of providing a satisfactory service to a community of users. 'Satisfaction' is frequently achieved by reaching a compromise among many conflicting demands. This compromise has implications for scheduling whether manual or automated, for determining **priority**, and for measuring performance by measuring throughput, **turn-around time** and **response time**.

If two or more processes execute concurrently, then *all of them will occupy primary storage along with parts of the operating system*. At the very minimum, the vital portions of the operating system must be protected from damage such as over-writing instructions with data, lest such damage halt all processing. Ideally, the operating system should be fully protected from such potential damage and each user should be fully protected from every other user. Such protection must not, however, prevent processes from communicating with each other nor should it prevent the sharing of data where this is necessary or desirable.

Potential areas of conflict

Which disk drive to use is not a question of great importance in microcomputer systems; the user indicates which of two, three or four is to be used if there is any choice at all. A large computer system, on the other hand, has, for example, tens of magnetic tape drives. If a programmer codes the absolute address of a particular tape drive in a program, situations will occur where a process requiring tape drive x must wait for another process using tape drive x to complete; this may be despite the fact that a half dozen other, idle tape drives are available at the same moment.

If several processes can be present in primary storage at the same time they cannot all begin at the same address. The operating system must have a means of deciding where each belongs in primary storage. This means that the object (machine language) program can contain *no absolute addresses* (there are minor exceptions). However, addresses in any program must be resolved *at loading time*, as the processor can only execute instructions referring to actual (that is, to absolute) addresses.

Minimizing the likelihood of conflict

The means of dealing with these two related problems are **device independence** and **relocatable programs** respectively. A related problem lies in having many copies of the same software in primary storage to serve many users simultaneously. This is wasteful of space, and can be solved by using **re-entrant code**.

Device independence

Device independence seems, unfortunately, to mean slightly different things when one looks at different operating systems. In general, however, it means that the relationship between the process and any physical device, such as a disk drive, it will use is postponed as long as possible. This may be as soon as the program is loaded and becomes a process or it may be when the process makes its initial request for action regarding a particular device. In order to accomplish this independence, all reference in a source program to a *specific* device is *symbolic*. That is, instead of referring to a specific disk drive in, for example, a Pascal program, you code:

    userfile := '*MYPROJ.TEXT';

and the relationship between that file and its physical location is *resolved* when the program actually executes, not before. The point at which the program is connected to an actual physical device is termed **binding time**.

Different operating systems establish binding at different times and allow the programmer different degrees of freedom in choosing the ultimate physical device to be associated with a particular file.

In source programs in which the programmer refers to the physical device directly by an absolute address, binding occurs as soon as the

Multiprogramming Systems 83

program is compiled and the program and physical device remain bound until the programmer alters and recompiles the program. This is totally inflexible.

When the programmer writes a source program using a symbolic reference to a physical device, in some operating systems binding time is deferred until the operating system begins creating the process. At that time the operating system establishes a link between the newly created process and the devices it uses.

In other operating systems, binding occurs when the executing process actually requests access to a device for the first time. This means that no process will tie up a device it refers to but does not actually use, and also that no process will tie up a device any longer than the minimum time necessary to accomplish its task. The later the binding time, the greater the degree of device independence.

However, the operating systems designer must balance the freedom allowed by a very late binding time with the possibility that a half-executed process will require access to a device reserved by a different process and may be delayed as a result.

Relocatable program code

A relocatable program is an object (machine language) program in which the assignment of absolute addresses is postponed until the object program is loaded for execution. At assembly or compile time all addresses in the program are treated as **relative** to the start of the program, which is given the address zero. The loader can then load the program beginning at any convenient address in primary storage and resolve addresses within the program in relation to its actual starting address. If such a program is loaded at an address of 077 A00, then its address zero becomes 007 A00 and another point in the program which is at relative address A2F now has the address of 00842F (007A00 + A2F). This method leaves the operating system free to locate any program within primary storage according to the program's need for storage space *and* the amount and location of space the operating system has available.

Re-entrant code

Another key concept to systems with a high degree of apparent concurrency (for example, interactive or real-time systems), is the concept of re-entrant code. In interactive systems, for instance, many activities access the same code: many users may access the same compilers, editors and so on.

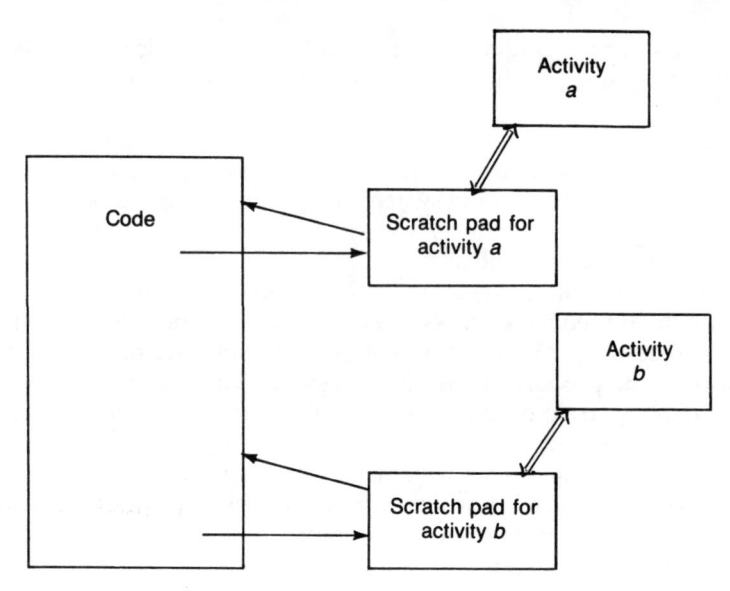

Figure 3.10 Re-entrant code and scratch-pad areas

Re-entrant code is written so that it is not self-modifying. It is easy, when writing code, to decide to set a signal or flag and to define that flag within the program. However, if the flag is actually a part of the program, the act of setting of the flag *will change the program* and hence only one activity at a time can use that code, since other activities will require a virgin copy in order to execute properly.

However, if the flag is defined outside the program and is associated with the activity that changes it, then modifying the flag does not result in any change to the program. In other words, the data used by an activity must be completely disjunct from the instructions executed to complete that activity. When several activities use one piece of re-entrant code and some data must be associated with each, the technique used can be termed *scratch pad*, with a small area of storage set aside for the data associated with each activity. The code simply uses the scratch pad for each activity to record any data pertinent to that activity. Most operating systems code is of the re-entrant variety.

Questions for review

(i) Why is relocatable object code necessary in multiprogramming systems? How is it accomplished?

(ii) What is meant by device independence? What is its chief advantage? What possible problem can occur where very late binding is allowed?

(iii) How is re-entrant code used? How does it ease the implementation of multiprogramming systems? How is code made re-entrant?

3.7 SCHEDULING IN MULTIPROGRAMMING SYSTEMS

Scheduling algorithms are very much a matter of carrying out a policy. They depend on considerations of: fairness to users, maximization of throughput (number of processes executed per unit of time), minimization of response time for interactive users (response time is the time between entering a command and receiving a response at a terminal), minimization of scheduling and related overhead, the balance of resource use, the enforcement of priorities and the avoidance of indefinite postponement (usually through a mechanism for increasing the priority of a request for work as it 'ages' while waiting). Scheduling can even be used to encourage or discourage certain behavior. For example, giving high priority to work requiring less than 30 seconds processor time tends to encourage users to break longer jobs of work into chunks which take 30 seconds or less.

An effective scheduling algorithm requires a careful look at a number of criteria, a good knowledge of the installation's work load, a firm description of a policy of use and a knowledge of queueing theory. The subject is a complex one, but let us look at it briefly.

Scheduling occurs at several levels in multiprogramming systems:

- when work is waiting to enter the system;
- when work is waiting to be initiated;
- when a suspended process is awaiting activation;
- when a running process is suspended or runs out of time (when time is the means of sharing the processor);
- when the process completes (that is, when it exits from the system).

The first two points above constitute **high-level** or **job scheduling**. Scheduling algorithms at this level decide what requests for work will be allowed to enter the *system*. (If you have ever tried to use a terminal to log on to access a multiprogramming system and have received a message saying 'try again later' you have been communicating with the high-level scheduler, which has found that the system cannot, at that time, support another interactive user, for whatever reason. Another common message in such a situation is 'system busy'.)

Priorities may be assigned to a request for work by hand or automatically. Priority determines the favoredness of a request for work. In large mainframe systems, especially in business and industrial environments, a user may also be able to purchase a higher priority than the request would normally be entitled to. By this means the system caters for those special circumstances such as emergencies or requests from the company's president. **Priorities** of this type are called **static priorities**; once assigned, they do not change.

Dynamic priorities, necessary in many instances, have a greater overhead than static schemes, but they respond to changes in work load or environment or both — for example by automatically increasing priority on aging requests for work.

A more problematic approach is **deadline scheduling** — scheduling any job so that it completes by a specific time. This requires intensive resource management and careful planning.

What I have just stated about all three types — static, dynamic and deadline — applies to high-level scheduling for batch processing as well as interactive processing.

Once the high-level scheduler has accepted a request for work and allowed that request to compete for resources of the system, the **intermediate-level scheduler** deals with which processes will be allowed to compete for the *processor*. This level of scheduling must be responsive to short-term fluctuations in the system's work load. It blocks or awakens processes.

The **low-level scheduler** determines which *ready* process will get the processor when it next becomes available. Some intermediate- and low-level scheduling strategies will be familiar to you from other contexts.

FIFO (first-in—first-out) is one of the simplest scheduling strategies. Once a request for work has been accepted by the high-level scheduler, it will be turned into a process once its turn in the queue comes. At the intermediate level, it will be made ready strictly in turn. At the lowest level, once a process has the processor, it runs until it completes or until it relinquishes the processor (for example by requesting I/O). FIFO is not much used in modern systems; however, it still remains imbedded within other scheduling strategies — units of work with equal priorities are usually dispatched on a FIFO basis.

Round-robin is a low-level scheduling strategy whereby ready processes are dispatched according to some other strategy initially, but once a process begins running, the low-level scheduler gives it a time-slice (also called a **quantum**) in turn with other running processes. Good service depends on the scheduling being tuned to provide the optimum quantum. This strategy is commonly used in time-sharing (interactive) systems.

Shortest-job-first scheduling favors requests for work which promise to take little time. Giving short-time requests preference quickly reduces the number of waiting requests and tends to minimize average turn-around time. However, it relies on the user's estimate of processor time, which may not be accurate. It may simply 'shut off' (guillotine) those jobs which grossly exceed the user's estimate. This avoids problems where programs have so-called endless loops and discourages users from

Multiprogramming Systems

purposely under-estimating the time required for their work requests in order to obtain better priority. Work so scheduled runs to completion.

Shortest-remaining-time scheduling means that a running process can be preempted from the processor by another process whose estimated time to completion is shorter. As with shortest-job-first, this method depends on the user's estimate (and as with shortest-job-first, work running grossly over the estimate is usually unceremoniously flushed from the system). Using this strategy requires that elapsed service times must be recorded for each unit of work, which adds to system overhead. Also, situations in which preemption of one process by another is only marginally worthwhile may occur with some frequency and the constant preemption will decrease throughput.

Highest-resource-ratio-next scheduling corrects some of the biases and short-comings of shortest-job-first scheduling. It was developed by Per Brinch-Hansen [4] as a scheduling strategy in which the priority (p) of each unit of work is a function of a combination of estimated service time (s) and waiting time (t) as given in the formula

$$p = \frac{t + s}{s}$$

The resource of importance here is time — time in the system and time in the processor.

Note that all of the scheduling strategies I have mentioned above are either non-preemptive — once a process has the processor it cannot be taken away, only relinquished voluntarily — or preemptive. Preemptive strategies are most useful in systems in which high-priority processes must have rapid or immediate attention, for example, real-time systems, where delay in processing an interrupt could easily be disastrous, and in time-sharing systems where such schemes provide a smooth, reasonable service to a large number of interactive users.

Even in non-preemptive systems, however, the operating system itself needs to use the processor in order to run itself so that it can make decisions about the control of the system. To prevent a user process from wholly monopolizing the processor the operating system sets an **interval timer** to generate an interrupt if one does not otherwise occur. This prevents any process from locking out all other processes indefinitely and allows the system to respond to time-dependent events.

Many computer systems combine more than one type of processing. For instance, it is common for larger systems to accommodate both batch processing and interactive use. In such cases, there may well be separate scheduling algorithms to deal at the high and intermediate level with both types of use, and the overall performance of such a system will depend upon how well the designers of the scheduling subsystems have managed to achieve a suitable balance.

Question for review

A data-processing system queues requests for work as they are presented to the system, but selects from that queue work to initiate as a process according to a policy of allowing a set number of tasks to be active (i.e. initiated) at one time. Among these active tasks, it divides processor attention equally, interrupting any task with a timer if it has not initiated its own interrupt (such as an I/O request). Once a job completes, its output is queued for printing (if any printing is required) and those with the fewest lines to print are processed preferentially, though an aging mechanism guarantees that no work sits on the output queue indefinitely. Describe the system in terms of the algorithms used in high-, intermediate- and low-level scheduling.

3.8 PROTECTION AND INTEGRITY

Issues of protection and integrity affect operating-system policies. Allocation mechanisms must not only effect policies regarding the sharing of storage, but where the philosophy of central data control is in place the system must also protect files from accidental or intentional damage or illegal access and must maintain the integrity of individual files and the system's data as a whole.

In microcomputer systems, the user is responsible for files on diskettes, for example. She or he may keep diskettes in a locked filing cabinet, a safe, a locked or unlocked desk drawer, at home on the coffee table or any other place. If the data need to be secured, it is up to the individual, perhaps at the direction of the organization, to do so, and failures in the 'system' are failures of individuals or of organizational policy. Similarly, if someone begins editing a file without making a backup copy and then inadvertently destroys the data, this is a matter for the individual or for organizational policy and its enforcement.

In looking at issues of protection and integrity as they apply to multi-programming systems with several processes sharing primary storage, operating systems designers must bear in mind that it is not only possible, but likely, that, for example, an applications program which refers to an address in storage outside its own bounds will occur. If the operating system does not contain measures to prevent or control any damage which might result, such damage will certainly occur. As an example, a program containing an array or table can easily compute an index value not only outside the bounds of the table, but of the program's allocated primary storage. Unless the operating system can detect this and take preventive or damage-limitation measures, the offending program can access data which does not belong to it or, worse, over-write part of another program's instructions or data, causing the innocent program to produce invalid results or to terminate abnormally. If this problem occurs to a part

Multiprogramming Systems

of the operating system, *everything could crash*, leaving all users without a system to use.

Two strategies exist for preventing problems of this kind. The first strategy can be applied to processes allocated storage in a single contiguous block. **Bounds registers** record the lower and upper addresses allocated to a process and the operating system verifies every address that process accesses to be certain that these addresses are within the upper and lower bounds of its allocated space as indicated by the bounds registers.

The second method can be applied whether or not a process's space has been allocated in a single contiguous block or discontiguous areas. The operating system assigns a value known as a *storage protection key* to the area(s) it allocates to a process. Any addresses generated by that process must refer only to areas with the same storage protection key value as its allocated space. Exceptions are made for certain areas common to all processes.

Applications and systems software programs themselves may also be worth protecting. Many systems software routines have facilities that the ordinary applications programmer might envy, but which might prove dangerous to system integrity in untrained, unscrupulous or unauthorized hands. For this reason levels of protection can be assigned to programs. A program which allows someone to alter the contents of storage dynamically, for example, would prove very tempting to an applications programmer in a hurry to fix a bug in a program. But this is obviously fraught with danger — hence such a program may be marked as: no read, no write, no execute except by special authorization.

Other programs might prove useful to the applications programmer but he or she would have no reason to read or update the code, only to execute it. Such programs can be marked as: no read, no write, execute only. In order to share programs or data, read can be allowed but write and execute disallowed. One may have a class of programs which can be freely read and freely executed, but which one wishes to protect from update — hence writing is disallowed. Since reading allows copying, anyone wanting a custom version of such a program can simply make a copy and ruin his or her own copy without being able to damage the original.

File management software will also provide the means of identifying who (user) or what (process) may access a file, and in what way the user or process may access it. Some files may be accessed by only a very limited set of users and processes. Any process which updates a file will require **authority** to do so, while other processes may read that file but not alter it in any way.

Different levels of *protection* must exist: no access, execute-only authority, read-only authority, update authority, or deletion authority. Deletion authority is the most dangerous and hence is usually the most restricted authority of all. Each level of access authority normally implies that the person having that level of access authority also has all levels below it; having the authority to update a file implies having the authority to read it as well.

The mechanisms by which a limited access policy can be carried out are varied. They may exist externally to the computer system itself in the form of limited access to computer facilities by means of locked or guarded areas in a building, by providing keys to switch on the equipment, or by levels of passwords which serve to identify the correct user or process beyond the identification provided by a name only. Or, an organization may apply a combination of these mechanisms depending upon how strict its security policies are. Only passwords have any implications for the operating systems software. The file management and interactive session management parts of the operating system record passwords, any associated levels of access authorization, file owners, authorized users and processes. It is the operating system which must verify that all that apply are correct before allowing access.

Integrity is another, but a related, matter. Integrity refers to the accuracy, validity and freedom from corruption of the data, and with the protection of the system as a whole from the effects of invalid, corrupt or inaccurate data. Integrity checks operate on many levels within the operating system and even in the hardware. Some brief examples follow.

Automatic parity checking is usually incorporated into the hardware, as doing this type of checking by software is normally too slow. For each byte of data, an extra bit is set aside (the parity bit). In even parity this bit is set to one if there are an odd number of one bits in the byte, otherwise it is set to zero. This way, all *correctly formed bytes will always have an even number of one bits*. Any corruption which causes a byte to have an odd number of ones will automatically be detected as an error. This simple check does not identify, of course, which bit has been corrupted and will not identify cases in which an even number of bits have been corrupted. However, such a basic check *does* identify the most common bit-level corruptions of data. An alternative to this is odd parity, which works in the same way except that the parity bit is set to one only when the byte contains an even number of one bits so that each correctly formed byte will always contain an odd number of ones.

Double read (write) and compare is another technique for assuring data integrity. Each record is read twice, into two different areas of primary storage and the results of the two read operations are compared. If they are identical, the record is assumed to be correct. If they are not, the read operation is retried. For a write, the record is written to the medium and then read back into an area different from the buffer from which it was copied. Again, the two are compared, and if identical the write operation is assumed to have worked properly and the record to be correct.

Making *backup copies or archiving* files is an important means of preserv-

Multiprogramming Systems

ing integrity. In microcomputer systems, users are usually cautioned to make copies of key diskettes and to use the copies, preserving the originals in a safe storage place. Though many people neglect to do this with their own data files, it is not very difficult to make a simple mistake (such as inserting the wrong diskette and starting to format it) which can wipe out many hours of work and a great deal of valuable data. In minicomputer and large mainframe installations, copies of key files (and often, of *all* files) are made and stored securely, often in a geographically separate place. The object of storing copies of key files in a different place from where the originals are kept is to preserve the data in the event of catastrophe such as fire or flood, and to prevent any saboteur or snooper from gaining access to all of an installation's data. The practice also provides a basis from which to recover data should the integrity of any file be compromised for any reason (head crash on disk, error in a program, etc.).

Analogous to mutual exclusion is the practice of *locking a data field, record or file to prevent multiple access*, particularly during updates. Integrity can be badly compromised by two processes each reading the same field, record or file at about the same time with the object of updating it. Mutual exclusion locks on a field, record or file can prevent the problem of double-updating, with other requests to read or (especially) to update queueing until the first update is complete. Such a locking mechanism can be applied at the volume, file, record or field levels, depending upon the software techniques used, but the finer the level of locking, the more carefully the lock must be constructed.

Questions for review

(i) Can you think of an application in which parity checking would be most useful?
(ii) Can you think of another reason than those given above for archiving important data?
(iii) Based on what you have learned already, what problem may occur with a poorly designed lock to prevent multiple access?

3.9 PERFORMANCE MONITORING AND ACCOUNTING

As well as any capital costs of purchasing or otherwise acquiring a computer system, an organization incurs revenue costs (ongoing necessary expenses or so-called *running costs*) in providing a computing service: electric power consumed, space in a building occupied, salaries and associated staffing costs, telephone and communication line rental, services, training, administrative overheads, maintenance, security. These costs must be incurred if the organization is to be able to offer a computing service to its other departments or outside organizations. In order to distribute these costs among users and recover them, the computing department charges for its services, with every organization having different charging criteria but all based on the consumption by users of some or all of the resources which can be measured. It is the function of the system's accounting routines to measure and record this.

System accounting functions superficially appear to be a means for charging users for the resources they use: processor time, space in primary and secondary storage, interventions by the operator (for example, to mount magnetic tape reels, demountable disk packs or reply to other special requests), number of lines of printed output produced. They do that, but are also more useful for monitoring the performance of both an individual applications program and the system as a whole.

The organization can use charges as a means of encouraging or discouraging the users of a system in certain types of behavior. Some behaviors can be allowed in order to make the system flexible to user demand, but those behaviors can be penalized by attaching a high price to them. Conversely, those behaviors which the organization wants to encourage can be made more attractive by making them a cheap alternative to others. In this function accounting and its associated charges to users for services help reinforce the policies embodied in most scheduling algorithms. High charges for operator interventions − for example to mount reels of tape − will encourage users to avoid requesting intervention as much as possible, while conversely, high charges for disk space will encourage the use of magnetic tape.

The data gathered by the operating system for accounting purposes are very useful for assessing the system's work load. This assessment, in turn, is needed in order to plan future facilities, to schedule, to design and build models of the system in order to predict *its* behavior as its environment changes, and in order to build sound test data streams for testing system changes.

Statistics gathered as a result of accounting routines may show: how long a request for work waited to enter the system, the duration of a job, its type and initial priority, its use of primary storage, the types of secondary storage used and I/O activity against them. These statistics may also show the times of day certain requests for work or types of requests occur, the frequency of their occurrences and the variation in workload through a measured period (for example, an 8-hour shift, or a 24-hour day).

A programmer can use these statistics to assess an applications program's own internal efficiencies. For example, would giving a large sequential file a higher blocking factor improve the I/O efficiency of the program? Is the program waiting as a request for a long time due to some resource not being available, and can that need be supplied by some other, more available, resource?

A systems programmer can use these statistics at a different level: to optimize the operation of the system as a whole. Some examples which come to my mind are as follows. How many small, frequently accessed files are on magnetic tape, which must be located in the library, fetched to the tape drive and mounted, when they would be better on a constantly mounted disk? How many large, sequential, seldom-accessed files occupy disk space which could more effectively be used by smaller, more volatile files? Given the installation's work load and mix, are the present scheduling algorithms optimal? Are the system's important linked lists ordered so that the most frequently sought items are at the beginning? If one data channel is excessively busy, can this problem be alleviated by moving some heavily accessed files to less busy channels?

The computer installation's manager must ask him- or herself: what factors affect system performance? Is performance as good (or bad) as its users perceive? Where are the bottlenecks to improved performance? Often, once such bottlenecks are detected, they can be relatively simple to eliminate. One can achieve significant performance improvements, for example, by distributing particularly heavily accessed disk files across disks attached to different controllers which are in turn attached to different channels.

This reduces or eliminates delays due to channel, controller or device-busy signals. Putting the most frequently accessed items at the head of a linked list rather than using some other order can improve performance in areas where heavy use is made of linked lists. Optimizing compilers can produce more efficient applications programs in an installation with a heavy production work load, whereas so-called quick-and-dirty compilers, because they are more efficient at producing object programs quickly, are more effective in an installation where the bulk of the work is program development, testing and debugging.

Question for review

What would be the likely effect of a high charge for short increments of processor time and a lower charge for longer increments (e.g. paying a unit charge for a unit of time-use, but, say, 1.8 unit charges for 2.0 units of time-use)?

3.10 SUMMARY

Throughout the 1960s and into the 1970s, the impetus behind much operating-systems development has been an effort to organize and manage the computer's storage so as to maximize the amount of work which could be accomplished. Organization is the way storage is viewed; management is the working implementation of that view.

Efforts to maximize the amount of work a system can do have meant the sharing of the system among several users apparently at once. This apparent concurrency has implications for all aspects of the computer system and has meant that more and more tasks have fallen to the operating system: scheduling, memory management (both for primary and/or secondary storage), responsibility for insuring integrity and protection, providing basic services — especially I/O support and file management, and finally accounting for what has been used so that it can be paid for *and* so that the system can be studied and tuned.

Note how sharing has been accomplished: first by looking at storage space as an undivided monolith which can be shared by dividing up the time that monolith is available so as to share it among many processes; secondly by looking at storage space as divisible. Some time-sharing systems combine both; this combined method of viewing the sharing of a limited or fixed resource has further implications which I shall discuss in the next chapter.

REFERENCES

[1] Weizenbaum, J. (1976) *Computer Power and Human Reason*, W.H. Freeman and Company, San Francisco, p. 27.
[2] Fano, R.M. and Corbato, F.J. (1966) 'Time-sharing on computers', in *Information*, eds. G. Piel *et al.*, W.H. Freeman and Company, San Francisco. (A reprint in book form of the September 1966 issue of *Scientific American*.)
[3] Brinch-Hansen, P. (1973) *Operating System Principles*, Prentice-Hall, Englewood Cliffs, New Jersey, pp. 93–4.
[4] Brinch-Hansen, P. (1971) 'Short-term scheduling in multiprogramming systems', in *Third ACM Symposium on Operating Systems Principles*, October, pp. 103–5.

FURTHER READING

Ben-Ari, M. (1982) *Principles of Concurrent Programming*, Prentice-Hall, Hemel Hempstead, UK. This short but excellent guide discusses semaphores, critical sections, message-passing and the Ada rendezvous, giving examples using a subset of Pascal (or of Ada for the rendezvous).

Brinch-Hansen, P. (1973) *Operating System Principles*, Prentice-Hall, Englewood Cliffs, New Jersey. Chapter 3 covers concurrent processes (concurrency,

Multiprogramming Systems

mutual exclusion, process cooperation and deadlocks). Section 4.2 pp. 134–51 covers short-term scheduling. Chapter 6 covers scheduling algorithms, with the discussion divided among queueing models, non-preemptive scheduling and preemptive scheduling.

Calingaert, P. (1982) *Operating System Elements: a user perspective*, Prentice-Hall, Englewood Cliffs, New Jersey. Chapter 2 ('Storage management') from pp. 11–29 covers the allocation and management of non-virtual storage.

Deitel, H.M. (1984) *An Introduction to Operating Systems*, Addison-Wesley, Reading, Massachusetts. Chapter 4 considers asynchronous concurrent processes, Chapter 6 looks at deadlock, and Chapter 7 looks at real storage management.

Gorsline, G.W. (1980) *Computer Organization: hardware/software*, Prentice-Hall, Englewood Cliffs, New Jersey. Chapter 6, pp. 190–8 considers concurrency at the instruction fetch and execute level in a single processor.

Lorin, H. (1972) *Parallelism in Hardware and Software*, Prentice-Hall, Englewood Cliffs, New Jersey. This is an advanced book on the subject of concurrency. Part 1 introduces fundamental concepts of coexistence in time. Chapter 6 looks at design concepts for high-speed single-stream systems. Chapter 7 looks at the elements of a processor and their functions in terms of introducing parallelism at the hardware level.

Lorin, H. and Deitel, H.M. (1981) *Operating Systems*, Addison-Wesley, Reading, Massachusetts. Section 6.2, pp. 164–6 describes interrupt handling in the IBM/370 architecture. Section 6.3, pp. 166–74 covers dispatching (low-level scheduling). Section 6.4, pp. 172–9 covers I/O support in some detail, within an IBM mainframe context.

Maekawa, M., Oldehoeft, A.E. and Oldehoeft, R.R. (1987) *Operating Systems: advanced concepts*, Benjamin/Cummings, Menlo Park, California. Chapters 2, 3 and 4 discuss process synchronization, language mechanisms for concurrency and deadlock at a more advanced level.

Peterson, J.L. and Silberschatz, A. (1985) *Operating System Concepts 2ed.*, Addison-Wesley, Reading, Massachusetts. Chapter 4 describes processor scheduling, Chapter 5, pp. 143–71 covers non-virtual storage management techniques, Chapter 8 covers deadlocks and Chapter 9 concurrent processes.

CHAPTER

4
Virtual storage systems

From the mid-1960s to the mid-1970s the cost of hardware relative to its performance declined precipitously. This decline in the *price—performance ratio* took a spectacular quantum fall when the microprocessor was introduced midway through the 1970s. By 1981 manufacturers found it possible to produce a general-purpose microcomputer cheaply enough to compete with the cost of a good electric typewriter.

During the same period, however, the cost of developing software had risen enormously. Furthermore, the scope and pace of automation also expanded very rapidly, as more and more organizations could afford computers and purchased or developed reliable applications software packages to carry out functions formerly done by hand in all but large firms. These trends had a profound impact on operating systems.

As processors became more powerful and cheaper, and as more applications were automated and the volume of data underwent a veritable explosion, the emphasis in software design shifted from making optimal use of the processor and primary storage, where costs were falling, to other areas where costs remained relatively great, such as the utilization of I/O devices.

Costs of hardware have declined, but labor costs have climbed. The productivity of people developing software has remained low, thus keeping the costs and time involved in software development high. It has become a common practice to use software, including the operating system, to aid in the production of applications software. This is done by providing tools for both the expert programmer and the relatively naive user.

Such user-friendly or powerful software has a high overhead cost. For example, a powerful text editor is often greedy of resources like primary storage space. Even if such software requires large amounts of supporting but cheap hardware, it can be used by people who are less computer-specialist and more application-specialist. This can still be a more economic option in many cases than would be true using less hardware and less highly functional software and needing higher-salaried computer specialists to carry out work.

The achievement of optimum overall system performance together with application-oriented, easy-to-use software has thus become increasingly important, as it allows more users with less knowledge to make increasing use of the powerful resource a computer provides in so many situations.

In this chapter I shall describe how multiprogramming concepts were extended in order to expand the apparent (though not necessarily the real) size of primary storage: this is called **virtual storage**. The use of virtual storage techniques in turn allowed two important developments to occur: the level of multiprogramming available in these apparently larger systems could be raised and applications were no longer limited by the real size of the primary storage available. This allowed more and larger applications.

4.1 PERFORMANCE AND VIRTUAL SYSTEMS

In Section 3.2 I described how several users could share a computer system simultaneously through swapping the various users' processes in and out of primary storage. In Section 3.10 I mentioned that the methods of time-sharing-type swapping and the method of subdividing space in primary storage could be combined together − perhaps quite simply, as in time-sharing systems which swap processes in and out but also allow several different processes to reside in primary storage concurrently. This combined method, I hinted, had important implications for future developments.

One of the problems inherent in the fixed partition and variable region methods of subdividing storage described in Chapter 3 is fragmentation of that storage and possible delay in executing very large programs which, in either form of storage organization, have to wait until sufficient storage was available in order to start.

A solution to both the problems of fragmentation and delay for large programs is the use of virtual storage techniques. I shall describe this in logical terms, since the actual mechanism is complex. Though virtual storage can be implemented using software alone, its high overheads mean that it requires changes to structures in the hardware to be effective.

Virtual is an over-used term in computing. The dictionary (*The Concise Oxford*) defines it as meaning: *as such for practical purposes though not in name or according to strict definition*. Virtual storage gets its name because, in practice, it allows one program to run when its storage requirements exceed, even greatly, the available amount of **real storage**, or many programs to execute concurrently when the sum of their space requirements exceeds what is actually available.

By *real storage*, I mean the physical entity I have hitherto called *primary storage*; this change of name helps me to differentiate clearly between *real storage*, a physically defined and clearly limited resource, and *virtual storage*. Virtual storage can also be defined as a method of storage management which blurs or even obliterates the distinction between primary and secondary storage for certain purposes, as I shall show.

Imagine a very large person attempting to wash in a bathroom wash basin. All of this person's body cannot possibly fit into the basin at once (at least, not without breaking something!). Yet that person can wash himor herself completely in the basin by immersing in the water only that portion of the body currently being washed: for example first one hand, then a forearm, then an upper arm, other hand, forearm and upper arm, left foot, lower left leg, and so on. This analogy applies to the technique of virtual storage in so far as only that part of a program/process which is currently executing *needs* to be in *real* storage; the rest can reside elsewhere. So a process needs only enough *real* storage to contain some minimum currently executing portion of itself.

A working virtual storage system was developed by a team at the University of Manchester, England and demonstrated in the very early 1960s: Atlas. Burroughs Corporation produced a commercially available computer with virtual storage operating system in the mid-1960s. However, the use of virtual techniques did not become truly widespread for nearly another decade.

How virtual storage works

In many virtual storage systems, real storage is divided into equal-sized pieces called **frames**. Each frame is 2 or 4 kilobytes (depending on the system) in size. Programs are also divided into pieces the same size as the frame; these pieces of a program are called **pages**. These, when the program has been initiated but is still inactive, are stored on a specially designated high-speed secondary storage device (disk or drum) in page-sized areas called **slots**.

When some code in a process is needed for immediate execution, the page containing the code is fetched from its *slot* on secondary storage and placed in a *frame* in real storage. If that page's code is executed with great frequency, the page will tend to remain, that is, to become *fixed* in that frame. Any page not in such frequent use will tend to be stored away again in a slot on secondary storage. It can be fetched again if it is needed again for execution. Otherwise, it will remain in its slot. Those parts of any program which carry out the bulk of the process's work will tend to become fixed in real storage and will then form what is called a **working**

Virtual Storage Systems

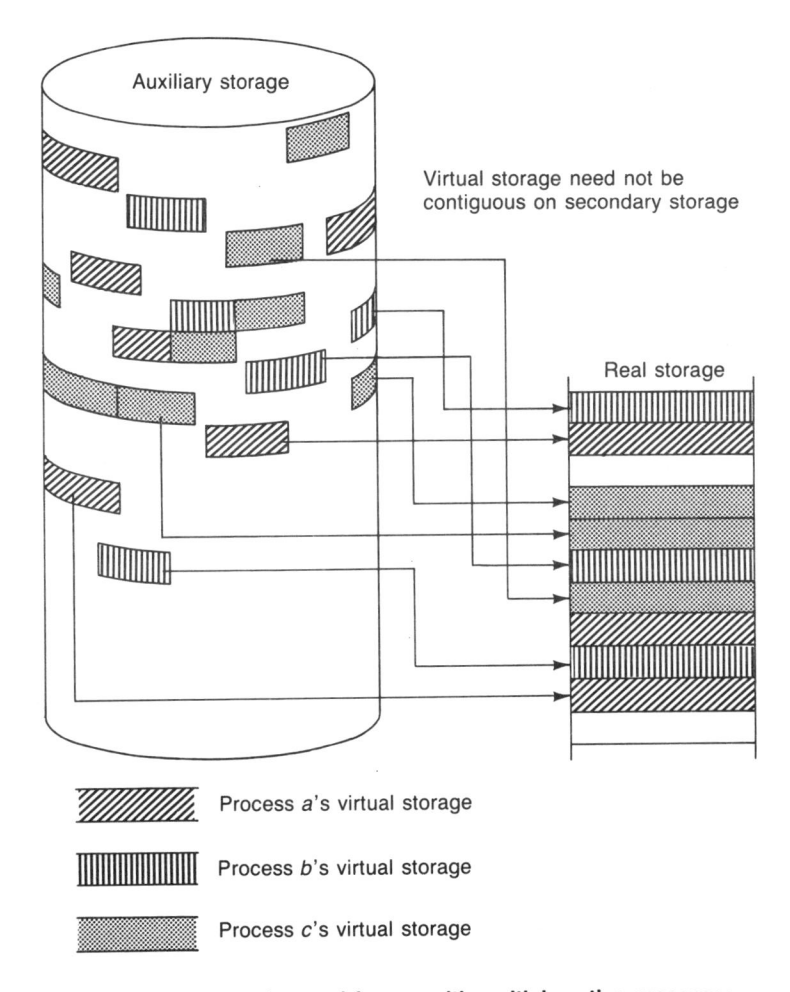

Figure 4.1 Page slots and frames with multiple active processes

set. Figure 4.1 shows three processes with pages residing both in slots on a secondary storage device and in frames in primary storage. Note that the pages in frames in real storage are scattered.

Many programs are largely or entirely serial in nature — instructions are executed one after another. When one part of a serial program's code is being executed, no other parts of that same program will be active. A significant part of any program's code, in fact, is executed once only during a program's execution. For example, code which initializes or terminates a program is executed once only: when the program begins or when it ends, respectively. Other code is executed seldom, for example error or exception-handling routines. Some parts of a program may not be used at all: redundant code which has been logically isolated but not removed, or code for dealing with extremely rare conditions.

When primary storage was a severely limited resource, many programmers made use of these common characteristics of program code to 'squeeze quarts into pint pots' using a technique called *pre-planned overlay*. In this technique, code used once would be brought into primary storage, executed, and then its space would be overlaid by another portion of the program. Any parts of the program which did not execute in quick succession could overlay each other. But the planning necessary to achieve good performance using this technique meant that it was best carried out by an expert programmer. The technique has some logical similarity with virtual storage techniques but is much less flexible and certainly not an automatic process carried out by the operating system and hardware.

The need for virtual systems grew out of the tendency to create ever larger and more complex programs for newer and more complex applications like database and from the shift to more and more interactive computer use. In terms of the effective use of an individual's time, the value of interactive computing is great. Work broken down into a series of short, individually trivial units allows a dialog between user and process. The user can enter a command, make decisions based on the outcome of that command and enter new commands in a matter of seconds. But to share a system among a large number of users, it becomes necessary to share primary storage among many more processes. In order to reduce overheads in swapping, more primary storage is required. The real storage available to a system begins to be a serious constraint as the level of concurrency increases.

Question for review

How is the concept of virtual storage different from that of the pre-planned overlay? How are these concepts alike?

Question for discussion

How do you see the concept of virtual storage as related to the concepts of device independence and relocatable code described in Section 3.6?

4.2 CONCEPTS OF VIRTUAL STORAGE

'The key to the virtual storage concept is disassociating the addresses referenced in a running process from the addresses available in primary storage.' [1]

Locality

Some programming techniques in early use were already based on the concept that a program's instructions could be composed into groups of instructions which had in common some subtask or operation on one particular group of data. These techniques were based on findings called the **property of locality**, though these findings do not describe a *property* so much as a *tendency*.

Studies of the executions of programs have shown that, over a relatively short period of time (in human terms) programs tend to make repeated references to the same data object(s). In other words, having once obtained, say, an employee's personnel record, a program will tend to make repeated references to that record over a short span of time, rather than jump from referring to that to, say, a stock-control record and then back again. This tendency is referred to as *temporal locality*.

Furthermore, programs tend to refer to new data objects which are in locations *adjacent* to those which have recently been referred to — this is termed *spatial locality*. And, of course, instructions in particular are found (with the exception of branches in the logic) in adjacent locations.

Relative addressing

Relative addressing is a commonly used technique in assembly-language programming. It involves using a two-part addressing scheme. The first part of the address is a **base address** — the starting address of some part of a program. The second part of the address is an offset or displacement from the base address.

This is, on a smaller scale, similar to the concept of relocatable programs mentioned in Section 3.6, where a program's first instruction is given an address of zero at the time the program is compiled into object code. Each instruction thereafter is assigned an address indicating its position relative to the zero starting point. The *real* address of any part of the program is computed as the program's true starting address in primary storage *added to* the relative address of the desired instruction. Thus an instruction to branch to +0ACD, in a program whose starting address in primary storage is 076000, will result in a branch to an actual address of 076ACD (076000 plus 0ACD).

In relative addressing, the programmer divides the program into pieces. The base address of each piece of the program points to the start of that piece of the program, and all instructions within that piece have addresses relative to the start. The base address of any piece of the program can then be loaded into a register for quick calculation of any address within that piece.

Let's say that a program has a piece whose base address is loaded into register 6. Any address within that piece of program can be calculated as the relative address added to the contents of register 6 — referred to as the **base register**. This means that that piece of the program need not be adjacent to the part which logically precedes it, or the piece which logically follows it, as those pieces can use other base registers which give the true starting addresses of their respective pieces.

This ability to dissociate different sections of the program from a rigid linear structure is called **artificial contiguity**. The logical contiguity of the program is maintained but physical contiguity is not necessary as the means to maintain it. The user need not be concerned about where procedures and data are positioned in real storage. It becomes possible to write programs in a more natural way. The programmer can concentrate on the details of algorithm design and program structure, can even write parts of the program in isolation from other parts of it, and can ignore the underlying structure of the hardware. The programmer becomes more aware of the computer as a tool for implementing algorithms and less aware of it in the sense of a device with unique physical characteristics. The computer becomes much more of a tool for solving problems in the external world and much less an adversary against which the programmer must struggle in the problem-solving task.

Re-entrant code

Another key concept, not just to virtual systems but to any systems with a high degree of apparent concurrency, is the concept of re-entrant code, described in detail in Section 3.6.

Virtualness

Just as the similar concept of making code relocatable (Section 3.5) allows the object program to exist without reference to real addresses until such time as it is loaded for execution, and makes it possible for the operating system to choose where in real storage to fix it, so the concept of virtual storage means that the running process is not tied to specific real addresses until this is actually required. A process is considered to refer only to **virtual addresses** — that is, to addresses formulated *as though* they referred to consecutive addresses within a program, the pieces of which are continuously adjacent. But processes still must run in real storage, using real addresses. Virtual addresses *map* to real addresses during the execution of the process.

This means that when a process is not executing it need not occupy

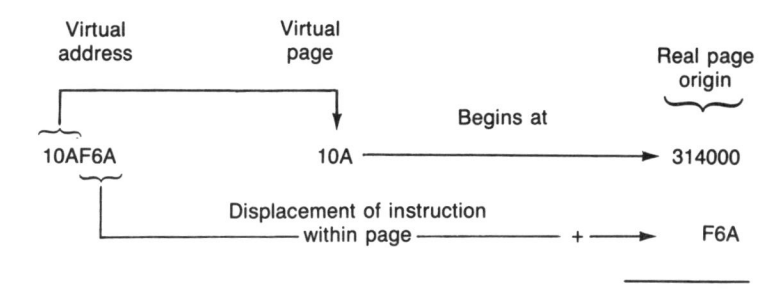

Virtual Storage Systems

```
Virtual              Virtual
address              page                          Real page
                                                    origin
10AF6A               10A  ─────────────────────►   314000
                                 Begins at
         Displacement of instruction
         ──── within page ──────────── + ────►     F6A

                    Real address for instruction   314F6A
```

Figure 4.2 Virtual addresses map to real addresses

any real storage (that is, it can be swapped out, as in an early time-sharing system). Further, *any part of a process not actively being executed need not occupy real storage either*, provided that part can be located (by using its virtual address), fetched from its storage slot and fixed to a frame in real storage with a real address when needed. This location and fetching must be done with extreme rapidity, or performance becomes unacceptably low.

Several methods of mapping virtual to real addresses have been developed. **Dynamic address translation (DAT)** is a software mechanism which provides high-speed mapping of virtual addresses to real. When

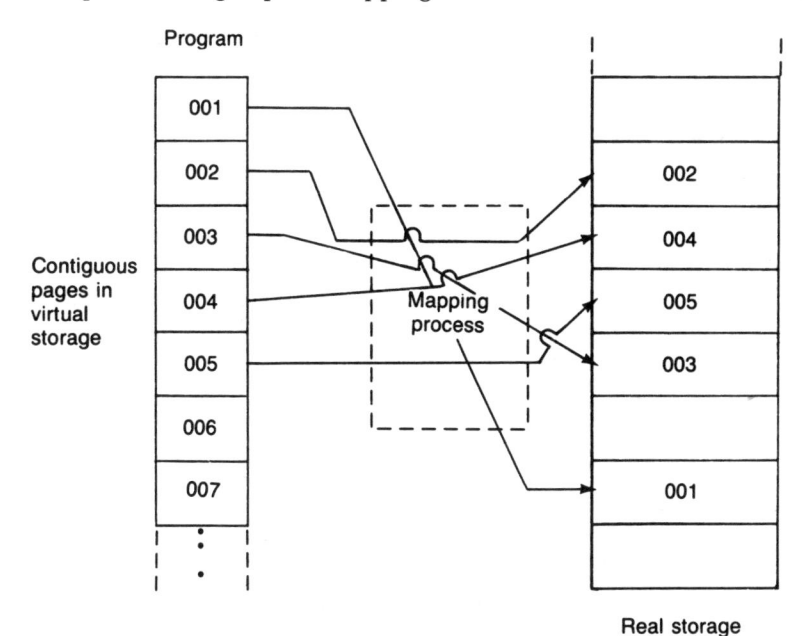

```
Program

                001
                002                        002
                003                        004
Contiguous
pages in        004    Mapping             005
virtual                process
storage         005                        003
                006
                007                        001
                 ⋮
                                        Real storage
```

Figure 4.3 Artificial contiguity

the process is freed from the limitations of real storage, several things become possible. Contiguous virtual addresses in a process need not be contiguous in real storage, since the mapping process provides the real address at the time of reference.

Freeing the process from real storage addressing also means that the size of the process can exceed the size of the real storage available. This also means, however, that those processes and parts of processes which often are not in real storage must reside elsewhere, whence they can be quickly accessed and retrieved; this requires a two-level storage scheme.

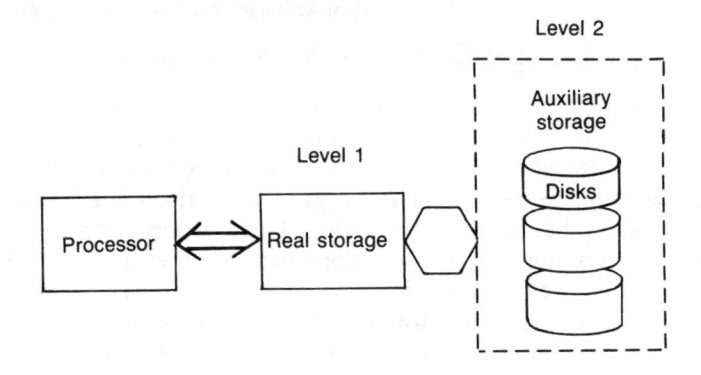

Figure 4.4 A two-level storage scheme (*Note:* Data file storage is not part of this scheme)

A high-speed device such as a disk or drum provides this second level of storage, the first level being real primary storage. As explained in Section 4.1, the process, real storage and second-level storage (auxiliary storage, a specially designated form of secondary storage) are all divided into small, standard-sized pieces of 2 or 4 kilobytes. This eliminates any delays inherent in having to employ a placement algorithm which includes *fit*. Recall, these pieces are called *pages* in the virtual process, page *frames* in real storage, and page *slots* in auxiliary storage. Indeed, it can be useful to picture code and data written on actual pages of paper, to be temporarily 'tacked' to a frame when being executed or referred to, and rolled up and stored out of the way in a slot or pigeonhole in auxiliary storage when not required.

Questions for review

(i) What is artificial contiguity? Why is it useful?
(ii) What are the two chief advantages to be gained from virtual storage techniques?

Virtual Storage Systems 105

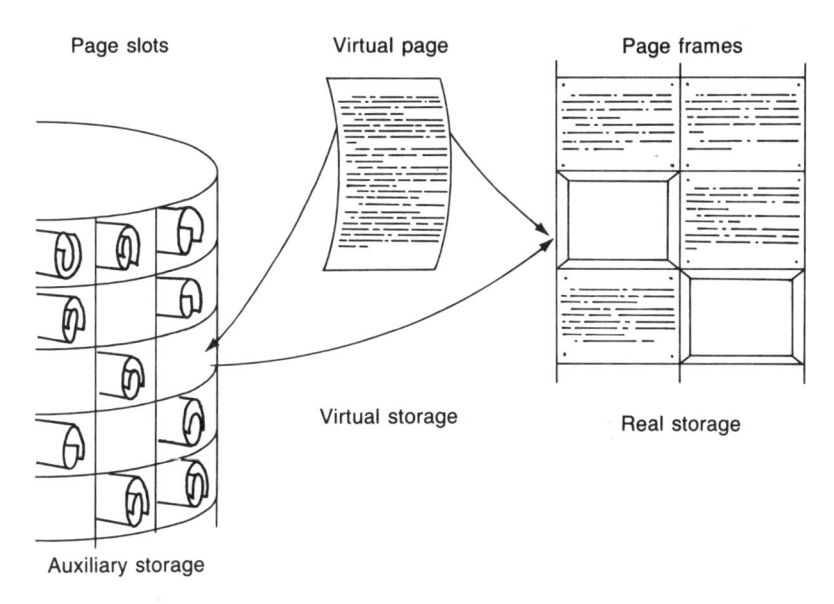

Figure 4.5 Pages, page slots and page frames

4.3 IMPLEMENTING VIRTUAL SYSTEMS

The dynamic address translation (DAT) mechanism keeps information for mapping.

Simple paged systems

Figure 4.6 shows a scheme for dynamic address translation using pages. In virtual storage, shown on the left of the diagram, pages appear, and are numbered, consecutively. Each page of virtual storage contains 4 kilobytes of instructions or data (or a mixture). A three-byte *virtual* address, consisting of six hexadecimal digits, refers to any point in a program from 000000 to the maximum possible with a three-byte address, FFFFFF — or a total of 16 megabytes.

This virtual address actually consists of three digits which designate a page number in virtual storage, while the remaining, low-order three digits are the displacement of the instruction or datum *within* the page. A virtual address of 0560AA refers to the byte that is the 171st byte from the beginning of the 86th page. (This assumes a byte-addressable architecture.) The page shown in Figure 4.6 actually resides in real storage at the

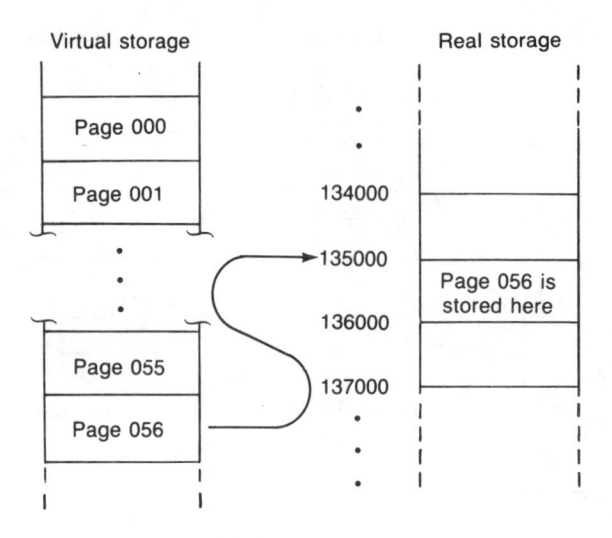

```
          Virtual storage                    Real storage
        ┌─────────────────┐              │                │
        │                 │          •   │                │
        │    Page 000     │          •   │                │
        │                 │          •   │                │
        ├─────────────────┤              ├────────────────┤
        │    Page 001     │    134000    │                │
        └─────────────────┘              ├────────────────┤
               •                ┌──────► 135000           │
               •                │              │ Page 056 is    │
               •                │       136000 │ stored here    │
        ┌─────────────────┐     │              ├────────────────┤
        │                 │     │              │                │
        │    Page 055     │     │       137000 │                │
        │                 │     │              ├────────────────┤
        ├─────────────────┤     │          •   │                │
        │    Page 056     │─────┘          •   │                │
        │                 │                •   │                │
        └─────────────────┘                    │                │
```

Page no. Displacement
Virtual address 056 0AA corresponds to real address 1350AA.

Figure 4.6 The simplest model of dynamic address translation

frame whose address begins at 135000_{16}, shown on the right. So 0560AA translates to 1350AA: page number 056_{16} is replaced by frame address 135000_{16} and the displacement 0AA is added to that.

This seems simple enough, but the mechanisms required to carry out the mapping of page number to frame address are more complex. For one thing, since pages can reside in slots on auxiliary storage, it must be possible to locate a virtual address in a page stored in a slot in auxiliary storage. Figure 4.7 shows how this is accomplished through the medium of a table.

The page table, sometimes called the block map table, is always maintained in real storage. It refers to a single process, and contains one entry for each page in the process. The entries in the table are in page-number sequence, so that entry zero contains data relating to page zero, entry one contains data relating to page one, and so on. Each entry contains three fields: the address of the slot in auxiliary storage in which the page is to be found, an indicator to show whether the page is also in real storage, and the frame address in real storage if the page is indeed there. In the figure, page 003 is in a slot at auxiliary storage address 065A0F000, and it is also in real storage in a frame at address 7A2000. Its indicator is set to 1 to indicate that it is, indeed, in real storage. The entry for page 002 shows that it is in a slot at auxiliary storage address 006221A00; its indicator is set to 0, indicating that it is *not* in real storage as well.

Virtual Storage Systems

```
Page table
origin register                                          Real storage
┌────────┐         Page table
│ 004200 │──┐  Auxiliary      Real storage
└────────┘  │  storage        location
            │  location
   Page no. 000  006218000   0
            001  002314000   0
            002  006221A00   0
            003  065A0F000   1   7A2000
             .     .         .     .
             .     .         .     .
                                                    Contents of
            055  006543000   1   122000              page 056
         →  056  043879000       135000
            057  002185000   0
             .
             .

With two words for each    In-real-storage
entry in the page table,   indicator
this entry has the address
of 004270₁₆
```

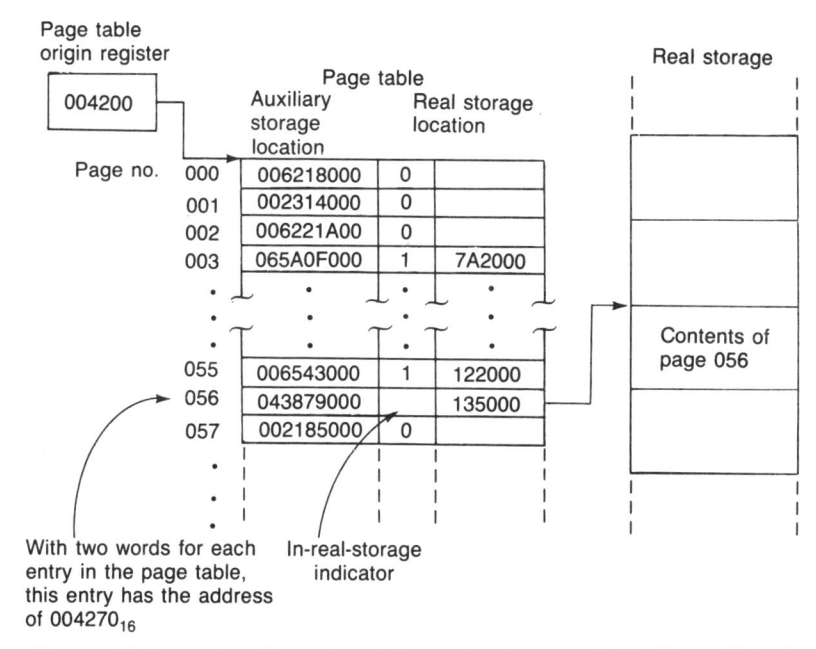

Figure 4.7 Dynamic address translation using the page table (*Note:* Virtual address 056 0AA is found at 1350AA)

If a process makes reference to virtual address 002AC0, the indicator shows that this page is not in real storage. So a free frame must be located, the page must be found on auxiliary storage in its slot at 006221A00, fetched into real storage and fixed to the frame, and the page table updated by changing the indicator to 1 and entering the frame address.

When a virtual address referred to is *not* in real storage, this is called a page fault. The resulting location of the page in its slot and the bringing of it into real storage is called a page fetch. Figure 4.8 shows the same page table as appears in Figure 4.7, but after the page fetch and page table update have occurred. Page 002 is now in a frame in real storage.

Page table lookups, and page faults and fetches, can consume a great deal of time, leading to unacceptable performance. Even when the page desired is already in real storage there is an overhead involved in searching the page table. One solution to this is a hardware solution — the use of high-speed **associative memory**. An associative memory is a highly specialized, very small and very fast memory in which all elements can be searched in parallel to each other. Associative memories are also called **content-addressable memories** because the parallel search of all cells within such a memory means that one is searching for particular contents. Figure 4.9 shows a search through a page table or parts of a page table held in such an associative memory.

108 Fundamentals of Operating Systems

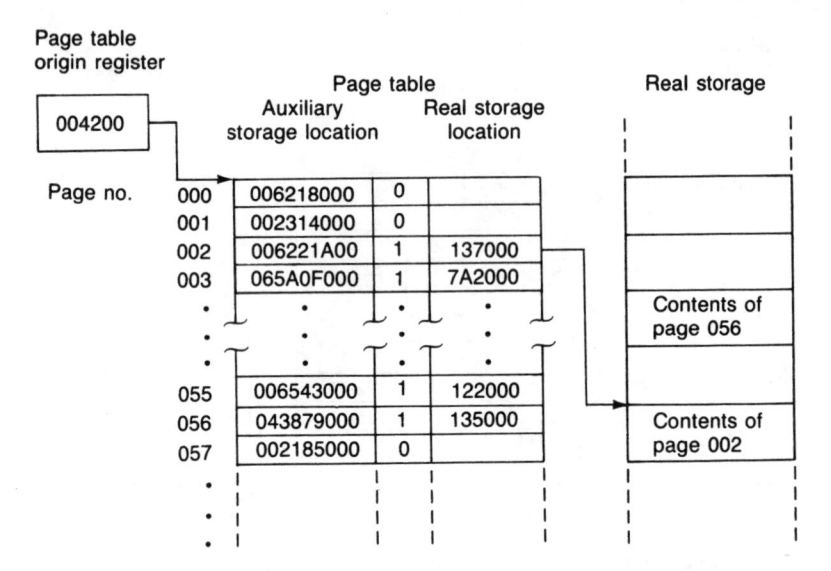

```
Page table
origin register
                          Page table                    Real storage
┌────────┐          Auxiliary      Real storage
│ 004200 │──┐       storage location  location
└────────┘  │
            │
Page no.   000   006218000    0
           001   002314000    0
           002   006221A00    1    137000
           003   065A0F000    1    7A2000
                                              ┌─────────────┐
                                              │ Contents of │
                                              │ page 056    │
                                              └─────────────┘

           055   006543000    1    122000
           056   043879000    1    135000
           057   002185000    0
                                              ┌─────────────┐
                                              │ Contents of │
                                              │ page 002    │
                                              └─────────────┘
```

Figure 4.8 **The page table after the page fetch for page 002**

All elements of the table in associative memory are searched in parallel. Since associative memories are normally very small, an entire page table (with up to 4096 entries in a three-digit page-numbering scheme) is unlikely to be small enough to be contained entirely. Hence only the most active pages are likely to appear in entries in the associative memory; this means that the page number must be one field in each entry. If the desired page is 003, the parallel search through all entries in the associative memory is looking for '003' and from that entry, if it is present,

```
                                                    Real storage
    Page table in an
    associative memory

    Page no.  Auxiliary storage     *    Real storage           ┌─────────────┐
              address                    address                │ Contents of │
                                                                │ page 002    │
     ──▶  003    006543000          1    72A000                 └─────────────┘
     ──▶  013    015673000          0
     ──▶  002    011432000          1    164000
                                                                ┌─────────────┐
                        In-real-storage                         │ Contents of │
                        indicator                               │ page 003    │
    Search starts on all elements in parallel                   └─────────────┘
```

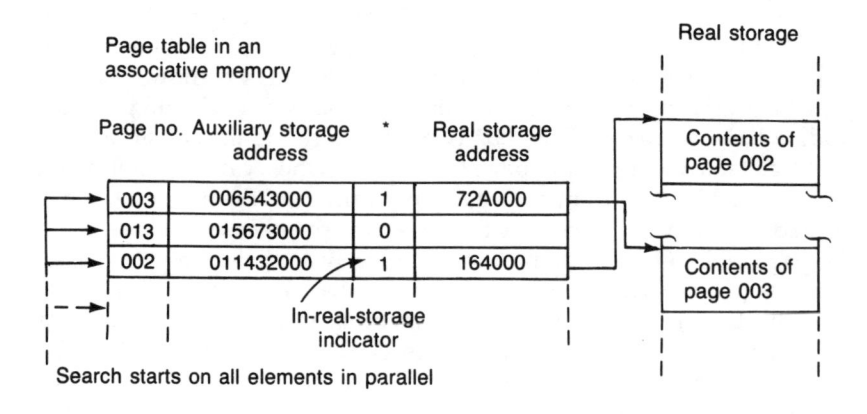

Figure 4.9 **Page table lookup using an associative memory**

Virtual Storage Systems

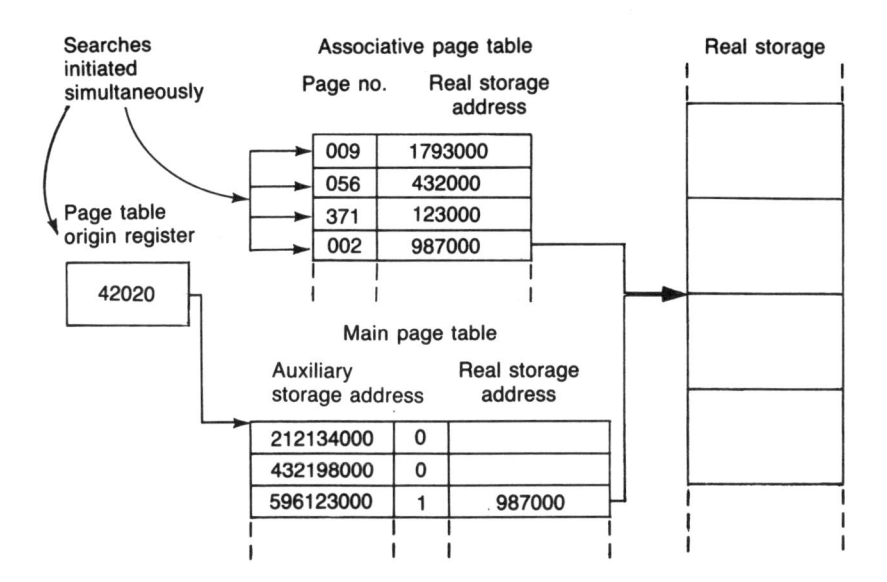

Figure 4.10 A combined system using a parallel search of both the associated page table and the main page table

the frame address is obtained. (Due to the small size of an associative memory, it is usual to record in it only as many as possible of those pages which are currently in real storage.)

However, there is a chance that the desired page may not appear in an entry in the associative memory. This means that a search must be made of the full page table in real storage. This is a much slower process. In order to reduce the overall time taken to locate *any* page — whether or not it appears in the associative memory — the system initiates *both* searches simultaneously, as illustrated by Figure 4.10. Thus, if the entry for the desired page is found in the associative memory, the search of the full page table in real storage can be aborted; if the entry for the desired page is not in the associative memory, then the search of the main page table has already advanced by some microseconds.

Segmented systems

Not all systems use pages as a means of dividing up virtual storage. Some use **segments** instead. A *segment* is a larger entity than a page and it may, or may not, be of fixed size. One relatively common segment size is 64 kilobytes. Segments, unlike pages, contain more than simply program code and data; they contain control information about the segment itself,

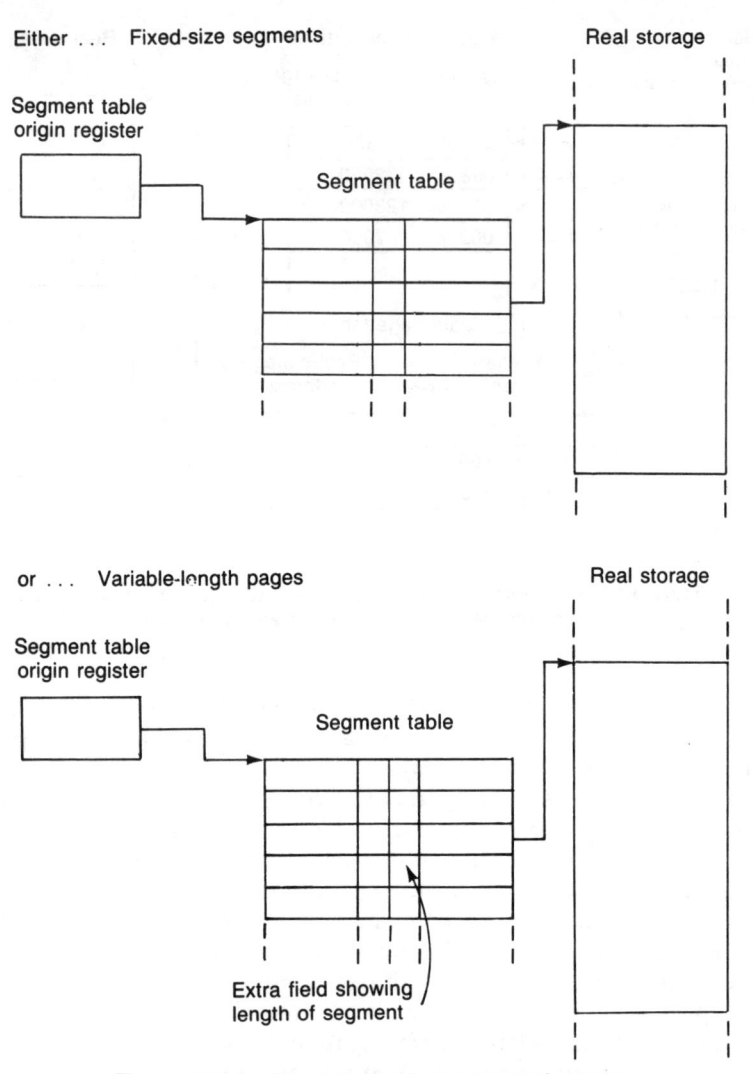

Figure 4.11 Two variations of a segmented system

such as access privilege rights and storage protection information. Otherwise, segments are used in a similar way to pages, with some differences. Figure 4.11 shows a segment system.

The table is called the segment table instead of a page table. If segments are of fixed size, the segment table entries are very similar to page table entries; they contain auxiliary storage location, an indicator showing whether or not the segment is in real storage, and a real storage address showing the origin point of the segment if it is in real storage.

Schemes involving variable-length segments require an extra field in the segment table entry showing the length of the segment. Lookup proceeds as for virtual pages in a page table, except that it is based on a virtual address consisting of a segment number and a displacement within the segment. The segment number maps, through the table, to a real storage address. When fixed-length segments are used, real storage can also be divided into segment-sized pieces. But when variable-length segments are used, the operating system must cope with an additional problem: implementing a placement algorithm such as first, best or worst fit in order to place a segment in real storage. The advantage of segmented systems over paged ones is that the tables are smaller and therefore more quickly searched, and any virtual address referred to is much more likely to be within the currently referenced segment than would be the case with the much smaller pages.

Combined segment-and-page systems

Many systems *combine* pages and segments, as Figure 4.12 illustrates. This scheme limits the size of a page table at the expense of having a segment table and several page tables for each virtual storage.

While this may seem more wasteful, it has advantages. In particular, whereas a page is a physical construct designed to facilitate the transfer of data between primary and secondary storage, segments can be regarded as logical constructs. Segments can be used for access control — for example by allowing a segment to be shared among several users without requiring multiple copies.

The virtual storage versions of the IBM System/370 and its successors use this scheme. The virtual address consists of six hexadecimal digits (three bytes). The high-order two digits are the segment number (so a program may have up to 256 segments). The third digit is the page number, allowing up to 16 pages per segment. The low-order three digits are the offset of any address within the page, allowing up to 4096 bytes per page. Each page is thus 4 kilobytes in size.

Address translation proceeds in two steps. The high-order two digits of the virtual address correspond to an entry (by position) in a segment table. But the segment table, instead of pointing to a location on auxiliary storage and perhaps a location in real storage, points to the start of the page table for all pages within that segment.

The page table contains entries (by position again) for each page, and these entries show the address of the slot in auxiliary storage for that page, the indicator showing whether the page is in real storage, and (if it is) the frame address where the page can be found. Lookup of a virtual address involves obtaining the address of a segment's corresponding page table, adding that address to the page number multiplied by the number

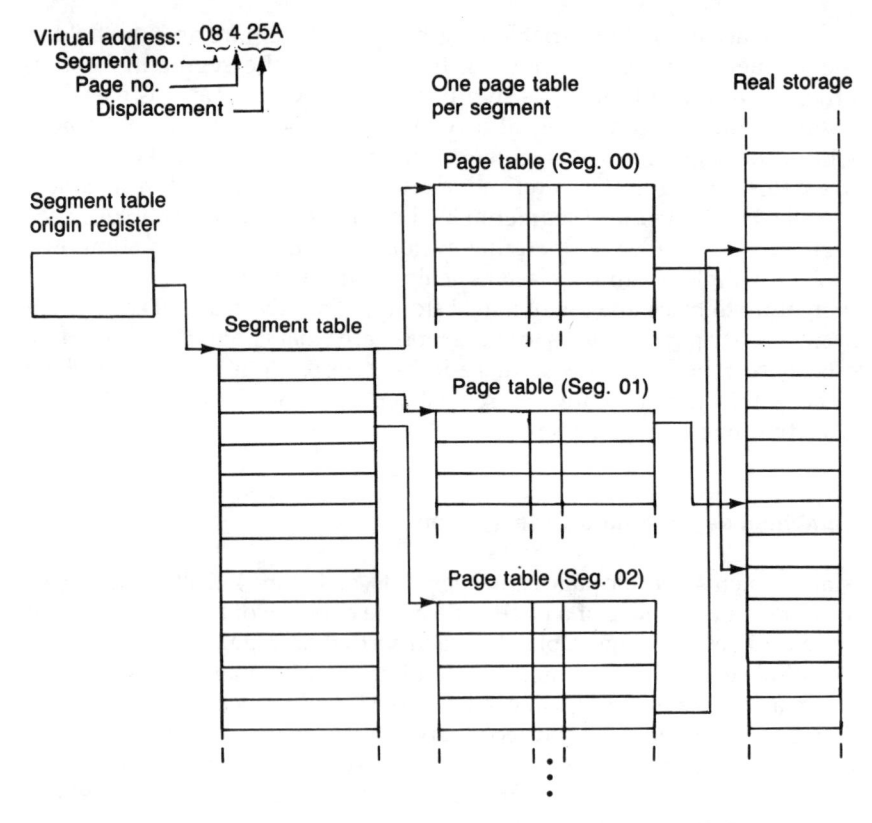

Figure 4.12 A system combining segments and pages, with fixed-size segments

of bytes in each page table entry, looking in the entry at the resulting address and finding the necessary information as to slot or frame address for the desired page.

Such a scheme is, for performance reasons, unworkable without the hardware assistance provided by an associative memory. Again, the associative memory is small, but tends to contain the most active pages. An associative memory entry contains the segment and page numbers, together with the frame address for a page. In order to reduce the time taken to locate a page which may not appear as an entry in the associative memory, the search of the associative memory and the segment table begin in parallel. If the page is represented by an entry in the associative memory, the search of the main segment and page tables is aborted; otherwise it has progressed some microseconds when it is found that no entry appears in the associative memory. Figure 4.13 shows this scheme.

Virtual Storage Systems 113

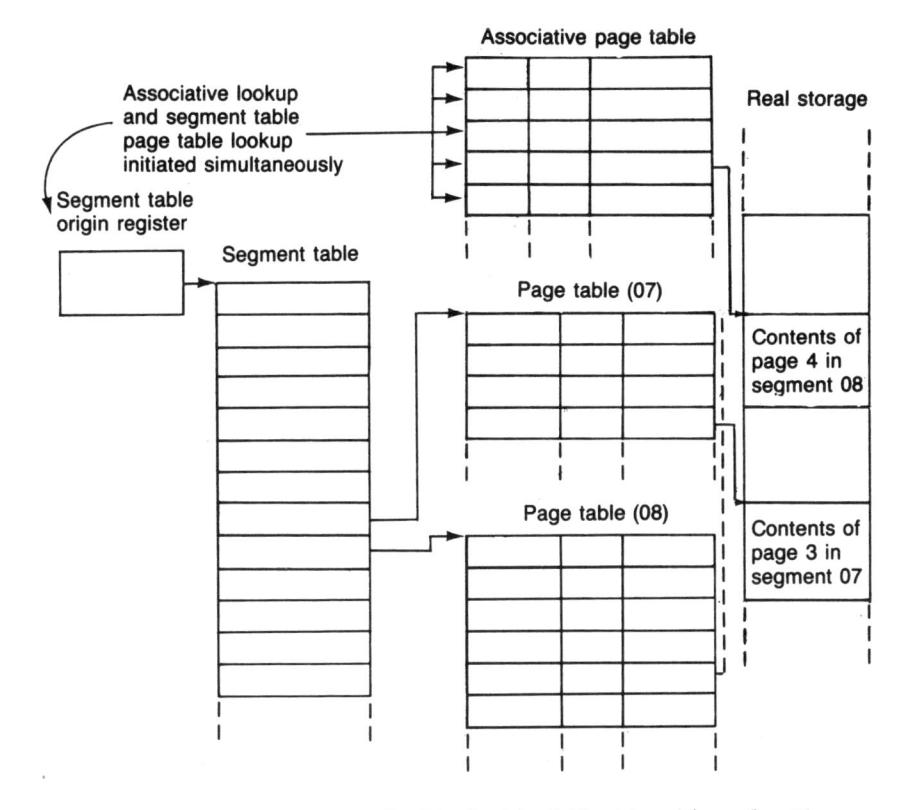

Figure 4.13 Parallel search with abort for failing/slower search path

So far, I have been talking as though only one process at a time is in virtual storage. I have not discussed how the system knows where to find the page table in a pure paged system or the segment table in a pure segment or combined system. Again, for the sake of speed, hardware must be used.

A register, called the page table origin register in pure paged systems and the segment table origin register (STOR) in segmented and combined systems, contains the address in real storage where the appropriate table begins. This is shown in Figure 4.14. Thus there is one additional level of address translation which I have not mentioned earlier.

In a pure paged system, the page table origin register contains the address of the start of the table. This is added to the page number multiplied by the number of bytes in each entry in the page table, giving the actual address of the entry in the table for the desired page. The same is true of segmented and combined systems, except in that case it is the

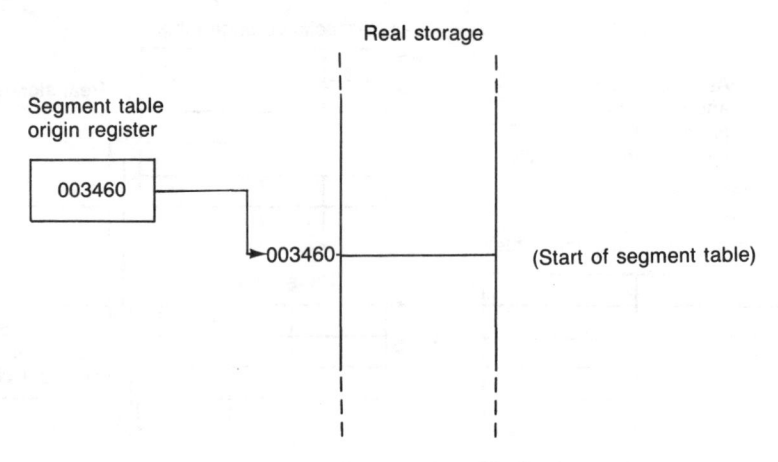

Figure 4.14 Segment (or page) tables in real storage, pointed to by the segment (or page) table origin register

address in the STOR which is added to the segment number multiplied by the number of bytes in a segment table entry. For example, page 00A is found by taking the address in the page table origin register (014500, for example) and adding that to the page number multiplied by the number of bytes in each entry, say four. Thus:

$$014500 + (00A \times 4) = 014500 + 28 = 014528$$

014528 is the address for the entry in the table for the desired page.

In order to make virtual storage schemes workable for multiprogramming systems, there needs to be a number of page or segment table origin registers — one for each active process — pointing to tables for each of the active processes. A *process table* provides the data necessary to track each active process. Any associative memory will thus contain entries for many processes — necessitating another field showing the process identification as well as segment or page (or both) numbers. In Figure 4.15, the diagram shows a schematic representation for an entire virtual multiprogramming system.

Questions for review

(i) What are the major differences between (a) a paged system, (b) a segmented system, and (c) a combined segmented and paged system?
(ii) What is the difference in the above three in the block mapping table?
(iii) What is the associative search technique and what advantage does it bring to the system?
(iv) In a combined segmented and paged system we wish to access a virtual address 084257. The STOR contains the value 024200. The segment table entry

Virtual Storage Systems

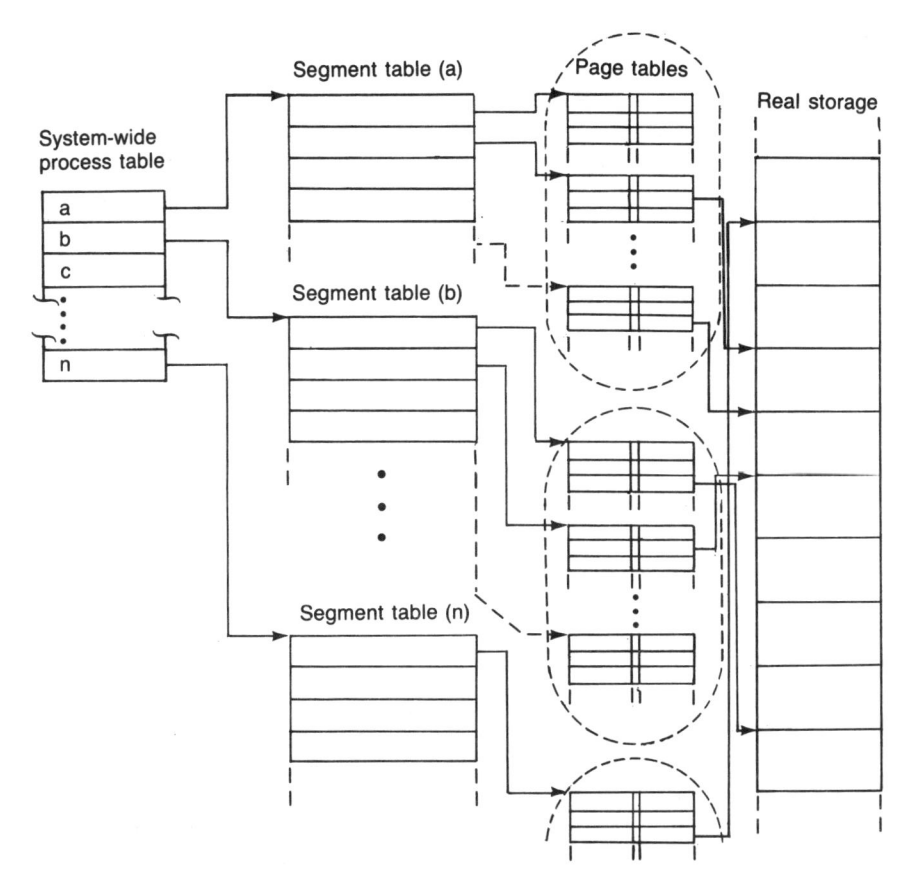

Figure 4.15 Table structure for a multiprogramming virtual storage system using combined segments and pages

for segment 08 contains the address 024430, and the page table for segment 08 contains an entry for page number 4 showing that the page is in real storage and the frame address is 133000. Write down the locations accessed in real storage when finding virtual address 084257.

4.4 MANAGING VIRTUAL STORAGE

Virtual storage concepts, however, complicate the management of primary storage. The operating system must have a strategy for determining when to bring the next page or segment into primary storage — a **fetch strategy**.

A fetch can occur upon explicit reference being made to a page or segment, called **demand fetch**. *Demand fetch* has the advantage that a page or segment will only be fetched when it is required, never at any other time.

Or the system can attempt to *forecast* which page or segment will be referred to next and fetch it. This is faster than demand fetch in that the forecast is made and the fetch begun *before* any actual reference is made to the page or segment, but at the cost of an occasional wrong guess. This method is called **anticipatory fetch**.

Whether demand or anticipatory fetch is used depends upon the types of program likely to be executed on the system under consideration (for example, those with many branches to widely separated addresses would degrade performance in anticipatory fetch) and the overheads of making the forecast.

Having fetched a page or segment, there is the problem of where to put it. Since (in paged systems) any free frame will do, this is trivial; it is merely a matter of locating a free frame, or, if none exists, freeing some frame. With variable-length segments, placement problems are the same as those occurring in multiprogramming real storage systems. A fit strategy must be used to find space for a segment being swapped in. The means of choosing placement, termed *placement strategy*, were explained in Section 3.2.

Lastly, when all page frames (in paged systems) or real storage areas (in segmented systems) are in use – a common occurrence – the operating system must have a **replacement strategy**. For optimal system performance, pages selected for replacement should be those which will not be required again soon. The operating system cannot determine this and it is therefore necessary to make inferences about the probability of any candidate for replacement being referred to at any time soon.

A simple technique with very low overhead is to select pages for **replacement at random**. It is seldom used.

Another technique is to select pages for replacement on a FIFO basis; each page is time-stamped as it is fetched and those in real storage longest are preferred for selection for replacement. The main drawback of this strategy is that it is more likely to select heavily referenced pages for replacement as they will tend to remain in real storage the longest. It is thus unsuitable for heavily used time-sharing systems.

A third strategy is to select **least recently used** pages. Each page is time-stamped when referred to, and the least recently used are selected for replacement. This strategy is detrimental to programs with very large loops involving multiple pages.

A fourth strategy is to select **least frequently used** pages for replacement. A use counter is necessary. A drawback is that the most recently fetched pages will be the least frequently used since they have not been in real storage long enough to run up a 'good' use count.

The last replacement technique I shall discuss is termed **not used**

Virtual Storage Systems 117

recently. Each page has a reference bit indicating that a recent reference to it has been made (0 = no, 1 = yes) and also a modification bit indicating whether any data within the page has been changed (0 = not modified, 1 = yes). Whenever a page is modified, the modification bit is set to 1. If a page is referred to, the reference bit is set to 1. All reference bits, but never the modification bits, are periodically set to 0, say once every 10 milliseconds. This gives some indication of whether reference has been recent.

Pages are selected for replacement according to their condition, as indicated by the pair of bits. First selected are those pages whose bits show that they have not been referred to since the last periodic bit-reset, and have never been modified. Should none of these exist, the next choice is those which have not been referred to since the last periodic bit-reset but have been modified. There is an overhead to replacing modified pages, as their contents must be preserved by copying the contents of the page back to auxiliary storage. For unmodified pages, the original copy in auxiliary storage is still valid and the page selected for replacement can simply be over-written. Should no pages of either of the above categories exist, the selection is made from those recently referred to but unmodified. Last to be selected are those which have been recently referred to and have been modified.

Questions for review

(i) Compare the two fetch strategies in terms of seeking optimum performance from a system.
(ii) List the four techniques for page replacement, and for each give one advantage and one disadvantage.

4.5 SYSTEM USES

Operating systems and support software have increasingly taken on the burden of more and more work. Time-sharing has become popular, though its use may decline with the advent of ever more powerful microcomputers. Hours of painstaking set-up and hours of (often fruitless) waiting for results have been replaced by simple but powerful commands carried out in a matter of seconds. Time-sharing has become both a tool for developing programs and a substitute for custom-designed programs. These commands present a face to the user which has become ever more powerful, and in many instances more friendly in the sense of becoming easier to use with more guidance given to the user by the system.

Collectively these commands are known as the **shell**, though the specific grammar and vocabulary are spoken of as the **command language**. The software which interprets the commands and thus deals 'face to face' with the user is termed the **command language interpreter**. Often a shell is all that a naive user with relatively simple needs is aware of.

Some recent uses of computer systems have included interactive, full-screen editors to allow the simple entry and modification of unformatted text on a screen rather than formatted text on a line-by-line basis, graphics and interactive debuggers (software framework for testing programs).

Frequently, control of time-sharing is an integral part of the operating system. Much early operating systems development in the late 1950s and early 1960s centered on general-purpose, time-shared systems to aid in program development and in the running of specially designed applications packages. These early systems proved the value of time sharing as an aid to both productivity and creativity.

Unix, as I describe it in Part II, is exceptionally strong in this respect, since the system itself can be so easily customized to a particular use. IBM, on the other hand, developed time-sharing systems separately from their OS family of operating systems, which initially were aimed at batch processing. Eventually, the company included TSO (for *Time Sharing Option*) with the operating system as an optional extra. With the introduction of OS/MVS, the only thing optional about TSO was whether or not the user chose to use it!

More power means increased ability to do work. Where once programmers were enjoined to save expensive disk and primary storage space and computer time, users can afford to expend space and time to gain enhanced function and to adapt data storage and presentation to human needs rather than to constrain human usage to the limitations of the computer system.

A major development made possible by this enhanced power is the database. Cheap and massive direct-access secondary storage was fundamental to the development of database systems.

> A **database** is an integrated collection of data which is centrally controlled; a **database system** involves the data itself, the hardware on which the data resides, the software (called a **database management system** or **DBMS**) that controls the storing and retrieval of data, and the users themselves. [2]

Such systems make data reference in applications independent of their physical storage.

Further, databases minimize data redundancy and the probability of inconsistency inherent in redundancy, maximize data-sharing capabilities while improving security control and standards enforcement, and improve integrity and help balance conflicts in applications requirements. The database management system is *not* part of the operating system, but must

Virtual Storage Systems

interface closely with it. A DBMS is most frequently used interactively. Users make short queries against the data, for example, in the nature of 'How many electronic subassemblies AX-21681-3717-90043 are in stock in the Chicago warehouse at this moment?' They expect a response within a matter of two to five seconds. Hence database systems depend heavily on the efficiency of the operating system.

Question for review

List some ways in which increased computing efficiency through hardware improvement and software techniques has benefited computer users.

4.6 SUMMARY

Virtual techniques were originally thought of as an extension of multiprogramming or as a way to accommodate the need for some very large programs. They grew from experiences gained with the techniques used in early time-sharing systems and techniques used to squeeze large programs into limited primary storage. An end result of virtual storage techniques was that even a very fast processor could, in a well-balanced system, be kept busy more than 90 per cent of its time by achieving a high level of multiprogramming. Furthermore, more work could be accomplished with the same real resources by making more clever use of them.

This added capacity could be used to develop powerful software for use by more naive users. It was no longer an economic necessity to design highly efficient, low-overhead software which was for use only by experts. Cheaper and faster computing power meant that it became possible to present carefully designed, highly functional, powerful software especially designed for people who did not have a deep understanding of the terse codes and complex methods of older-style computing; in other words, computing could be made available for nearly everyone. It could be made to suit the specific needs of specific groups of people, and could easily be made to adopt the familiar language of the application rather than computing jargon.

Cheaply available secondary storage devices, especially direct access devices like disks, have freed data from rigid notions of records and files and allowed users to dictate how one data field should relate to another without much regard for any physical requirements of storage and retrieval.

By making it technically possible in many organizations to place a computer terminal connected to a large, powerful computer system on

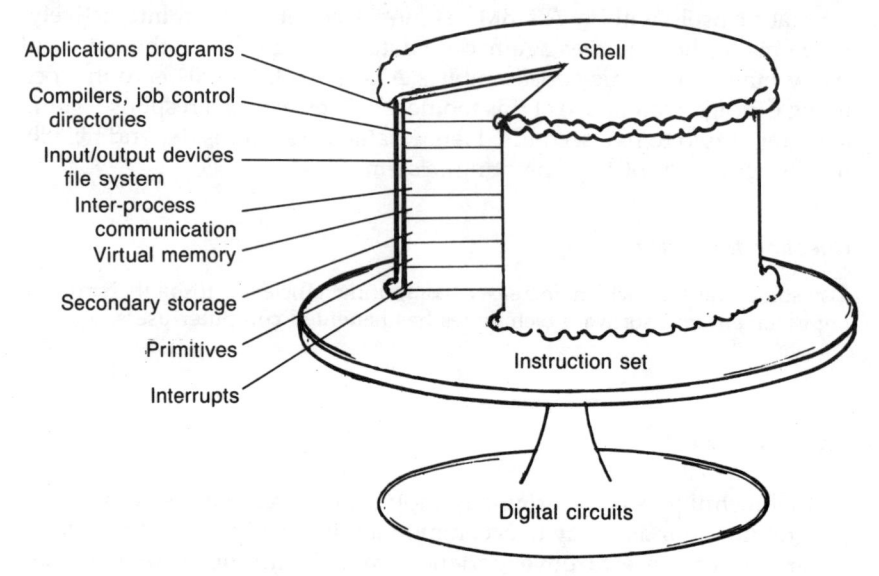

Figure 4.16 A model of a computer system

nearly every desk in an organization, virtual systems paved the way for the notion of computing for everyone. Such systems transformed many tasks which were formerly too expensive for computing solutions; for example, word processing is quickly replacing typing, and electronic files and mail are quickly replacing massive filing cabinets and innumerable memoranda.

Figure 4.16 shows a conceptual drawing of a computer system, beginning at the bottom with the fundamental digital circuits and proceeding upwards and outwards to the shell. It is now possible to enjoy the 'cake' without knowing all the ingredients that go into the different layers, fillings and frostings.

REFERENCES

[1] Deitel, H.M. (1984) *An Introduction to Operating Systems*, Addison-Wesley, Reading, Massachussetts, p. 181.
[2] *Ibid.*, p. 338.

FURTHER READING

Calingaert, P. (1982) *Operating System Elements: a user perspective*, Prentice-Hall, Englewood Cliffs, New Jersey. Chapter 2 from Section 2.3 (pp. 28—48) looks at non-contiguous allocation schemes, control techniques, dynamic storage allocation and housekeeping.

Deitel, H.M. (1984) *An Introduction to Operating Systems*, Addison-Wesley, Reading, Massachussetts. Chapters 8 and 9 look at virtual storage organization and management.

Lorin, H. (1972) *Parallelism in Hardware and Software*, Prentice-Hall, Englewood Cliffs, New Jersey. Part 7, especially Chapter 34 onwards, looks at the concepts and principles of primary storage management with especial emphasis on dynamic management, policies, strategies and techniques.

Lorin, H. and Deitel, H.M. (1981) *Operating Systems*, Addison-Wesley, Englewood Cliffs, New Jersey. Chapter 14 looks at virtual storage.

Maekawa, M., Oldehoeft, A.E. and Oldehoeft, R.R. (1987) *Operating Systems: advanced concepts*, Benjamin/Cummings, Menlo Park, California. Chapter 5 is an extensive, advanced discussion of virtual memory background, algorithms and models.

CHAPTER

5
Multicomputer and multiprocessor systems

In pushing out the frontiers of what a computer system can do, time and again the same constraint appears — *there is only one processor*. After clever techniques for storage management, the balancing of the workload, and the management of other resources bring a processor's utilization to levels closely approaching its fullest possible capacity for work, very little further performance can be wrung from it. Furthermore, the law of diminishing returns begins to bite increasingly hard as performance improves: ever-greater and more costly efforts are required to squeeze forth ever-smaller improvements.

In most computer installations catering for a number of simultaneous users, the amount of work a computer system does varies over time: from minute to minute, hour to hour and day to day. For example, in a time-sharing, interactive computing environment it is common for peaks in use to occur at certain times of the day — early in the working day, just after the lunch break and just prior to going home time in the evening.

In batch-oriented systems, many of which are accounting applications, there may be a daily load which arrives after closing time and the day's business is entered in journal files, a monthly load as each month's business is 'closed' and monthly statements of account are prepared, and an annual load to carry out year-end processing, produce the year's ledgers and compute taxes. The month-end and year-end loads coincide in the twelfth month of the accounting year, and in businesses with seasonal peaks (for example, firms making Christmas decorations), there may be three or four peaks occurring on top of each other. Thus, the planning function of a computer installation must take into account two different types of loading on a computer system: **average load** and **peak load** (see Figure 5.1).

As more work within an organization comes to depend upon com-

Multicomputer and Multiprocessor Systems

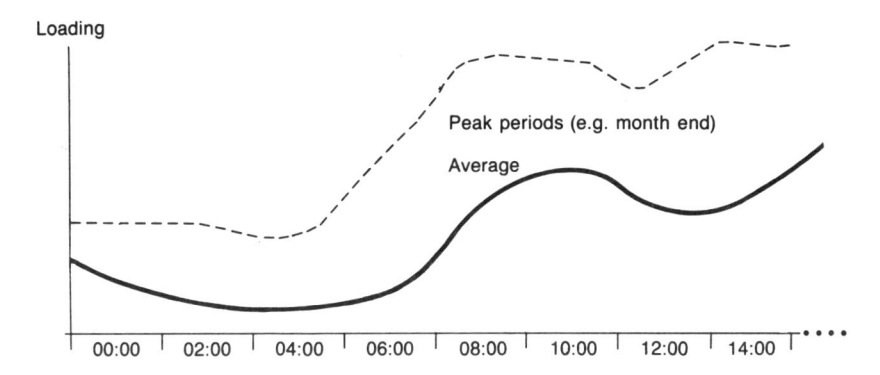

Figure 5.1 Workloads as function of time in a hypothetical system

puting power and (increasingly) upon *interactive use* of that power, the contribution to a computer system's total maximum throughput made by the system's reliability comes to have increasing importance.

Early multicomputer and multiprocessor systems were extremely expensive, hence very rare. They tended to be systems in which hardware redundancy was necessary in order to accommodate high peak loads (when one computer was sufficient for average loads) or to achieve a high level of reliability — in critical real-time systems like defense radar. (The nature of such critical systems is such that high levels of utilization are unimportant and even counter-productive, considering the functions of such systems.) An obvious answer to requirements for high peak loading or a high level of reliability is to have two or more computers or processors available to do the work — a **multicomputer system** or a **multiprocessor system**.

Though I discuss both types and you should clearly distinguish between them, the latter are, in the mid-1980s, for the first time appearing widely on the market and are gaining in importance. Multicomputer systems link, in some way, two or more *computers* which are otherwise capable of full independence from each other in that each has its own processor and storage. Multiprocessor systems link two or more *processors* together but such linked processors may share other resources, such as storage, to a very high degree, as I explain below.

Because writers tend to blur distinctions between processors and computers neither of these two terms has an exact meaning. I shall use the convention that a computer is *capable* of independent operation and a processor is not because it has no useful amount of storage available to it. A multiprocess*ing* system refers to a system containing more than one processing element, and the processing element may be either a processor or a computer, or the system may consist of some combination of processors and computers.

Microcomputers and microprocessors have made systems composed of more than one computer or processor cheap. Their small size means that several can be effectively packaged into a single *system*.

A multiprocessor or multicomputer system has three significant advantages over single computer or processor systems: first, the extended computing capability provided by having more than one processor available, secondly, enhanced flexibility in processing tasks with highly variable resource requirements, and, increased system throughput, reliability and availability, especially for critical tasks. However, the failure of one or more units in a multiprocessor or computer system will mean that the system gives a degraded performance.

I shall describe network and distributed systems as a separate category in Section 5.5. In reality, the distinction between multicomputer systems and distributed networks of computers is unclear, especially when viewed from the user's point of view. Often, the sole differences are those mechanisms necessary to deal with the distances involved. For example, multiprocessing systems may actually share secondary storage, while networked computers may *appear* to share secondary storage — in reality sharing data from secondary storage in a network involves encapsulating data and sending it as a message over the network. Networked and distributed system computers evolved somewhat differently from multiprocessing systems, and for somewhat different purposes. This historical fact has made a difference in how networks are used as opposed to how they are perceived.

5.1 DEFINITIONS AND CLASSIFICATIONS

Multiprocessor and multicomputer systems allow two or more processors to have, at least, an interconnection mechanism in common and, in varying degrees, to share data, instructions and storage. In multicomputer systems, each computer has a large degree of potential independence, as well as some interdependence.

A **symmetric independent multicomputer system** such as the one illustrated in Figure 5.2 combines two or more wholly independent single systems. Such a multicomputer system consists of two or more *identical* computer systems which, from the user's point of view, are completely anonymous — that is, no single computer within the system does any specialized work, and any computer within the system is fully capable of undertaking any job. The user does not, and usually cannot, specify a preference for one computer over the other. A university's computing

Multicomputer and Multiprocessor Systems 125

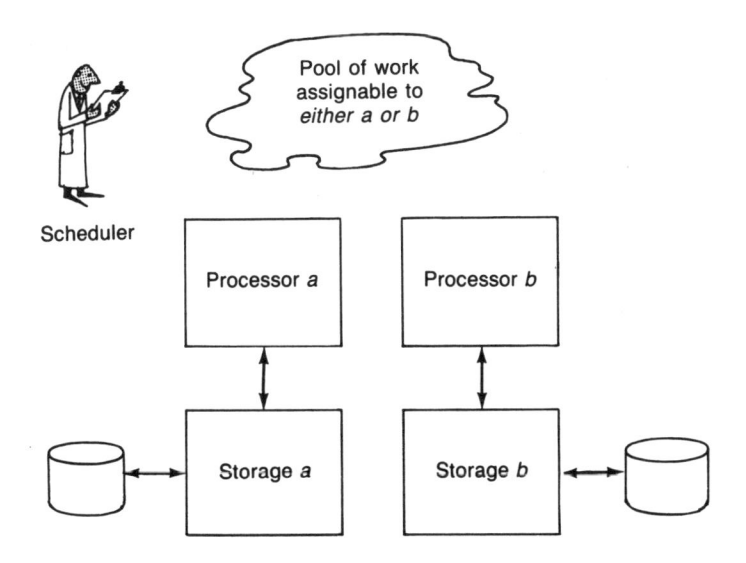

Figure 5.2 Symmetric independent multicomputer system

laboratory with several identical microcomputers for student use conceptually is such a symmetric independent multicomputer system. Chance, and perhaps a preference for being near a window, determines which student will use which microcomputer. The term also describes larger computer installations where two or more identical mini- or mainframe computers exist in the same identical, anonymous and independent relationship. In the latter case, it is the job of the operator or the scheduling supervisor to determine which computer will be assigned which tasks.

Why have such an arrangement? Such symmetric independent multicomputer systems commonly exist to provide redundancy in the case when one computer fails, or because a single computer would be loaded to the point where performance is adversely affected, or because a capability for high-priority express work must exist without seriously disturbing the normal flow of work, or because peak loading requirements exceed a single computer's capacity.

Notice that symmetrical independent multicomputer systems have no interconnection (other than that they may be used by the same person) and share no resources. Therefore, although they are called multicomputer systems, they do not meet the definition I have given above. I have included them here because they demonstrate the use of two or more independent computer systems to meet certain overall throughput and performance requirements. For example, a university computing laboratory with a large number of microcomputers helps ensure that no one student should be kept waiting indefinitely and that many students can work simultaneously. The minicomputer and mainframe systems commonly exist to accommodate peak loads well above the average loading for which a single computer system is available. In all cases, if one computer breaks down, others are available to carry on the work and, though not as much work may get done as if all the computers in the system were functioning properly, at least work continues in some form.

Once one begins to look at multicomputer and multiprocessor systems which have some degree of *inter*dependence, the many possible degrees and methods for obtaining interdependence mean that it is necessary to attempt to classify such interdependent systems in order to be able to discuss them in a meaningful way.

The problem of classifying such systems has bedevilled writers on the subject for years. This is because such systems vary so much in the way in which they are constituted. For example, multiprocessor systems have processors which range from the very simple to the very complex, the processing elements in a single system may be identical or heterogeneous, there may be local storage for each processing element or all elements may access a global storage — or a system may combine both, the degree of **data coupling** between elements may vary from very tight (with a great deal of or total sharing of data) to very loose (little sharing of data) to simple shared communication channels, the arrangement of processing elements can range from a strict hierarchy of master and slave processors to a 'fully democratic society of equals', the different processing elements may do specialized work or may be general-purpose, and there are differences in the types of workloads possible.

One of the earliest and most commonly seen classification schemes was that suggested by Michael J. Flynn [1]. This scheme classifies a system according to the way its instructions and data streams are organized. The scheme has four broad classifications.

SISD stands for *s*ingle *i*nstruction *s*ingle *d*ata. This classification described the classic von Neumann architecture: the single processor relates each data operand to the single instruction that manipulates it. Writers in the field argue about whether or not this classification also covers pipelined architectures, where several instructions and several data operands are manipulated by the processor at once, but are *always* at different stages. (The fetch and execution of instructions and fetching of data are overlapped to a great extent, but no two instructions are actually executed simultaneously, nor is an operand simultaneously related to two or more instructions.)

Another of Flynn's classification is **SIMD**, which stands for *s*ingle *i*nstruction *m*ultiple *d*ata. A system which uses several processing elements to process the elements within vectors in parallel fits this category. For example, a single instruction to *multiply* may be executed

Multicomputer and Multiprocessor Systems

simultaneously by several processing elements upon as many elements of a vector. The so-called *distributed array processors* such as the ICL DAP or the IBM 3090 Vector Facility fall into the SIMD category. However, it is difficult to know whether to include array processors among multi-processing systems since the processing elements are not independent processors in their own right, capable of fetching, decoding and executing instructions. They are components of systems, and must have a 'host' computer system and a master controller.

Flynn's third category, **MISD** (for *m*ultiple *i*nstruction *s*ingle *d*ata) is not in general use. It appears that a single data stream must be replicated before it can be presented to a multiple instruction stream.

The final category is **MIMD** − *m*ultiple *i*nstruction *m*ultiple *d*ata. All multiprocessor and multicomputer systems fall into this category. Each processing element can operate on its own data stream, with its own instruction stream.

Another classification scheme was proposed by J.E. Shore [2]. This scheme is based on the organizations of instruction storage, control unit, processing element(s) and data storage, and links between processing elements. It is an interesting classification scheme from the architectural point of view, but does not shed much light on multiprocessor and multicomputer systems from an operating-systems point of view.

Another means of classifying multiprocessor systems is to talk about them in terms of the degree of data coupling that exists between major elements. In the symmetric independent multicomputer systems I described above, there is no coupling − no interconnection mechanism at all. Figure 5.3 shows a very simple example of **loosely coupled multiprocessing** between two largely independent computer systems. The diagram shows two computer systems which are not identical and therefore not anonymous, which have a common communications path. This allows each system to pass messages to the other: messages *can* but don't necessarily have to contain signals, data or instructions.

In the case shown, both computers share, via this common communications path, a common input stream. In such a system requests for work could arrive designated as belonging either to a or to b, or such requests could be for either a or b where the destination system did not matter. **Local area networks** (LANs) and other networks (the geographic extent of such a network makes no conceptual difference to the degree of coupling) are also examples of such loose coupling; perhaps the degree is only one of the exchange of simple messages between users over an electronic medium such as coaxial cable or a telephonic transmission medium.

Figure 5.4 shows another form of loose coupling, an input/output linked system. The processors of the two computers communicate with each other as though the other were simply an input/output device. In

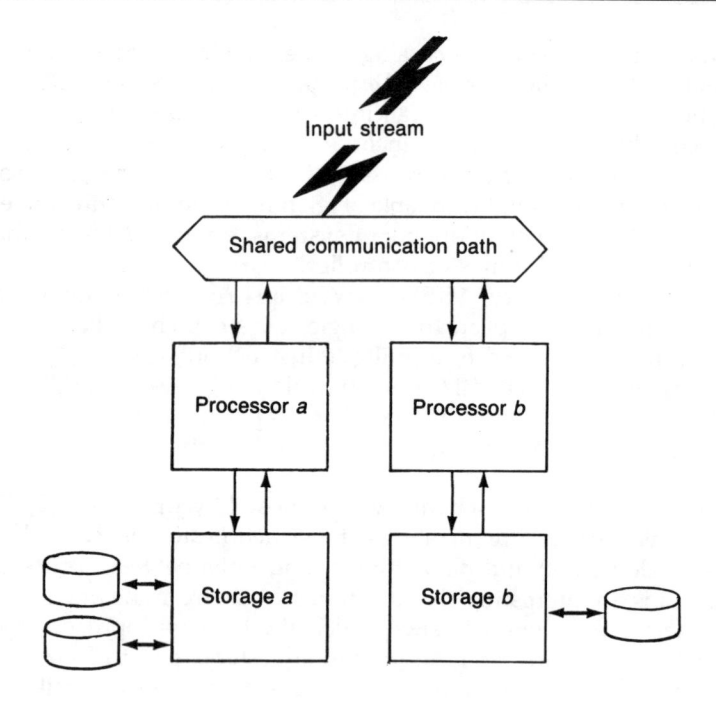

Figure 5.3 Multicomputer system with common input stream

such an arrangement it is somewhat simpler to share data in greater bulk than in a scheme such as that illustrated in Figure 5.3, because the communication path between the two is organized on a one-device-to-one-device basis, whereas the communication path shown in Figure 5.3 may be shared by many elements.

Tightly coupled multiprocessing means sharing much or all of

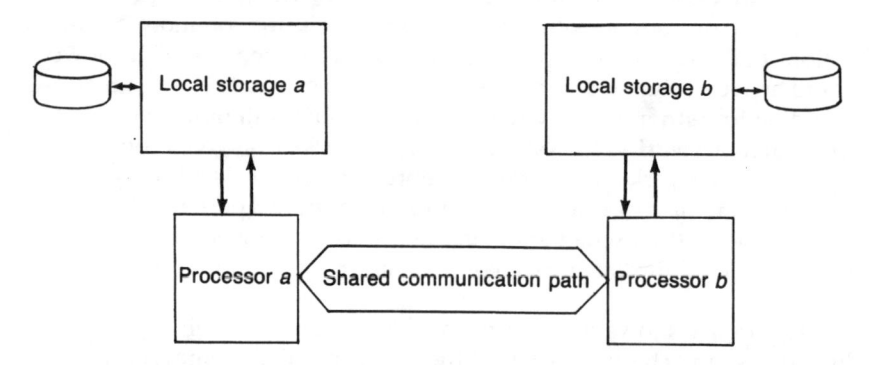

Figure 5.4 An input/output linked, loosely coupled system

Multicomputer and Multiprocessor Systems 129

secondary, and especially primary, storage, giving each computer or processor access to most or all of the same data and storage resources as any of the other computers or processors in the system.

The disadvantage of this classification scheme is its inexactness; the advantage is that the inexactness itself indicates the wide range of possibilities. Figure 5.5 shows a partial sharing with partial independence between processors. Figure 5.6 shows an arrangement whereby all storage is global to every processor in the system and no processor is independent of the others.

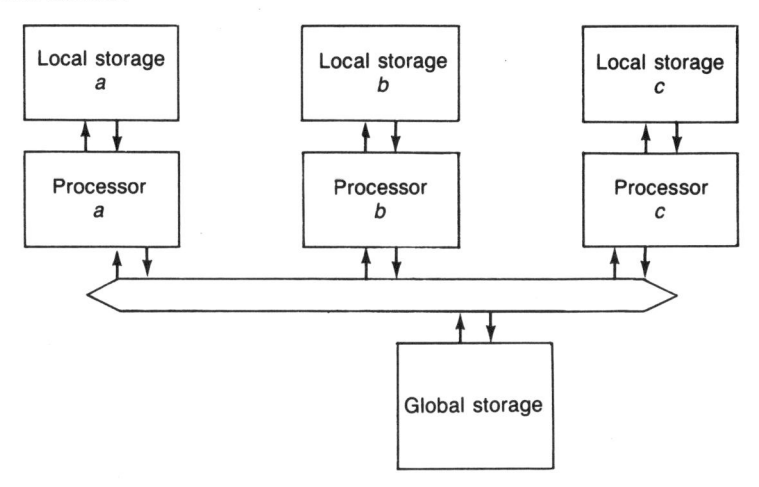

Figure 5.5 Partial sharing with partial independence

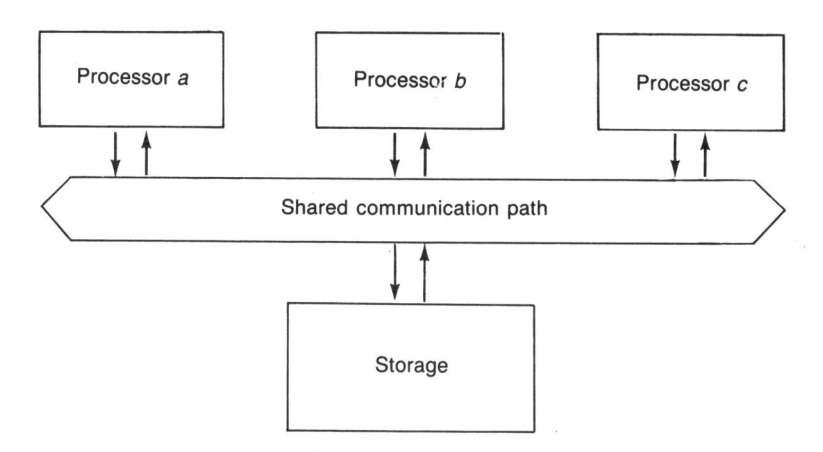

Figure 5.6 A simplified multiprocessing system: each processor may also have local (its own) storage. The shared communication path may become a performance bottleneck in such a system

Finally, one can view such systems in terms of the relationship between the processors or computers that comprise it: that of a society of equals or that of master and slaves.

Only if all the elements are logically identical (they may be physically different, as in a network comprising different makes and models of microcomputers) can a system be considered fully democratic. Figure 5.6 shows an arrangement which can potentially be fully democratic.

In any system where some elements have more power or more storage (or both) there may be some degree of democracy but there is also likely to be one element which has some degree of control or precedence over the others.

In a hierarchically organized system the higher levels of the hierarchy have control over those levels beneath them. In some cases a system of disparate elements can be very strictly defined as a master–slave system. Figure 5.7 illustrates a system in which one processor has control of all the storage and allocates tasks to a slave processor. An example of such an arrangement is IBM's large mainframe (System 370 and up) Attached Processor (AP), in which any interrupt occurring in a task running in the AP must be passed as an interrupt to the main processor for the main processor to process.

Questions for review

(i) What resource is shared in a symmetrical independent multicomputer system?
(ii) What determines which computer in a symmetrical independent multicomputer system will run a particular task?
(iii) What do the elements in a very loosely coupled system share?
(iv) What would happen to a request for I/O from a task running in a slave processor of the sort shown in Figure 5.7?

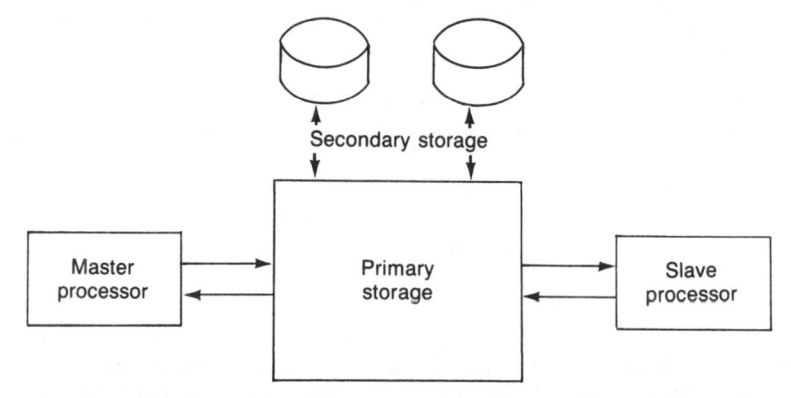

Figure 5.7 A master–slave system with tightly coupled processors

Question for discussion

Why are different classes of computer architecture, such as those proposed by Flynn, desirable?

5.2 PRINCIPLES OF MULTIPROCESSOR AND MULTICOMPUTER SYSTEMS

All the systems I described in Chapters 1—4 are often called **single server** systems: one server (processor) does one sequential task at a time, though it may switch its efforts between a number of similar sequential tasks whenever any one task pauses. Resources are also likely to be treated sequentially, and tasks are likely to have a high degree of dependency, hence be rigidly time-dependent.

A model of such a single server system might be one person in a kitchen preparing a meal of several dishes, watching a small child and feeding pets. This individual must prepare each dish of the meal according to a set of ordered subtasks: break the eggs into a mixing bowl and discard the empty shells, beat the eggs until they are frothy, add a small amount of water, salt and pepper, beat again, melt some butter in a frying pan set over low heat, add the egg mixture slowly to the warm pan, and so on. Any serious deviation from the order of subtasks (for example beating the eggs before breaking them) would result in a very odd omelette.

The one server can, however, switch his or her attention between tasks whenever a task does not require immediate attention: for example, as the eggs are cooking put some water in the kettle and put it on to boil, pour some frozen peas into a pan and put that on the hob at low heat while waiting for the kettle to boil, put a filter paper in the filter cone, add ground coffee and set that on the coffee pot, when the water boils, pour some into the coffee filter, gently turn the eggs, admonish the child to stay away from the hot stove, get a can of dog food from the cupboard and find the dog's feeding bowl, give the child a piece of fruit to keep it occupied, . . . etc.

Not least of the constraints in fully exploiting multiprocessor systems is the pervasiveness of the often unconscious model for computing in general: the human mind. Serious conscious thinking tends to be (or we feel it to be) sequential — a fact reflected in such expressions as 'train of thought', 'straight thinking', 'line of thought' or 'thinking along those lines'. Since we consciously think and work sequentially (though we are quite capable of interrupting one train of thought or line of work in order to devote our energies to a more critical or more attractive thought or task) we find we are not geared to thinking consciously about parallelism.

Yet parallelism does exist in the human model; we need not devote conscious thought to those functions controlled by the autonomic nervous system, and most people have had the experience of successfully walking or driving over a familiar piece of road while all 'conscious' thought was apparently devoted to pondering some problem totally divorced from navigation and watching other traffic.

To date, most common programming languages are sequential in nature and sequential in the way in which they describe problems even when implied parallelism is possible, as it is in vector arithmetic and array handling. Indeed, the correct sequence of instructions is paramount in much computing. However, most programmers at one time or another have realized that, if a and b must be summed and both a and b are derived quantities, it will make no difference to the end result which is derived first so long as both are derived prior to the summing. The programmer is free to choose which to derive first. What is less obvious because of the strictly serial nature of most computer systems is that, were *two* processors available, *both a and b could be derived in parallel*.

There are four major steps to developing program code:

- design an algorithm to solve the problem at hand;
- express that algorithm in a programming language;
- compile the source program into machine-readable code;
- execute the code on the target computer system.

The earlier parallelism is introduced into this development process, the more effective the ultimate solution will be. It is simple to translate a parallel process into a sequential one. This can be done by assigning an arbitrary sequence to parallel processes. It is much more difficult to attempt to introduce parallelism into a sequentially defined process, since this requires careful and extensive analysis to exclude any sequential dependencies from any processes selected to be run in parallel. Parallel algorithms can run on any computer, but will achieve maximum performance when the parallelism can be sustained through all the stages in program development, including the last.

Some programming languages are inherently parallel in nature, and the design of algorithms for such languages also requires or implies parallel thinking. APL, which was originally developed as a concise mathematical notation and not as a programming language, is one language with implied parallelism; it introduces sequential operation only at the stage where source code is compiled into machine code. Occam is a newer programming language using a somewhat different approach; parallelism in occam is explicit and the language constructs assume that complete tasks will be carried out in separate processors.

Other languages are beginning to develop parallel structures — FORTRAN has long been pressed into service for this purpose, and others have had vectorizing compilers introduced for the language. These compilers are capable of recognizing independent instructions which can be executed in parallel: for example the repetitive DO loops in FORTRAN used to carry out vector operations. The design of parallel algorithms and the methodology for doing so are current areas of research.

The definition of the task to be done and the nature of the resources for doing it have a critical influence on any appreciation of concurrency. The significant elements in any model of concurrency of activity are:

- the task(s). The order of dependence between subtasks is fundamental to the definition of the task. The more there exists logical order between tasks, the less opportunity there is for concurrency.
- The processor(s) available.
- The resource(s) required to carry out a task, together with some consideration of its (their) possible parallelism.
- Time. 'We can never, by its very nature, invoke a time-independent notion of parallelism.' [3]

Thus, it is possible to describe multiprocessing systems by taking into account these elements.

Multiple servers (**multiservers**) — that is, several linked processors and computers — imply a potentially high degree of concurrency. I have described both the real concurrency of two processors — in terms of the processor and its data channel — and the apparent concurrency of multiprogramming systems earlier. I am now speaking of *combining, expanding* and *unifying* the two.

Hardware redundancy and recovery

One of the justifications of a multiprocessing/computing system is its increased reliability due to the redundancy of its major components. In the event that a single processor or computer in such a system fails, work can shift to those processors or computers which continue to function.

A shift of this type is a far from simple matter. The system must somehow detect any processor or computer which fails. Either a failing element must be able to recognize that its own failure is imminent and signal this to the other elements in the system, or the other elements must be able to detect its failure. Once failure has occurred, the operating system must rebalance the workload so that the degraded system continues to provide some service to its users and so that the sudden shift in workload does not cause the entire system to seize up. Similarly, the operating system's allocation strategies must be adjusted in order to prevent what is effectively a smaller system than that which was originally configured from becoming overwhelmed by incoming work.

A multiprocessor or multicomputer system allows its elements to be reconfigured into forms which are highly reliable. Some elements in the system may exist solely as backup to other elements, particularly to those performing critical tasks. An additional advantage of such systems is that all elements can perform any non-critical, preemptable tasks, providing extra computing power in addition to increased reliability.

In systems where one element may be engaged in executing critical tasks and the redundant elements are either idle or engaged in executing non-critical, preemptable tasks, the element engaged in the critical activity is termed the *primary*. The status of *primary* can be switched to one of the non-critical elements in case of failure of the primary or according to a schedule to allow periodic maintenance. In some applications it is necessary for the backup element to be kept 'up-to-date' with the activity of the primary; the backup can receive and process the same data and merely suppresses output. Such an arrangement can be valuable for cross-checking critical results but calls for massive duplication of data.

Several models of reliability, around which multiprocessor and multicomputer systems are designed, exist. All systems are subject to periodic component failure, but in some applications failure of the entire system is undesirable or even unacceptable. It is useful here to make a distinction between **fault** − an abnormal hardware or software condition which results in a reduction of performance or capacity − and **failure** − the complete loss of capability. The need to avoid failure, even if at great cost, is true especially of critical systems. Air traffic control systems are an example of systems in which failure is extremely dangerous and intolerable.

Non-stop computing describes those systems where total system failure is intolerable. Such a system must have a high degree of redundancy in all components in order to prevent total failure. This extends to protection of the power supply across power failures usually by having a backup independent power supply available or by using an uninterruptable power source that bridges power failures through stored electricity and backup electrical generators. Multiple data paths around the system prevent system failure due to inter-component communications failure. Hardware redundancy provides backup against component failure, and software redundancy may also be used to provide protection against catastrophic software failure. Such systems are extremely complex and costly.

Another term which applies to such systems is **fail-safe**. In the case of fail-safe systems, a failure in any element is tolerated *only* when such a failure cannot result in any dangerous condition or loss. Thus, the term *fail-safe* does not have exactly the same meaning as *non-stop*. However, the high degree of redundancy necessary in either case means that a fail-safe system could probably perform in a non-stop manner, if necessary.

Another common justification for multiprocessing and computing systems is that it becomes possible to provide an uninterrupted, if somewhat degraded, service to the systems users. Such systems are called **fault-tolerant** or **fail-soft**, the latter meaning that, as components fail, service continues at a reduced level and allows a controlled shut-down.

Data

In other applications the preservation of correct data may be of paramount concern. The system can tolerate failure so long as that failure is detected before data are corrupted. Such systems also make use of redundancy to provide fault detection and recovery, though the level of redundancy is unlikely to be as great as it is in non-stop systems.

Combinations of hardware and software help guarantee data integrity. The concept of **stable storage** recognizes that *any* component can fail, whether primary storage (which, usually being volatile, is 'wiped clean' in any power failure) or secondary storage, where disks can fail. *Stable storage* may be a type of memory which is non-volatile and therefore not subject to data loss in power failures, or it may consist of pairs of disks updated with new or changed data simultaneously. In the event one disk fails, the other will contain uncorrupted, accessible data.

Algorithms which guarantee **failure atomicity** can be used. This means that any critical action with regard to data becomes an 'all or nothing' proposition. Given the possibility that a failure can occur part way through an update to critical data such that the data might be corrupted, the algorithm guarantees either that the update can be completed successfully, *or* that the update can be wholly nullified and the data returned to *exactly* the same state it was in before the update sequence began.

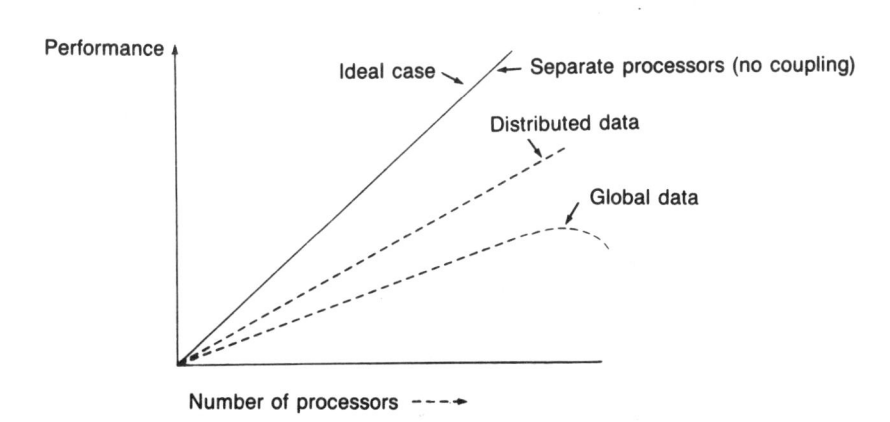

Figure 5.8 Multiprocessor performance

Whatever advantages in reliability may accrue from a multiprocessor or multicomputer system, the goal of most such systems is increased throughput. Increasing throughput means making the system do more work, but the way in which the work is structured and the way in which the availability of several processors is exploited is conditioned by a number of factors, some of which are illustrated in Figure 5.8. In any case, two interdependent processors or computers do *not* perform at twice the capacity of two independent processors or computers, as I shall show in the next subsection.

Questions for review

(i) Why is it important to introduce parallelism early in the program development cycle?
(ii) What process is necessary to introduce parallelism into a sequentially ordered program?
(iii) Describe the nature of a non-stop computing system. For what kinds of applications is such a system necessary and suitable? Why do relatively few of these systems exist?
(iv) What are the goals of fault-tolerant and fail-soft system designs?
(v) What techniques are used in non-stop and fault-tolerant systems?
(vi) What is *stable storage*?
(vii) What is meant by *failure atomicity*?

Question for discussion

What bearing do you feel the distinction between *fault* and *failure* may have on hardware design? Software design?

5.3 MULTIPROCESSING OPERATING SYSTEMS

Multiprocessing operating systems share many functions with multiprogramming systems: resource allocation and management, data protection, deadlock prevention, handling abnormal terminations of user processes, I/O and processor load balancing and reconfiguring subsystems (for example, disk secondary storage or the I/O subsystems).

Multiprocessing systems have the additional problems of load balancing among several processing elements and system reconfiguration. Automatic support for the exploitation of parallelism in hardware and software is the key. Since the addition of hardware to any system adds to its cost, the operating system (itself more complex and hence more expensive) must manage the resources effectively in order to generate the added benefits to balance against the increased cost.

One major difference between operating systems for multiprogramming and multiprocessing systems is that the latter must be organized to take into account the existence of multiple processing elements and the relationships and interconnections between them.

Master and slave

One possible organization of a multiprocessing system is that of master and one or more slaves. The degree of data coupling in master–slave organizations may be loose or extremely tight. The master, however, directs all slave processing elements and as such usually executes the operating system. A slave usually executes only user processes.

Such an organization is relatively easy to implement; it can be a fairly direct adaptation of a multiprogramming system. Its advantages are that deadlock prevention is no more difficult than in a multiprogramming environment and that there is no need for re-entrant code in the operating system because only one processor executes that code and on behalf of only one user process at a time. It is particularly suitable when the slave is less powerful than the master, when there is a great deal of computation and little or no I/O work (called **CPU**, **computation** or **processor bound**) and where the workload is steady, well understood, and scheduling is straightforward and tunable. Its disadvantages, however, are several. The slave can only run relatively processor-bound jobs, since I/O demands *two levels of interrupt*. In poorly scheduled systems large queues can build up at the master. Failure of the master proves catastrophic to the system as a whole. Utilization will be poor if the scheduling algorithms are poor or the master is inefficient.

IBM's large mainframe attached processor system (AP) is an example of an extremely tight master–slave organization. The system consists of two processors with one primary storage and with one secondary storage subsystem. The master processor runs the operating system and has complete control over I/O and secondary storage. The attached (slave) processor runs only user processes which, when they require the services of the operating system, must request an interrupt of the master, and then must wait for the master's action on their requests.

A somewhat looser master–slave organization is realized by having the operating system of the master element have directive powers over the slaves, but the slaves may also have their own operating systems. Loosely coupled master–slave organizations may be a network of computers (discussed more fully in the next subsection) each with its own copy of the operating system, but with one node in the network (the master) having the power to direct the slaves whenever any inter-computer action is required.

Separate executives

In the organization known as **separate executives** each processing element has its own operating system and processes interrupts generated by user processes running only on itself. Each processor, in addition, controls its own I/O devices and files. Any process assigned to a processor runs to completion on that processor and each processor executes its own operating system; thus, the processors do not cooperate on the execution of any one process. I/O devices may be switched between processors, but this requires an operator's or a master operating system's intervention. Certain system information, such as the table of processing elements known to the system, are global to the entire system. Access to such global information must be tightly controlled using mutual exclusion techniques.

Loosely coupled master—slave or democratic organizations both make use of separate executives.

An example of such a system is one in which two or more large, and quite possibly asymmetric, IBM mainframes each runs OS/VS2 MVS as an operating system. However, input and output functions (except to or from interactive terminals) and I/O queueing, syntax-checking and partial translation of job control language, and high-level scheduling are parts of a Job Entry Subsystem (JES) which provides these functions for *all* linked computer systems.

Such a system can be both very large and very complex, with high, but economically tenable, overheads. Auslander *et al.* [4] mention one system with seven computers, over 450 direct access devices serving nearly 15 000 terminals in over 50 locations with a total instruction execution capacity of over 40 MIPS (*m*illion *i*nstructions *p*er *s*econd). The authors note that IBM-provided software (consisting largely of the operating system) uses 90 per cent or more of such a system's total capacity; what remains is left for the users!

Such systems may need to resolve conflicts, but this clearly is difficult when several copies of the operating system are in existence. One common method used in such systems to resolve conflicts is *voting*. Each processing element in the system *votes* on the resolution of the conflict. In some cases, a majority rule is acceptable. In others, such as votes occurring within distributed operating systems on questions of failure atomicity, a veto system prevails: a single 'no' vote is sufficient for a 'no' decision. In failure atomicity algorithms, for instance, where several nodes in a geographically distributed transaction system are involved in making a data update on distributed data, the update must not proceed unless all nodes are in agreement that all necessary sub-actions within the transaction are fully complete. If even one node signals a failure of a sub-action, this constitutes a *veto* on the transaction in question and the data are returned to the state they had prior to the beginning of the transaction.

This ensures against partial updates.

Another possible mechanism for resolving conflicts is to allow the part of the system involved to make a decision. For example, in the JES-linked IBM systems described above, any conflict regarding resources controlled by JES would be resolved by JES, whereas any conflicts with resources controlled by an MVS system would be resolved by that MVS with no reference made to any other of the linked systems.

Symmetrical systems

I have already described one form of symmetrical system: the symmetrical independent multicomputer system. A more evolved form of this is **symmetrical multiprocessing**; it is the most powerful organization and also the most complex to design and implement. All processing elements in such a system are identical, and are managed by an operating system which *floats* between them. Since the processing elements are identical, any one of them can host the operating system. The element which hosts the system tables and system-wide functions is termed the **executive** processor. Only one processor is the executive at any instant. This prevents conflicts over information which is global to the system from arising. Any member of the pool of identical processing elements may be used to control any I/O device or to refer to any storage unit. Any user process may execute on any processing element and several elements may cooperate to execute any user process.

In such a system, resolving conflict at both the hardware and software levels is vital to the smooth functioning of the system. Conflicts between processing elements attempting to access the same I/O device or storage unit are usually resolved by hardware, whereas conflicts arising from attempts to access system global information are resolved in the operating system's software. Because there is only one copy of the operating system but many processors can execute its code simultaneously, code must be re-entrant and mutual exclusion is necessary.

Such a symmetrical organization offers several advantages:

- increased reliability and **graceful degradation** in the event of a processor failure;
- better load balancing and improved utilization (since *any* task can be routed to *any* available processor);

but it has its attendant disadvantages:

- contention problems can become severe;
- **lockout** may be excessive.

Questions for review

(i) What is the major difference between multiprogramming and multiprocessing operating systems?
(ii) List the three organizations possible in multiprocessing and for each of the three list one advantage and one disadvantage.
(iii) Describe both kinds of 'voting' systems. Which applies in failure atomicity algorithms?

5.4 MULTIPROCESSING SYSTEM PERFORMANCE

Studies of the performance of multiprocessing systems using the three organizations I have just described have shown that two processing elements in such a system do *not* provide twice the processing capacity of one processor. Additional operating-system overhead, increased contention for system resources and the delays inherent in switching and routing transmissions between an increased number of components cause this, as indicated in Figure 5.9.

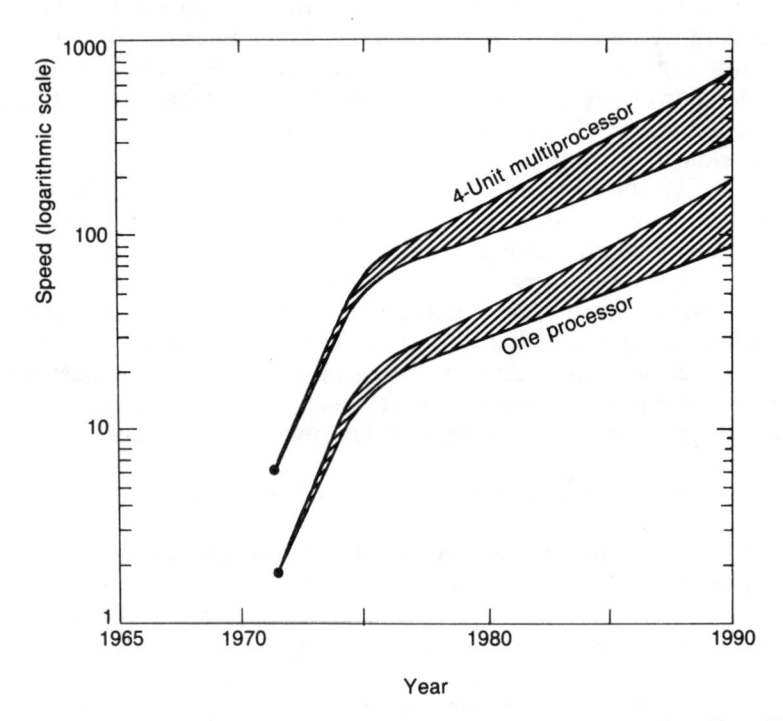

Figure 5.9 Projected multiprocessor performance, adapted from Turn [6]

Multicomputer and Multiprocessor Systems

The allocation of processes to processors or computers in multiprocessing systems is one problem related to concurrency. In most multiprocessing systems the processing elements are not fully interconnected. That is, in a system consisting of six processing elements it would be unusual for element 1 to be directly connected to elements 2–6, and for element 2 to be directly connected to elements 1 and 3–6, and so on (see Figure 5.10).

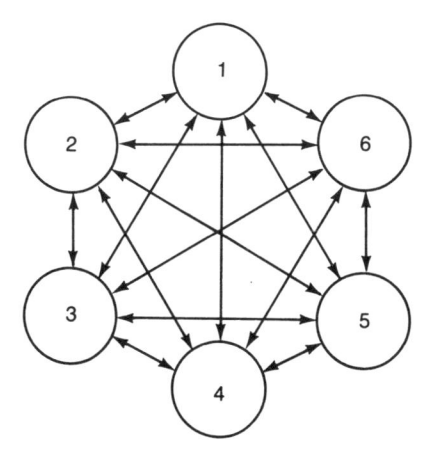

Figure 5.10 A fully interconnected multiprocessor arrangement

This means some kind of routing information is needed for directing inter-element communications within the system. This results in additional overheads, though these overheads can be kept to a minimum if a process can be allocated to a processing element in a way that reflects the topology of the system and the needs of the process to communicate with other processes.

Many applications do not have a sufficient degree of internal concurrency to exploit the power of multiprocessing systems fully. It may be necessary to increase an application's degree of internal concurrency in order to achieve optimum multiprocessing performance [5].

Performance is especially of interest when processing elements cooperate in executing a single process. Performance is usually even lower than that of multiprocessing systems in which the elements execute separate processes. This occurs because the interactions within a process executed cooperatively take place through more remote means than would be the case for the same process running in a single processor.

In any case, effective utilization of a multiprocessing system requires a steady stream of tasks for the processors. Turn [6] gives two formulae of interest in determining performance. The first expresses the performance of the multiprocessor as

$$S_{MP}(N) = (N - k_N)Sp$$

where N is the number of processors, k_N represents the fraction of processor activity devoted to system overhead tasks, and Sp is the speed, expressed in MIPS, of the component processors. He notes that it is difficult to assess the dependence of k_N on N. The shortfall in performance found in cooperating systems is highly dependent upon the interconnections of components of the system and upon the nature of the task, but can be broadly identified with a multiplicative factor (k_i) which is less than one, such that the gross speed of the system S_N is

$$S_N = \sum_{i=1}^{N} k_i S_i$$

where S_i is the speed of an individual processor in the multiprocessing system. Studies have shown that, if a single processing element is taken to have a performance factor of 1, two elements will increase productivity to a factor of 1.8, but three will increase that to a factor of only 2.1. However, new architectures are emerging which should improve these figures.

Justification for multiprocessors vs. multicomputers

Whether an organization chooses to adopt a multiprocessor rather than a multicomputer approach depends on a large number of factors which are different for each organization.

One advantage of either approach is that new processors or computers can usually be added to a system without adding to the work force, providing that the new processing elements draw on the staff's existing skills. (If not, the organization may have to hire new staff or engage in some training of existing staff.) Adding processor capacity can be more economical than adding a new computer system *if* it is more processing capacity that is required. Adding a new processor can be done quickly and smoothly, and multiprocessor systems can be more cost effective over a wide range of tasks.

Multiservers for a single queue of work are more effective in improving throughput than several single servers serving discrete queues. Imagine going to the bank and choosing to join one queue of several possible — when the person in front of you turns out to have bags full of small change to be counted and deposited, and then wants to find out the current balance of another three accounts. If instead you join a single long queue, each individual advances quickly up the queue when the person at the head of the queue can proceed to the next free teller.

However, multiprocessors are more complex than multiple computer systems, both in terms of hardware and in terms of software. Error recovery capabilities are very important for multiprocessors and must be carefully designed, and it will probably be necessary to duplicate or even multiply crucial systems data in the event of processor failure.

Because of the precipitous decline in processor costs, advances in research in the automatic detection of parallelism and the rapid development of programming languages (occam, Ada, concurrent Pascal, etc.) which allow the explicit expression of parallelism, the trend towards multiprocessor systems is accelerating rapidly.

In addition, the physical limits of even the largest single processors are being reached and exceeded. The development of yet larger and more complex single processors is a difficult task, since increasing complexity and size mean that design and testing efforts are greatly multiplied.

Recent impetus has gone into using simpler, cheaper processors in parallel to achieve the same results. Design and testing time are reduced, as is the manufacturing cost of the final system. New developments point to combined symmetric and asymmetric multiprocessors joined into a single system with a hierarchical arrangement.

Questions for review

(i) What factors influence the performance of a multiprocessor system such that each additional processor does not 'deliver' a processor's worth of power to the enlarged system?

(ii) What factors might influence an organization's choice of multiprocessor versus multicomputer systems?

5.5 NETWORK AND DISTRIBUTED SYSTEMS

In 1969, work began on putting together the world's first computer **network**, Arpanet. It still exists today, linking over 100 computer systems. Arpanet and other early networks were initially undertaken as research projects; today private networks and newer commercial and public networks offer users wide access to computing resources. This trend will, no doubt, continue and accelerate.

Networks can be considered as a form of multicomputer system in which the physical connections are communications links between otherwise largely independent computer systems. The user may perceive that, for example, secondary storage is shared between one computer system and another; however, this occurs indirectly through the communication of data from one computer system to another, rather than directly by providing a physical link from one computer system to another's secondary storage. The user may also perceive, in the same network, nodes which appear to be fully uncoupled, in the same way a telephone appears to be disconnected from the telephone network until the caller begins to dial.

In networks, a number of individual computers are connected by a **communications subsystem**. The subsystem consists of **hosts** (*hosts* are those parts of the system which provide computing power), **nodes** (the category of *node* includes both *hosts* and 'dumb' devices like printers), and various types of communications links ranging from a simple twisted pair of wires to satellite transmissions. Some networks include special **communications processors**. *Communications processors* are themselves computers whose tasks are to effect communications between hosts by assuming communications tasks and defining the interface between any host and the network. Each host supports the running of user processes for its local users.

A network connects geographically dispersed processing elements and input and output devices. This allows processing elements to cooperate, often by allowing users to share resources such as data, or hardware and software resources which any individual user cannot afford and which he or she may need or want only occasionally.

Such sharing is often complicated by the need to know a great deal about access to the network's communications and about the target host. This means the user must have access to expensive and cumbersome documentation and a not-infrequent struggle with complex accounting systems. Fortunately, this complication is disappearing as more and more network designs attempt to minimize the amount of host- and network-specific knowledge needed by a user to access and share resources.

An essential part of any network, however small or large, is communications. These communications can be described in terms of models. Models are abstract descriptions; communications models are abstract descriptions of the operations available to programmers on networks for communicating between processes and processing elements.

Models for communication

One model is the message-based model. Cooperating processes send messages to each other by using *send* and *receive* primitives. *Send* is designed as a reliable function; it will continue to retransmit a message until it is successfully received at its destination. That is, *send* does not wait for any acknowledgement from the recipient; it will not block itself to wait for an event (an acknowledgement).

A second model is that of remote procedure calls. This model is now

Multicomputer and Multiprocessor Systems 145

a widely accepted communications method. It extends the **procedure call**, where one process invokes another, from multiprogramming to multiprocessing and networked systems. A remote procedure call causes the parameters to the call to be assembled in the form of a request message. The request is transmitted to the appropriate processing element, where a process is created and executed. This in turn creates a reply message which is transmitted back to the calling element, where it is 'unpacked' (communications data are stripped from the basic reply data) and used.

Both of these models have limitations. The message-based model's actual behavior is difficult to document precisely, while the remote procedure call is less flexible. Neither model suits the transfer of bulk data, that is data consisting of more than a thousand bytes.

A third model which addresses these limitations is the remote pipe and procedure communication model. I describe *pipes* more fully in Part II, in the Unix case study. A **pipe** is a process which accepts data from another process as they are produced. As a remote process, the *pipe* resembles the process in the remote procedure call model. Unlike the remote procedure call, however, the pipe does not block the calling procedure, which continues to produce data. The pipe acts as a kind of 'sink' into which data can be sent for processing. Pipes process data sent to them in strict FIFO order while the calling procedure continues execution and production of data. Hence the degree of concurrency achieved in this model is higher than that achieved by the remote procedure call model, where the calling process is blocked until a reply is received from the remote procedure as it ends [7].

Categories

Network applications fall into three broad categories:

- **resource-sharing networks**, in which the resources of any host are made available to the other hosts in the network, for example, files and output devices, as though these files and devices were actually a part of the user's local system;
- **remote-communications networks**, in which the use of geographically remote computing facilities is effected as cheaply as possible, usually by exploiting batch processing capabilities with **remote job entry** (**RJE**) and remote printing; these normally involve a small number of geographically dispersed, very large hosts perhaps linked to smaller, more local subhosts; and
- **distributed-computation networks**, for example real-time process control systems where individual tasks are performed concurrently on

several hosts in the system and where resources are placed close to their users but applications software and database are distributed throughout the network. Distributed computation networks are most frequently found embedded in factory automation, process control and telecommunications.

Hybrid applications, involving two or even all three of the above categories, exist and are rapidly becoming more common in large organizations.

Operating systems

Operating systems for the control of networks can be classed as either **network operating systems** or **distributed operating systems**.

Network operating systems are those in which each of the hosts runs its own non-network operating system and network control functions are carried out by communications processes which run on the various hosts.

Distributed operating systems have a single operating system which is run on all the hosts in a network.

Network operating systems are best where architecturally diverse, widely dispersed, large-scale computer systems have been connected into a network. System developers tend to favor distributed operating systems in implementing **local area networks** (**LAN**s) consisting of mini- and microcomputers. Distributed operating systems offer the bonus of integrity of design, whereas network operating systems utilize existing but heterogeneous hardware and software.

Both kinds require an underlying network. The network itself can be either *visible* to the user, as it often is in network operating systems, or *transparent*, as it most often is in distributed operating systems. If a network is *visible*, the user must be aware of the different hosts and must refer to them explicitly in commands, e.g.

RUN MYJOB ON HOST Q

whereas, when the network is *transparent*, the user should be unaware which host is accessed, or even that it has been necessary to access another host. The comparable command on a transparent network would be

RUN MYJOB

and the operating system would select the appropriate host for the user.

In either case, a common approach to implementing networks is to interpose another layer of software, in the form of a process called the **agent process**, between the user and all the network's hosts, so that the

Multicomputer and Multiprocessor Systems 147

access will be the same for any host in the network. Such an *agent process* is a facilitator, linking logical names of files with real files on real devices, and holding common bases for accounting for each user *and* each host.

Questions for review

(i) What relative advantages accrue to: (a) a transparent network, and (b) a visible network?
(ii) What are the three models for communication? What limitations does each have? What strengths?
(iii) List the three categories of applications of networks.
(iv) Which of the categories above is the most likely to have a distributed operating system? Which category is least likely to be able to use a distributed operating system?

5.6 SUMMARY

Multiprocessor and multicomputer systems are a means of obtaining the benefits of greater reliability, greater capacity and greater performance. The performance of such a system is not, however, an incremental increase on the performance of a single processor or computer system — two are not twice as good as one. Rather, two are about 1.8 times as good as one, and three are about twice as good as one.

The reason for this failure to extend performance to such a degree is the operating system and communications overheads in such systems. Though the simplest multiprocessor or multicomputer systems use simple extensions of multiprogramming techniques, most do not, depending upon the objectives the organization has in mind when it begins assembling such a system.

The objective may be to achieve fault-tolerance, fail-soft or fail-safe systems or non-stop computing. If that is the case, then performance and especially full use of a system's capacity is not a consideration. In other cases, the goal may be to provide for peak loads beyond a single system's capacity, or to respond, in the case of network and distributed systems, to the geographic spread of the organization.

To understand the multiplicity of arrangements possible, it is necessary to apply some form of classification. Some commonly used classifications are useful for distinguishing one hardware organization from another. Other classifications apply more to the software or to the degree to which parts of the system share data. These classifications often apply regardless of whether the parts of the system are enclosed in the same cabinet, sit in the same room, or are half a world away from each other.

REFERENCES

[1] Flynn, M.J. (1966) 'Very high speed computing systems', *Proceedings of the IEEE*, **54**(12) (December), 1901–9.
[2] Shore, J.E. (1973) 'Second thoughts on parallel processing', *Computers and Electronic Engineering*, **1**, 95–109.
[3] Lorin, H. (1972) *Parallelism in Hardware and Software*, Prentice-Hall, Englewood Cliffs, New Jersey, p. 7.
[4] Auslander, M.A., Larkin, D.C. and Scherr, A.L. (1981) 'The evolution of the MVS operating system', *IBM Journal of Research and Development*, **25**(5), 471–82.
[5] Baiardi, F. and Vanneschi, M. (1987) 'Design of highly decentralised operating systems', in *Distributed Operating Systems: theory and practice*, eds. Y. Paker, J-P Banatre, M. Bozyigit, Springer-Verlag, Berlin, pp. 113–46.
[6] Turn, R. (1974) *Computers in the 1980s*, Columbia University Press, New York, pp. 90–3.
[7] Gifford, D.K. (1987) 'Communication models for distributed computation', in *Distributed Operating Systems: theory and practice*, eds. Y. Paker, J-P Banatre and M. Bozyigit, Springer-Verlag, Berlin, pp. 147–74.

FURTHER READING

Calingaert, P. (1982) *Operating System Elements: a user perspective*, Prentice-Hall, Englewood Cliffs, New Jersey. Pages 198–213 of Chapter 8 ('System Configurations') looks at multiprocessing operating systems, design issues.
Deitel, H.M. (1984) *An Introduction to Operating Systems*, Addison-Wesley, Reading, Massachussetts. Chapter 11 discusses multiprocessing.
Gorsline, G.W. (1980) *Computer Organization: hardware/software*, Prentice-Hall, Englewood Cliffs, New Jersey. Pages 198–226 covers MISD, SIMD and MIMD computer organizations.
Gotlieb, C.C. (1985) *The Economics of Computers: costs, benefits, policies and strategies*, Prentice-Hall, Englewood Cliffs, New Jersey. Chapter 4 discusses the economics of centralized, decentralized and distributed systems.
Lorin, H. (1972) *Parallelism in Hardware and Software*, Prentice-Hall, Englewood Cliffs, New Jersey. Chapter 11 discusses multicomputer configurations. Chapter 18 covers symmetric multiprocessor systems, Chapter 19 looks at alternative designs, Chapter 26 looks at reliability.
Maekawa, M., Oldehoeft, A.E. and Oldehoeft, R.R. (1987) *Operating Systems: advanced concepts*, Benjamin/Cummings, Menlo Park, California. Chapter 6 covers distributed systems and Chapter 7 covers distributed concurrency control, deadlock and recovery.
Peterson, J.L. and Silberschatz, A. (1985) *Operating System Concepts*, 2nd edn, Addison-Wesley, Reading, Massachussetts. Pages 449–50 describe multiprocessors. Chapter 13 discusses many aspects of distributed systems.

CHAPTER

6
A brief look into the future

Operating systems have evolved steadily since the 1950s. Their initial purpose was to provide the means to control and make the best possible use of the hardware available. As hardware itself has evolved rapidly, one role of an operating system has been to ease the users' and applications' transition to new hardware by making the new compatible with the old at the interface between users or applications software and the computer system. In part, the operating system has increasingly cushioned the user from the hard realities of the hardware itself, first by allowing the user to assume that certain functions such as the details of I/O would be automatically taken care of, and later by expanding the functions available to the user to make the system appear less and less 'computer-oriented'.

The operating system has also attacked time: first to make the disparity between the speeds of the processor and its input and output devices shrink to near insignificance, and then to make use of idle time by sharing the processor among competing processes to achieve apparent concurrency.

The virtual storage operating system has also attacked the limitations imposed by restricted real storage space through its virtual techniques.

But most of all, an operating system embodies a policy about how the computer system should be used. In general-purpose operating systems, some aspects of the system may be used to encourage, discourage or forbid certain behaviors on the part of the users. This is done in order to achieve the goals set by the organization which controls the system when the system is large. In small, unnetworked microcomputer systems, the policy reflects what the system's designers *think* is required by the small system user, combined with the compromises made necessary by the small system's more limited capacity and power. A special-purpose operating system enforces adherence to a limited set of goals. That the goals are limited is itself a manifestation of policy.

But an operating system, however closely it meshes with the architecture of a computer system, is software, and software, though highly flexible because changeable, is relatively slow, and can be cumbersome. I mentioned an example where 90 per cent of the capacity of a computer system was taken up by the operating system and other systems software — a high price to pay in overhead.

Some future developments

The cost of hardware will continue to decline, speed and capacity will increase, but physical size will continue to decrease. It seems reasonable in view of the declining cost of hardware that those functions of the operating system which: (i) are most clearly defined, (ii) require no change once installed, and (iii) are performance bottlenecks will migrate into microcode and become embedded in the hardware. (This type of 'programmed' hardware is called **firmware**.) Those parts which are less critical to performance, require flexibility or are less well defined will remain as software.

In looking at the future of operating systems, Brown et al. [1] note that the success of operating systems lies in the fact that the software provides levels of abstraction that hide non-essential (from the user's point of view) details from the user. These abstraction levels form a hierarchy which ideally shields the users, who are at the highest level in the 'system', from everything but that which they need to accomplish their own tasks. Thus, the definition of an operating system, from their point of view, becomes 'a set of software extensions to ... hardware ... culminating in a virtual machine' [1].

The exploitation of concurrency will grow. Languages which incorporate explicit concurrency, such as Ada, concurrent Pascal, occam and others are being developed, and users are gaining experience with them. Languages which allow *implicit* concurrency have long existed (for example, LISP and PROLOG), but only now is it becoming possible to exploit this fully in the underlying system.

There has been considerable research into methods for dealing with parallelism, for example, MASCOT — *M*odular *A*pproach to *S*oftware *C*onstruction *O*peration and *T*est. MASCOT provides:

> 'a formalism for expressing the software structure of a real-time (parallel processing) system ... a methodology based on the formalism for design, implementation, testing and documentation ... applicable during all stages of a computer-based system life cycle ... a small kernel to provide a run-time (executive level) set of facilities which supports the formalism and provides scheduling and synchronization.' [2]

Another approach has been to use Petri nets to represent the flow of control in and between processes. A Petri net is a representation of possible system states, with information about how the system can progress between states. The net consists of circles representing places p and transitions t (represented by short vertical lines) with the places and transitions connected by arrows showing the direction in which progress can occur. If a condition represented by a place is valid, it is said to hold a *token*. If all arrows leading to a transition derive from places with tokens, the transition can take place, or 'fire' (see Figure 6.1). Research on such tools for representing concurrency is currently very active [3].

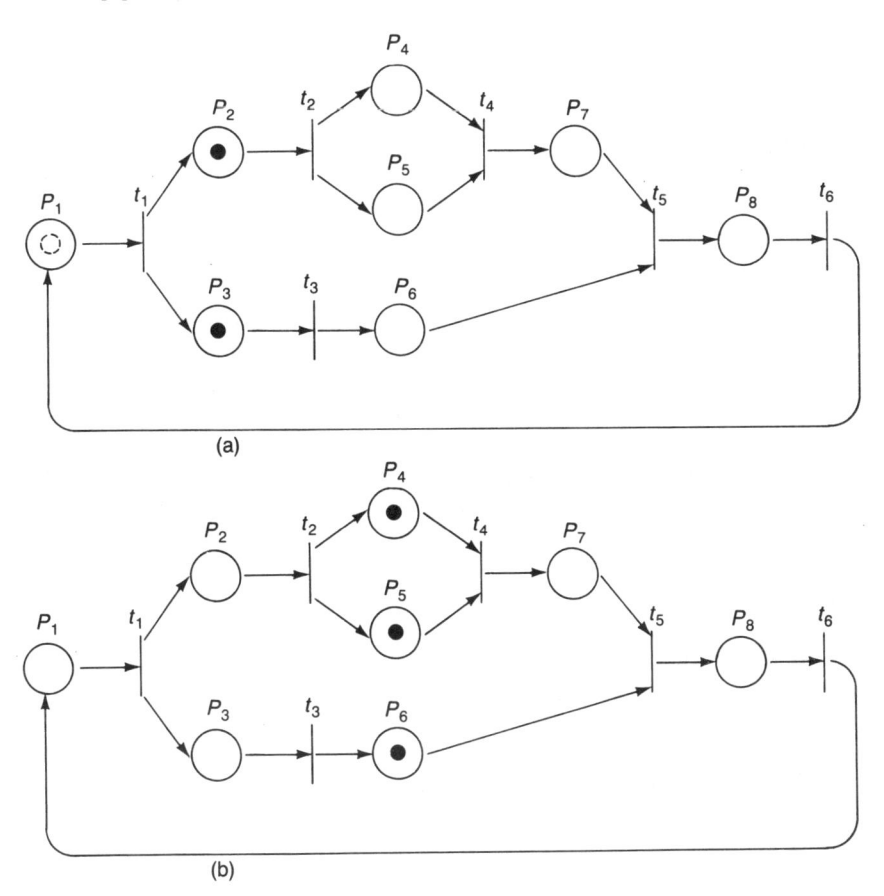

Figure 6.1 The Petri net as a tool for describing concurrency: (a) after transition has 'fired' (in its previous state the net showed a single token in P_1); (b) after transitions t_1 and t_3 have fired concurrently (*Note:* t_4 is now in a position to fire, but t_5 cannot until a token is present in P_7)

Virtual computers will also become more common. They will be *virtual* in the sense that they will present similar or even identical appearances to the user regardless of the underlying real hardware (see the p-System, Unix and VM case studies in Part II) and will make it possible for a single computer to present several different 'faces' to its user depending upon the task at hand. This virtuality (or virtuosity!) will be accomplished by means of both the computers themselves and their operating systems.

Operating systems will increasingly be designed, constructed and tested according to the principles of software engineering and will, as a result, be simpler, more comprehensible, more reliable and easier to maintain.

Massive hardware parallelism and multiprocessing will also become much more common.

More and more users will gain access to powerful personal computers. As hardware costs drop, full utilization of the computer will become less important than its availability and ease of use.

Computers, whether small or large, will increasingly be tied into networks due to the decreasing costs and increasing availability and speeds of data transmission. Network use will become increasingly transparent to the user.

An interesting development in operating systems in this area is currently the subject of research: making the operating system capable of detecting free computing capacity in a network and 'growing' into unused computers in order to carry out, for example, very large computations utilizing the high degree of parallelism provided by 'idle' computers in a network.

Such an operating system builds on the 'worm' program concept. A worm program is one which can propagate itself or parts of itself in idle computers in a network in order to make full use of the processing resources available in a network, to use those resources for parallel processing, and to provide some fault tolerance. A worm adapts to network changes automatically, without having to be informed about the structure of the network. To do this, a worm is made up of individual program units called segments, each of which can run on a single processor. Work is being carried out to develop a worm operating system, Wormos [4].

Design issues

For the designer of operating systems, two ways forward exist and are presently the subjects of argument in discussions of future developments.

Should operating systems, and indeed the underlying architectures, now be designed from the top down, beginning with a definition of the user's needs and expanding and refining that downwards through applications, support and operating systems software to the underlying hardware in order to present a fully integrated and internally consistent computer system?

Or should operating systems be designed as a series of simple, modular functional blocks which can be joined together in a predefined interface to provide a 'custom' operating system easily at low cost?

Can both these approaches be combined successfully?

One of the important design issues will remain the clear definition and understanding of any particular system's goals. 'More than one system has proved unsatisfactory because its goals were either not clearly understood, or not taken properly into account during the design phase' [5]. One can state simplistically that an operating system's goal is to manage a given pool of resources according to a stated or implied policy for their use. However, in any community of users there is conflict over which of several different policies should prevail into the design.

Another consideration is the extent to which the prospective workload of a system is predictable and controllable. Differences also exist between what users want and what they can afford.

Flexibility is the second important issue in operating systems design. Each community of users has different needs from every other, although they often have much in common, and in any one community needs alter with time due to alterations in hardware or changes in the nature of the application, or even changes in the users' apprehension of what applications and methods are possible and desirable. The system must have at least some degree of flexibility built in, if only to allow correction of errors, upgrade, additions or changes to peripheral hardware. In Part II you will see how some operating systems failed in their initial designs to allow sufficient flexibility to accommodate, for example, the Winchester technology large-capacity disk in microcomputers.

Ranged against the drive for flexibility is the reduction of complexity and its resultant benefits: lower cost and higher performance. Flexibility can mean different things — a single 'all-singing, all-dancing' operating system, an operating system which exists in variant forms (where perhaps the kernel and some higher functions form the essential part of the system, which can then be 'tailored' by means of modular, add-on options) or an operating system such as Unix in which the implementation is intentionally flexible and the users themselves tailor the final implementation.

Lastly, the designer must choose between competing policies for managing the resources of the system.

> For example, a policy of not requiring users to state resource needs in advance precludes the selection of avoidance as the policy for coping with deadlock [and also] eliminates SJN [shortest-job-next] as the dispatching

mechanism for enforcing the policy of equal service. The operating system designer must therefore take a global view and make policy decisions that are not independent, but interdependent. [6]

REFERENCES

[1] Brown, R.L., Denning, P.J. and Tichy, W.F. (1984) 'Advanced operating systems', *Computer*, **17**(10), 173–219.
[2] Jackson, K. (1983) 'MASCOT and multiprocessor systems', in *Distributed Computer Systems*, eds. Y. Paker and J.-P. Verjus, Academic Press, London, p. 228.
[3] Peterson, J.L. (1977) 'Petri nets', *Computing Surveys*, **9**(3) (September), 223–52.
[4] Kindberg, T., Sahiner, A.V. and Paker, Y. (1987) 'Worm programs', in *Distributed Operating Systems: theory and practice*, eds. Y. Paker, J-P Banatre and M. Bozyigit, Springer-Verlag, Berlin, pp. 355–79.
[5] Calingaert, P. (1982) *Operating System Elements: a user perspective*, Prentice-Hall, Englewood Cliffs, New Jersey, p. 211.
[6] *Ibid.*, p. 213.

FURTHER READING

Lamport, L. (1987) 'A formal basis for the specification of concurrent systems', in *Distributed Operating Systems: theory and practice*, eds. Y. Paker, J-P Banatre and M. Bozyigit, Springer-Verlag, Berlin, pp. 3–46. Lamport describes systems as behaviors and defines behavioral semantics, describes them with axioms and discusses correctness, formal description and specification.

Peterson, J.L. (1977) 'Petri nets', *Computing Surveys*, **9**(3) (September), pp. 223–52. This paper contains an extensive description of Petri nets and their application.

PART II

CASE STUDIES

CHAPTER

7
CP/M: a microcomputer operating system
(BY GORDON DAVIES)

In this chapter I shall briefly describe one of the more important microcomputer operating systems, CP/M. CP/M was one of the earliest operating systems to be developed as a simple single-user operating system for 8-bit microcomputers using floppy disks (1975). The system was implemented originally by Microcomputer Applications Associates, the predecessor of Digital Research, using the Intel 8080 microprocessor and PL/M (Programming Language for Microcomputers). CP/M became a very popular operating system (CP/M-80) for personal computers and is now in such widespread use that it will be difficult to replace. It is also now available for hard-disk systems and 16-bit micros (as CP/M-86).

7.1 STRUCTURE

CP/M consists of three modules, as shown in Figure 7.1.
- the Console Command Processor (CCP)
- the Basic Input/Output System (BIOS)
- the Basic Disk Operating System (BDOS)

When a user gives a command to the system, then the CCP interprets the command and issues a response. Thus the CCP is the user's interface with the CP/M system and its underlying hardware. The user perceives CP/M as it is portrayed by the CCP.

Some commands are 'built into' CP/M. These commands reside in the part of primary storage reserved for the system and are executed

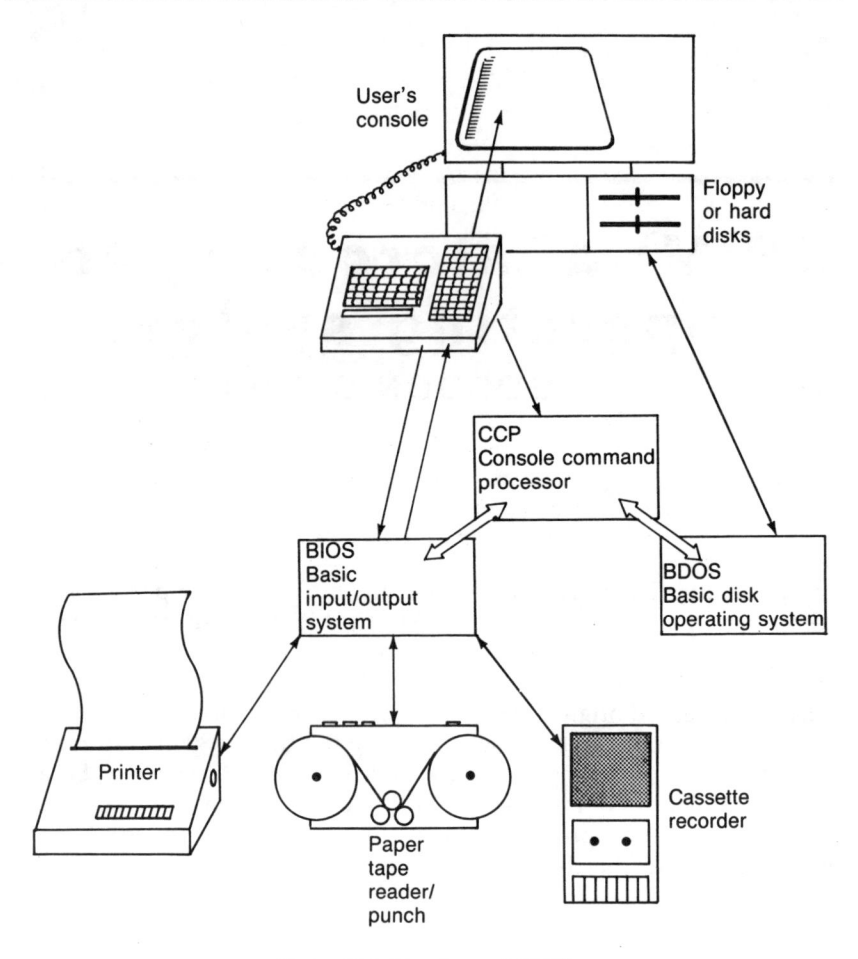

Figure 7.1 Structure of CP/M

directly. Examples of built-in commands are:

TYPE — list a file
DIR — list files in a directory
REName a file
ERAse a file
SAVE a file (not built into CP/M-86)

If the command is not built in, CCP assumes it to be a *transient* command, and therefore that it is a file on disk. In effect, these transient commands are more exactly called *utility programs*. When the user enters one of these commands, the CCP attempts to find the file on disk; if the search is successful the file is copied into primary storage and executed.

CP/M: A Microcomputer Operating System   159

The problems associated with input and output are considerably reduced for the user by CCP calling on the other two modules, the BIOS (Basic I/O System) and the BDOS (Basic Disk Operating System).

BIOS handles transfer of information between primary storage and all peripherals. It therefore contains the various device drivers for those peripherals. For example, BIOS can read characters from a keyboard or write characters to a printer. Only these sorts of primitive I/O operations can be handled by BIOS; it does not deal with any I/O operations concerned with files and is not aware of the existence of files.

The CCP invokes the BDOS for transfer of data between primary storage and disk. The problems of record blocking in files and of having files scattered throughout the disk are handled by BDOS. Thus the management of files and directories, and the allocation and freeing of secondary storage are made invisible to the user. BDOS, therefore, is concerned with operations such as reading and writing files, creating files, searching directories and so on.

The BIOS and BDOS together are commonly referred to as the Functional Disk Operating System (FDOS). The combination of FDOS and CCP make up what is generally thought of as CP/M.

Question for review

What are the three major modules of CP/M and what are their major functions?

7.2 STORAGE ALLOCATION

Figure 7.2 shows how primary storage is divided up between the three CP/M modules just described, other systems information and a user program.

The FDOS module and the CCP module are placed at the top (high address) end of storage. At the lower end, 256 bytes of system parameters are stored. As you will note from other case studies, this organization is somewhat unusual in putting the bulk of the operating system at the top end of primary storage. Between these two lies the largest part of storage, where users' programs and the transient commands are placed for execution. This area is called the Transient Program Area (TPA). The size of the TPA will depend on the size of the primary storage available. However, it is possible for a user to **overlay** much of the CP/M-80 system in order to execute programs larger than the available TPA. When such a program finishes executing it must reload a copy of CP/M before exiting (called a **warm start**). In CP/M-86 the CCP area *cannot* be overlaid in this way; all CP/M-86 modules remain in primary storage at all times and do not get reloaded in a warm start.

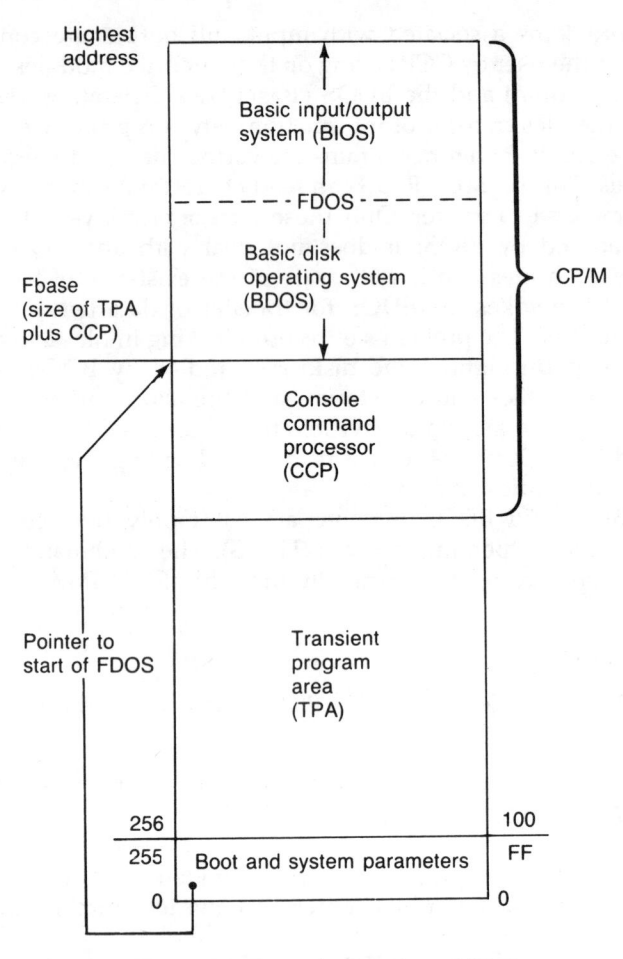

Figure 7.2 Storage allocation of CP/M

As the structures of the two systems are very similar, it is possible to change from CP/M-80 to CP/M-86 with very little effort. Because of the increased addressing capability of the Intel 8086 processor, however, CP/M-86 allocates storage for the three modules in a different way — it does not use absolute addresses for system variables. The modules can be placed in any position in storage and users' programs can then be run from any *non-reserved* region of storage.

The CCP allows multiple programs to reside in primary storage simultaneously. This allows background tasks, such as a print **spooler**, to run. When CP/M-86 receives a request to load a transient program (for example, a transient command) it checks the program's space require-

CP/M: A Microcomputer Operating System 161

ments. If sufficient free space exists, it allocates that to the program and loads it. Once loaded, the program can request further space from the BDOS for buffers. When the program ends, CP/M-86 frees *all* its allocated space.

Questions for review

(i) What is the transient program area and what is its size?
(ii) How can the storage allocation of CP/M-86 differ from CP/M-80?
(iii) Why does converting from one system to the other impose a possible restriction on the storage organization used?

7.3 FILE ORGANIZATION

When a user enters a file name the CCP calls on BDOS to access the file and copy it into primary storage.

Files are identified by means of a file control block (FCB). All files have at least one of these control blocks; how many a file has depends on the size of the file. Figure 7.3 shows the structure of a file control block.

This is a simplified diagram; some information contained in the FCB is not shown. The file name is the name given to a file by the user. The disk allocation map gives the physical location(s) of the file on disk. A standard floppy disk has tracks divided into sectors of a given number of bytes each, for example, 128. CP/M files consist of records of 128 bytes. Note that these records are *physical* CP/M records used for allocating storage; a user may consider logical records to be of any size. As the records are unlikely to be stored in consecutive locations on the disk, the locations of the records that make up the files are stored in the FCB.

A file's space is dispersed throughout the disk. Each FCB can refer

Byte numbers:

| 0 1 | 8 9 | 11 | 13 14 | 16 | 31 32 |

| ← File name → | ←Type→ | not used | ← Disk allocation map → |

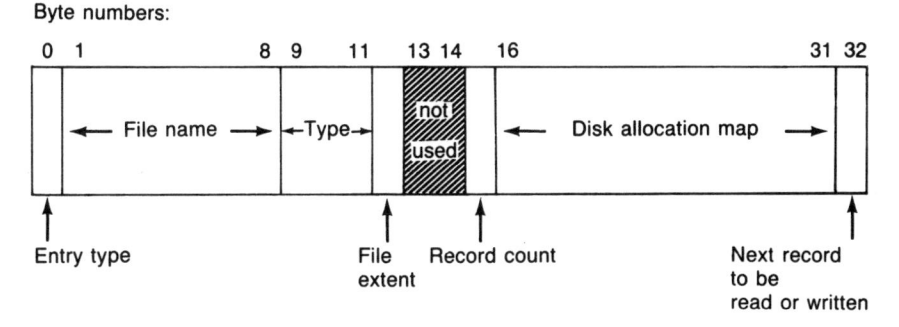

Entry type   File extent   Record count   Next record to be read or written

Figure 7.3 CP/M file control block

Case Studies

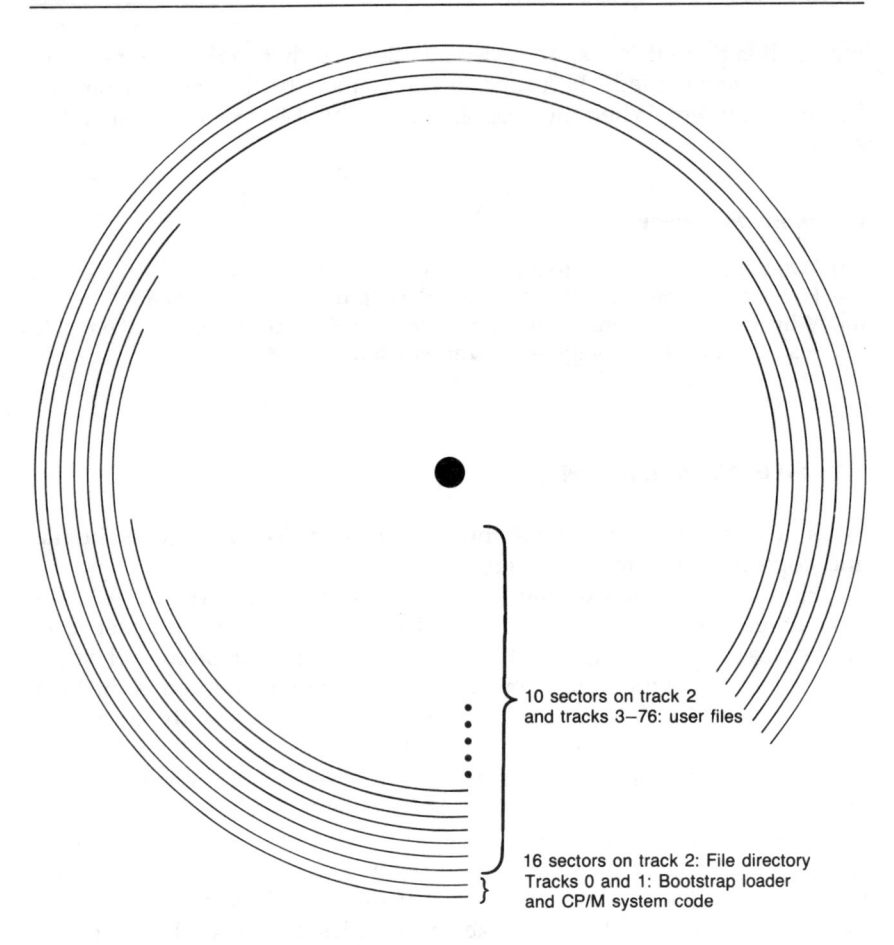

Figure 7.4 Allocation of space on a floppy disk

- 10 sectors on track 2 and tracks 3–76: user files
- 16 sectors on track 2: File directory
- Tracks 0 and 1: Bootstrap loader and CP/M system code

to up to 16K bytes of a file; a larger file will have at least one additional FCB. When a file is referred to, its FCB is located on disk, read and the disk allocation map for the file is used to locate the records of the file which are then transferred. The disk is divided up as in Figure 7.4.

When a file is created BDOS accesses an allocation **bit map** that is maintained by BDOS. When a disk is first accessed, the allocation bit map is copied into primary storage. This is a representation of the disk storage, whereby one bit represents a sequence of contiguous locations called a *cluster*, that is, eight 128-byte records (probably identical with sectors) on a disk. If a cluster is in use the corresponding bit is set to 1, otherwise the bit is set to 0. Figure 7.5 shows a bit map on a small scale. In the figure, clusters x, y and z are in use, while clusters a, b and c are free. Allocating

CP/M: A Microcomputer Operating System 163

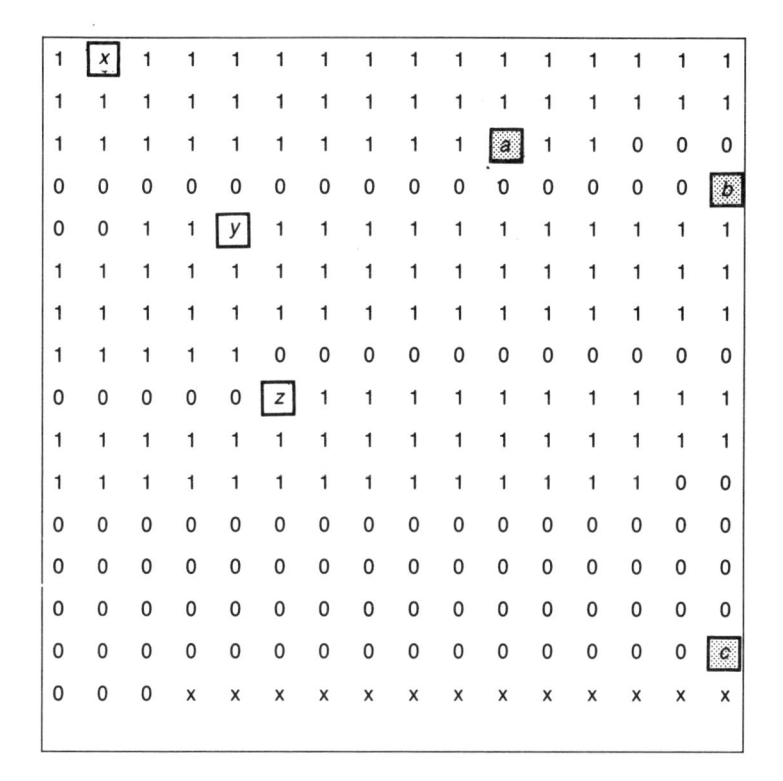

1	x	1	1	1	1	1	1	1	1	1	1	1	1	1	1
1	1	1	1	1	1	1	1	1	1	1	1	1	1	1	1
1	1	1	1	1	1	1	1	1	1	a	1	1	0	0	0
0	0	0	0	0	0	0	0	0	0	0	0	0	0	0	b
0	0	1	1	y	1	1	1	1	1	1	1	1	1	1	1
1	1	1	1	1	1	1	1	1	1	1	1	1	1	1	1
1	1	1	1	1	1	1	1	1	1	1	1	1	1	1	1
1	1	1	1	1	0	0	0	0	0	0	0	0	0	0	0
0	0	0	0	0	z	1	1	1	1	1	1	1	1	1	1
1	1	1	1	1	1	1	1	1	1	1	1	1	1	1	1
1	1	1	1	1	1	1	1	1	1	1	1	1	1	0	0
0	0	0	0	0	0	0	0	0	0	0	0	0	0	0	0
0	0	0	0	0	0	0	0	0	0	0	0	0	0	0	0
0	0	0	0	0	0	0	0	0	0	0	0	0	0	0	0
0	0	0	0	0	0	0	0	0	0	0	0	0	0	0	c
0	0	0	x	x	x	x	x	x	x	x	x	x	x	x	x

Figure 7.5 Allocation bit map

storage for a file then becomes a matter of searching through the bit map for a cluster with its bit equal to 0. The file is stored at that cluster and the bit is set to 1. In fact, it is the cluster address that is stored in the FCB.

When a file is requested by a user, an *open file* operation activates an FCB specifying that file, provided it exists in the directory of the disk. BDOS scans the directory on the currently referenced disk for a match of an 11-byte ASCII file name. (A question mark will match any character in the corresponding position.) When a match occurs, the relevant directory information is copied into the FCB. This constitutes a successful *open file* operation, after which records may be read or written, sequentially or directly. When a file is accessed directly, the FCB has an additional three bytes (bytes 33 to 35) holding a random record number in the range of 0 to 65 535, with an overflow possible.

The *close file* operation is the reverse of the *open file* operation. It records the new FCB information in the disk directory. If a file has been accessed in a read-only mode, it need not be closed, but if write operations have occurred, then the *close file* operation is necessary. The current record field must be set to zero if the file is to be accessed sequentially from the first record for any subsequent open. In a sequential read, the current record field in the FCB is automatically incremented to point to the next record position.

A new file is created by a *make file* operation, which is similar to the *open file* operation except that the FCB must contain a file name which *does not exist* in the currently referenced disk directory. BDOS then creates the file and initializes the directory entry on the disk. An *open file* is unnecessary, but to be properly accessible subsequently, the file must be closed as I have described.

Questions for review

(i) What is the function of a file control block?
(ii) What is the function of the disk allocation map?
(iii) How are individual records within a file located?

7.4 DEVICE MAPPING

To make the use of CP/M easy, the system uses *logical* devices for input and output. Logical devices don't actually exist but a user reads from and writes to them; the system maps the logical devices onto real physical devices, thus making input/output much simpler.

CP/M considers these to be four logical devices:

- CON: (console, e.g. terminal) for low-speed communication between user and CP/M. Typically, this is a device such as a CRT.
- RDR: for paper tape reader, punched cards or teletype input or a simple optical reader.
- PUN: for paper tape punch or teletype output.
- LST: the 'listing' device, usually a printer or teletypewriter.

The RDR and PUN logical devices can also be used to connect a CP/M system into a network of CP/M systems, CP/Net.

The mapping of logical to physical devices is controlled by the contents of one byte at an address reserved for CP/M. Each of the four logical devices corresponds to a pair of bits in this byte

```
0  1   2  3   4  5   6  7
CON:   RDR:  PUN:   LST:
```

The value of the pair of bits determines the logical-to-physical mapping. For example, if bits 6 and 7 have the value 01 (in binary), then the LST device becomes the CRT; if it is 00 then it becomes a teletypewriter device.

CP/M: A Microcomputer Operating System 165

If the value is 2 (10 in binary) LST becomes a line printer device; if 3 (11) LST becomes a user-defined list device. The contents of this byte can be changed to accommodate a particular configuration.

A single device can be assigned as LST, PUN and RDR simultaneously. *Some* device *must* be assigned to one of these or the system gives an error message to prevent the system from 'hanging'.

Questions for review

(i) Explain how the use of logical devices helps a user of CP/M.
(ii) How does CP/M relate logical devices to their physical counterparts?

7.5 PORTABILITY

CP/M was designed to be as portable as possible. To this end the system is divided into two parts. There is an *invariant* part which contains the disk operating system (BDOS) written in PL/M, and a *variant* part (written in the particular processor's assembly language) which contains the I/O device drivers for the configuration.

Another aspect of the system helps with the portability of the system. As peripherals became more powerful, ranging from floppy disks to 'hard' Winchester disks, the system evolved to support these devices. To simplify matters the system was redesigned to be **table-driven**. For example, the parameters relating to disk devices were removed from the invariant part of the system and stored in tables in the variant part. Implementing CP/M on different hardware configurations means that the relevant tables must be altered accordingly.

When the system runs it refers to these tables for the parameters of the devices it can access rather than having these parameters **hard-coded**. Modification of the system is then easier as changes to tables are required rather than changes to code.

Question for review

How is portability achieved in CP/M?

7.6 MP/M

MP/M or its 16-bit version, MP/M-86, is an on operating system designed by Digital Research to provide a real-time processing facility and a multi-user, multiprogramming system. In this section I shall describe only those parts of MP/M concerned with process management. I do not intend to describe the inner workings of the whole system.

Process scheduling

A process has associated with it a descriptor in which is stored information about the process. (Compare this with a process control block.) The system assigns a priority to a process and stores it in the descriptor. If a process is allocated the processor (in other words, is allowed to run), it continues to use the processor until:

- it finishes, or
- it issues a system call, or
- it is interrupted, or
- the interval (quantum) expires.

At this point a part of the system called the dispatcher looks at the descriptor of the process to decide whether its priority is higher than the priority of any currently suspended process. The dispatcher chooses the process with the highest priority to execute next. A way of organizing processes so that the dispatcher can choose a new process is shown in Figure 7.6.

The dispatcher chooses as the next process to run the process with the highest priority. In the figure process x will be run next, followed by process y. All processes at priority z will be run before any other processes. Figure 7.6 represents a list of active processes, processes that are candidates for the dispatcher. Another list is kept of processes that are suspended or blocked. MP/M refers to the latter as **dormant processes**.

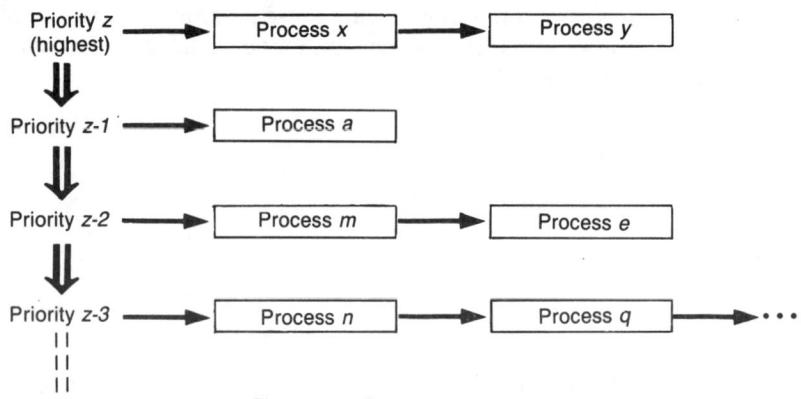

Figure 7.6 Process priorities

CP/M: A Microcomputer Operating System

The system refers to processes through their descriptors; the descriptors are stored in queues while the processes await execution. A *queue* is a waiting list and is used to control the operation of peripheral devices as well as the scheduling of processes. For example the **spooling** (temporary storage on disk) of files to a printer uses a queue. Queues are also used by MP/M for process synchronization. A process may need access to the line printer *exclusively*. The process which controls the printer can set up a message queue and, when the printer is available, place a message on it. The process requiring the printer must wait until the message appears in the queue. An empty queue indicates that the printer is busy and therefore unavailable.

Questions for review

(i) What *data structure* is used to represent the processes on MP/M?
(ii) What similarities are there between the MP/M representation of a process and the process control block described in Part I?

Multitasking

MP/M version 1.0 can handle up to 16 consoles. Thus there can be up to 16 people using the system simultaneously. A user may also run several processes simultaneously from a single terminal; the facility is provided for a user to *detach* a program from a terminal (this means that the terminal is freed to execute another program and the output from the detached program does not appear on the terminal). It is also feasible to *reattach* a program to the terminal from which it was detached.

Questions for review

(i) How can one process communicate with another process?
(ii) What interaction can occur between a user at a terminal and a detached program?

7.7 CP/NET

CP/Net is a network operating system derived from CP/M. CP/M is a single-user/single-computer system; MP/M is a multiple-user/single-computer system; CP/Net is an evolution to a multiple-user, multiple-computer system.

CP/Net was designed, like CP/M and MP/M, to be as portable as

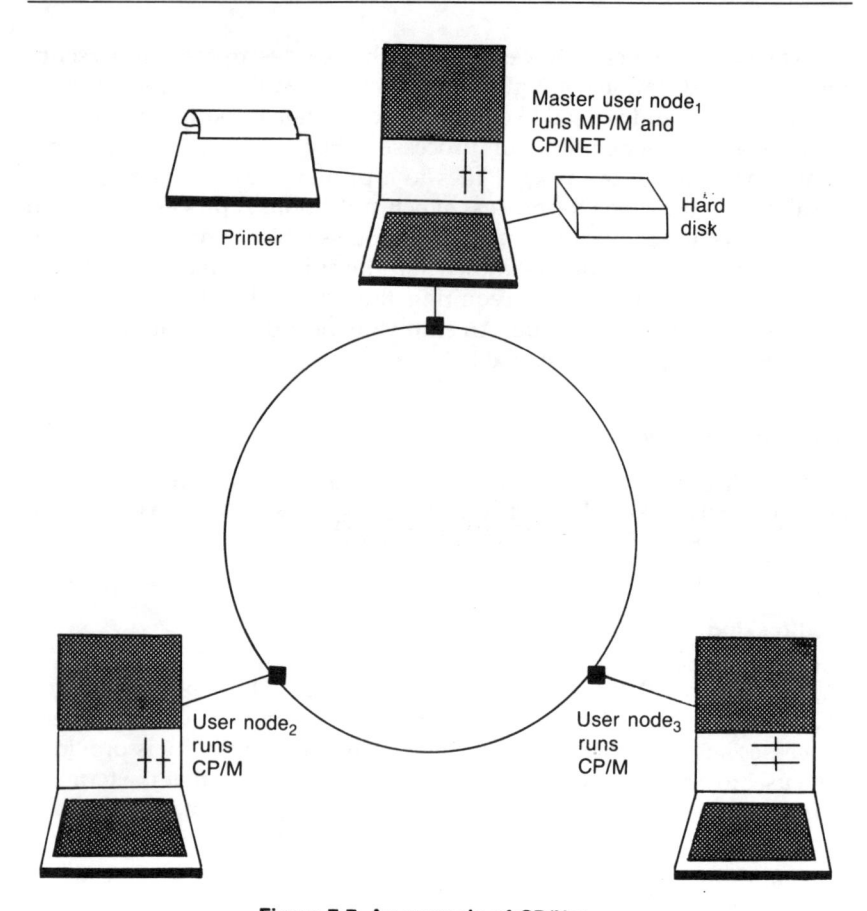

Figure 7.7 An example of CP/Net

possible. It connects CP/M-based users or requesters (possibly on different types of processors) with MP/M-based servers (at least one, but perhaps more than one on different kinds of processors). Figure 7.7 shows a typical CP/Net network.

A CP/Net network has at least one master node that has the responsibility for managing the whole network. This master node must have substantial disk storage and runs the CP/Net system together with MP/M; the remaining nodes need consist of nothing more than a processor and 16K of primary storage, but in an office environment may consist of high-quality printers and facsimile transmission equipment.

Thus CP/Net can enable an organization to give access to a large database from separate sites or to share expensive peripheral devices.

Using such a network allows the sharing of all resources: hardware, software and information. CP/Net then is a *resource-sharing network*.

GENERAL REFERENCES

Anon. (1981) *CP/M-86 Operating System: System Guide*, Digital Research, Pacific Grove, California.
Anon. (1981) *CP/M-86 Operating System: User's Guide*, Digital Research, Pacific Grove, California.
Deitel, H.M. (1984) *Introduction to Operating Systems*, Addison-Wesley, Reading, Massachussetts, pp. 535–66.

FURTHER READING

Deitel, H.M. (1984) *Introduction to Operating Systems*, Addison-Wesley, Reading, Massachussetts. Chapter 20 is a case study description of CP/M.
Zaks, R. (1980) *The CP/M Handbook with MP/M*, Sybex, Berkeley, California. An entire book for the programmer interested in CP/M.

CHAPTER

8
MS-DOS and PC-DOS

MS-DOS and PC-DOS are very similar systems: PC-DOS is a trademarked off-shoot from MS-DOS written especially for the IBM PC family of computers. Unless I state otherwise, when I mention a feature of MS-DOS, what I say will apply to PC-DOS as well.

The relatively inexpensive 8-bit microcomputer appeared in 1975, packaged together with the newly developed floppy diskette disk drive and floppy diskettes. The combination of these two items with a standard keyboard and a television screen or CRT (cathode ray tube) monitor meant that the power of larger computers could be bought for the home or small office. To make such a product truly marketable to a wide audience, though, it had to be reasonably easy to use. CP/M appeared in 1975 for use on 8-bit microcomputers based on the Zilog Z80 or the Intel 8080 or 8085 microprocessors. It quickly became popular and remains a 'standard' for 8-bit micros.

Though they represented a considerable step forward when they appeared in 1979, the larger 16-bit microprocessors were not well received in the marketplace. Until, that is, IBM decided to enter the market with a 16-bit personal computer. This sparked a competition to develop an operating system for 16-bit computers.

The company that markets and supports CP/M developed CP/M-86, which you read about in the preceding chapter. A company called Microsoft developed MS-DOS. IBM decided to adopt MS-DOS, but they renamed it PC-DOS. Subtle differences have been introduced into PC-DOS subsequently.

All three of these systems: CP/M-86, MS-DOS and PC-DOS, appear very similar, and by design. Microsoft attempted to make MS-DOS similar in nature to CP/M so that software developers could more easily develop products for both operating systems. These systems are similar — but *not* compatible.

When IBM announced the IBM PC/XT which exploits directly the size and power of the rigid Winchester-technology disk, its later versions of PC-DOS departed even further from the original CP/M model. These later versions begin to incorporate an increasing number of features of Unix, which is described in Chapter 10.

8.1 STRUCTURE

As with CP/M, MS-DOS has a command-driven interface with the user. In fact, the interface appears very similar, as MS-DOS designers based the outward appearance of MS-DOS on the outward appearance of CP/M. The commands available to a user consist of a few letters entered in response to a prompt. The prompt usually indicates the default disk drive; this can be altered by entering the new default disk drive as a command.

Commands are divided into internal and external commands, respectively the same as the built-in and transient commands of CP/M. Internal commands are loaded into primary storage during the bootstrap process; a user can execute one of these commands without having to load the system disk into a disk drive. External commands, as is true with transient commands in CP/M, are loaded from the system disk into primary storage at the time the user first requests that function by entering the command. Should you have one of CP/M, MS-DOS or PC-DOS you can hear this happening − the noise is from the reading of the disk. (Once the command has been loaded, however, the user may execute it multiple times without having it fetched from the system disk each time.)

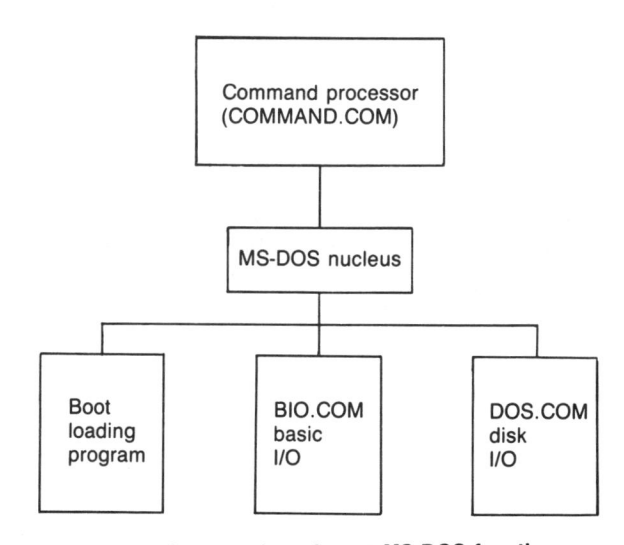

Figure 8.1 Organization of most MS-DOS functions

Some examples of external commands are CHKDSK (which analyses the directories on the disk and produces a status report), COMP (which compares files to see whether they are identical), FORMAT (which initializes a disk for subsequent file storage), PRINT (which prints a queue of data files on the printer while the user does other tasks at the keyboard).

MS-DOS is organized, at its most basic level, into basic I/O and disk I/O parts called, respectively, BIO.COM and DOS.COM. Whereas BIO.COM is responsible for basic input and output functions such as keyboard, CRT screen and slow device (e.g. printer) I/O, DOS.COM contains the low level disk management routines.

These two functions make up the MS-DOS nucleus or kernel. The boot loading program is also part of the nucleus. So is the command processor, called COMMAND.COM. This responds to interrupt commands from the user (for example, to stop or restart scrolling), recognizes user errors such as misspelled commands and issues error messages. It also contains the *internal* commands mentioned above. Figure 8.1 shows the organization of the MS-DOS kernel.

8.2 STORAGE ALLOCATION

By convention, much of an operating system is loaded beginning in the lowest possible address in primary storage, though some very low addresses are 'reserved' or are made up of read-only memory (ROM), depending on the architecture of the processor.

In MS-DOS on the iAPX86 and iAPX88 processors the interrupt vectors are at the very lowest addresses. A *vector* is a pointer to something else; in this case the interrupt vectors contain the addresses of the start of each of the interrupt handlers. Intel's own interrupt vectors are at addresses ranging from 00 to 1F — these are hardware interrupt vectors. The interrupt vectors of MS-DOS are located between addresses 20 and 3F. There are more interrupt vectors, but these are the most fundamental.

The nucleus or kernel, consisting of the basic I/O and disk operations, is loaded by the bootstrap beginning at the lowest possible addresses in primary storage above the various interrupt vectors. The bootstrap then loads just above this the command processor.

Everything above the command processor is called the transient area. This area of memory is available for programs and data which can be brought into and taken out of primary storage as they are needed or not. If a user uses a spreadsheet, the command (s)he gives would cause the program to be loaded into the transient area, with its data to be loaded above that.

The transient commands are, by contrast, loaded into primary storage

MS-DOS and PC-DOS

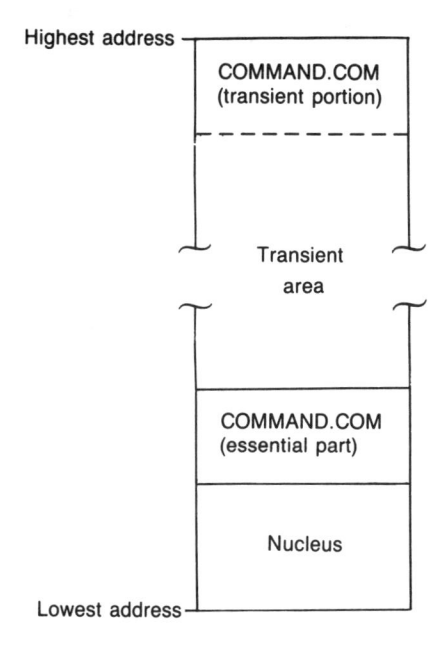

Figure 8.2 Primary storage organization in MS-DOS

from the highest possible address downwards. This has an advantage; if a user's program needs more space, the space can be 'stolen' from this upper portion of the operating system, while the essential (internal) commands which allow the system to continue to function are protected as a part of the command processor in the low addresses just above the kernel. See Figure 8.2.

Notice that no fixed size is given for the transient area. Since computers come with different amounts of primary storage or can have their primary storage expanded, the size of the available transient area can be increased to make the increased space available.

Before I leave this subject, let us look at what happens to a program and data in primary storage. Figure 8.3 shows this, beginning with the loading of MS-DOS in the lowest and highest addresses. Then a program is loaded. As the program opens a file, the data from the file is loaded above the program. The blank area in the diagram indicates unused space.

Questions for review

(i) What are two advantages for loading much of the operating system into the lowest areas of primary storage?

Case Studies

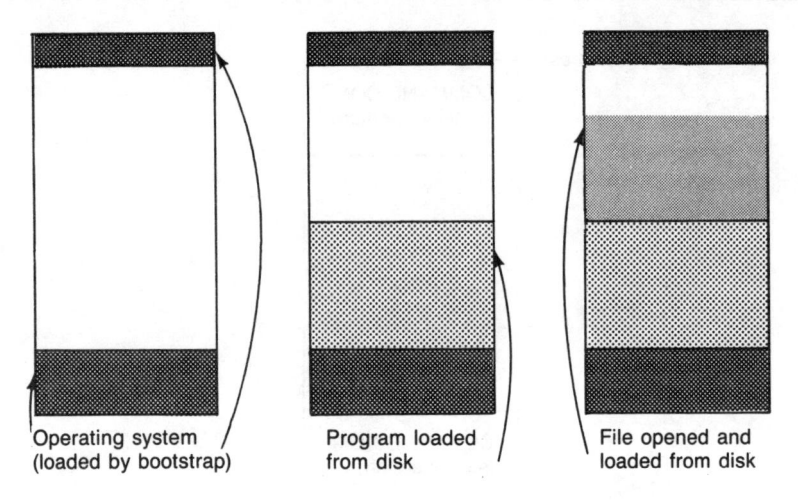

Operating system (loaded by bootstrap) | **Program loaded from disk** | **File opened and loaded from disk**

Figure 8.3 The program and file in primary storage

(ii) What advantage is there to loading some of the operating system into the highest addresses in primary storage?
(iii) What advantage is there to the system of loading a program above the main part of the operating system, leaving any empty space above that?

Questions for discussion

(i) What do you think happens if a program opens two or more files simultaneously?
(ii) How might you go about making certain that, no matter how much or how little space is left after a program is loaded, there is room for at least some data from each and every file that program has open at any one time?

8.3 FILE ORGANIZATION

When a user formats a disk under MS-DOS or PC-DOS, he or she is given the option of creating a volume label on the disk. This allows a user to distinguish one otherwise identical disk from another — for example to distinguish which is used for file backup and which is the 'working' copy where any directory information on the two disks might otherwise be identical.

When a disk is newly formatted, except for the space occupied by the volume label, it is empty. All the remaining disk space is available both for the VTOC (volume table of contents, described in Section 2.4) and for any directories and data files.

MS-DOS and PC-DOS

Byte no. offset:	0 7	1 1 8 . 0	1 1	1 2 . . . . 2 1	2 2 2 3	2 2 4 5	2 2 6 7	2 3 8 . . . 1
Contains:	file name	file extension	*	Reserved for system use	Time †	Date	‡	File size
Example:	M S P C D O S	T X T	0 0		6 F 8 4	1 8 F D	0 1 0 A	0 0 F F 0 0 F 8

* The attribute byte: normal (user) files show hexadecimal 00.
† Time in binary format — the value shown is 68F4, which translates to 1:07:20 p.m.
The date is similarly held in a binary format, with the value shown (1F8D) translating to the 31st of the 3rd month of the 6th year after the base year of 1980, i.e. 31 March 1986. The scheme for the date will work until 2099.
‡ Starting allocation unit.

Figure 8.4 An MS-DOS VTOC entry

The *number* of directories and data files which can be held on a disk is limited to the amount of space available on the disk for the VTOC. For example, the index on a single-sided floppy diskette has a VTOC which will hold 64 entries, so the diskette can contain, at most, a total of 64 files (some of which may be directories). A double-sided floppy diskette in a PC-DOS system has a VTOC with room for 112 entries. Most other MS-DOS versions have room on a double-sided floppy diskette for 128 directory entries — so the limit to the number of files a disk can hold is 128, no matter how little room those files might actually take.

The MS-DOS system allocates disk space in blocks. Unfortunately, it doesn't call these blocks, but AUs, or *a*llocation *u*nits. To make things more confusing, the PC-DOS version refers to *clusters*. They are all the same thing.

In addition to the VTOC, each disk in an MS-DOS system has something called a *file allocation table* or *FAT*. The FAT indicates the use of each AU (allocation unit/cluster/block) on this disk. Each entry in the FAT consists of 12 bits. If all the bits are set to zero, this indicates that the AU corresponding to the entry is unused — it is free space. If the entry in the FAT has the hexadecimal value of FFF (all bits set to one), this means that the AU corresponding to that entry is the *last* AU in a file. Any other value in an entry is the number of the FAT entry which corresponds to the next AU in a file.

This means that MS-DOS uses the block-oriented file-mapping technique of keeping track of both unused (free) space and blocks in a file. The FAT is a logical description of space on a disk.

For MS-DOS to access any AU on a disk, it is necessary to establish the relationship between the FAT's *logical* description and the underlying physical reality. Different computers which can run MS-DOS can have disks of different characteristics, and the mapping from the simple logical description of the FAT to the correct position on a disk can be quite complex.

Let us assume that each track of a disk is divided into an equal number of sectors, say eight. If an AU contains four sectors, then the relative AU number must be translated into a physical location consisting of track and sector number. In the scheme I have just described of four sectors to an AU and eight to a track, AU number 47 is the 48th AU from the beginning of the disk (AU number being relative, the first AU is number 0). The 48th AU starts at 4 × 48 = 192nd sector. Since each track contains eight sectors, this number must be divided by eight to give the track number. 192/8 = 24. So the AU wanted is on the 24th track. Since 24 is evenly divisible by eight, this AU starts at sector 0. But as the number of the track is also relative (the first track being numbered 0) the track *number* is 23.

The problem becomes more complex on certain computers which do not have the same number of sectors on each track. These usually have a larger number of sectors on the tracks furthest from the center of the disk, with a decreasing number of sectors each as the tracks are closer to the center. An example of such a computer is the Sirius 1, where the outermost tracks have 19 sectors each and the innermost have only 11 sectors each. Obviously, it becomes no simple matter to convert the AU position in the FAT's logical map to a real location on such a disk!

Question for review

What information for using the disk appears on a disk in an MS-DOS system?

Questions for discussion

(i) Since MS-DOS supports various different computers, what file compatibility problems is a user hoping to use more than one type of computer likely to encounter?

(ii) In what ways could a complex mapping of the FAT to the real disk be made to work? How might you deal with mapping on a system like that of the Sirius?

(iii) MS-DOS uses block-oriented file mapping. What does this imply for information necessary to point to a second-level directory? What does the second-level directory need to know about a data file?

8.4 PORTABILITY

As with CP/M (and you will find this method common to many portable operating systems), the lowest levels of MS-DOS (which also occupy the lowest levels of primary storage) must be written for a particular processor and particular configuration of computer. That is, the sections BIO.COM and DOS.COM are written in the machine code of the processor which this version of MS-DOS controls and are written for specific configurations of keyboard, disk, monitor and other devices. The higher levels of the system, the command processor and the external commands, can be written in a higher-level language and can be transported in source form without change. Only the BIO.COM and DOS.COM parts of the system need to be modified in order for the system to run on a computer with a different processor or different configuration.

GENERAL REFERENCES

Lucy, S. (1984) *MS-DOS User Book*, Sigma Press, Wilmslow, Cheshire (UK).
Microsoft Corporation (January, 1984) *Disk Operating System (IBM Personal Computer) Version 2.10*, 1st edn, IBM.
Murtha, S.M. and Petrie, G.R. (1983) *The PC-DOS Companion*, Howard W. Sams, Indianapolis, Indiana.
Texas Instruments (June, 1985) *Getting Started with MS^{tm}-DOS3* (for the Texas Instruments Business-Pro^{tm} Professional Computer), Texas Instruments, Dallas, Texas.

FURTHER READING

Lucy, S. (1984) *MS-DOS User Book*, Sigma Press, Wilmslow, Cheshire (UK). A programmer's guide to the ins and outs of MS-DOS.
Murtha, S.M. and Petrie, G.R. (1983) *The PC-DOS Companion*, Howard W. Sams, Indianapolis, Indiana. A user's view of PC-DOS and the IBM PC family.

CHAPTER

9

The p-System
(BY MARK WOODMAN)

9.1 THE UNIVERSAL OPERATING SYSTEM?

By now, you realize the task of choosing a computer system is extremely complex. Would not the task of selection be made easier by standardizing on a single operating system, leaving only the computer architectures to be evaluated and selected from?

There are a number of problems with this utopian suggestion. First, how could the implementers of such a universal operating system ensure that all the versions of the system be functionally *identical*, and not merely compatible? Secondly, how could a universal system be provided on computers of different word sizes? Lastly, bear in mind while reading this and subsequent chapters the question of whether one operating system can meet all requirements.

The UCSD p-System discussed here has attempted to be a kind of universal operating system.

It has overcome the problems of functional identity and differing word sizes by 'hiding' their cause: real computer architectures. The operating system has been designed and implemented for an ideal, or *pseudo*, machine and architecture. (The 'p' in p-System stands for pseudo.) The pseudo-machine has its own machine code — *p-code* — and the p-System is a p-code program which can be executed on any *p-machine*. To provide the p-System on any processor therefore requires the implementation of software which *simulates* the imaginary p-machine — the *p-machine emulator* (*PME*). This will then execute any p-code program, including the operating system itself. (Note that the use of the term *emulator* here differs from its definition in Part I; this confusion of terminology is a common problem in computing!)

This approach not only eases the portability problem, but is productive since the p-System is implemented only once. The real discriminators between computers running the p-System are their performance, cost and reliability.

In this case study I shall examine the architecture of the p-machine, the facilities provided by the p-System and how these facilities are made available to the user. I shall also look at how the p-machine is implemented on real machines, particularly at the difficulties encountered and how they were overcome. The relationship between the operating system and p-machine emulator (PME), and the operating system and the programming language UCSD Pascal will also be discussed.

Question for discussion

What are two major problems to be solved when implementing a portable operating system?

9.2 A BRIEF HISTORY

The history of the p-System is linked with the development of the programming language Pascal and the advent of microcomputers.

The development of Pascal in the early 1970s was a milestone in computing: the language provided facilities for the emerging technique of structured programming. Pascal first found favor because of its suitability for teaching this technique. At the University of California at San Diego (UCSD), Pascal was being used on an overloaded time-sharing system when the decision was taken to move to the newly available microcomputers, and in 1974 a group of students working under Ken Bowles began the project which resulted in the p-System.

A number of fundamental design decisions were taken early in the project. First, the team decided that a complete Pascal program-development environment would be required. This involved such objects as operating system, editor, compiler and file manager. They decided that this software should be fully integrated — thereby achieving a harmony between parts not usually available in systems developed on a more piecemeal basis.

Secondly, they decided that the system must be congenial to both the novice student and the more experienced programmer. Unlike many systems existing at that time, they assumed the user's terminal was a CRT and not a teletypewriter.

Thirdly, as a standard for Pascal had not yet emerged, the team felt it was acceptable to extend the language to provide for teaching requirements and systems programming. It is because of this close relationship between the UCSD p-System and UCSD Pascal that you will find it convenient to have a rough idea of what a UCSD Pascal program is like.

Finally and crucially, because the design team expected a boom in low-cost microcomputers, they did not wish to make any premature decisions on hardware. They decided to design the system around a pseudo-machine. This approach had already proved successful in facilitating the production of Pascal compilers: a single Pascal compiler could produce p-code for a pseudo-machine — requiring only that *code generators* (which translate p-code to the machine code of a particular real machine) be written.

The first three decisions would result in a software system which would be relatively large compared to the typical microcomputer primary storage of the day (48K−64K bytes). Compilers for the programming language Pascal would produce large object programs due to the primitive instruction sets of available microprocessors. Therefore, a technique known as **interpreting** was chosen: rather than translating p-code to machine code (as happens in a compiler), an **interpreter** 'translates' a program *as it executes it*. The machine code executed is actually part of the interpreter software, and the particular code executed depends on the p-code instructions encountered. By compiling Pascal to a space-efficient p-code and then interpreting p-code rather than translating it, the implementers could squeeze a quart into a pint jar!

The project team soon produced successful *adaptations* (so-called because only a part of the software needs 'adapting' for any particular computer architecture) of the Pascal system on PDP-11, LSI-11, Z80 and 8080 processors. Interest outside UCSD grew, culminating in an avalanche of enquiries following an article in *Byte* magazine in 1978. As this interest grew various releases of the system found their way out of the university. The versions up to I.3 (Roman numeral one) had had some element of federal funding and were therefore available to the public on demand. Subsequent versions (up to version II.0) began to make the University of California money. By 1979 the Federal Government began to take an interest in a possible return on its investment. The university gave Bowles a choice: close down the project or license development and exploitation to an outside company. Eventually SofTech Microsystems Inc. was licensed.

The way in which early versions of the p-System were released has caused a number of different manifestations of the UCSD Pascal system to develop; a number of companies were licensed to develop the system separately from the 'mainstream' UCSD, and later SofTech, work. Therefore it is worthwhile looking at part of the p-System family tree.

The Western Digital Version III p-System on the Pascal Microengine is interesting because the PME became a real machine! The Pascal Microengine actually executes p-code as its machine code. Moreover, Version III also saw the introduction of concurrency facilities into UCSD Pascal; this had direct impact on the development of Verson IV of the system.

Throughout this case study I shall discuss Version IV.2, although I

The p-System

```
                    Version I.3 (UCSD, public domain)
                                 |
                    Version I.4 (UCSD)
                                 |
                    Version I.5 (UCSD)
         _____|_____
        /                |                  |             \
  Version II.2      Version II.0      Version II.1    Version III
(Volition Systems) (Softech Microsystems) (Apple)  (Western Digital)
                         |
                    Version IV.0
                    (Softech Microsystems)
                         |
                    Version IV.1
                    (Softech Microsystems)
                         |
                    Version IV.2
                    (Softech Microsystems)
```

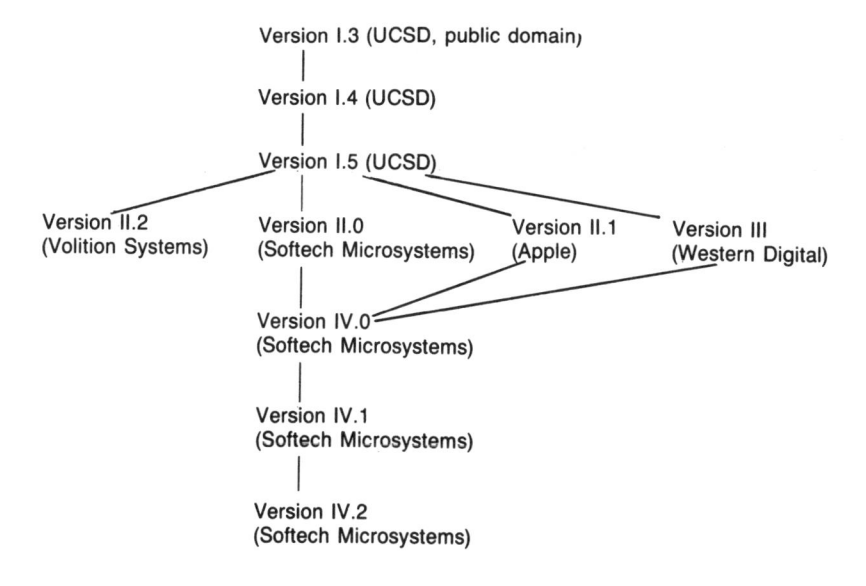

Figure 9.1 The p-System family tree

make some references to other versions. In 1985 Versions IV.2 and IV.21 were released, with significant improvements to performance, programming language facilities and, most importantly, with the capability for networked operation.

Question for discussion

Why do you think that realizations of the p-System are called adaptations rather than implementations?

9.3 USING MENU-DRIVEN COMMANDS

Typically, the p-System is run on microcomputer systems whose configuration consists of:

- primary storage of at least 64K bytes;
- direct access secondary storage — typically at least two floppy disks of about 320K bytes capacity each;
- a CRT capable of scrolling and of having the cursor move to any position on the screen;
- a printer.

Operation using smaller-capacity disks or a single disk is possible.

On starting up the system the user sees a prompt to enter a command which looks like Figure 9.2. The prompt appears at the top of the screen and lists some of the commands available at this 'highest' command level. The commands can be selected by pressing the single key corresponding to the upper-case letter preceding the left parenthesis in the command. For example, to enter the file manager (called the filer) the user would simply press F.

```
Command: E(dit, R(un, F(ile, C(omp, L(ink, X(ecute, A(ssem,? [IV.2 R1.6]
```

Figure 9.2 Top-level command prompt

When a command requires parameters, the system prompts the user for them. This relieves the user of the burden of learning complex command syntax. For example, to *compile* a program requires the user to first press C; the p-System then prompts the user for the name of the file containing the source code of the program, and then prompts the user for the code file name and compiler listing file:

Compile what text? EXPNS
To what codefile? EXPN1
Output file for compiled listing? (⟨cr⟩ for none)

The first prompt will assume a text file (with its name ending in .TEXT), the second will assume a code file (.CODE) — see Section 9.4. Simply pressing the escape key in response to any of the prompts will abort the command. At any later stage the user can press the system's break key, which will cause system reinitialization. This method aids the novice, while the expert could respond with a dollar sign ($) to the second prompt to indicate that the same name as the text file should be used for the code file.

The exact display on the command line is determined by the p-System depending on how many characters wide the screen of the CRT is. For example, the top-level prompt is actually what is shown in Figure 9.2 *plus* the terms from 'D(ebug' to 'S(et' of Figure 9.3 replacing the '?' of Figure 9.2. Because the number of characters in the whole prompt is greater than the number which can be displayed across the screen (80 in this case), the system divides the prompt: it only displays the prompt up to the last comma which will allow a '?' and system version number (the code

```
Command: D(ebug, H(alt, I(nitialize, U(ser restart, M(onitor, S(et [IV.2 R1.6]
```

Figure 9.3 Continuation of top-level command prompt

between brackets) to be displayed. The '?' indicates that there is at least another line's worth of prompt available. If the user presses the question-mark key, the next line will appear. With a screen width of 80 characters used above, pressing ? will produce Figure 9.3.

In this way, system prompts do not need to be tailored to a particular CRT.

The advantage of this type of system is that the novice can see all choices available by looking at the command names on the screen. The expert, on the other hand, can type a series of single-letter commands in quick succession.

Commands are grouped logically according to function. For example, to list the directory of a disk would require a filer function: the user would type F and be presented with the filer prompt shown in Figure 9.4.

```
Filer: L(dir, R(em, C(hng, T(rans, D(ate, Q(uit, B(ad-blks,? [6R3.5-1]
Filer: E(xt-dir, K(rnch, M(ake, P(refix, V(ols, X(amine, Z(ero,? [6R3.5-1]
Filer: O(n/off-line, F(lip-swap/lock [6R3.5-1]
```

Figure 9.4 File prompts

From the filer prompt the user will select L for 'list directory' or E for 'extended directory listing'. The system will then prompt the user for the disk name (more on these names appear in Section 9.4). Figure 9.5 shows the interaction using E.

In response to the directory listing prompt, the user has selected the disk named PSYS and its contents, in order of storage, have been displayed.

The extended directory listing in Figure 9.5 displays nearly all that is held in a p-System directory: the volume name (PSYS), the size (in blocks), the start and end block and the number of files. A date field

```
Command: E(dit, R(un, F(ile, C(omp, L(ink, X(ecute, A(ssem,? [IV.2 R1.6] F
```

[screen cleared]

```
Filer: L(dir, R(em, C(hng, T(rans, D(ate, Q(uit, B(ad-blks,? [6R3.5-1] E
```

[filer prompt cleared]

```
Dir listing of what vol ? PSYS: [return]
```

[screen cleared]

```
PSYS:
SYSTEM.PASCAL     199 15:19 24-May-85     6 512 Datafile
SYSTEM.MISCINFO     1 17:54 20-May-85   205 512 Datafile
SYSTEM.LIBRARY     41 16:54  5-Dec-84   206 512 Datafile
SYSTEM.FILER       45 10:00 18-Sep-84   247 512 Codefile
SYSTEM.EDITOR      59  9:31 26-Nov-84   292 512 Codefile
SYSTEM.COMPILER   114  9:48 18-Sep-84   351 512 Codefile
SYSTEM.SYNTAX      16        20-Dec-83  465 512 Textfile
SYSTEM.STARTUP      6 12:36 10-May-85   481 512 Codefile
USERLIB.TEXT        4        1-Apr-85   487 512 Textfile
LIBRARY.CODE       13        9-Dec-83   491 512 Codefile
DECTALK.CODE       33 18:08 20-May-85   504 512 Codefile
ENDBOOT             1       13-Sep-82   537 512 Datafile
SYSTEM.INTERP      24       11-Jun-84   538 512 Codefile
SPOOLER.CODE       11        2-Apr-84   562 512 Codefile
< UNUSED >         34                   573
SETUP.CODE         84        5-Jan-84   607 512 Codefile
< UNUSED >        589                   691
15/15 files<listed/in-dir>, 657 blocks used, 623 unused, 589 in largest
```

[filer prompt replaced at top of screen (above line starting with "PSYS:")]

Figure 9.5 Extended directory listing interaction

indicates when the volume was last used. First, the file name appears. The second column shows its length. Next comes the time and date the file was last written. Columns five and six represent the start block of the file and the number of significant bytes in the last block, respectively. The final column indicates the file's type.

The p-System

The commands available to the user thus form a hierarchy of command levels representing the context (or mode) in which the user finds him- or herself. Part of the hierarchy for version IV.2 is shown by the tree in Figure 9.6.

The most useful aspect of a menu approach is that all the valid choices available at any point can be displayed. Command-driven systems (such as Unix or MS-DOS) require the user to have a substantial 'vocabulary' before starting to use the system.

Also, menus may be used to display the names of options which suggest their function. 'C(omp' (for compile), selected by pressing C, needs no further explanation. However 'U(ser restart' is not so clear: it means start the user program (or even a system one) already in primary storage. 'R(estart program' might have been better, but R is used for 'R(un', which means compile and then execute the resulting code file.

This illustrates a problem with menus which use letters rather than require the user to position the cursor at an option and then press a select key. The most obvious command names may be excluded by having first chosen other names which start with the same letter. This is particularly obvious in the filer. Here, R is used for 'remove' (to remove a file); D for 'delete' cannot be used since D is used for setting the date. Since R is not available for rename, C for 'change' (to change the name of a file) is used; this eliminates C for 'copy', and so T for 'transfer' (a file) must be used. Such command name clashes sometimes force menu designers to create a new level in the hierarchy. The same letter has different meanings at different levels. This is sometimes cited as a weakness of menus. In practice, if the levels have some logical coherence users are not confused easily.

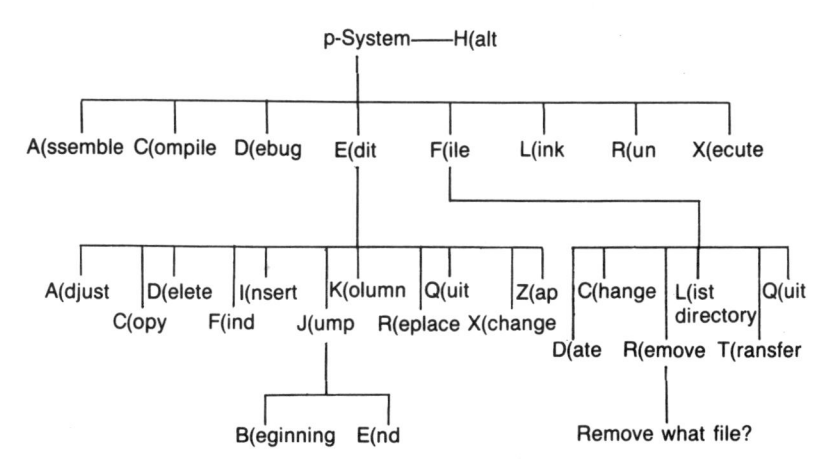

```
                    p-System────H(alt
         ┌──────┬────────┬──────┬─────┬─────┬─────┬─────┐
    A(ssemble C(ompile D(ebug E(dit F(ile L(ink R(un X(ecute
         ┌────┬─────┬─────┬─────┬─────┬─────┬────────┬─────┐
    A(djust D(elete I(nsert K(olumn Q(uit Z(ap C(hange L(ist    Q(uit
         C(opy   F(ind   J(ump  R(eplace X(change         directory
                           │                    D(ate R(emove T(ransfer
                      ┌────┴────┐                     │
                   B(eginning E(nd              Remove what file?
```

Figure 9.6 Command menu hierarchy

Clearly, the choice of a menu-driven system imposes a restriction on the number of commands available to the user — in the p-System they are built into the system and cannot be added to. A number of utility programs are therefore provided for less-used functions. The system can also be directed to take commands from a *script* file.

Menus can also be provided by applications programs. Facilities exist for a menu program to start up other programs. Thus a naive user need not know the names of individual programs. In fact, applications developers can provide an alternative top-level menu. On system startup, if a program called SYSTEM.MENU is found it will be executed in place of the standard menu.

Question for discussion

Compare the command interpreters of the p-System and MS-DOS: state two ways in which the p-System menu could be argued to be better than MS-DOS's commands, and two in which a command interface like MS-DOS's is better.

9.4 THE FILE SYSTEM

The constraints of microcomputer architectures for which the early adaptations were made resulted in a simple, but efficient, file system for the p-System.

Conceptually, files are stored in *volumes* of data. These volumes are associated with various devices which may be classified as *block-structured* (floppy and hard disks), *interactive* (a terminal) or *write-only* (a printer). Each device is numbered, and may be referred to by its number. More importantly, each volume has a name of up to seven characters followed by a colon (:).

Disk volumes are block-structured devices: they are considered to be an array of directly addressable blocks of 512 eight-bit bytes. These blocks usually correspond to a physical sector on a disk. The disk directory and

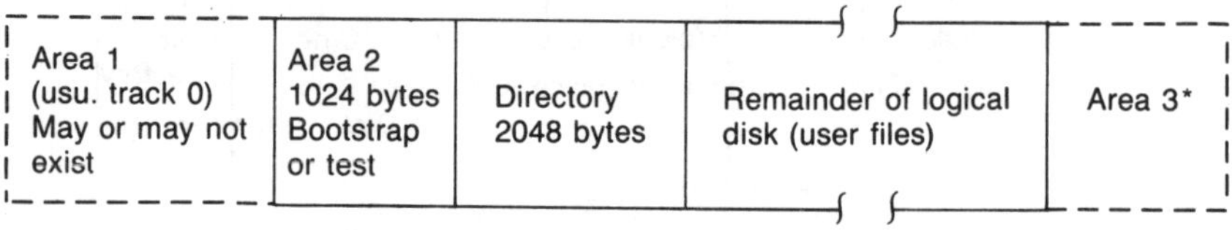

| Area 1 (usu. track 0) May or may not exist | Area 2 1024 bytes Bootstrap or test | Directory 2048 bytes | Remainder of logical disk (user files) | Area 3* |

* Remainder of any physical disk not used by the logical disk, area 3 can be nonexistent.

Figure 9.7 Logical structure of a p-System disk

file system are superimposed on this logical array structure. Schematically, the directory and files are held as shown in Figure 9.7.

Files are stored in *contiguous* blocks. This causes fragmentation of disk space. If you refer back to Figure 9.5, you will notice that the first file SYSTEM.PASCAL has a 6 in its row: this refers to the number of the block at which it starts — two blocks are used for the bootstrap, four for the directory. The unused disk space after the file SPOOLER.CODE is probably the result of a file having been removed.

While fragmentation can be a nuisance, the storage method provides very efficient file access. On opening a file which is to be read sequentially, for example, the file system need only look in the directory for the start position and length of the file; the file can then be accessed block by block. The system uses the largest space — the *worst-fit* algorithm described in Part I, Section 3.2 — by default, but half the largest or a specific size may be specified. The command 'K(runch' is provided to **compact** a fragmented disk.

In order to specify a file fully, the name of the volume on which it is stored must be given. For example, the full specification of the file DECTALK.CODE on the PSYS disk shown in Figure 9.5 is:

PSYS:DECTALK.CODE

The volume name may be up to seven characters long, and the file name up to 15 characters. Any characters after the rightmost period (.) denote the file's type. The system recognizes a number of file types: in particular TEXT files (lines of ASCII characters) and CODE files (p-code programs).

When the p-System is started up, the disk which has been used to bootstrap the system and which contains the interpreter and the operating system code file (SYSTEM.PASCAL) is designated the *root* volume and may be abbreviated to asterisk (*). It is also assumed to be the default, or *prefix*, volume. The latter means that if the user omits a file's volume name the system substitutes the prefix. The prefix may also be abbreviated to colon (:). Files, particularly frequently used programs on the root volume, can always be referred to using an asterisk, while files on any other disk named as the prefix need not be explicitly qualified by the volume name. A common example of how these facilities are used is the situation where a number of people share a computer: a 'system disk' can remain with the computer (it will be the root — *), while each user will keep his or her private 'user disk' which will be the prefix (abbreviated to :) for that user.

Another shorthand notation is provided for the user: file names may be *wild carded*. That is, special characters (*wild cards*) may be used to provide a *pattern-matching facility*. For example, to transfer the contents of disk MYDISK to the disk BACKUP1 might mean specifying dozens of files, but with wild cards it can be done by selecting the 'T(ransfer' command and then:

> Transfer what file? MYDISK: =
> To where? BACKUP1:$

The equal sign (=) will match all files on MYDISK; the dollar sign ($) indicates that for each file the same name must be used on BACKUP1 as was used on MYDISK.

Only 77 files may be stored on a volume. This is the maximum number of entries which will fit into the two blocks used to store the directory. The restriction is not too serious for floppy disk systems. On mass storage devices such as Winchester-technology hard disks the restriction is intoler-

```
Vols on-line:
 1    CONSOLE:
 2    SYSTERM:
 4  # IBMDISK:    [ 1280]
 6    PRINTER:
 7    REMIN:
 8    REMOUT:
 9  # PSYS:       [ 1280]
10  # SYSUTIL:    [ 1280]
11  # RAMDISK:    [ 1634]
12  # PART3:      [32000]
13  # PART4:      [29680]
16  # UNITS:      [  320] on volume SYSUTIL: starting at block 11
17  # MISC:       [   64] on volume SYSUTIL: starting at block 331
18  # FS:         [ 1280] on volume PART3:   starting at block 10
19  # UTIL:       [ 1280] on volume PART4:   starting at block 10
20  # COMMS:      [ 1280] on volume PART4:   starting at block 1290
21  # DOC:        [ 1280] on volume PART4:   starting at block 2570
22  # USUS:       [ 1280] on volume PART4:   starting at block 3850
23  # RECS:       [ 1280] on volume PART4:   starting at block 5130
24  # SOLO:       [ 1280] on volume PART4:   starting at block 6410
25  # ATMSEAS:    [ 1280] on volume PART4:   starting at block 7690
26  # SEMNET:     [ 1280] on volume PART4:   starting at block 8970
27  # SYNTAX:     [ 1280] on volume PART4:   starting at block 10250
28  # FOREX:      [ 1280] on volume PART4:   starting at block 11530
29  # SPRINT:     [ 1280] on volume PART4:   starting at block 12810
30  # W7:         [ 1280] on volume PART4:   starting at block 14090
31  # TEMP:       [ 1280] on volume PART4:   starting at block 15370
124   SERIALA:
125   SERIALB:
126   SERIALC:
127   SERIALD:
Root vol is - PSYS:
Prefix is   - USER:
```

Figure 9.8 Volumes held on a 33-megabyte hard disk divided into four partitions (numbered 9-13 above)

able. The solution has been to introduce *subvolumes* with Version IV of the p-System. Subvolumes are files, with the type SVOL, with the same logical structure as real disks, as shown in Figure 9.7. They are 'mounted' (made known to the system) or 'dismounted' using the filer's 'O(n/offline' command. Once mounted, they can be referred to just as other volumes. Subvolumes introduce a nice distinction between a physical volume and a logical volume of data which was not previously present, but which is extremely useful. This distinction is also in evidence in VM/SP.

Many hard disk systems divide the disk into *partitions* which can be treated as separate physical devices. However, the number of partitions is often small and this results in large volumes. Many users prefer to have control over the number and size of volumes in order to impose some sort of structure on the information they hold. Figure 9.8 illustrates this with the output from the 'V(ols' command on a system which has a 33-megabyte hard disk.

The volumes PSYS, SYSUTIL, PART3 and PART4 correspond to hard disk partitions. The other volumes are subvolumes of these four. This is clearly seen in Figure 9.9, the directory of PART4. It should be noted that subvolumes do *not* provide a hierarchical file system.

So far, I have discussed only block-structured volumes. Those which are not block-structured are less visible in that the user does not usually refer to them explicitly. The user uses CONSOLE but needs to refer to it explicitly only if, for example, he or she wishes to look at a file: the 'T(rans' command transfers the file to the console. The PRINTER volume is usually configured to be the parallel port on the real computer (if available) since many printers use this type of communication. REMIN and REMOUT are used for remote communications. Utilities are provided with the system for connecting it to other computers via these ports.

```
PART4:
UTIL.SVOL      1280 11:31 10-May-85     10   512 SVolfile
COMMS.SVOL     1280 11:31 10-May-85   1290   512 SVolfile
DOC.SVOL       1280 11:43 10-May-85   2570   512 SVolfile
USUS.SVOL      1280 11:46 10-May-85   3850   512 SVolfile
RECS.SVOL      1280 12:00 10-May-85   5130   512 SVolfile
SOLO.SVOL      1280 12:02 10-May-85   6410   512 SVolfile
ATMSBAS.SVOL   1280       11-Mar-85   7690   512 SVolfile
SEMNET.SVOL    1280 16:52 10-May-85   8970   512 SVolfile
SYNTAX.SVOL    1280 11:50 13-May-85  10250   512 SVolfile
FOREX.SVOL     1280 12:42 13-May-85  11530   512 SVolfile
SPRINT.SVOL    1280 15:19 15-May-85  12810   512 SVolfile
W7.SVOL        1280 15:21 15-May-85  14090   512 SVolfile
TEMP.SVOL      1280 14:56 24-May-85  15370   512 SVolfile
< UNUSED >     13030                 16650
13/13 files<listed/in-dir>, 16650 blocks used, 13030 unused, 13030 in largest
```

Figure 9.9 Listing of a physical volume containing subvolumes

Question for discussion

What is the main difference between CP/M's, MS-DOS's and the p-System's organization of secondary storage, and what are some pros and cons of each?

9.5 ARCHITECTURE OF THE P-MACHINE

Up to this point I have only looked at how the p-System 'feels' to the user — the facilities it provides and the user interface it employs. Before I show the underlying architecture of the p-machine you will need some idea of the structure of a UCSD Pascal program. The language is coupled so closely with the p-System that a discussion of one without the other is difficult. The outline of a UCSD Pascal program is shown in Figure 9.10.

```
PROGRAM accounts;
USES io_unit(get_answer);
TYPE (* definition of global data types... *)
VAR  (* global data structures... *)
     command: char

SEGMENT PROCEDURE startup;
   VAR (* local data... *)
   BEGIN
      (* code for startup *)
   END;

FUNCTION valid_command(option: char): boolean;
   BEGIN
      valid_command := option IN ['A', 'a', 'B', 'b']
   END;

BEGIN (* accounts main program *)
   startup;
   get_answer('What system A or B ?', command);
   IF valid_command(command)
   THEN
      ...
      ...
END.
```

Figure 9.10 An example of a UCSD Pascal program

The p-System

The statements correspond to those in most other programming languages: assignment, condition, repetition, and procedure call statements. What they compile to is more significant. A compiler on a real machine would produce machine code for that particular machine. For example, a simple assignment statement like $i := i + j$ would often be translated into several instructions; these instructions might transfer values from primary storage to registers, where the addition takes place before the result is transferred back to primary storage. The p-machine does not use its registers in this way; instead it uses a **stack**. A *stack* is a data structure which implements a last-in–first-out queue.

The UCSD Pascal compiler would, for this assignment, generate p-codes to place the values of i and then j onto the top of the stack. A p-code to add integers would perform the addition with these top-of-stack values, leaving the result on the top of the stack, whence it could be 'popped' off and stored back in i.

To execute p-code on a real machine requires a p-machine emulator (PME) which implements a stack and the operations on it. The user's p-code program (or a portion of it) must be in primary storage for the PME to fetch each p-code instruction in sequence and to perform the appopriate action.

It is important to note that Pascal is a stack-oriented language. All static data structures in a program (those whose sizes are known when a program is being compiled) are held on a stack. As procedures are called, their local data are placed on the stack; on exit the data are removed. On the other hand, dynamic structures are built on the *heap*.

A feature of UCSD Pascal is important to our discussion — *segments*. The word SEGMENT preceding PROCEDURE in Figure 9.10 denotes that the code subroutine *startup* does not have to be in primary storage prior to its execution. If it is not, it will be swapped in, and if primary storage becomes exhausted and that procedure is not being executed the space it occupies may be reclaimed as free space. In fact, a p-code program is itself a segment. Code files are therefore organized into segments.

Note how the system is organized in primary storage — shown in Figure 9.11.

The stack may expand as procedures are called, while the heap may grow up towards it as dynamic structures are built. In the free space between the two is the *code pool*, where the segments or units of p-code reside.

The process stacks shown as part of the heap are extra stacks for the data areas for special procedures called *processes* which may be executed concurrently. Concurrency on the p-System is provided using a semaphore model and is used in implementing the operating system.

Global data segments hold data structures which are global to programs; that is, they are available to all procedures in a program. The

```
                  High address  ┌─────────────────────┐
                                │  Operating system   │
                                │ (subset always      │
                                │    resident)        │
                                ├─────────────────────┤
                                │       Stack         │
                                │▓▓▓▓▓▓▓▓│▓▓▓▓▓▓▓▓▓▓│
                                │▓▓▓▓▓▓▓▓│▓▓▓▓▓▓▓▓▓▓│
                                │      Code pool      │
                                │▓▓▓▓▓▓▓▓│▓▓▓▓▓▓▓▓▓▓│
                                │▓▓▓▓▓▓▓▓│▓▓▓▓▓▓▓▓▓▓│
                                │                     │
                                │       Heap          │
                                │                     │
                                ├─────────────────────┤
                                │   Process 1 stack   │
                                │▓▓▓▓▓▓▓▓│▓▓▓▓▓▓▓▓▓▓│
                                │   Process 2 stack   │
                                │▓▓▓▓▓▓▓▓│▓▓▓▓▓▓▓▓▓▓│
                                │Global data segment 1│
                                │Global data segment 2│
                  Low address   │     Interpreter     │
                                └─────────────────────┘
```

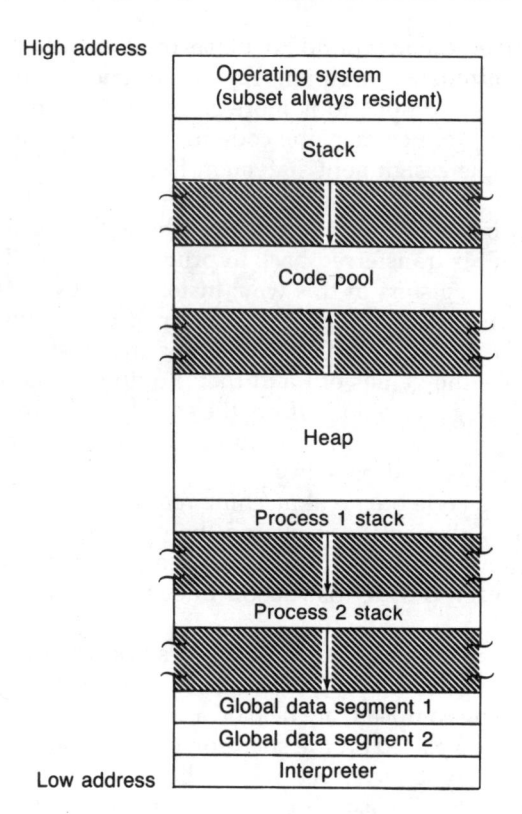

Figure 9.11 The architecture of the UCSD p-machine (version IV)

global data segments also hold the operating system's global data structures.

The use of the code pool provides a powerful, though occasionally time-expensive, primary storage management system. The code pool is organized as a contiguous area of primary storage in which the segments of the operating system and user's program are placed. Within the code pool the segments are connected in a **linked list** structure. The pool can be modified in the following ways:

(i) an attempt to expand the stack fails (called a *stack fault*): the code pool is moved 'down' (towards the heap) in order to free space;

(ii) an attempt to expand the heap fails (called a *heap fault*): the code pool is moved up (towards the stack);

(iii) an attempt to make room after either a stack or heap fault fails: one or more segments are discarded and the remaining segments are moved together; then repositioning is attempted;

(iv) discarding segments and repositioning fails to create space: a fatal system error (called *stack overflow*) has occurred and the system must be reinitialized.

These primary storage management faults are handled by a subsidiary process of the p-System. This fault-handler process cannot itself cause faults because its stack space is permanently allocated on the heap (see Figure 9.11) and it causes the execution of only that part of the operating system which is permanently resident in primary storage.

Fault handling works as follows. If the PME detects a stack fault or a *segment fault* (a call made to a segment which is not in primary storage), the fault-handler process is activated. It processes the fault by manipulating the code pool or, in the case of a segment fault, by reading in the required segment. It then switches back to the PME, which re-executes the instruction which caused the fault. Heap faults are detected by the operating system, which activates the fault handler.

Like other processors, the p-machine has registers which are a fundamental part of its architecture. These are not general-purpose but are used for managing the p-machine efficiently. They are used for functions like pointing to the next p-code (instructions in p-code are called 'p-codes') to be executed, pointing to the current procedure, and pointing to the top of the stack. The stack is used for general computation.

Questions for review

(i) What causes a stack fault and what effect does it have on a running program?

(ii) Compare primary storage management of the p-System with that of MS-DOS or CP/M. How does each allow for objects (for example data files in primary storage) to grow dynamically?

9.6 P-CODE PROGRAM EXECUTION

In order to execute p-code programs on this stack architecture, code files must hold sufficient information for the PME to be able to place local data on the stack, to access them there and to remove them upon exiting from the procedure. The system must also be able to gather all the information it needs on a program's component segments. So a code file must contain segments; in fact a *segment dictionary* is also held. This is shown in Figure 9.12.

The segment dictionary contains the name of each segment in a program and where in the code file it is stored. The dictionary is held as a linked list of sequences of dictionary entries, which are held in a block between segments. Segments are aligned on block boundaries: although

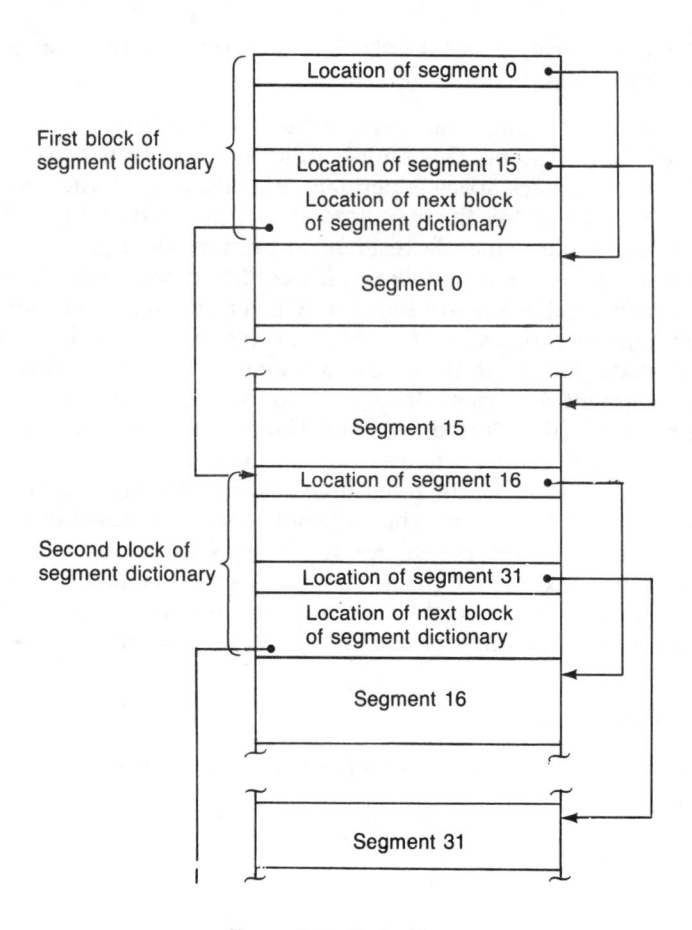

Figure 9.12 Code file format

this increases the size of code files slightly, it provides fast access to the segment dictionary and to the segments themselves. Each segment contains sufficient information for managing the stack. The format of a segment is given in Figure 9.13.

The *procedure dictionary pointer* at the bottom points to an array of pointers (the *procedure dictionary*) to the code for each procedure in the segment. The *procedure code* contains the p-codes which implement whatever computation is to be performed in that procedure, the space required for local data, and a pointer (EXITIC) to code which must be executed when the procedure finishes. When a procedure is called, an *activation record* is generated and placed on the top of the stack. The activation record contains space for parameters, local data and housekeeping

The p-System

High address

```
┌─────────────────────────────┐
│      Relocation list        │
├─────────────────────────────┤
│    Number of procedures     │
│    Pointer to procedure 1   │
│    Pointer to procedure 2   │
│            ...              │
│    Pointer to procedure N   │
├─────────────────────────────┤
│       Constant pool         │
├─────────────────────────────┤
│       Procedure code        │
├─────────────────────────────┤
│        Procedure 2          │
│        Object code          │
│        Data size            │
│          Exitic             │
├─────────────────────────────┤
│       Procedure code        │
├─────────────────────────────┤
│        Part number          │
├─────────────────────────────┤
│          Realsize           │
├─────────────────────────────┤
│    Constant pool pointer    │
├─────────────────────────────┤
│   Byte sex indicator word   │
├─────────────────────────────┤
│    8-character symbolic     │
│      Name of segment        │
├─────────────────────────────┤
│    Relocation list pointer  │
├─────────────────────────────┤
│ Procedure dictionary pointer│
└─────────────────────────────┘
```

- Procedure dictionary: spans from Number of procedures through Pointer to procedure N
- Procedure code for procedure 2: spans Procedure 2 Object code, Data size, Exitic

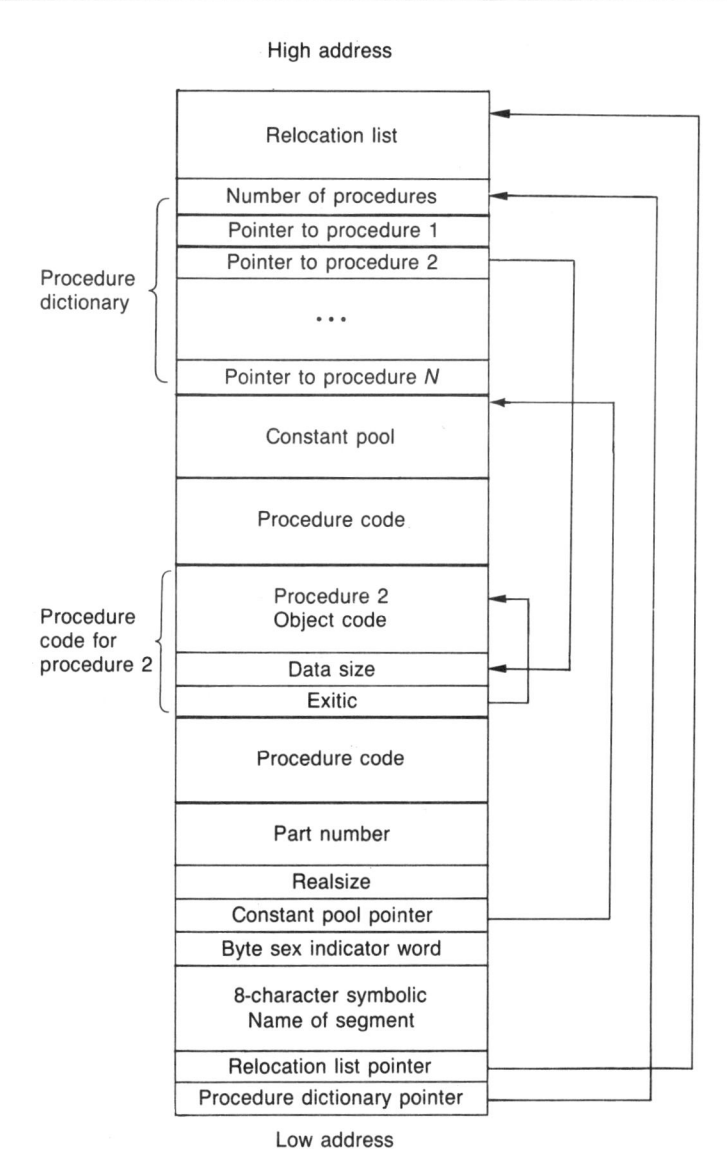

Low address

Figure 9.13 Code segment format

information for managing transfer of control to and from the procedure.

Of the other fields shown in Figure 9.13, three have particular importance to implementing a p-machine: real size (called REALSIZE), constant pool and byte-sex indicator.

REALSIZE indicates how large real numbers are: two or four words. Although there is an IEEE standard for floating-point representation, many existing processors do not use it. Therefore, the PME converts the processor-independent form to the processor-defined format when a segment is loaded. Provided that the size of the real numbers is the same, code files may be moved with impunity to p-Systems running on other processors.

To explain the byte-sex indicator word I must first discuss **byte-sex**. In order to address 16-bit words, for example, a byte-addressed machine will require *either* the least *or* most significant byte of the word as the address of the pair making up the word. Thus a pair of characters stored at (byte) addresses 400 and 401 will be accessed as 'No' or 'oN', depending on whether the processor uses most-significant-byte-first or least-significant-byte-first byte-sex respectively. The indicator word in a segment will determine the segment's byte-sex according to whether the value read is 1 or 256.

Byte-sex is a major problem for portability. By using an indicator, the p-System can remain independent of byte-sex, and code files of 'mixed sex' are commonplace. The problem can be solved for data files, if programs explicitly write indicator words in files and explicitly check them when reading those files. If such a program finds that a file is of the wrong byte-sex for the computer on which it is running, then the program will need to 'flip' the bytes.

To execute a p-code program, therefore, the p-System finds the program's code file and builds a *run-time environment* which maps the local segment numbers to global numbers and records whether its segments are already in the code pool.

Question for review

How does the structure of a code file make code pool management efficient?

9.7 THE P-MACHINE EMULATOR

The PME can be considered to consist logically of two parts:
- the *interpreter*, which fetches each p-code and its parameters and performs the appropriate action on the stack;
- the *run-time support package* (*RSP*), which performs machine-level operations such as moving or searching large sections of primary storage, moving segments in the code pool and performing low-level input and output.

The p-System

One part of the RSP, in particular, is well organized for portability — the part responsible for input and output, the RSP/IO. It is machine-independent except for the portion called the *Basic Input/Output Subsystem* (*BIOS*). The BIOS varies depending on the peripheral devices being used, but the interface between RSP/IO and BIOS is standard. Therefore a hierarchy of I/O processing exists, as shown in Figure 9.14.

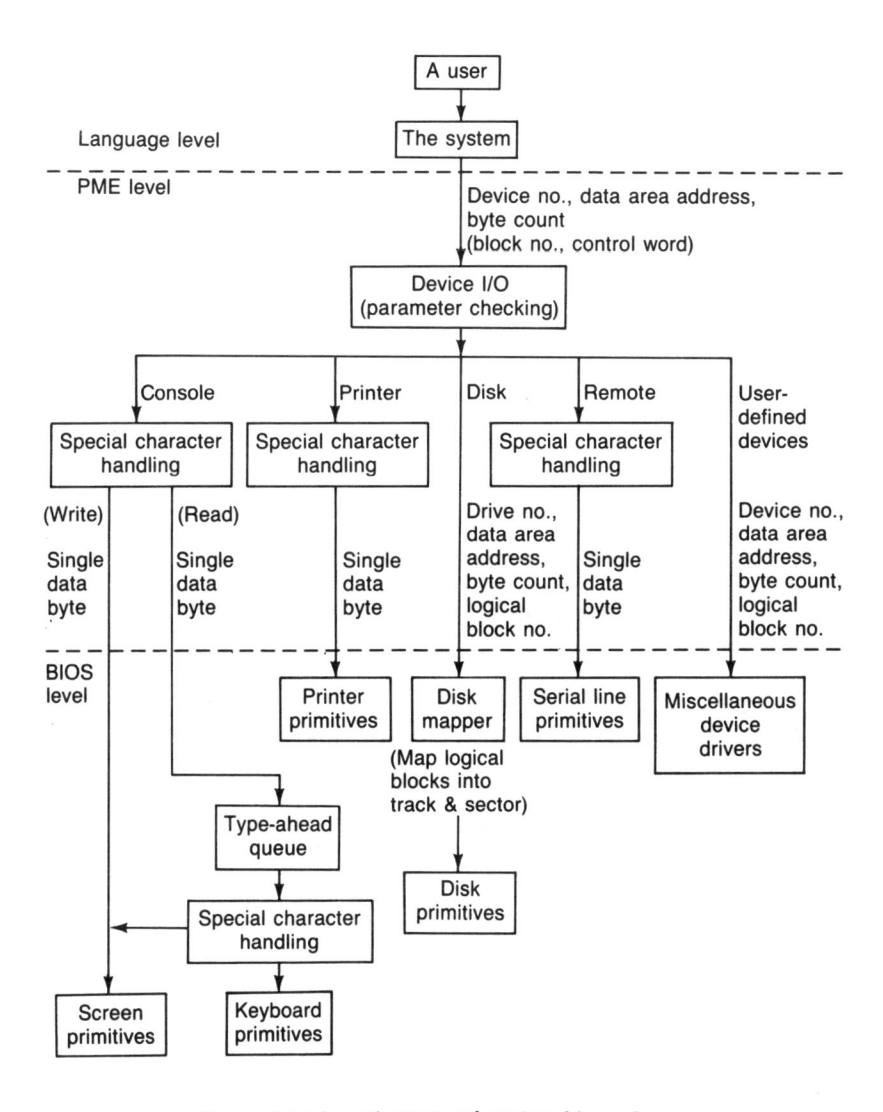

Figure 9.14 Input/output subsystem hierarchy

A program's input or output statement is translated into a call to an RSP/IO routine which converts the parameters to the appropriate BIOS routine calls and parameters. The use of a BIOS to implement low-level I/O came about fairly early in the development of the p-System. The first PDP-11 implementation did not need such a portable strategy; the adaptations for the Z80 and 8080 processors used existing CP/M BIOS code for low-level I/O. It became clear when adapting the system for other processors that some analog to the BIOS of CP/M was needed.

Another important aid to portability was the development of the SBIOS (simplified BIOS). Implementing a BIOS is a difficult task and requires the p-System already to be operational on the new hardware. Therefore, the so-called 'adaptable system' can be used to produce a preliminary adaptation of the system quickly; it is supplied with a BIOS which makes calls to the SBIOS, thus effectively adding a layer to the hierarchy shown in Figure 9.14. The implementor only needs to write an SBIOS. Once the system is running with SBIOS it can be used to develop a more efficient BIOS adaptation.

Question for review

How is the seemingly hardware-dependent I/O of the p-System made portable?

9.8 OVERCOMING WEAKNESSES AND RESTRICTIONS

One of the common objections to the p-System is that because it is interpreted code it is slow. This is true. However, the performance of a computer system is measured not only by its computational power; its data throughput can be crucial. While very efficient native machine code can easily outperform p-code when both are processor-bound, the differences for relatively I/O bound code are not so great. Also, native code programs are necessarily larger than those in p-code: this is because p-codes exist which implement high-level features of Pascal, while native code compilers need to produce large amounts of machine code to implement such features. (Recall the examples in Figures 1.5 and 1.7 in Part I.)

The large size of native code relative to p-code can mean that the transfer of native code to and from secondary storage or within primary storage can degrade overall performance. This is an important factor where primary storage management schemes are employed for program overlay (such as the UCSD Pascal segment procedure facility).

Native code generators, which convert p-code to native machine code, have been provided for many processors, but their use can itself incur penalties. First, a native code program is bigger than its p-code counterpart. Secondly, when the PME transfers control to native code it must save its working data, which must be restored when control is returned to p-code. This context switching is itself an overhead. However, new code generators are emerging which are more efficient.

The single greatest weakness of the system is that it is byte-addressed and the p-machine word-size of 16 bits only allows addresses up to 64 kilobytes. This is not really sufficient to support the stack, heap and code pool architecture shown in Figure 9.11, especially if the PME occupies some of the 64K. Although large applications can be accommodated, excessive code pool manipulation occurs. Also, developers have been unable to take direct advantage of increased primary storage available on 16- and 32-bit processors. A partial, but effective, solution has been to split up the data area (stack and heap) and code pool into separate 64 kilobyte areas, as shown in Figure 9.15.

The configuration in Figure 9.15 is called an *external code pool*, as distinct from the *internal* arrangement shown in Figure 9.11. Since stack and heap faults in the external arrangement no longer cause swapping, performance is much improved. Multiple code pools are also possible, but the real problem is data storage and access.

Good use can be made of large primary storage in another way: a 'disk' volume can be provided in primary storage. This is called RAM disk. On booting the system, the operating system files (SYSTEM.PASCAL, SYSTEM.MISCINFO, SYSTEM.LIBRARY, etc.) and any user files are

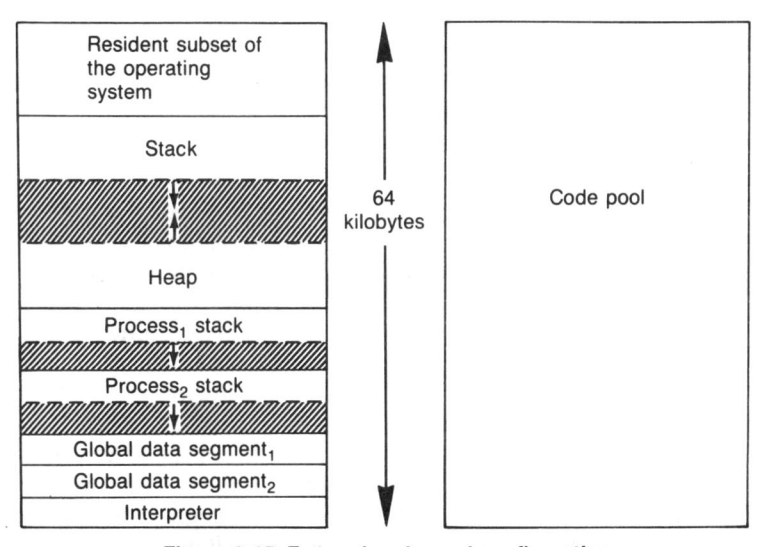

Figure 9.15 External code pool configuration

transferred (often at high speed by the PME) to the RAM disk. The RAM disk then becomes the root volume. There are several advantages to this strategy.

(i) Transfers to and from primary storage are extremely fast so program loading, file processing and swapping are speeded up dramatically.
(ii) The RAM disk is always ready to transfer data — there are no mechanical start-up and seek times.
(iii) The RAM disk can never be removed and irritating operating errors can thus be avoided.

The first point even allows computers without disks but with slow tape-loop devices to run the p-System. Everything required can be loaded at boot time. Only when the user has finished and is about to switch off the power will the data need to be permanently stored on an external device. The problem with RAM disks is that the primary storage medium in which they are implemented is usually **volatile**.

An addressing restriction applies to disks as well. A volume can have only 32 767 blocks (16 megabytes), which could be a limitation on Winchester-technology hard disks. On large disks extra partitioning must be used.

Question for review

How do the provision of RAM disk and external code pools speed up the performance of the p-System?

9.9 P-SYSTEM COMPONENTS

A *unit* is a module of UCSD Pascal compiled separately for later inclusion in programs. Units may be stored in libraries to make them generally available. Units consist of an *interface part* and an *implementation part*. The former includes declarations which describe data structures, and procedure headings which describe operations on them. The latter is the code which implements these data structures and operations, and which is hidden from the user. In Figure 9.10 the program uses the unit *io_unit* and has indicated that it only needs the procedure *get_answer* from the facilities on offer through this unit's interface part.

Since units are managed by the p-System as if they were segments, I have not needed to treat them separately until now. Units are relevant to the way in which the p-System has been designed for portability because their use as components of the system allows programmers to access operating system software through the *unit interface mechanism*. Furthermore, in order to make the system portable over a wide range of console devices (CRTs), one unit may be user-supplied (see Section 9.10). The code-file organization discussed earlier also provides for libraries: a library is, in fact, a code file whose segments are mostly units. A program supplied for managing libraries can be used to build code files with separately compiled units already incorporated. This is how the operating system is constructed.

Two aspects warrant description. First, note that the kernel unit (called KERNEL) contains permanently resident code (see Figure 9.11) which maintains the code pool, handles faults, reads in segments, and reads in swappable segments for accepting commands, loading programs, initializing the system and printing errors.

The way in which the p-System starts a user's program is the second point to note here: when a program is to be executed, its principal segment is mapped into a unit called USERPROG, the run-time environment record is built and the system calls the user's program as if it were one of its own segments.

Some of the system's units, such as KERNEL and SCREENOPS (see next section) are accessible to the programmer. Others, such as those which implement the file system, may be used only through units of the system library.

Question for review

What are the differences between library files and program code files?

9.10 DEVICE INDEPENDENCE

The decision of the UCSD project team to use a CRT as the user's terminal was, at that time, remarkable and adventurous. The problem in making a screen-based system device independent is almost as great as making the operating system portable over a number of computers; effectively a pseudo-CRT had to be specified.

Consider what codes a user might have to enter when operating the system. He or she might want to halt a fast-scrolling display to read it, and then restart scrolling, or discard output, or abort a running program by pressing some kind of 'break' key. Even the most suitable keys to delete a character or line might vary from CRT to CRT. When using the standard screen-based editor the user will want to press the cursor directional keys to move the cursor up, down, left or right. The codes generated by these keys might not be the codes which have to be sent to the screen to move the cursor up, down, left or right! The editor and other programs also requires codes which are distinguishable from ordinary text. Typically these codes will be control codes or *escape sequences* (the ASCII ESC code followed by a printable character).

The problem is greater when one considers a screen-based editor or applications with a screen-oriented user interface (for instance a 'form-filling' program). These require a method of specifying how random cursor addressing is achieved − what codes need be sent to make the cursor go to column x, row y of the screen.

Two mechanisms have been used to solve these problems. The first uses a file called SYSTEM.MISCINFO which holds miscellaneous information on the codes sent from the keyboard and the codes to be sent to the screen for the various functions. The file also holds information, for example, about whether an external code pool is to be configured and, if so, where in primary storage it is to be placed. When the system is started, the values in SYSTEM.MISCINFO are read and those which are needed while the system runs are stored in a global data systems communication record held on the heap. These values can be accessed by the user through the system unit KERNEL.

The screen-addressing problem is solved by requiring the system's supplier or user to provide a Pascal procedure in a GOTOXY unit. Once compiled, this unit can be placed in the operating system code file for use by the system or programmer.

All the system's screen-handling facilities, including the prompt display software described in Section 9.3, are available to the programmer via a unit called SCREENOPS.

Question for review

Why is the configuration file SYSTEM.MISCINFO not referred to every time a device-dependent code has to be transmitted by the p-System?

9.11 NETWORKING THE P-SYSTEM

Liaison is an extension of the UCSD p-System which permits computers running it to be connected in a local area network. Its prime functions are to provide the means by which portable distributed programs can be written and by which existing p-System software can share resources which may be hardware or software. Large file storage on Winchester hard disks and fast floating-point processors are examples of hardware resources; a database and database management system are examples of software resources.

The p-System

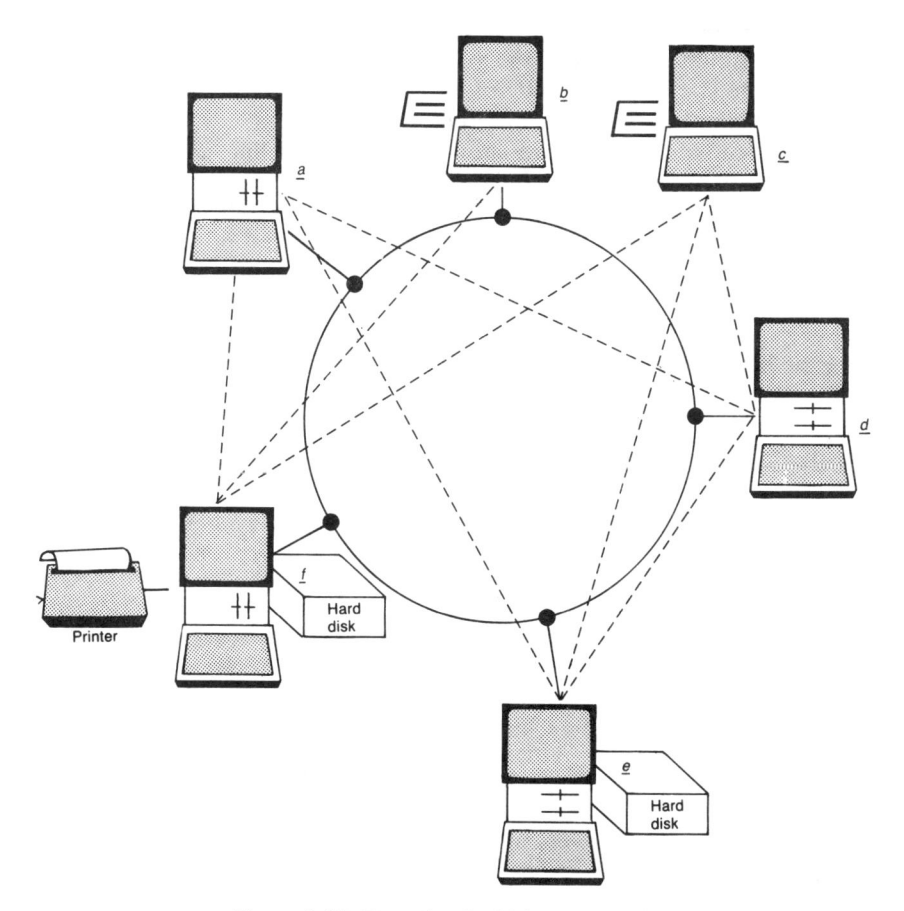

Figure 9.16 Example of a Liaison network

In the same way that the p-System abstracts machine architectures to a pseudo-machine, Liaison abstracts network architectures to a pseudo-network which may be implemented on real architectures such as Omninet or Ethernet through an extended p-System BIOS. Liaison networking facilities are provided by adding appropriate network units as components of the p-System. These units provide the high-level functions such as transmitting and receiving specifically addressed or broadcast messages, while network drivers in the BIOS provide the interface to the network hardware.

Liaison is based on a 'client/server' network model. In this paradigm a p-code program or process may provide a service of which other programs on the network can take advantage. Thus a *service* is provided by a *server* and used by a *client*. A server may provide its services to many clients simultaneously; a client may use many services simultaneously. Figure 9.16 shows an example of a Liaison network. Each of the micro/ personal computers can be different.

Physical connections are shown with a solid line, and the logical connections are shown by broken lines. The diagram depicts several different computers built around different processors which are the nodes of the network. (Because they are often used as general-purpose computer systems, these nodes are usually termed **work stations**.) One computer, e, has a large-capacity disk; another, f, has a high-speed printer and a large-capacity disk; all the others have floppy disks and operator consoles but no other peripherals. Computer e may be used as disk server, while f may be either a disk server or printer server. The other work stations may use the services provided by these two, or may communicate directly with each other while executing a distributed application program.

Liaison provides dynamic location of servers and clients; they are able to identify each other prior to interaction. This flexibility allows services to be moved to different work stations if required.

One of the most important features of Liaison is its facility for allowing existing non-distributed software to make use of network services. This facility is offered by supplying the system with servers and programs to access those servers. There are three standard servers: a disk server, a semaphore server and a print server. Clients may use the services offered by them by a menu-driven utility, SHARE, which has a menu level for each type of server.

Disk servers

A disk server is a program which provides access to disks local to the server for any Liaison user's client program on the network. Any p-System volume to which the server has access may be offered to clients provided that the volume is not being shared out by another server. In other words, if two or more servers have access to a volume of data, only one of them can offer it as a service at any moment. When the disk server is executed on a work station the operator (usually the network manager) specifies which of the work station's local volumes are to be offered to the network. These volumes are then available to any client while the server program is executing. The server cannot finish execution until there are no clients using it.

To use a disk server, a client user must execute the SHARE program to establish contact between the client's p-System and the server's. The user may obtain a list of all volumes on offer by any of the disk servers on the network. He or she can then gain access to one or more by 'mounting' the *remote volumes* in place of any of the local *major volumes* (subvolumes may not be replaced). This mounting is a *logical* operation which makes the remote volume known to the p-System: the volumes must already be physically on-line to the server for the server to offer them. Once the user has mounted the remote volume locally, he or she may then use it as if it were a local one. In this way the user may use the filer to manipulate the remote volume or execute a program to process data on it. Thus, mounting a remote volume for local use is analogous to replacing a floppy disk in a disk drive.

There are two main restrictions to this access. First, no user may extend or delete a file that is already open. Secondly, if the byte-sex (see Section 9.6) of the server and client computers differs, then the client program will have to detect this and transform the data when reading and writing.

When a client user has finished using a remote volume, he or she must execute SHARE again and sever the (logical) connection to the server; otherwise the server may not be able to terminate.

Semaphore servers

The semaphore server permits clients to indicate that they require exclusive use of a resource. It is of most use when more than one user on the network needs access to a specific file. If all of these users precede the execution of the program to process the file by the execution of SHARE, they can test whether the file is available. The user who first attempts to wait on the semaphore which has been associated with the resource will get access; subsequent users who wait will be denied it. Because the semaphore server is used mostly for file access control it is run as a concurrent process with a disk server. There can only be one semaphore server on the network at once (to prevent two clients using the same semaphore on different servers).

The weakness of the semaphore server is its voluntary nature. Unless all users who want shared access to a resource agree to use such a server and abide by some protocol access control will fail.

Printer servers

A printer server is similar to a disk server, but its purpose is to provide spooled output services to *serial* devices. It is a separate program from the disk server and cannot be run simultaneously at a work station. The print server uses its local disk space to spool its clients' output for printer-type devices. The client may select a device on offer by a print server, and *mount* (attach) it in place of one of his or her own local serial volumes (e.g. PRINTER). Any of the client's output to that device will be spooled to the server's local disk until a *break* command is issued to the server. This forces it to print the file as soon as a printer accessible to it becomes available. A *break* command may be issued explicitly from a program. It is also normally issued when the program which has created the output terminates.

Writing software for the network

Liaison may be used by programmers at a number of different levels.

It may be ignored. This does not mean that the user of a program cannot use the network but that the programmer need not be concerned with whether the service is provided locally or over a network.

The programmer may make use of the units of the Liaison operating system. These provide high-level interfaces to the network for sharing disk, printer and semaphore services. These units provide the means to interrogate remote servers to find out what services they offer (a disk server would return the server name and the volume names that it has to offer), and the means to establish the service. Units are also provided which implement client requirements, such as forcing the printing of a document before the client program terminates when using the print server. The programmer could thus program the use of network services without the user even being aware that they were being used.

The programmer may implement network services by writing a server program and a client program or unit so that some new service may be offered to the network. For example, a database server could be implemented to channel database access requests from any user to a single database management program. One advantage of this approach is a substantial reduction in network usage.

Network services may themselves be written at a number of levels: these levels are provided explicitly by Liaison for inter-user communication. These levels are as follows:

- *Low-level network transmission and reception routines.* These routines try to send or receive a message but do not guarantee success. This is the lowest level — the so-called 'socket level'.
- *Reliable user-to-user communications.* These routines take the responsibility to ensure that messages have arrived and that their communication can be assumed by the sender. Routines are provided to establish, allow use of and finally disconnect a user-to-user link. This is the 'channel level'.
- *Remote server location.* These routines help to establish the existence of and to set up communications with a remote server.

The p-System

Thus Liaison provides an environment for network software development. The programmer or user need not be concerned as to which networking hardware will be used, only that Liaison is implemented on some real network.

As an example of how transparent Liaison can be when a user executes software written to run on it, consider how the network shown in Figure 9.16 might be used: the owner of microcomputer d wants to write a letter. The owner executes a small menu program on d's system and selects the option *word processing*. The menu program selects remote microcomputer b (at the top of the figure) which contains the word-processing program and data storage; it mounts the appropriate volumes automatically and executes the software immediately. When the owner of d finishes, the word-processing program returns to the menu program and thereby releases all the volumes required for word processing. The menu program on d waits for the next menu selection. The owner is not aware of running network software. If b is not available for some reason, then d's owner is told that the server is not available and is returned to the menu program.

I stated above that software can be considered a scarce resource. Since microcomputer software is often priced on a per copy basis an organization may wish to buy only one copy of a program and to make it available on the network. The software developer, on the other hand, will want to be paid as though n copies of the program had been supplied for n individual work stations. A facility to control program usage, the Liaison monitor, is therefore provided.

The Liaison monitor allows a software developer or a network manager to prevent the same piece of software being run on a network by more than a fixed number of people. For example, a limit of three users may be set for a database management program; if a fourth user tries to execute the program when three are already using it, he or she is told that the network limit has exceeded and that someone must finish using the program first. The network limit can be set for a program by running a utility supplied for the purpose.

The advent of the Liaison version of the p-System is a step forward in the development of the p-System. Liaison is one of the first hardware-independent products to arrive for networking, and its further development and use should be of great interest.

Question for review

What is the weakness of using a voluntary semaphore server for implementing resource access control?

Question for discussion

What kind of mental model will the naive user form of a Liaison network? Why?

9.12 VARIATIONS ON A THEME

The simplicity of design and functional power of the p-System has made it a prime candidate for novel implementation.

In Section 9.7 I mentioned how CP/M was used to provide a BIOS for the Z80 and 8080 adaptations. In fact CP/M has been used for bootstrapping the adaptable p-System onto machines which use these processors; a CP/M program is executed from a CP/M disk which starts the p-System running. This system can be used to develop a proper adaptation.

More recently the market dominance of MS-DOS has been acknowledged by an MS-DOS-hosted version of the system. In this configuration the p-System is provided as an MS-DOS program and MS-DOS files are used as p-System volumes called *virtual volumes*. Real p-System volumes may also be used. A DOS filer is provided as well: it allows MS-DOS files to be transferred to p-System volumes and allows p-System files to be transferred to MS-DOS. The MS-DOS-hosted p-System also allows user programs to manipulate MS-DOS directories and files directly.

Storage allocation of virtual volumes is slightly odd under MS-DOS. Since the MS-DOS file system allows dynamic disk space allocation a p-System virtual volume can contain a large number of blocks which have not yet been allocated by the MS-DOS file system. p-System software may then record that it has space available on the virtual volume which is not actually available on the MS-DOS disk. A system crash results.

Another company (NCI of Vancouver, Canada) has implemented the PME using the MS-DOS file system. The p-System is not hosted by MS-DOS; the user boots the p-System directly but the p-System can access MS-DOS files since its own files are MS-DOS files.

There has been considerable development of the p-System in Europe. The Open University (UK) has implemented two DECsystem-20 (TOPS-20 operating system) adaptations and a VAX VMS adaptation. All of these use virtual volumes and no real ones: they are defined prior to starting the p-System and are permanently mounted while it is running. TOPS-20 and VMS files are imported and exported through REMIN and REMOUT and software has been developed to manipulate p-System volumes. The most innovative aspect of these adaptations is that programs written under TOPS-20 or VMS (rather than under the p-System) may be run directly from the p-System. This is provided by calling a small p-code program which accesses the external program through a special device.

In Germany, Focus Computer has implemented a Unix-hosted

p-System. A Unix filer is provided, as is software for manipulating the p-System volumes from Unix. The multitasking and multiple-window facilities of Unix System V offer the p-System user the possibility of having four 'windows' on a CRT screen running the p-System, each performing different tasks concurrently.

The Swedish company Versal has microcoded an AMD 2901 chip in the processor so that it 'knows' about p-code and can optimize the performance of the interpreter. They have a small p-System and resource managing operating system, VOS, which allows up to 32 'p-worlds' to execute concurrently. A user may have any number of p-worlds allocated to him or her, and, thanks to the screen mapping of the system, he or she can switch instantly between these systems at the touch of a button.

Versal has successfully tackled the problem of security for p-System devices which multi-user p-System environments do not usually do well. On a microcomputer, the only way to prevent access to a system is often by removing the disks containing it. This is not possible with a hard disk, and once the system is running all volumes become accessible. VOS allows a system manager to specify which volumes, both block-structured and non-block-structured, may be used and whether they can be used in read-only or read/write mode. VOS also allows the system manager to specify that a p-System program be loaded and run immediately a p-world is started and that access to the command interpreter be prevented. Thus a secretary might be given access only to a word-processing package which would start executing immediately the secretary's p-world starts. The secretary would never see a p-System prompt.

Two versions of the p-machine have also been microcoded. The Western Digital Microengine implemented version III of the p-System in hardware, while Volition Systems implemented their version II.2 PME in microcode on an AMD 2900 chip.

The Volition Systems p-machine is worth mentioning. They added p-codes to facilitate the implementation of the programming language Modula-2. It must be seen as a weakness that the p-machine, and hence p-System, is so dependent on the requirements of one particular programming language. Ideally a p-machine which would suit other languages should be designed. The Volition system executes both Pascal and Modula-2, but their p-machine is not compatible with the Version IV p-machine. (Other languages such as FORTRAN-77, BASIC, SNOBOL and PROLOG have been implemented for the p-System.)

9.13 SUMMARY

The problems involved in designing a portable operating system are considerable. The p-System is a portable operating system whose developers have identified and solved many of these problems. As a portable program development system for small computers it is an undoubted success. As a vehicle for portable applications software it is equally successful. Its weaknesses of performance and limited data storage have only become apparent in the early 1980s.

GENERAL REFERENCES

Anon. (1984) *Liaison Operating System Reference Manual*, SofTech Microsystems, San Diego, California.
Anon. (undated) *TDI p-System: Internal Architecture Reference Manual*, SofTech Microsystems, San Diego, California.
Anon. (1984) *TDI p-System: MS-DOS Hosted p-System Supplement*, SofTech Microsystems, San Diego, California.
Anon. (1983) *TDI p-System: Operating System Reference Manual*, SofTech Microsystems, San Diego, California.
Bowles, K.L. (1980) *Beginner's Guide for the UCSD Pascal System*, Byte Books, Peterborough, New Hampshire.
Buckner, K., Cookson, M.J., Hinxman, A.I. and Tate, A. (1984) *Using the UCSD p-System*, Addison-Wesley, Reading, Massachussetts.

FURTHER READING

Bowles, K.L. (1980) *Beginner's Guide for the UCSD Pascal System*, Byte Books, Peterborough, New Hampshire. A user's guide.
Buckner, K., Cookson, M.J., Hinxman, A.I. and Tate, A. (1984) *Using the UCSD p-System*, Addison-Wesley, Reading, Massachussetts. A slightly more detailed user's guide.

CHAPTER

10
Unix
(BY GORDON DAVIES)

Unix is a general-purpose, interactive multi-user operating system originally written for the PDP-11 series of computers but since made available on a wide variety of machines ranging from larger microcomputers to mainframes.

The Unix system was developed by programmers for the task of programming; it provides a powerful user interface with a broad variety of compilers, editors, assemblers, debuggers and document preparation aids. As such, Unix has come to stand for the whole user environment it provides.

History

In the 1960s Bell Laboratories, the research arm of AT & T, were involved with the Multics project — a project to develop a large multi-user operating system. When Bell Laboratories withdrew from the project, an employee named Ken Thompson wrote an operating system for the PDP-7 to support a team of programmers working in a research environment. Multics influenced that design. Since the original system supported only one user, it was named Unix.

With Bell's encouragement, further versions were built. In the early stages all the code was written in the particular assembler language necessary, but in 1973 Dennis Ritchie used the language C to produce a new version. Parts of the code remained in assembler — for example those parts dealing with low-level I/O. However, because C can be compiled into a number of different machine languages, Unix is relatively machine independent and as a consequence has appeared on a variety of processors ranging from the Intel 8046 and Motorola MC68000 to the IBM 370 and Amdahl 470.

Question for discussion

What problems are inherent in using a high-level source language as the means of making an operating system portable?

10.1 THE SHELL COMMAND LANGUAGE

To aid your understanding of the explanations which follow, you must know something of Unix's interface to the user — the *shell command language*. If you have experience of Unix, you may ignore this section and continue reading at Section 10.2 on page 215.

Commands

Once the user has logged in and received the prompt character (usually a dollar sign), the system is ready to process commands. For example, a user might enter

$ date (followed by ⟨return⟩)

A response such as

Fri Apr 12   10:48 GMT 1985

should appear.

To list the names of files, a user can type

$ ls

This will list the names of the files in alphabetical order.

fortran
letter
message
resume

It is possible to get more detailed information about files by using the *ls-l* command. The -l in the command is known as an **argument** to the command *ls*. Because this argument is prefixed by a hyphen, it specifies more precisely or modifies what the command is to do. Such arguments are known as **flags**. Arguments without a hyphen are usually file names, as will be seen in the next section.

To copy a file, the *cp* command is used. For example to make a copy of *fortran* in the file *oldfort*, you could type:

$ cp fortran oldfort

Note that *oldfort* need not exist; it will be created by the *cp* command. If *oldfort* did exist before the *cp* command, then its original contents will have been lost and it will now contain a copy of the file *fortran*. The *cp* command is an example of a command which operates on one or more files. In the example above, *fortran* and *oldfort* are the arguments to the command *cp*.

Printing files

The Unix system provides several ways to print a file. The simplest one is *cat*, which stands for conCATenate. To see the contents of the file called *message*, the user can type:

$ cat message

The *cat* command simply *copies* the contents of the file onto the terminal.

Redirecting input and output

Up to this point, I have assumed that all the input to the shell and all the input to a command came from the terminal and that all output has been directed to the terminal. The input is said to be coming from the **standard input** and the output going to the **standard output**. However, it is possible to have the input come from a file and to place the output in a file. Essentially, *Unix treats the terminal as a file*. In fact, to Unix a terminal is a file. This is a very powerful capability, one of several which gives Unix the reputation of being so flexible.

If the user types

$ ls > outfile

the output of *ls* (the names of the files) will be redirected to the file, *outfile*. The 'greater than' sign (>) tells the shell to redirect the standard output to a file called *outfile*. Nothing will be printed on the terminal, except for the prompt character, which indicates that the command has finished executing. *Outfile* can now be manipulated (printed, edited, copied) as if it had been created with an editor.

Input can also be redirected. If a command normally expects input to come from the terminal, then the input can come from a file instead by using the symbol < (the 'less than' sign). For example, consider the situation where the user uses an editor, *ed*, to modify several files in the same way, by using the same editor commands. It is possible to create a file and put the commands in this file. Call the file *script*. Then, to edit a particular file, *newprog*, using these commands the user would type

$ ed newprog < script

where *ed* is the command to invoke the editor, *newprog* is the file to be edited and the file *script* contains the set of editor commands to be applied to the file *newprog*.

Script is an example of a **command file**, a file consisting of a frequently used sequence of commands. The sequence can then be invoked by using the command file name.

The user's terminal is treated by Unix as though it were a file. The terminal is the standard input file and also the standard output file. Writing to a terminal is logically the same as writing to a file, reading from a terminal is the same as reading from a file. This is what makes redirection possible, because when the user redirects input or output he or she is telling Unix not to use the standard input or output file, but to use instead the files named in the command.

The redirection is done by the shell and is independent of any associated commands. Therefore, the programs to execute such commands ignore such redirection and are thus simplified. This applies equally to programs that a user might write.

Pipes

You have seen how to redirect both input and output to a file. In this way, a user could use the output of one command as the input to the next one by means of an intermediate file. With the use of pipes, this need not be an explicit intermediate file, as the pipe connects the standard output of one program to the standard input of another program.

A pipe is an open file connecting two processes. Information written into one end of the pipe may be read from the other end. The synchronization, scheduling and buffering is handled automatically by the Unix system.

You can think of data passing through a Unix pipe as water going from the spigot through a hose to a sprinkler. The spigot continues to emit the water. At the same time, however, the water is being used at

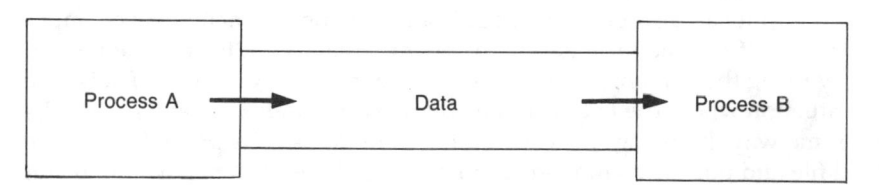

Figure 10.1 A Unix pipe

the sprinkler. Similarly, process *b* is accepting and using the data as process *a* generates them. Process *b* does not have to wait until all data have been generated by process *a*. To continue the analogy of the water coming from the spigot and through the hose, the water is the data and the hose is the pipe, that is, the open file.

A pipe is denoted by |, a single, vertical bar, as follows:

a | b

This means that the output of the command *a* becomes the input to the command *b*.

Filters

It is possible to eliminate data which the user doesn't want or need to see. When used this way, a command is known as a **filter**. A filter is any command that reads the standard input, selects from it in some way and passes the output as standard output.

The idea of pipes and filters is part of the Unix philosophy of breaking down a problem into small, well-defined tasks and using Unix utility programs linked together to accomplish the whole task.

10.2 FILES ON UNIX

Now that you have seen how to communicate with Unix, let us see how the information is stored by the Unix system. This involves an understanding of the facilities Unix provides for storing and retrieving files in its filing system.

Directories

Users logging on to Unix have access to their own personal directory, called a **home directory**. The home, and indeed any, directory is itself a file and can therefore be recorded in another directory at a higher level.

The filing system is then a hierarchical structure. At the top of the hierarchy is a special directory called the **root**, which contains the system-related directories such as *bin* and *usr*. Figure 10.3 shows the directory structure of a Unix system. As a user it is not necessary to know of the existence of most of the directories in the system.

As a directory is a file, so where a file exists the user can have a directory. For example, the user's directory could contain another directory

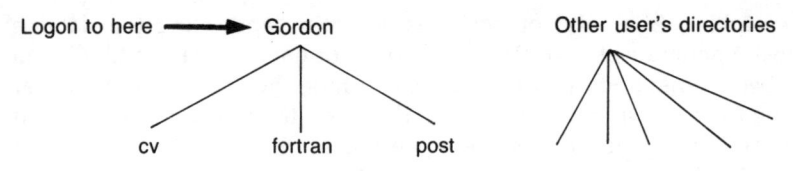

Figure 10.2 The home directory

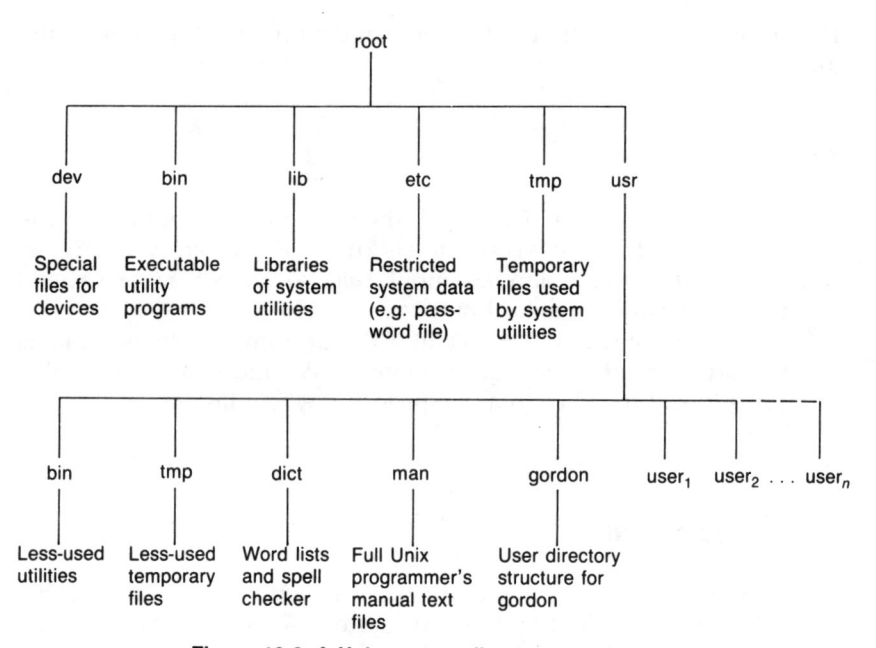

Figure 10.3 A Unix system directory structure

called *book*. This is created by using the *mkdir* (make directory) command. Type

    $ mkdir book

then the directory structure appears as in Figure 10.4.

There are no files as yet in the directory *book*. To create files in this directory it is more convenient to first position oneself at the directory, although not essential. This is done using the *cd* (change directory) command.

    $ cd book

Now any files created will reside in the directory *book* and hence *another* level in the hierarchy is created. For example, the user may be producing

Unix

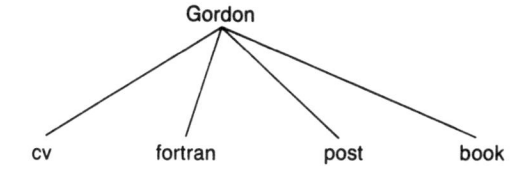

```
        Gordon
       /  |  \ \
      /   |   \  \
     cv  fortran post  book
```

Figure 10.4 The home directory after adding the directory *book*

```
         book
        / | \
       /  |  \
  chapter 1  chapter 2  chapter 3
```

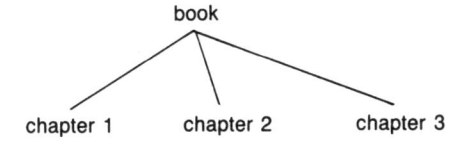

Figure 10.5 The directory *book*

a book with several chapters. This can be organized by arranging for each chapter to be a file within the directory book. See Figure 10.5.

Path names

It is not necessary to position oneself at a directory to access a file within that directory. Access can be through specifying the file's path name. A path name for a file is a path through the file system that leads to a file. If the user wants to access a file called *chapter1* in directory *book* then *chapter1* can be accessed by its path name

book/chapter1

Path names are formed by listing the directory names, separated by slashes as necessary, to define the path.

Question for review

Suppose you want to divide the chapters of your book into separate sections and make each section a separate file. How could you achieve this using additional levels of directories?

Files

The structure of the Unix file system encourages users to group their files together logically into units called directories. The directories can become large and a Unix system may have hundreds. To simplify further the maintenance of files and directories, a strict hierarchical structure is used: the whole file system is organized as a tree structure. Figure 10.3 above shows the hierarchy 'tree' for a typical Unix system.

There are three types of files; ordinary files, directory files, and **special files**.

Ordinary files are typically texts of programs, administrative records or program data and are normally used as long-term storage. These files can be of readable text, e.g. text files where the file is a stream of characters separated by the new line character, or **binary files** where the file is perhaps executable code. Although it is possible to store records such as those used in many administrative applications, the concept of a record does not exist in Unix files — a file is a collection of randomly addressable characters, its size being exactly the number of characters in the file, up to about a billion (10^9).

A file in a Unix system has *no intrinsic structure* at all. Any structure it possesses is imposed by the user. Unix files will use less space than a file system that stores fixed-length records, where space is wasted by filling blanks. A system that uses variable-length records with character counts uses time to keep a count of the number of characters processed. A Unix file's lack of structure is convenient for text-processing programs that usually deal with streams of characters. The Unix philosophy of general-purpose program tools would be more difficult to implement if its files existed in a variety of forms. This common text form helps in the writing of software tools, as all of them essentially convert one text file into another text file.

File sharing and file protection

Directories are considered to be files, but they are manipulated in a different way. The organization of the directory system is the responsibility of Unix; *user programs* are unable to access the directories, all changes being made by system commands.

A directory can only appear within one directory at the next level higher in the hierarchy. Ordinary files, however, can exist in more than one directory, and can be known by more than one name. This is useful in a multi-user community such as a research group, where all the members of the group perhaps need to read a particular data file. Only one copy of the file exists but each user has a link to that file and can regard it as his or her own. This can, of course, cause problems if users wish to write to the file simultaneously.

There are occasions when a user may wish to ensure that files are private and therefore inaccessible to other users. Also, there are many system files that need to be protected from damage such as over-writing or deletion, either accidentally or deliberately, by users. To protect files from intrusion or damage, Unix has a scheme for file access permissions.

Access to a file can be given at any of three levels of permission: read (r), write (w) and execute (x) for each of three categories of potential users of the file: the owner, a selected group of users, and the remainder of the Unix user community.

Special files

Special files do not contain information in the usual sense; they act as an interface between application programs and the kernel of the operating system. As programs have the facility to move data between files, assigning a file name to an I/O device means that a program can transfer data to the I/O device as if it were transferring data to a file. Each I/O mechanism is connected to a special file.

Mountable volumes

Any empty directory at any level can be replaced by a whole new branch of the filing system corresponding to the files on a completely new volume (disk or tape), thus extending the file system.

Once any volume is incorporated into the system its physical identity is lost to the user and it becomes difficult to find out where files actually reside. This could cause problems if files on a removable volume were cross-listed in directories on other volumes, i.e. a file has a link to it from a directory on another volume. What happens if a volume is removed? Consequently, such *cross-linkings* are prohibited.

Questions for review

(i) What is the purpose in having three different file types?
(ii) What limitations can a user place on others' use of his or her files?
(iii) What mechanisms are necessary for a file to be read simultaneously by different users?

Questions for discussion

(i) How does the hierarchical nature of the filing system provide a measure of data privacy for a user?
(ii) What needs to happen for several users to share a file which one or more might want to update? Does it make a difference if there is a rule that they cannot share in this fashion simultaneously?

10.3 IMPLEMENTATION OF THE FILE SYSTEM

A Unix directory is not the repository of all the information about the files within it; it contains only the file name and a reference number. More detailed information is contained in the **i-node** for a file. An i-node is a file definition and contains user ID, protection status, disk block addresses where the file is stored, file size and other information.

I-nodes are stored in **i-lists**. The offset of the i-nodes from the start of the i-list is the i-node's **i-number**. It is this i-number which is the reference number stored in the directory along with the file name.

A directory consists of 16-byte entries for each file (14-byte name, two-byte i-number). As it is a file, a directory is referred to by its i-node as with any other file. A file's name is stored only in the directory.

If a path name is specified for a file, then accessing the file involves searching a directory for the name and i-number for the directory at the next level down. The i-number specifies the i-node for the directory; the i-node for the directory specifies where the directory resides on disk so that that i-node is brought into primary storage. The directory pointed to by that i-node is then brought into primary storage. The process continues until finally an ordinary file name is specified in the path name rather than a directory.

Secondary storage organization

The disk on which the files reside is structured as shown in Figure 10.6. The first block, block zero, is unused by the file system — it is used to contain booting procedures. Block one is the superblock and contains the file system header. Such information as the size of the file system, the number of i-nodes and free space parameters are stored there. Next comes the i-list for that disk volume, containing one i-node, occupying 64 bytes, for each file. Following the i-list are the blocks used for storage of files.

The i-nodes contain block addresses for accessing a file. There are 13 block addresses stored in each i-node. For a file of up to 10 blocks, the corresponding block addresses are stored in the first 10 block address locations in the i-node. For a file larger than 5120 bytes (10 blocks) the eleventh address is the address of a block (an **indirect block**) that contains the addresses of the next 128 blocks. This addresses a file of up to 70 656 bytes.

For a still larger file the twelfth block contains the address of a block (a *double* indirect block) which contains the addresses of 128 further blocks. Each of these 128 blocks contains the addresses of 128 blocks used to store the file. This will allow access to a file of up to 8 459 264 bytes (10 + 128 + 128^2 blocks). The thirteenth address in the i-node is used for triple

Unix 221

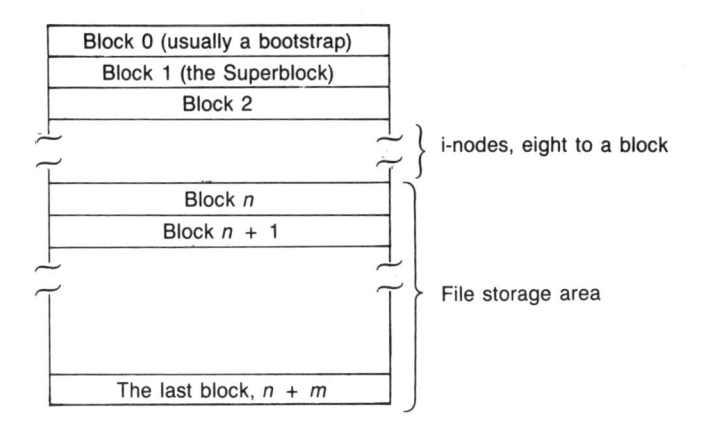

```
┌─────────────────────────────────┐
│  Block 0 (usually a bootstrap)  │
├─────────────────────────────────┤
│   Block 1 (the Superblock)      │
├─────────────────────────────────┤
│           Block 2               │
├─────────────────────────────────┤  } i-nodes, eight to a block
│                                 │
├─────────────────────────────────┤
│           Block n               │
├─────────────────────────────────┤
│          Block n + 1            │
├─────────────────────────────────┤  } File storage area
│                                 │
├─────────────────────────────────┤
│       The last block, n + m     │
└─────────────────────────────────┘
```

Figure 10.6 The physical layout of a Unix disk

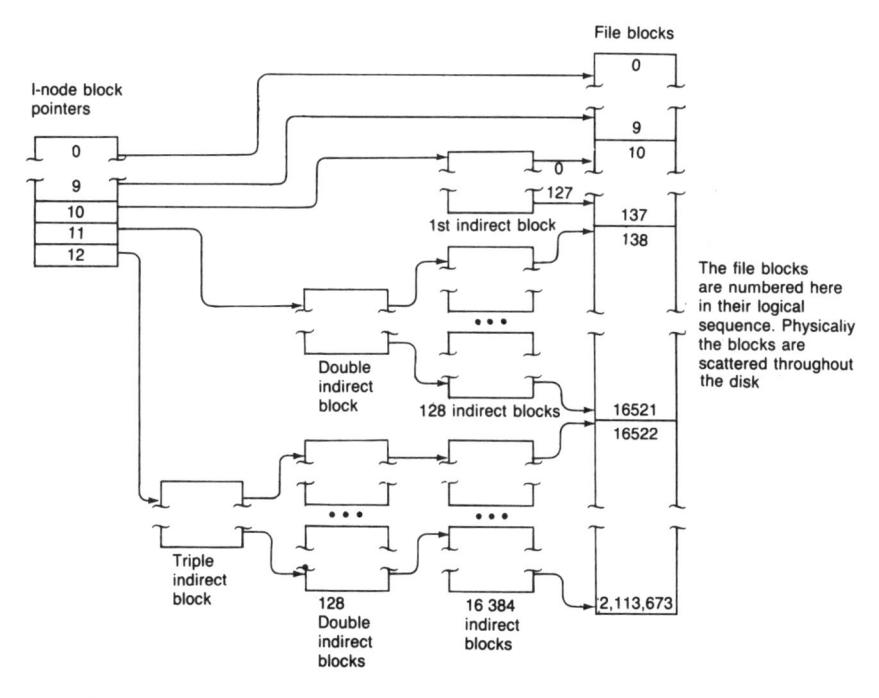

Figure 10.7 How the i-node block pointers actually reference the blocks of a file

indirection, giving a maximum file size of 1 082 201 087 bytes (10 + 128 + 128^2 + 128^3 blocks).

For the system to allocate storage for a new file or an enlarged file, it is necessary to know where the free blocks are. The free blocks are maintained as a linked list of blocks — a free block will contain a pointer to (the address of) the next free block. In addition a block will contain the addresses of up to 50 additional free blocks. Access to this chain or linked list is from the superblock. When a file is removed, its space is freed and the blocks used by the file must be added to the free block linked list.

Efficiency

The transfer of a file into primary storage is more efficient if blocks are allocated for a file so that they form a contiguous sequence. This is done, if possible, but it can happen that both files and free blocks become scattered over the volume. Periodically it may be necessary to compact files. All the files are moved to form a contiguous sequence of blocks, so that the free blocks are also contiguous. This compaction reduces time required to access files and improves the system's ability to allocate contiguous blocks. Although the problem of fragmentation exists it may be preferable to storing files *only* in contiguous blocks as occurs in some systems.

Such a method of storing files, involving up to triple indirection, could be thought inefficient. However, use of a cache memory can reduce the I/O necessary to retrieve a larger file and the space overheads (i-nodes, indirect blocks, partially filled last blocks) on one particular system totalled less than 10 per cent.

Question for discussion

Compare the overheads of the Unix method of storing files with other methods you know about, for example that used by MS-DOS. What relative advantages and disadvantages are there?

File access

Before a file can be processed by reading or writing, it must be opened. A non-negative integer value called the **file descriptor** is returned in response to a system call to open a file. The file descriptor is the reference number of the file in a table called the **system file table**. The entry in this table contains a pointer to the corresponding i-node for the file in the system i-node table.

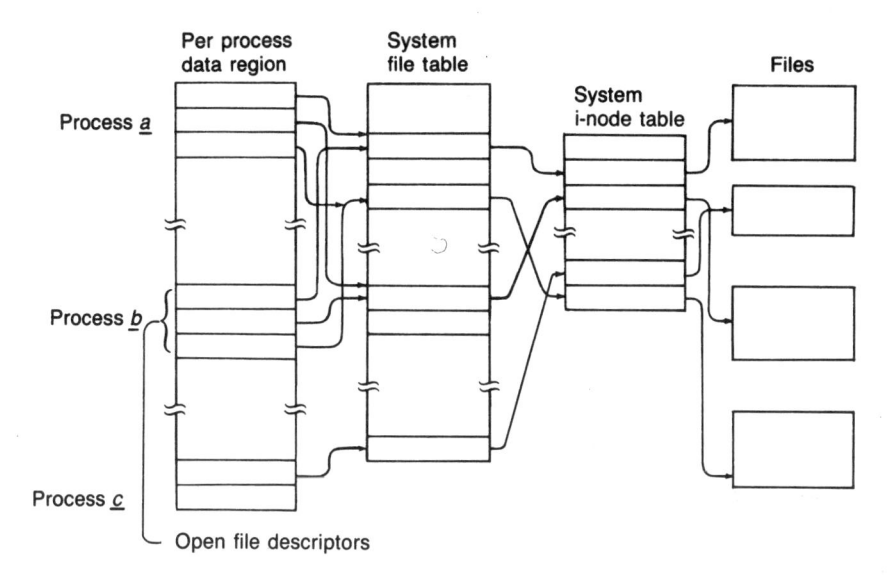

Figure 10.8 The kernel's data structures for accessing files

When a file is opened, the i-node for the file is fetched and placed in the **i-node table**; a pointer to the i-node is placed on the system file table and finally another pointer to the system file table *entry* is placed in the user's per process data area (explained in Section 10.5, on page 228) for the process. There appears to be an extra level of indirection here, the function of the system file table not being obvious. However, each file has associated with it a file pointer which is the byte offset from the beginning of the file to where the next read/write operation is to be performed on the file.

Related processes must be allowed to share files and therefore have a common file pointer. At the same time it is also necessary to allow independent processes access to the same file. Consequently, the system file table is used to hold the file pointer as the file pointer of a sharable file cannot reside in the i-node table nor in the open file section of the process table.

Consider what happens when the shell runs a program. It executes a new process and waits for its termination. The new process may read and write from the same files that the shell uses. The shell and the new process share the same file pointer, stored in the system file table, so that when the new process terminates the file pointer is positioned correctly for the shell to continue.

A *read* or *write* operation specifies the file descriptor and the number of bytes to be transferred. A *read* or *write* starts from the current position of the file pointer. To facilitate direct access it is necessary to position the file pointer at the appropriate byte in the file. This is done with the *seek* system call, which sets the file pointer to the required position in the file.

Questions for review

(i) What functions do the following have?
 (a) directory
 (b) i-node
 (c) i-list
 (d) i-number
 (e) i-node table
(ii) Since all files are essentially sequential files, how is direct access accomplished?

Device independence

Unix brings about ease of use and device independence by means of special files and **device drivers**. Each I/O device is made available to a user by making it appear to be a file. The actual communication with the physical device is brought about by the device driver, which supervises the transmission of data between primary storage and the peripheral device.

The I/O subsystem of an operating system poses two problems that Unix attempts to minimize. First, peripheral devices vary in their operating characteristics — a magnetic tape drive is obviously different from a disk drive — and so each type requires different low-level techniques for access. Secondly, the peripheral devices themselves can be constantly rearranged; the physical connections are changed, and the I/O subsystem needs modification.

Unix helps to overcome these two problems by using a set of tables to allow the kernel to communicate with the software modules, the device drivers, that control the peripheral devices. Normally Unix is delivered with device drivers for the more common peripherals. The tables are the system's source of information about the system's configuration, and they are connected to the device drivers. Consequently, a subsequent change in the configuration will involve altering the tables and the writing of software for any particular new type of peripheral device.

There are, in fact, two tables of interest, one for the block I/O subsystem, **bdevsw**, and one for the character I/O subsystem, **cdevsw**. The block subsystem is used for devices that can support block addressing (in blocks of 512 bytes), and the character system is used for other devices. In effect, the two subsystems are disk-like and terminal-like respectively.

Block-structured I/O

The block subsystem regards a device as having up to any number of addressable blocks; the device driver must then emulate this idea on a real physical device. The block subsystem allows the kernel to make full use of buffering techniques.

Normally, buffers are not permanently assigned to a particular user, but are allocated as required to a process from a pool. A request by a process for a particular block of data entails a search of those blocks currently resident in buffers belonging to that process. If it is found, then no data transfer (physical I/O) need take place.

Conversely, a block write is first a write into a buffer. The physical transfer will take place only when all buffers are full and buffer space is required. If the block is required again before this time, then no transfer will take place. Read-ahead techniques usually keep the buffers filled and writing is often delayed. This cuts down on physical I/O. However, unexpected system crashes may result in there being data in the buffers that have not been transferred physically even though the process generating those data has completed. There exists a system function which periodically will flush all the buffers.

Character-oriented I/O

Character-type I/O is carried out by creating a queue of blocks of characters to be processed, e.g. 14 characters per block for terminals. The queue is created from a storage pool of character blocks and the block is returned to the storage pool when the characters are actually transferred. The queue is built up until a fixed number of characters are on the queue, or, in the case of terminals, a line is complete.

Terminal I/O differs from other character I/O in that some preprocessing of the queue may be necessary, e.g. performing erase editing to incorporate changes the user has made during the time he or she has entered the line, so that the transferred line is the *corrected* line of data intended by the user rather than the 'raw' line of data with correction characters such as backspace imbedded.

Figure 10.9 shows how special files and device drivers are connected: i-nodes are associated with special files, just as with ordinary files and directory files. However, the information in a special file i-node differs from that in ordinary and directory files. Devices are identified by a major device number, a minor device number and a class (block or character) and this information is stored in the i-node. The major device number is used as an index into either the character type table *cdevsw* or the block

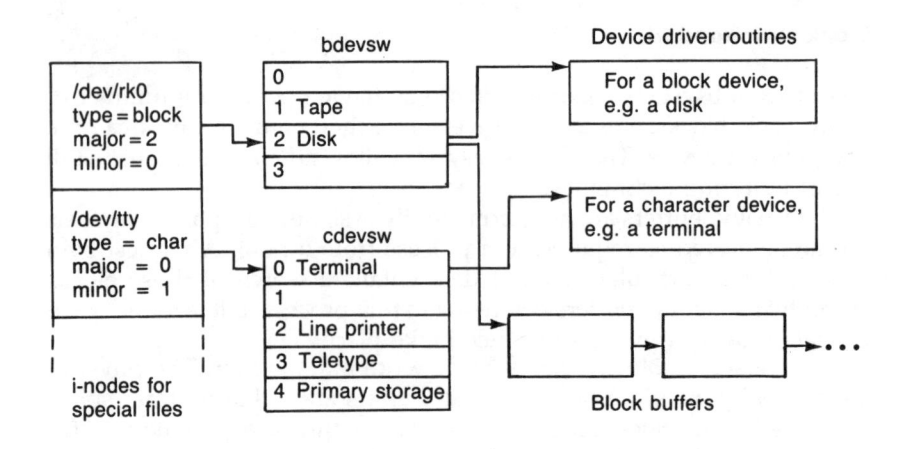

```
                        bdevsw           Device driver routines
/dev/rk0          ┌──────────────┐    ┌──────────────────────┐
type = block      │ 0            │───▶│ For a block device,  │
major = 2         │ 1  Tape      │    │ e.g. a disk          │
minor = 0         │ 2  Disk      │    └──────────────────────┘
                  │ 3            │
                  └──────────────┘
/dev/tty                               ┌──────────────────────┐
type  = char          cdevsw           │ For a character device,│
major = 0         ┌──────────────┐     │ e.g. a terminal      │
minor = 1         │ 0  Terminal  │────▶└──────────────────────┘
                  │ 1            │
                  │ 2  Line printer│
                  │ 3  Teletype  │
i-nodes for       │ 4  Primary storage│     Block buffers
special files     └──────────────┘
```

Figure 10.9 The kernel's data structures for accessing I/O devices

type table *bdevsw*. Usually, the minor device number identifies one of several identical physical devices.

The entry in the *cdevsw table* defines the addresses of the driver routines for communicating with a character device, e.g., open, close, read, write. Similarly, the entry in the *bdevsw table* is used to connect I/O routines for block devices with the kernel. There is also a routine for optimizing block reads and writes for block devices. In addition the table contains a pointer which is used to access the buffers for that device.

Questions for review

(i) Unix claims to have a high degree of device independence. How does this affect:
   (a) the user?
   (b) the person who must manage the overall system?
(ii) What two differences in the way that the data are processed affect the buffer sizes for character and block input/output?

10.4 SHELL PROGRAMMING

In Section 10.1 you saw how a user communicates with Unix using the shell as a command language interpreter. Normally, a programmer will write programs in a suitable language and contact with the shell can be limited to the sort of communication described earlier. However, the shell can be used as a programming language itself, the Unix commands being connected together not only by using pipes and filters, but by the use of the usual high-level programming language constructs. For example, do—while loops and parameter passing are two of the features of the shell when used as a programming language.

Thus the shell is a very important and very powerful system utility. There is far more to the shell than I can describe here.

To apply a command such as *ls* to more than one directory, the use of a loop is required.

```
for i
   do
   ls -1 $i | grep '^d'
   done
```

Here the *for* loop means that the body of the loop is executed for each of the parameters.

As a precaution a user might wish to test whether any parameters have been passed. Hence

```
if test $# = 0
then lsdir
else
   for i
      do
      ls -1 $i | grep '^d'
      done
fi
```

The test $# tests the number of parameters passed; if this is zero then the current directory is searched. If it is non-zero then the directories named as arguments are searched.

This small shell program should give you some idea of what can be done. When a programmer should use the shell rather than writing a program in assembler or a high-level language is not always obvious. If a normal programming language can be used for a problem, then the execution speed penalty of the shell high-level features may favor the use of the programming language. However, if the application involves operations that are standard Unix commands, then the shell might be more appropriate.

Another consideration concerns the Unix idea of all data being lines of text. If data are in this form, then the shell may handle them. If the data are numbers, then handling them may be difficult for the shell and a high-level language may be more suitable.

There are several features of Unix that I have not described; space precludes a full description of the system. However, you have seen how Unix encourages programmers to think of using software tools and standard programs to perform a specific task, linked together to perform a more complex task. Unix provides many utility programs for this purpose and is different from some other operating systems in that these programs are independent of the underlying operating system.

10.5 THE UNIX KERNEL

A Unix kernel consists of about ten thousand lines of C code and a thousand lines of assembler code. The kernel is hidden from the user by the shell program so that users perceive a virtual computer whose evident characteristics are those of the shell. *Virtual* in this sense means that the computer as it appears to its users is the computer as its operating system makes it appear, a conceptual machine. In the case of Unix it is done by enclosing the kernel within the shell, while the kernel itself hides the underlying computer rather as scenery and lighting hide the reality of a stage from a play's audience. There can be many different versions of the shell, each presenting its own virtual computer to the user.

The machine-specific part of the Unix system is comparatively small, and it is this that makes Unix a relatively easy system to move to other, dissimilar, computers, these few programs being all that are necessary to recode for a new computer.

The kernel is responsible for two major areas: the management of processes and the management of devices, including files. The former involves the allocation and scheduling of resources and servicing of requests made by processes; the latter is concerned with the supervision

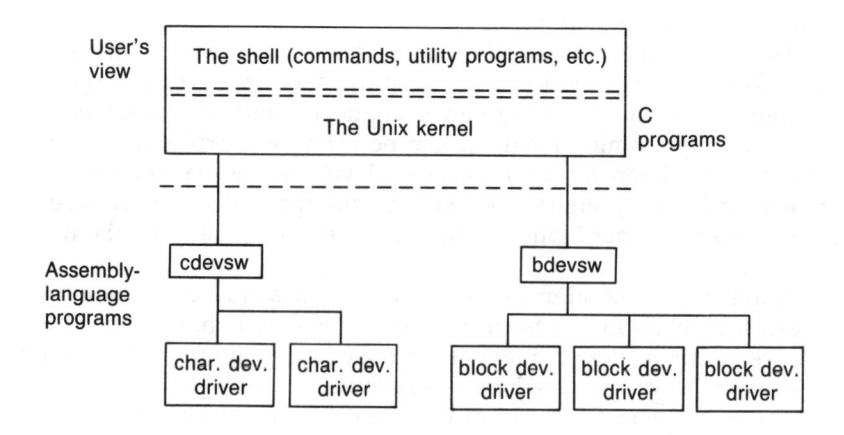

Figure 10.10 The structure of Unix

of the movement of data between primary storage and the various types of secondary storage. One of the achievements of Unix is that although it is available on several different types of computer, the process management sections of the kernel are very similar *and hence machine independent*. However, the device management section includes code for each type of peripheral device, so that adding a new type of peripheral device entails writing new code. To move the system to a new type of computer usually means a completely new device management section, as computers vary greatly in their treatment of peripheral devices. This section of the operating system is therefore *machine dependent*, although this has no effect on users of the system.

Process management

A process, remember, can be considered as a program in a state of execution. A program may exist on disk or in primary storage, but it is only when a program is executed that a process is created. Usually, there is more than one process associated with a particular program; for example, if there is to be any input or output to or from the program, then a further process will be generated. Unix is a multiprogramming system so there will be several programs executing simultaneously, each having processes associated with it. In addition, the kernel itself is a program and therefore generates processes.

For the kernel to look after a process, it must be given some information about the process. Unix uses two data structures used to store such information, the **process table** and the **user structure** (also called the **per process data area** (**PPDA**)). See *process control block* in Chapter 2.

When a process is created, details are entered in the process table, which is permanently resident in primary storage. The information stored includes the identifier for the process (an integer), the indentifier of the user (user ID), the size of the process and where the process is currently residing (in primary storage or swapped out).

When a process is in primary storage it has with it its user structure. In this structure is stored such information as saved registers (when the process is blocked), user IDs for file access and directory information. Figure 10.11 below shows that the process table and the user structure are under control of the kernel, in the kernel's address space, and are not accessible by user programs.

The user data region is where the user's program is stored during execution. In practice, both the user structure and the user data region are swapped in together and form a contiguous part of storage – the **process image**.

A user process may also execute from **read-only code** (also called

```
                Process table
                ┌──────────────┐
                │              │
                ├──────────────┤
                │active process│
                └──────────────┘
```

```
                                             Resident
─ ─ ─ ─ ─ ─ ─ ─ ─ ─ ─ ─ ─ ─ ─ ─ ─ ─ ─ ─ ─ ─ ─ ─ ─ ─ ─
                                             Swappable
```

```
  ┌──────────────────────┐         ┌──────────────────────┐
  │ Per process data     │         │ User data region     │
  │ area (user structure)│         │ (data and instructions)│
  └──────────────────────┘         └──────────────────────┘
```

          Kernel address | User address
          space | space

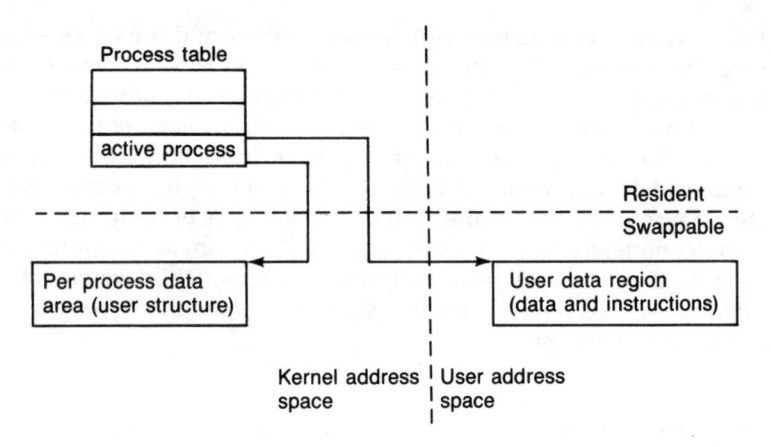

Figure 10.11 The data structures for managing ordinary processes

re-entrant code and described in Chapter 3). A program is read-only code if it can never be modified during execution. It may thus be executed simultaneously by more than one user. Unix sets up programs so that instructions and data are in separate areas of primary storage. Read-only code need not be copied to disk when a process is swapped because, being read-only, it cannot have changed. Also, in the case of programs like the editor, there is no need for each user to have a copy of the program.

To deal with the situation of shared read-only code, referred to by Unix as **pure text**, another table is used, the text table, which is linked to the process table. The process table uses the text table to access a separate text region containing pure text. If several processes are using the same piece of pure text, the editor for example, then each process table entry will have a pointer to the approximate entry in the text table.

```
┌─────────────────────────┐
│                         │
│      User stack         │
│                         │
├─────────────────────────┤
│                         │
│                         │
│   User data and code    │
│                         │
│                         │
├─────────────────────────┤
│                         │
│   Per process data area │
│   (user structure)      │
└─────────────────────────┘
```

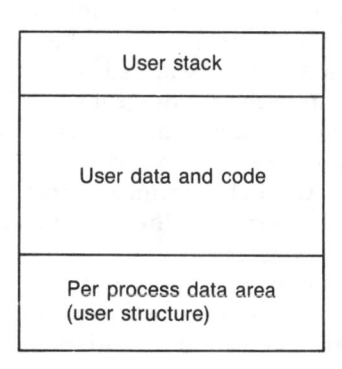

Figure 10.12 The process image

Unix

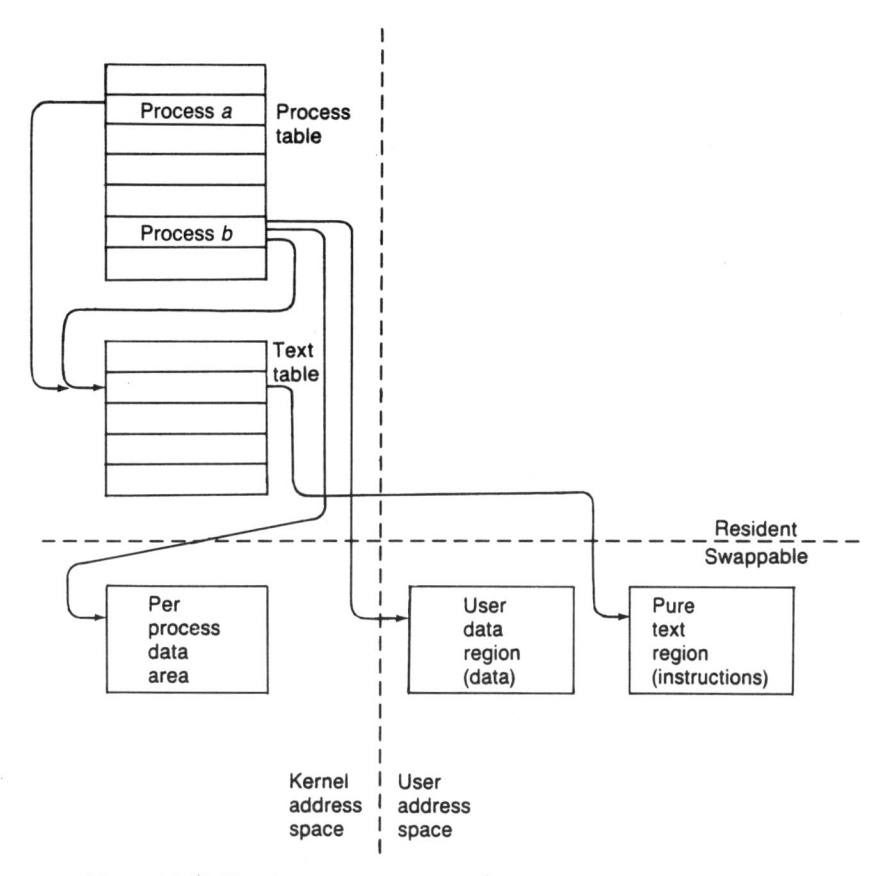

Figure 10.13 The data structures for managing processes with pure text

The information stored on the text table entry includes the number of pointers from the process table that are referring to it, i.e. the number of processes using it. When this number is reduced to zero, that part of the pure text space can be released and allocated to another process.

In Figure 10.13 you can see that process *a* and process *b* each has a pointer into the same entry in the text table; processes *a* and *b* are both using the same piece of pure text. The other pointers associated with process *a* are not shown.

Question for review

In Part I the idea of a process control block is introduced. What is the equivalent of a process control block in Unix?

Question for discussion

What purposes are served by having separate data structures for process id and such items of data as saved registers? What implications would there be for a plan to combine such data into a single data structure?

User mode and kernel mode

A process will execute instructions in the user program until some system facility is required or an outside event, such as a clock interrupt, occurs. Up to that point the process is said to be in **user mode**; after the event the process switches to **kernel mode**.

Put differently, when the computer is executing instructions in a user process, then the computer is in *user mode*. If a switch to execute instructions in the kernel has been made, then the computer is in *kernel mode*. When the execution of instructions in the kernel is complete another process will resume and the computer will return to user mode. This may not occur immediately as other processes may be selected for running.

One of the causes of a switch to kernel mode is the interrupt generated by the system clock. On servicing the interrupt the priority of the current process is re-evaluated by the kernel and the process may be suspended or blocked. (The clock 'ticks' at a rate of 50 or 60 times a second, depending on the frequency of the local electricity supply. A 'tick' is not, however, the same as a quantum, and it is the expiry of the quantum which results in an interrupt. In early versions of Unix a quantum was equal to one second; from version 4.2 BSD (Berkeley Software Distribution) a quantum has been a tenth of a second.)

Another cause is a request for one of the system calls mentioned earlier, such as an I/O operation, which usually means the suspension or blocking of the calling process while the I/O is dealt with. Both of these mechanisms result in the sharing of processor time amongst several processes.

The switch between user and kernel modes due to, for example, a clock interrupt, are Unix's manifestation of context switching. The system *must suspend* the active process (change its state from running to blocked) either because the active process has initiated such an action through a system call such as an I/O request or because the low-level scheduler requires it.

The operating system must first see that the active process is suspended, and that it is marked as suspended; that the current PC (program counter) is saved on a stack; that other vital process data (such as the contents of registers) are saved; and finally that the new PC (address of the next instruction which will be fetched and executed by the processor) associated with the processing of the I/O request is placed into the current

PC. The processor then fetches the instruction at the address pointed to by the PC and executes it. This must be reversed to restore the suspended process when the I/O request has been completed by the system.

Questions for review

(i) What principle underlies the switch between user and kernel modes?
(ii) Why does Unix's kernel evaluate a process's priority on servicing an interrupt?

Process creation

When the user communicates with Unix using the shell there is a process associated with the shell that interprets commands. When the user types a command a new process must be created that is associated with the program invoked by the command. Unix uses two system calls *exec* and *fork* to create new processes.

If a process requires the execution of another program, then a system call *exec* (*file*) is issued to execute *file*, where *file* contains an executable program. A copy of *file* then overlays the current process and assumes the process identifier (pid — see below) of the overlaid process. This is a one-for-one replacement so the number of active processes does not increase. *Exec* can be used to chain processes together serially, but one process must terminate before another can begin. To get around this the system needs a mechanism for increasing the number of processes and allowing one process to wait for the completion of others.

The *fork* system call, used in conjunction with the *wait* system call, fills this purpose. Upon a process calling *fork*, a copy of the calling process is made. The original is called the *parent* and the new process is called the *child*. When started, each process is allocated a **process identity** (in Unix called the pid). This is the integer which uniquely identifies any process. When forking the pid of the child is returned to the parent. The child is returned the value zero. This is how the two otherwise identical copies of the program can be identified as the parent or the child.

The most common use of *fork* is for it to be followed by an *exec* in the child process, thus overlaying the child process with a new program. This way one process produces another to do some specific task. If it is required that the parent process should wait for the child process to terminate before it can resume, then another primitive, *wait*, is used by the parent process. In this case the child process will communicate to the parent that it has terminated and the parent will then proceed.

The only difference between the two is that each knows whether it is the original (the parent) or the copy (the child) and they have different process identifiers. Now two identical processes are running.

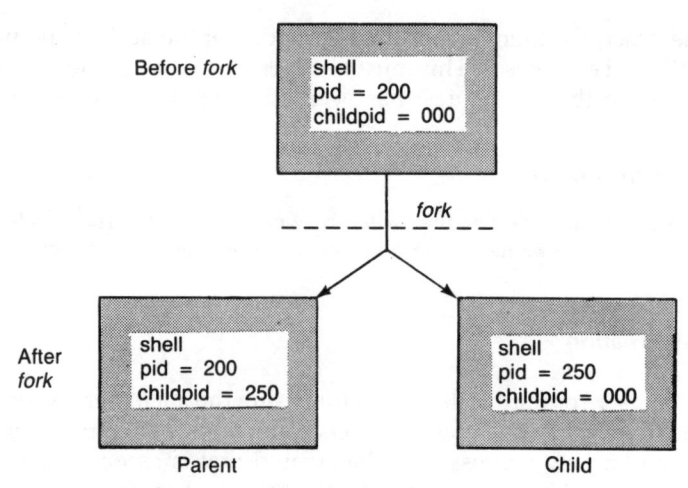

```
                Before fork    ┌─────────────────┐
                               │ shell           │
                               │ pid = 200       │
                               │ childpid = 000  │
                               └─────────────────┘
                                        │
                                       fork
                               - - - - -┼- - - - -
                                    ↙       ↘
        ┌─────────────────┐                   ┌─────────────────┐
 After  │ shell           │                   │ shell           │
 fork   │ pid = 200       │                   │ pid = 250       │
        │ childpid = 250  │                   │ childpid = 000  │
        └─────────────────┘                   └─────────────────┘
              Parent                                 Child
```

Figure 10.14 The *fork* system call

The parent process now *waits* until the child finishes (the parent issues a *wait* call) while the child shell *exec*utes a new program, which in the illustration (Figure 10.15) is *date*. The *date* program overlays the child copy of the shell, thus becoming the child process, as the *exec does not change the process identifier of the child*. The successor process is now executed.

When the *date* process terminates, it *exits* and dies. Once the child dies, the waiting parent wakes up. It does a bit of tidying up and then gives the next prompt.

Process switching

A process is interrupted for one of two reasons: (i) its time slice is up — it has not finished, so it is an immediate candidate for consideration on the next round of scheduling, (ii) it cannot continue, perhaps because of an I/O request, i.e. it is blocked.

The process is suspended and, in Unix terminology, it goes to sleep. Before it does this, arrangements must be made for it to be awakened

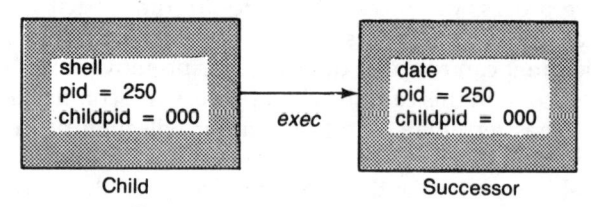

```
    ┌─────────────────┐              ┌─────────────────┐
    │ shell           │              │ date            │
    │ pid = 250       │   ──────→    │ pid = 250       │
    │ childpid = 000  │    exec      │ childpid = 000  │
    └─────────────────┘              └─────────────────┘
          Child                           Successor
```

Figure 10.15 The *exec* system call

as explained above. It is waiting for an event to take place and the event it awaits is noted in the process table. If the event never happens, the process never wakes up.

Once a process is suspended or terminated another process must be selected to run next. The low-level scheduler will select a process from those in primary storage. There may be processes which are ready, according to their process table status, but are not currently in primary storage. Some mechanism is therefore required to enable these runnable processes, currently on secondary storage, to be brought into primary storage to be given the chance to run. This is the function of the **swapper**.

The swapper looks for the processes and tries to bring them into primary storage by swapping them with processes in primary storage that are currently suspended. The process with the longest secondary storage residence time is normally swapped in. The process to be swapped out is chosen according to the event that it is waiting for, how long it has been in primary storage and also by its size.*

Priorities

Priorities for processes are determined dynamically, so that, for example, processes that have already used a lot of execution time have a lower priority than processes that have so far used little. Processes that have not been executing, such as those waiting for I/O and those that have just been swapped in, consequently have relatively high priorities.

The result of this is that **I/O bound** processes, those with a large amount of I/O (e.g. interactive programs), tend to run until they need to wait for the I/O. Processes with large amounts of computation (processor bound) then fill the gaps created. The user with a great deal of interactive work should then get a good response from the system.

Question for review

Which of the scheduling algorithms described in Section 3.7 is Unix using? Defend your answer.

Question for discussion

It is theoretically possible for the swapper to bring in a process to primary storage,

---

*Earlier versions of Unix, for example those that were pre-3 BSD, used swapping exclusively. Later versions use demand-paged virtual storage management. I shall concentrate on the earlier versions here, as paged systems are described in detail in the case studies in Chapters 12 and 13.

but for the process to be swapped out before it gets a chance to run. Why might this happen?

10.6 PRIMARY STORAGE

Every time a system call *fork* is executed, the new process (child) requires space in primary storage. Parent processes and their children *do not share a single area of primary storage*. Thus each child process must be allocated its own space. (I shall concentrate in this decription on those versions of Unix which do not use virtual storage management techniques.)

This is done in Unix using a first-fit strategy. Having, in a sense, been born, the child usually immediately executes a system call *exec (file)* in order to overlay itself with new code for execution. There is no guarantee that the file of code thus invoked will be the same size as, or smaller than, the child it is to overlay. Hence the child can 'grow' by this means, and space to accommodate that growth must be found by the operating system. The growing process thus requests more storage. The system (using first-fit) then gives the process a *new* allocation of storage large enough to hold the expanded process. The entire contents of the old storage locations are copied to this new allocation and the old area is then freed.

If the process seeks to grow when there is insufficient free primary storage available, then sufficient secondary storage is allocated (also using first-fit). A separate area on secondary storage is selected for swapped out processes and is known as the **swap area**. The process is swapped out to secondary storage, and subsequently will be swapped back in when sufficient free primary storage becomes available.

Background processing

When a user logs in, the shell reads the commands that the user enters at the terminal and then carries them out. The user gets a fresh copy of the shell. Most of the commands are totally independent of the shell. The shell starts them running, giving them their arguments, then waits for them to finish. Then it gives the user the next prompt sign.

It is possible for a single user to run more than one process at a time and not have the parent shell wait for the child. This is useful if one wishes to execute several commands that take a long time.

To do this, the user ends the command line with & (ampersand). The ampersand causes the user's copy of the shell not to wait for the child command to execute. When a **background command** is started with &,

the shell returns the process identifier (pid) of that process. That number can then be used to identify the process or to terminate it.

Questions for review

(i) What steps does Unix take to ensure sufficient space for a growing child?
(ii) Briefly describe background processing.

10.7 COMMUNICATION BETWEEN PROCESSES

You have seen above that one process can generate another process and then wait for the termination of the generated process. Therefore some method of communicating between processes is required. At its simplest a child needs to let its parent know that it has finished, whether successfully or not. Communication between processes varies according to whether the process is in kernel or in user mode.

User mode

The simplest form of communication between processes is by using the *exit* call when a process successfully terminates. Such an *exit* can be explicit, or there is an implied *exit* in the process which terminates by executing the last line of its code. A parent process waiting for the event is informed by the *exit* call in the child that the child process has terminated.

Another form of communication is by means of a *signal* — a form of software interrupt. Signals are used to inform a process that an error has occurred; this will usually mean the termination of the process. Examples are illegal instructions or a terminal interrupt initiated by the user. However, it is possible for a process to be told to ignore any signal. The shell process ignores an *interrupt* signal from the terminal keyboard. If the *shell* could be interrupted in this way, the user would be logged off immediately.

A signal to a process is stored in the process table entry for this process and is not referred to until the process is next reloaded to be run. Hence this cannot be considered as a form of instantaneous communication.

Kernel mode

There is only one kernel process being executed at any one time. (There is of course only one process *ever* being *executed* at any time in a single processor system.) When a kernel process is suspended the reason for its suspension is stored in the process table, coded as an integer. This integer then represents an event for which the process is waiting before it can resume. The event could be the termination of a child process or the release of primary storage, if the process was waiting for extra space.

Once an event takes place a *wakeup* procedure is called and the process table is searched for a process waiting for that particular event. If one is found that process is awakened and becomes a candidate for execution. An event may wake up more than one process if several are waiting for the same event to occur. If no process waits for that event, then the event's occurrence will have no effect. Thus the event-wait mechanism is very simple. Because of its simplicity little information can be transferred. In the case of processes waiting for more storage for example, all processes awaiting that event would wake as no information about the *quantity* of primary storage now available can be transferred.

Question for discussion

Given the above methods of process communication, why is Unix not appropriate for a real-time control system?

10.8 AN EVALUATION OF UNIX

Security

Security is the ability to protect against unwanted access to or destruction of data and against denial of service to other users, for example, by causing a crash. Unix was designed for a rather open environment. As a result, there are several security problems. Most versions do not check for over-consumption of certain resources, such as file space, total number of files, and number of processes. These things do not cause a crash, but can make the system unusable for a time.

It is relatively easy to write a user program that interprets the contents of a physical disk drive as a file system volume. Unless the special file referring to the disk is protected, the files on it can be accessed in spite of their protection modes.

Questions for discussion

Listed below are some ways in which a person intent on penetrating an operating system might go about doing so. Evaluate which are easily possible under Unix and which would be more difficult. Assume none are truly impossible.

Unix 239

(i) Modify parameters with one process which another process has already validated but not yet used.
(ii) Search the computer system in a general way, looking for information.
(iii) Attempt to masquerade as the systems manager or system programmer.
(iv) You as an authorized user seek to crash the system in order to disrupt processing for a time.

Structural weaknesses

Unix cannot be used easily as a real-time system because its structure makes it impossible to lock a process in primary storage to guarantee rapid response to events. Nor can it be connected directly to I/O devices. MERT, a real-time system which in a sense is a generalization of Unix, does allow these operations. One of its standard processes is a Unix simulator, making ordinary Unix software available.

In Unix, there is no generalized inter-process communication, nor are there semaphores.

Primary storage is not shared between processes (with the exception of the read-only program text). There is a requirement, however, for better inter-process communication (both by means of messages and by sharing primary storage). For example, the effective use of database requires a high degree of inter-process communication and data sharing.

Question for review

What limitations in the standard Unix system precludes generalized inter-process communications?

Question for discussion

In Section 3.1, IBM's use of microcode to provide a uniform assembler/machine language for dissimilar architectures (to make a family of computers) is mentioned. Evaluate a recommendation made by Ritchie and Thompson [1] that all operating systems '... should be written in a high-level language that encourages portability' based on consideration of a 'portable' low-level language.

Language dependencies

There is a strong link between the C language and Unix. Although its designers claim C is a structured language, it has more of the flavor of a high-level assembler. C has a very distinct view of how the underlying machine looks. To some extent this has prevented programs written in C from being as efficient on some machines as its designers might have wanted. As a language C is ideal for expert programmers working in small groups. C is not well suited to average programmers as it encourages tricky techniques that can produce unreadable and unmaintainable code.

The language itself is not as portable as is claimed by its designers. Some basic features of the language definition rely on the underlying machine for which the compiler is generating code, e.g. byte-addressing as opposed to word-addressing. Because it relies on programmer know-how to produce efficient code rather than on a good compiler, C has a long learning curve.

Question for discussion

What are the different approaches to diverse architectures taken by IBM, the UCSD p-System and Unix? What problems does each approach have? What advantages does each approach provide?

Files

The designers recognized the fact that most files are quite small and so for reasons of efficiency they decided to make use of this fact when designing the file system and some utilities. Designing a file system around this small file observation occurs quite often in operating-system file-system design and for the most part it is invisible to the user, the transition from small to large files being handled by the system.

The Unix file system considers files to be a stream of bytes. This has the advantage that text files and binary files are held in an ideal form. However, although database users form a large proportion of computer users, Unix does not provide any form of intrinsic database structure. This means that database system designers have to become involved with operating-systems internals in order to provide efficient database tools for a Unix system. One of the most serious drawbacks in this area is file locking. The ability to lock a file when updating it in order to prevent access is crucial to database systems. Many systems houses have implemented such a feature but it is not yet standard in Unix.

Storage management

From the user's point of view, the primary storage allocation scheme (particularly in the pre-virtual storage management versions) is very primitive. The maximum amount of space that a program may use is decided at program start-up time, usually by a constant fixed by the system. Most utilities are configured to a maximum likely value; an attempt to exceed this limit will cause the program to fail. For utilities that could potentially use a large amount of memory this is a major problem. There is no true dynamic allocation and re-allocation of space. It is thus common to find a utility existing in two versions.

For example, *diff* is a utility for finding the differences between two files. When an attempt is made to resynchronize after a difference is found it is possible to use a large amount of primary storage. For comparison of large files a utility called *bigdiff* is supplied; this is identical to *diff* with the exception that it has a larger space allocation.

Questions for discussion

(i) What problems might occur if the utility program with the larger space allocation were *always* used because a user was unsure which to choose?
(ii) What drawbacks are there to the practice of having two versions of such programs?

Secondary storage

At the systems level, the interface of peripheral devices is very clean. However, a consequence of Unix's design is that all users have access to the device driver ports. The smooth running of the system demands that users use these devices through the standard utilities only. This means that, on the whole, security is poor. An errant user can write to any terminal and directly to disks and line printers. It is even possible to write a command file to read what other people are entering on their terminals without their being aware of it, using the standard utilities.

User interface

That silence is golden is a basic tenet of Unix design. No messages are displayed unless things go wrong and even then they are very cryptic. Things run smoothly when programs, scripts and utilities are debugged and working.

The command names, formats and syntax have no relationship to their function. There is no support for truly novice users. This silence can appear as unfriendly to many people. To be able to use the full power of Unix, utilities cannot display user information. A channel is supplied for standard input, standard output and error messages, but there is no separate channel for user messages. Consequently any job running in the background may access the user terminal, with messages interfering with the user's interactive session.

Resource sharing

The operating-system control structures have a tree form. When users log on to the system a process is started. This process has the program *init* as its parent. *Init* has all logged-on users as children. When a user starts one or more jobs running they become children of the user and so on down. Within this tree structure there is only a limited form of communication up and down the tree, parent to child and child to parent. There is no easily accessible form of interprocess communication. Two running programs can only communicate with each other via temporary files or if they know each other's process numbers. Process numbers are allocated sequentially, starting at one on system start-up. A process can find its own number but because this value is different at every invocation two processes which are not parent and child cannot use it for communications.

In any computer installation where a range of users are going to be using the system some form of resource sharing is needed. Resources that are usually allocated are disk space, processor time (by the day or week), connect time and so on. Unix has none of these facilities. It grew up in an environment in which the number of people using a computer was low. This lack of control means that it is possible for a user to fill up an entire disk or to start several background tasks running, each using a portion of process time, thus excluding other users to a greater or lesser degree. For this reason Unix users rely on good will and well-behaved colleagues. It is quite common for systems to be accidentally disrupted when new users start using Unix, simply because they make mistakes.

The Unix view of hierarchic files and their protection is limited. The hierarchy is concerned solely with the cataloging of files: grouping files together for a particular purpose. It is not possible to form groups of users or groups of files within the hierarchy for access permission purposes. Systems which do this (e.g. GEORGE3, MULTICS) are much more powerful but are correspondingly more difficult to implement.

Software tools and programming

The idea of using Unix utility programs as software tools to produce a larger piece of software has been referred to in this chapter as one of the good points of the Unix system. A contrary view is that writing software in this way can be detrimental to the production of a good final working version. A working piece of software may be quickly developed using this approach, perhaps for prototyping or testing purposes, and then become the *de facto* final version. A version which more closely meets the original specification should be produced from the analysis of the problem and should not be affected by the particular software tools that Unix provides. There is a strong tendency for the prototype piece of software to become the finished product.

While it may be quicker to use the tools provided this will not always result in the most efficient software; some of the utility programs are too general-purpose. This results in a proliferation of flags for utilities, with no systematic specification for such flags. Maintenance of software incorporating Unix tools is generally difficult — it is not possible to modify a few lines in a program when the basic unit is a Unix utility.

Conclusions

Hence there are situations in which Unix is not appropriate, and there are criticisms of the Unix environment for producing software. There are problems in the real world connected with resilience, security, process communication and segmented/paged system architectures. Unix does not address itself to these problems and hence is a simpler system than the more complex systems provided by many major manufacturers. It is not a system for a large data processing environment. However, Unix is extending itself downwards to the 16-bit microcomputer market and, although its performance on a small computer degenerates considerably as the number of users increases, it is perhaps in this area that future developments will take place.

In conclusion one can say that Unix is a good tool for programmers or software designers working in small groups. It has none of the features necessary for managing large installations, those making heavy use of database or for groups of users not knowledgeable in computing.

Some interesting offshoots

Having said that Unix is not suitable for novices in computing, it should be noted that its history lent itself to Unix as an *object* of study in the universities. This was due to the fact that, until version 7 was released, the source code for the Unix operating system was widely available and could be studied on a detailed basis.

The fact that the source code for AT & T's standard Unix is no longer available means that students are unable to study recent versions because, in the eyes of AT & T, Unix is a product to market and as such ought to remain a 'trade secret'. But by the mid-1980s a number of computer-science organizations were involved with Unix-based work and produced

Unix versions. One such was the University of California at Berkeley. I have referred to their versions 3 BSD and 4.2 BSD (BSD stands for Berkeley Software Distribution). [2]

Another approach was taken by Andrew Tanenbaum at the Vrije Universiteit in Amsterdam. He has written a Unix look-alike operating system called Minix which runs on IBM PCs, PC-clones or a PC simulator. Tanenbaum wrote with the express purpose of providing each student with a source-code copy of the software on either a microcomputer or a time-shared computer so that the student can modify, compile and test parts of the system. Even when this is not desirable, students can read and learn from the Minix source code. [3]

REFERENCES

[1] Ritchie, D.M. and Thompson, K. (1978) 'The UNIX [sic] Time-sharing System', *Bell Systems Technical Journal*, **57**(6), pp. 1905–29.
[2] Peterson, J.L. and Silberschatz, A. (1985) *Operating System Concepts*, 2nd edn, Addison-Wesley, Reading, Massachussetts, pp. 507–10.
[3] Tanenbaum, A.S. (1987) *Operating Systems: Design and Implementation*, Prentice-Hall, Englewood Cliffs, New Jersey, pp. xiii–xvi.

GENERAL REFERENCES

Bell Telephone Laboratories: Unix Time-Sharing System (1983) *Unix Programmer's Manual*, vols. 1 and 2, Holt, Reinehart & Winston, New York.
Christian, K. (1983) *The Unix Operating System*, John Wiley, New York.
Bell System Technical Journal (1978) **57**(6), July–August.

FURTHER READING

AT&T Bell Laboratories (publishers) (October, 1984) *Computing Science and Systems*, **63**(8), Part 2, 1571–910. This journal replaced the *Bell System Technical Journal*. The issue mentioned devoted itself to Unix and is worth reading.
Banahan, M. and Rutter, A. (1982) *UNIX – The Book*, Sigma Technical Press, distributed by John Wiley, New York. This book contains a good description of Unix and its uses.
Bell System Technical Journal (1978), **57**(6) (July–August). This entire issue was devoted to papers on Unix and contains a wealth of information.

Bourne, S.R. (1983) *The UNIX System*, Addison-Wesley, Reading, Massachussetts. This book makes clear the close relationship between the C language and the Unix system and describes everything from simple commands to systems programming, document preparation and data manipulation tools.

Bugden, D. (1985) *Making Use of UNIX*, Edward Arnold, London. A good book for users of Unix who are anxious to get the best from the system.

Christian, K. (1983) *The Unix Operating System*, John Wiley, New York. This is probably the best book currently available on Unix.

Deitel, H.M. (1984) *An Introduction to Operating Systems*, Addison-Wesley, Reading, Massachussetts. Chapter 18 is a case study of Unix.

Norman, D.A. (1981) 'The trouble with Unix', *Datamation*, November, 139–50. This is a very readable criticism of Unix, coupled with a laudable defense of the system.

Peterson, J.L. and Silberschatz, A. (1985) *Operating System Concepts*, 2nd edn, Addison-Wesley, Reading, Massachussetts. Chapter 14 is a case study of the Unix operating system.

Sylvester, P.P. (1984) *The Unix System Guidebook*, Springer-Verlag, Berlin. This book, while not as comprehensive as Christian (1983), is a good description and explains some of the Unix ideas in a sufficiently different way to make it worth reading.

Tanenbaum, A.S. (1987) *Operating Systems: Design and Implementation*, Prentice-Hall, Englewood Cliffs, New Jersey. This book described the Minix operating system, which looks, from the user's point of view, like Unix. It contains an introduction to the C language, a user's guide, an implementor's guide, an introduction to the IBM PC, and complete source code listings for the system, as well as considerable general teaching material on operating systems. It describes how to obtain a copy of the Minix system from Prentice-Hall.

CHAPTER

11

TPF/II: a high-performance system

In the chapter that follows, I shall talk about TPF/II (for *Transaction Processing Facility*), a special-purpose system quite different from the general-purpose systems discussed so far.

TPF/II is an operating system whose entire structure is dictated by special needs, which I shall describe in a moment. It has undergone considerable development since its first appearance in 1968, but as the functional requirements which the system must meet have remained substantially the same, it has remained close to its origins. On the other hand, the architectures which underlie it have changed radically, but according to a philosophy which can be described as one of maintaining compatibility with earlier architectures while at the same time enhancing function and performance.

TPF/II is a high-performance, real-time, message-driven operating system. **Message-driven** means that its actions are triggered by the arrival of a message which must be answered by a message (this is called a *message pair*, an *interaction* or a *phase*).

Typically, the message which initiates an action is an enquiry from an operator at a remote station, and the response message is that which is returned by the computer system to that operator. Technically, an input message is a string of characters entered at a terminal and terminated by a special end-of-message character.

The response (output message) may contain the information requested by the initiating message, indicate problems encountered (such as science fiction's popular computer response of 'insufficient data'), request further action by the remote operator or simply confirm that the required action has been taken.

Note that a *transaction* can be a collection of messages; the terms are not synonymous. The transaction of reserving a place for a passenger on an airline's system, for example, may mean that the agent must collect several items of data: the passenger's name, telephone number, address,

246

TPF/II: A High-performance System   247

number travelling in party, itinerary, etc., each of which may be entered as a separate message. The agent indicates the completion of a transaction by entering a special 'message' indicating the fact.

The environment in which TPF/II and functionally similar systems operate is one characterized by a large volume of unpredictable initiating messages which individually require very little function or flexibility, where the availability of the environment must be maintained 24 hours a day, where data must be available (online) and current. Due to the 24-hour-a-day online requirement, any system failure or shutdown must be dealt with so as to minimize, to the greatest extent possible, the amount of any down-time. This requires processor redundancy (since all computers must be 'taken down' periodically for maintenance) and, for software and general operations, extremely fast **fallback**, restart and recovery. (*Fallback* is the switch of work to the standby processor.)

Ideally, the user — the remote terminal operator and any customer waiting for the terminal operator's responses — should scarcely be aware of any failure or planned outage (as when one system is switched offline for maintenance and its backup is switched online). This means that such a switch, planned or not, should require no more time than it takes for a few words of conversation to pass between the remote terminal operator and waiting customer — a few seconds at most. Any impact on the system's ability to perform should be truly negligible.

In order to achieve such a high degree of availability and performance, systems such as TPF/II have a number of unusual features: a high degree of hardware, software and (often) data redundancy, use of special techniques to boost performance, and very limited function with related but less critical functions off-loaded to other processors.

In addition, TPF/II's design philosophy has been to include the remote terminal operator as a functioning part of the system — an intelligent component in the overall system. The operator is encouraged, and even required, to be knowledgeable about the application and to make human judgements. At the same time, however, the operator cannot be allowed to make a decision or take an action which can adversely affect the system's ability to perform its functions or which can interfere with any other actions (message pairs and associated system actions). In what follows, I shall show how this is accomplished.

Questions for review

What implications for

(i) load planning and
(ii) scheduling

do you think a message-driven system has?

11.1 HISTORY OF TPF/II

In 1963 [1] an 'experimental' airline passenger name reservation system developed jointly by IBM and American Airlines went live. Its original name was an acronym for Semi-Automatic Business Environment Research or SABER, later changed to SABRE. The system was intended to automate the airline's seat reservations, a function which previously had been primarily a manual one. The system was implemented on an IBM 7090 processor, a second generation computer using disk files and specialized terminals and terminal concentrators. The last two were developed especially for this application.

Some important technical achievements resulted from work in developing SABRE: development of line concentration techniques and of medium- and low-speed data sets (**modems***), the uses and techniques of **front-end processing**, development and improvement of large-capacity, rotating storage media, fast direct-access techniques for data stored on extensive disk files (important in the continuing development of database methods), and the techniques of writing relocatable, re-entrant software (which I described briefly in Chapter 3).

Two similar systems which built on the original experience gained with SABRE were developed by IBM jointly with other airlines: Deltamatic with Delta Airlines using IBM 7074 processors, and Panamac with Pan American Airlines using IBM 7080 processors, both of which went live in 1964. The major differences between the three were the systems' capacities.

The following year IBM began development of a *generalized* airline reservation system using knowledge of the application and new techniques gained from SABRE, Deltamatic and Panamac coupled with System/360 technology. (See Section 3.1 for the impact this technology had on computer architecture and systems design.) The system, PARS (*P*rogrammed *A*irline *R*eservation *S*ystem), would be modular and could be used by an airline of any size. (The three predecessor systems differed primarily in their capacities. To accommodate this difference required different processors and 'custom' implementations.)

PARS was implemented on the System/360 family of processors ranging from the Model 40 (not the smallest member of the family) to the Model 75. Most commonly it was implemented on a System/360 Model 65 coupled with a Large Core Storage unit (LCS), also often known as 'slow core'. The LCS provided an electronic random-access memory extension to the processor's own integral primary storage with slower

---

*A *modem*, short for *mo*dulator-*dem*odulator, translates digital electrical signals to or from analog signals suitable for transmission over a medium such as the telephone system lines. Its function is to convert a signal suitable for digital computer or terminal to a signal the characteristics of which match the requirements of the analog transmission medium.

TPF/II: A High-performance System   249

access times than the latter but faster access than that provided by disk. This served to store frequently accessed records, with less active records stored on disks.

The system included a number of special features: for example purpose-designed CRT terminals with keyboards especially created for the function of airline reservations, modified terminal concentrators and transmission control units, and a special buffer for the storage control unit so as to free the channel for a major part of the access time, thus allowing more accesses.

In 1970–72 the system control functions of PARS and utilities related to them were separated from the airline passenger reservation application, and the control program portion (i.e. the operating system) was desginated ACP (*Airline Control Program*). The application continues to be called PARS. However, now ACP was maintained by IBM, enhanced to provide functional and performance improvements and to support new devices as these became available for attachment to the system. (This enhancement has included the shift to the newer architectures of the System/370, 303x and subsequent descendants such as the 308x and the 3090 which grew out of the System/360 family.) The user, that is the airline, can write its own applications programs for PARS, such as seat assignment, boarding control, and so on.

In the more recent past, ACP has come to provide the fundamental operating system in other environments requiring high-speed response to high-volume message traffic: areas related to airlines such as car rental and hotel room reservation systems, online 24-hour banking and credit authorization applications, and also police work such as rapid identification of reported stolen cars or wanted suspects and the dispatching of police personnel in response to emergency calls. Airlines commonly use ACP to support fare quotation, ticketing, seat assignment, boarding pass production and cargo handling. Thus its name has shifted first to ACP/TPF, the latter standing for Transaction Processing Facility, and then to TPF/II, as it has to suport applications other than PARS.

Question for discussion

What advantages do you think accrue from separating such a special-purpose application as PARS from its underlying operating system? What disadvantages exist?

11.2 FUNCTIONAL REQUIREMENTS

The functional requirements which shaped TPF/II and its predecessors are few.

- The system must serve geographically dispersed centers.
- Data must be online 24 hours a day, seven days a week.
- Data must be accessible by anyone with access to the communications network within a very short time (less than 5 seconds). This is because the terminal operator (*agent* in airline terminology) is dealing with a customer over a telephone with many other customers waiting to be served, or at a counter under the same conditions.
- Updates to data must occur in immediate response to a request to do so. Thus, one agent selling, say, the last four seats on a flight must have the update recording this fact occur immediately in order to prevent another agent elsewhere from selling the same four seats. (*Note:* over-subscribing flights is a matter of policy — an attempt to avoid flying with empty seats which could have been sold — since a portion of the passengers on any flight will possibly not appear to claim the seats they've reserved. It is not a technical problem.)
- The database is very large, as it involves every passenger and the passenger's necessary data (such as name, telephone contact number, credit card number, etc.), an inventory of all flights, all seats available on any flight, all fares, and perhaps ancillary information about hotel reservations, connecting flights, car rental, etc.
- There must be many logical paths to any item of data. For example, an enquiry may be of the form: 'I want to fly from Chicago to Spokane'. A list of flights from Chicago to Spokane with times should result. The enquirer may then say, 'I'd like to reserve two seats on the flight leaving at 9.43 for next Tuesday. Is there a cheap fare available for that flight?'. And then, 'Can I order two vegetarian meals please?'. All such enquiries may require many paths to the same, related or similar items of data.
- If several physical paths to data exist, due to data duplication or the duplication of data transfer paths through the system's configuration, this will avoid degradation of service caused by queues building up at points on the path to any heavily accessed data.

Let me discuss some of the functional requirements in terms of one specific TPF/II system in order to illustrate the more general requirements I have listed above. The figures I use below pertain to Trans World Airlines. These figures were extracted from a case study of TWA's system which appeared in the *Communications of the ACM* in 1984 [2].

- The system has attached to it 11 to 12 thousand communications terminals — worldwide.
- Unlike banks, which often maintain a flow of paper documents in parallel with any electronic processing, the only paper backup for the airline is the passenger's ticket. The airline cannot operate unless the system is available. Thus, TWA works to maintain fully backed-up power systems to avoid **downtime** due to power outages. All data are

TPF/II: A High-performance System   251

kept, online, in duplicate. In 1976 (the last year for which figures were available) the system had 131 incidents of outage, but the estimated losses from such outage in terms of revenue (a highly subjective measure), were considered very small when compared to 1972's 548 outages, where revenue losses were estimated to be nearly 10 times as great. Looked at another way, the system was *scheduled* to be available 98.7 per cent of the total 8784 hours in that year. It was *actually* available 99.85 per cent of the scheduled time. On 270 days there were no system outages, and the mean outage was 6.0 minutes, though one single outage lasted 230 minutes [1, p. 190].

- The system is thus accessible to an individual user 98 per cent of the time, and TWA guarantees travel agents connected to its system an availability of 95 per cent or no payment will be required. A typical daily volume of transactions is 7 million, and at peak times is around 170 transactions per second with maximums of over 200 per second. (Another airline peaks at about 1000 per second.) Average response time is 1.5 seconds, and the airline attempts to guarantee that 90 per cent of transactions will have a response time of no more than 3 seconds.
- The online database contains one to one-and-a-half million passenger records, each consisting of 1.2 to 1.5 kilobytes. Passenger records are not all, but do constitute the bulk, of the system's data. Thus passenger records make up a database of two billion (1 billion = 1 giga-) bytes, fully duplicated. In addition to this is the inventory database. Secondary storage on disk has a capacity of over 45 gigabytes. Using native mode IBM 3350 disk drives with a capacity of 317.5 megabytes each, this would require 142 such disk drives (3350s contain non-removable disk packs) each about the size of a domestic washing machine.
- Reservations are indexed by passenger name, flight number and date (all three being necessary to retrieve a particular reservation) while inventory can be accessed by date, departure time or city.

As you can see, requirements such as TWA's place enormous demands on a system. In the next chapter, I shall discuss how these requirements influence operating-system (and configuration) design and how TPF/II meets these requirements.

Questions for discussion

Physical paths between items of data are established by their adjacency (in serial files), or by the 'translation' of a key to a location either through lookup in an index or by direct equivalence between a function based on the key (or the key itself) and a location.

(i) What do you think is meant by logical path?
(ii) Can you think of a means of establishing such a path?

11.3 MEETING SYSTEM REQUIREMENTS

TPF/II, then, can be described as a high-performance, real-time, message-driven operating system. This last term means that the source of input is remote devices (concentrators, which 'concentrate' input from a number of terminals) and this input is obtained by *polling* these devices. Therefore the occurrence or timing of any specific input is unpredictable.

There are several key factors to be considered in providing service in a high- but unpredictable-input, fast and reliable response environment.

- Certain decisions and functions can be done *either* by the software, or by some other means (including the 'off-loading' of these decisions and functions to the people who operate the terminal). This involves the operating-system designer in determining the relative value of having these decisions made by software versus the relative value of the *time* which would otherwise be devoted to work on those decisions and functions.
- All large computer systems need some flexibility in the matter of **configuration**; that is, the arrangement of the components of the system. Large systems frequently have a need, which the designer of the system must address, to add, change or remove devices. For example, disks may need to be upgraded from a smaller-capacity model to a larger-capacity model, or additional disks may need to be added to the system to accommodate growth in the database. A system's configuration can be part of a process known as **system generation** (**sysgen**), in which the variable portions of the operating system are set for some time to come (often known as a **release**), or more dynamically at initialization: that is, when the system is bootstrapped to begin running. A system will be bootstrapped if, for example, it is shut off during the night because it is not used, or after a power failure. The designer must decide whether the flexibility of configuration at initialization is worth the extra time it will take. In the case of TPF/II, where every emphasis is placed on limiting *any* outage to as small a minimum as possible, configuration takes place only at sysgen time. This allows very fast and simple restart. The restart procedure and the procedure required to switch from a primary system to the backup (fallback) are identical, as well, to avoid any confusion. This improves overall reliability.
- TPF/II is a highly structured operating system. By making each unit of work small, using few resources, and doing trivial amounts of computation, it is possible to have many units of work active simultaneously; that is, TPF/II has a very high **degree** or **level of multiprogramming**.
- A backup computer must be available in the event of any outage, whether scheduled (as computers are regularly switched to allow

maintenance) or unscheduled. This backup computer is thus available for other work, provided that work can be preempted very quickly in the event of an unplanned fallback. Since, however, most switchovers are of a planned nature, it may be deemed acceptable to use the backup computer for important work on the grounds that loss of processing capability due to emergency switchover will be acceptably rare.
- The database can be, as it is at TWA, completely duplicated. Less expensively, a database can be selectively duplicated instead (thus saving on storage space and, to a small extent, on processing overheads). The decision of whether fully or only partially to duplicate, and if the latter, which data to duplicate, depends upon a number of factors. First, there is a decision to be made as to what data types are to be duplicated, and what their relative importances are. Then there is a decision about the need for extra storage space. However, when data are duplicated, more than one path exists to any datum which has been duplicated and this may improve access.

In TPF/II, the unit of work to be done is called an **entry**. An entry is initiated by a message coming in in response to a poll. As many entries as possible (as many as the system's resources can accommodate) can be active. *All applications programs must be re-entrant and relocatable.* Re-entrant code is code in which no changes occur as the result of its execution. From reading Chapter 3 you should realize that this means that the code in any applications program can be shared between two or more entries.

The kernel

An external interrupt due to the interval timer causes the system to poll and to accept messages. Any message enters a queue called the *input queue*. It has not yet become an entry. Messages are added to the queue by network services interrupt routines which service message input processing needs.

From the input queue a message will be selected (FIFO) to initiate an entry by assigning an entry control block (ECB) which is unique to the specific input message. It is the ECB which defines the entry. A pointer to the input message is placed in the ECB. Within the ECB a routing control parameter list (RCPL) identifies the origin, destination and characteristics of the message. Indirectly through pointers a link to the application which processes the data content of the input message is established.

Once initiated, an entry will cause code in an application process to execute until it requests I/O on behalf of the entry. The *entry* will then be blocked. (*Note:* the process, being re-entrant, is not blocked.) When I/O completes, an interrupt occurs for that entry and the I/O interrupt service routine places that entry on another queue called the *ready queue*. Other services may be required by the application; for example, it is generally necessary to retrieve some segment of the application program *package* (a group of closely related functions) from secondary storage, in which case the necessary I/O will be started in order to obtain the necessary program segment.

If an entry has continued execution after interruption, the application process may need (depending upon what has occurred so far) to fetch work blocks written out to secondary storage which contain temporary data: these are collectively called the scratch pad area (SPA). Whenever this happens, execution returns to the kernel which may return to the ready queue, return to the input queue or solicit input messages by polling.

From the *ready queue* a waiting entry will be selected (FIFO again) to continue executing. When an entry completes, the application issues an EXIT macro-instruction which causes the system to release all primary storage allocated to processing the message and to perform other housekeeping tasks. The application process generates a message to the originating terminal which is passed to a system formatting services routine, an integral part of this operating system though quite separate from the kernel, which transmits that message or, in the event that it cannot, places it on the appropriate *communications line queue* for transmission to the terminal whose message originated the entry.

The average processing time for a message under Model 5 of the operating system (first available in 1972) was 4.7 milliseconds. Tests at that time showed that the processing time per message was fairly constant regardless of the message rate (the number of messages arriving each second). This meant that it was fairly simple to extrapolate performance of any system up to its maximum capacity. Message processing capacity is thus a function of a processor's speed rated in MIPS (*m*illion *i*nstructions *p*er *s*econd). [1, p. 174]

One other important queue appears in TPF/II, the *deferred queue*. This queue contains entries which are designated by the application as being of low priority. Processing of such low-priority entries can be deferred by placing them on this queue, perhaps by setting a timer so as to allow each one a very brief execution time before it is placed back on the queue. Thus, such low-priority entries use no system resources beyond queue space while they wait. (If, instead, such an entry were simply to loop to kill time, it would use up processor cycles which are better used by higher priority work.)

The mechanism for controlling execution is called the **cpu loop program**. It is a simple one, based on a simple philosophy. The philosophy

TPF/II: A High-performance System

is that it is better to give priority to work in progress than to initiate new work. The cpu loop program checks the queues in turn and also checks certain status indicators, the most important of which is a time-to-poll indicator, also called the time-to-solicit-input-messages indicator.

This is 'flip-flopped' as a function of time and the interrogation of the communication facilities. The cpu loop begins by, say, checking the ready queue. (Since the kernel is a loop, it cannot actually be said to *begin* or *end* at any one point.) If any entries appear on the ready queue, *all of them are dispatched before the cpu loop program proceeds to the next queue.* This is consistent with the philosophy of giving priority to work in progress before initiating new work.

When the ready queue has been emptied, the cpu loop program proceeds to interrogate the input queue. If there are any messages queued there *all of them are initiated before the cpu loop program proceeds to the next queue.* When all queued messages have initiated entries, the cpu loop program proceeds to interrogate the deferred queue. Again, if any entries are on this queue, they are all dispatched before the cpu loop program returns to the ready queue to interrogate it again. Figure 11.1 shows the cpu loop program and queues.

The entry point of the cpu loop program ensures that the ready queue will always be the first to be interrogated.

The scheduling in TPF/II is thus carried out through the simple mechanism of the cpu loop program cycling around the three queues, emptying them in turn and carrying out periodic polling. Entries (messages in the case of the input queue) are placed on queues by the communications or SVC (*supervisor service call*) interrupt handlers, but the interrupts themselves have no scheduling function since the queues are strictly ordered by time of arrival on the queue.

In the case of input messages, it is the network interrupt program which adds messages to the input queue. In the case of ready entries, it is the I/O interrupt program (signalling completion of I/O) which places entries on the ready queue. In the case of low-priority entries, it can be a timer interrupt which places the entry on the queue.

In addition, it is assumed that no entry will require an interval of uninterrupted control of the cpu (called a processing interval) greater than 500 ms at a time – though this is adjustable to any value during the system generation process. This eliminates the need for complex time-slicing algorithms, but means that several processing intervals are likely to be needed to complete the processing of one entry.

Questions for review

(i) Which of the scheduling algorithms described in Section 3.7 does TPF/II use?

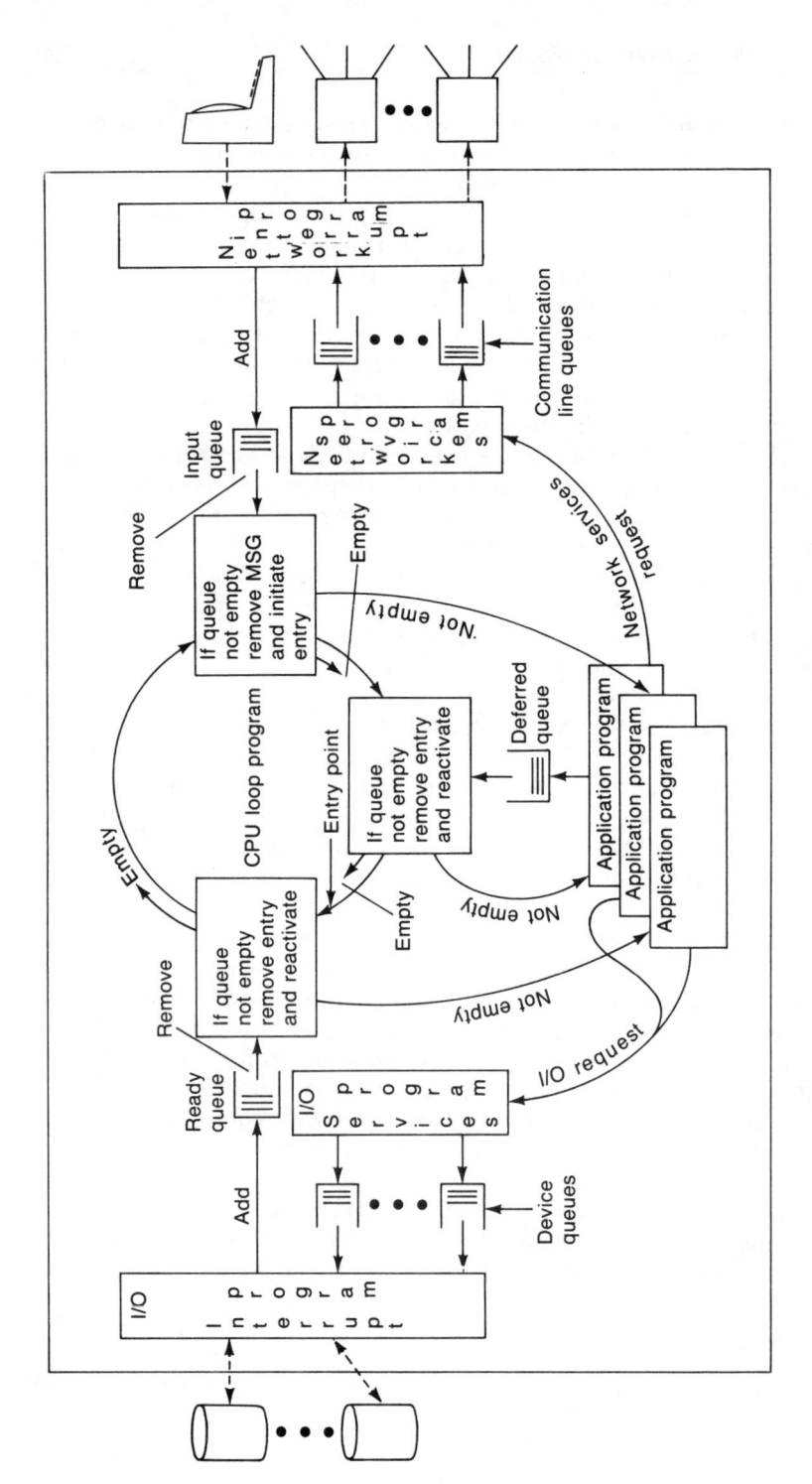

Figure 11.1 The CPU loop program of TPF/II

(ii) In what way does the scheduling algorithm ensure fairness in a system where *every* message requires a very low response time?
(iii) What sets the upper limits of the system's capacity to process?

Questions for discussion

(i) Briefly describe what you think the role of the interrupt mechanism is in the scheduling of work in a TPF/II system.
(ii) How is this different from, say, Unix?

Primary storage management

Storage management in a system which, like TPF/II, seeks to achieve goals of high performance, is best kept simple. This avoids the overheads which result from flexible schemes of storage management which tend to be complex; it does, however, restrict the options the systems designer and the programmer have in using storage.

TPF/II does not distinguish between different uses of storage. Thus, it does not have one rule for, say, programs and another for data. In using primary storage, it does not differentiate between storage used to contain a process, storage which represents a buffer, storage containing data, or storage containing control blocks. All primary storage in active use has two characteristics: it is divided into homogeneous blocks so far as the management of it is concerned, and a storage block is part of an active entry and thus 'lives' only so long as the entry does. When an entry completes, any storage block associated with it is returned to a *storage pool* of available space for use by another entry.

For simplicity, storage is divided into small, fixed-size blocks. There are four different sizes and each of these four groups provides a pool of storage for particular uses.

- Blocks of 40 bytes in size are used exclusively by the kernel to control I/O operations.
- Blocks of 128 bytes are used primarily as input buffers for network control and as work space for the application or the operating system.
- Blocks of 381 bytes are used as: entry control blocks, message blocks, data blocks, program blocks or work space. This is one of the two most common groups of blocks.
- Blocks of 1055 bytes are used in the same way as the 381-byte blocks, except not for entry control blocks.

The number of blocks in each group is a function of the type and volume of system activity for a particular system; this is set when TPF/II is initialized. Thus, it is important for any TPF/II installation to be able to predict activity. It is also important to measure activity to improve system performance by adjusting the numbers of blocks in each group to correspond to previous activity levels each time initialization is required.

The groups of blocks are called **pools**. Thus, there are four pools. These pools represent free blocks available for use by entries. Blocks within each pool are represented in a 'list' associated with that pool.

The 'list' is actually a procedural stack containing the addresses of all the blocks within the pool. A stack pointer contains the address of the entry in the stack which contains, in turn, the address of the next available block within that pool. Such a stack is thus simple to maintain: addresses of blocks are removed from or returned to the stack and the stack pointer is incremented or decremented accordingly.

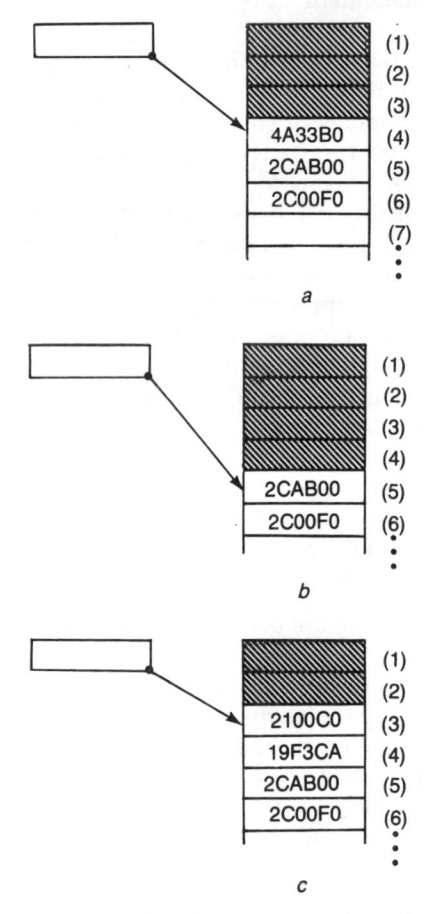

Figure 11.2 Allocation and release of blocks: (a) list pointer at start of GETC; (b) list pointer at completion of GETC; (c) list pointer after completion of two RELCs

TPF/II: A High-performance System

For each time an application issues a **macro-instruction** to obtain a block of primary storage (GETC), the stack pointer is incremented by one ('pushed down' to the next entry in the stack) and the address of that block is put into the entry control block of the entry requesting space. Each time an application issues a macro-instruction to release a block of primary storage (RELC) the pointer is decremented by one (made to point to the entry above in the stack) and the address of the released block is placed in that entry. Thus, if the pointer is, say, pointing at entry 17 and two applications in quick succession issue GETCs, the pointer will advance to 18 and then 19. If an application then issues a RELC, the pointer will return to 18.

The addresses of blocks below the pointer represent available blocks of primary storage, while the total *number* of entries above the pointer represent the number of blocks which are in use. Addresses allocated from the pool are unique, therefore addresses returned to the pool are also unique. When the pointer is decremented, the returned address is placed in the stack at the position specified by the pointer. Thus addresses of blocks will migrate around in the stack as they are allocated and released. See Figure 11.2.

The pointers and stacks are located in protected storage, while the storage pools themselves are in unprotected storage. Early designs used chained blocks, but often chain pointers were altered by applications in such a way that chains were broken, with a resulting loss in available storage. By separating the pointers from the blocks and thus protecting pointers from erroneous modification this problem has been reduced significantly.

Question for discussion

How does the storage management mechanism of TPF/II compare with that of Unix?

Processing

A message, in becoming an entry, is removed from the input queue and 'chained' to a 381-byte block called the *entry control block*. There may be multi-block messages, in which case the message will occupy more than one block, with all such blocks chained together. The entry control block contains pointers to associated blocks such as the 128-byte message block and some 381- and 1055-byte data, program and work blocks. Note that, while the program block is pointed to by the entry control block, *it is not*, strictly speaking, *part of the entry*. It is this collection of message, data and work blocks which constitutes an entry.

The application process (say, air fare quote) then processes the entry, using work space in the form of work blocks. The application process requests the retrieval and update of data from the operating system, responds with a message to the originating terminal and then exits.

In the TPF/II environment, then, the application process is treated very much like a second-level system service: it is re-entrant and therefore usable by a number of messages requiring the same service. It is only necessary, in such a scheme, for such services to be addressable by the entry through its control block. If an entry becomes preemptable (for example, by requiring too much time) the system must provide whatever is necessary for the preempted entry to continue from the point where it was preempted when it once again is scheduled for execution by the processor. In some systems mentioned in Part I this was done by saving key registers and pointers in storage, perhaps in a stack. In re-entrant coding a common method is the provision of work space for the values which are local to a given process. In TPF/II this method is effected by assigning work blocks to an entry. [3]

The entry control block is pointed to by a 40-byte I/O control block which allows the operating system to perform I/O operations on behalf of that entry. This I/O control block is in turn an item in a *device queue*. Figure 11.3 shows an arrangement of control blocks where one application program is being shared between two entries.

Questions for review

(i) What is the relationship between the application and the entry control block? Describe briefly.
(ii) What does the entry control block need to contain or have access to regarding the application when the applications code is re-entrant?

Auxiliary storage management and database support

In any system meeting the same requirements as TPF/II there is a need to provide rapid access to a very large database, and to do so concurrently for many processes.

In TPF/II, data are arranged across all the available devices (disk or drum) rather than grouped according to any concept of discrete files. This method is common in many database systems, where it is known that requests for data will be entirely random. (In fact, in most such systems requests are not wholly random, but 'bunch' around certain data: for example, flight data for the near rather than the distant future will be the target of more enquiries.)

However, the application's view of the data it accesses is as though

TPF/II: A High-performance System

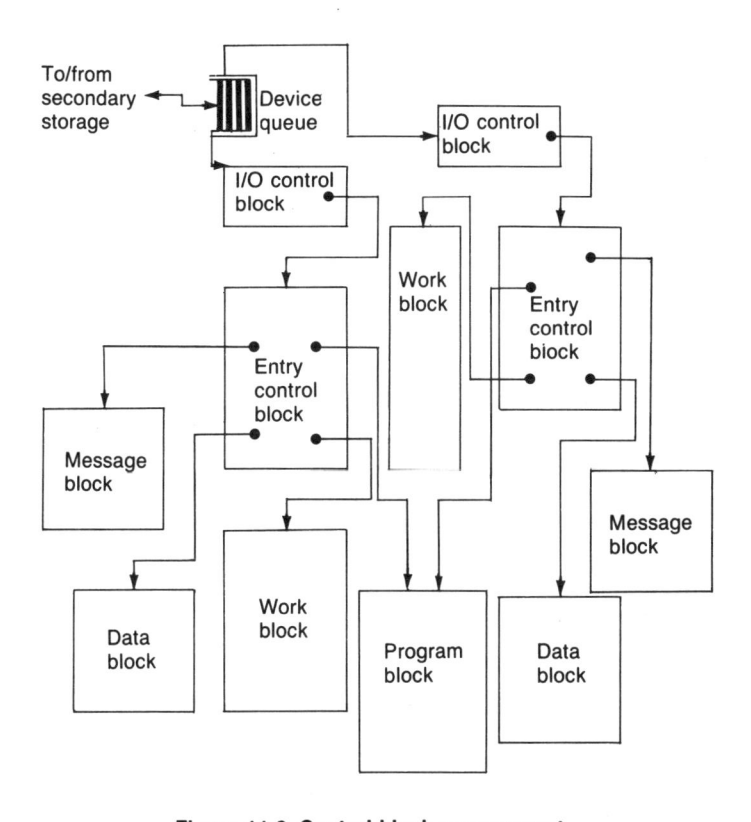

Figure 11.3 Control block arrangement

the data were arranged in a sequential file. By spreading the data, as I mentioned in Section 1.2, across all channels, control units, controllers and devices, potential bottlenecks are avoided and a better arrangement of data is achieved in terms of their accessibility. In effect, the paths to a datum are multiplied by this arrangement. As with most database systems, no one application 'owns' the data, and no one application is responsible for opening or closing any 'file'; 'ownership' and responsibility for access fall to the operating system.

Logically, the database consists of a group of disk packs, each identical in format and type of content. Each disk pack holds an equal percentage of the total logical file, evenly distributed. Records in TPF/II are arranged by record type; there is one 'logical file' for each record type spread evenly across all the disks.

Addressing of individual records within this logical file is accomplished using a base address (starting point) plus ordinal number of the desired record. (Since all records of one type are of exactly the same size, there are no complications to this method of locating a record.) A table resident in primary storage contains the base address of each of the record types ('logical files'). The ordinal number of a record indicates its relative position within the record type 'file'. The ordinal number of a record is assigned to it when the record is initially allocated. The application program subsequently passes this number and the record type as arguments (parameters) when requesting retrieval.

This arrangement insures that a large number of concurrent accesses to any particular logical file create no problems for the system. The spreading of the logical files throughout the disk packs available reduces the likelihood of excessive queueing at a device. This method also frees the applications programmer from any concern with I/O performance (see Section 1.2).

Two record sizes are used in auxiliary storage: 381-byte records and 1055-byte records. (Note the implications for simplifying the allocation of buffer space.) These records are also divided into two other categories: *fixed*, which contain permanent or static data, and *pool*.

In fixed records, the contents of a record may change, but the number of records generally will not. Pool records contain data which are more ephemeral; these data will occupy space only while they are active. For example, fixed records may contain an inventory of seats on a flight,* while pool records will contain the names of intending passengers reserving seats on that flight on a particular date. Since flights are flown on a periodic schedule over a relatively long period of time, the records for a flight will remain static so long as that flight continues to be flown by a particular configuration of aircraft. Passenger names, on the other hand, become history once the flight on which they were reserved has flown. In such a case, the data are copied to a history file and the disk records they occupied are returned to the free space *pool*: hence the name.

Service routines within the operating system manage pool record availability using a **bit matrix** (or bit map) technique to locate a record and show its use. In such a bit matrix (in reality a pool directory) each bit corresponds to a record and when set (bit = 1) indicates that the corresponding record is in use. Pool records are allocated on an as-needed basis. The application process obtains a pool record address (i.e. is allocated the record) when it needs the space, not before.

---

*A *seat inventory* is a function of the type and configuration of the aircraft assigned to that flight, a *flight* being a periodic – usually daily – one-way trip between a starting and an ending point, though it may have intermediate stop-overs. A flight has a designator of a flight number, e.g. TW001. It is the combination of flight number *and date* which designates the *event* of a flight as the passenger commonly perceives it, e.g. TW001 on 3SEP87.

TPF/II: A High-performance System

Pool records are further categorized as short- or long-term. Short-term records are allocated only during the life of a transaction — at the most a few seconds. *Long-term* means time measured in days, weeks or months.

Either the applications process or the operating system frees pool records. Records are reclaimed when necessary by on- or offline utility programs. (Such programs might occupy the *deferred queue* mentioned earlier.) The bit matrix must be manipulated to show which records are free. Some utilities constantly scan through the database following chains and recovering records whose addresses were never returned to the pool or those from broken chains.

Actual I/O is effected through a simple interface between the application process and TPF/II. To do this, the application process issues a macro-instruction to TPF/II. These instructions are simple from the applications programmer's point of view: for example, FIND to retrieve a record, FILE to write a record, FINH to 'find and hold' a record (this blocks any other attempt to update this record but does allow simultaneous read-only access).

Question for review

What common performance problem does TPF/II attempt to address in spreading a very restricted number of logical files evenly over the whole population of disks belonging to the system?

Question for discussion

What purpose do you think is served by classifying records according to the length of their lifetimes? Can you think of ways in which this classification can affect a system's performance?

Communications support

Data communications are an integral part of the TPF/II environment. Hence, they are integral to the overall architecture of the system. By *architecture* I mean the combination of the hardware and software which constitute the entire system, the components of the system, their interconnections and interactions.

The communications portion of TPF/II is called the communications control program or CCP. It

- polls attached devices (usually *not* the terminals themselves) and assures the integrity of circuits;
- executes all communications I/O operations on behalf of applications processes;

- allocates primary storage (obtains the proper sized block(s) on input operations) and releases message block(s) to the appropriate pool on output operations;
- translates input transmission codes to the single, common internal code and translates the common internal code to the appropriate transmission codes for output;
- does the preliminary assembly and editing for invalid characters in incoming messages;
- detects hardware errors and attempts corrective action;
- reconfigures communications hardware;*
- performs the queueing of an input block;
- queues outgoing messages for communications lines in main storage;
- controls the network in a manner which allows terminals, lines and other communications facilities to be shared by other processors (this portion is called the message router — see below);
- enables communications between the processor and the operator.

The need for efficient communications and the need to handle many terminals was recognized by the system designers from the time of the initial SABRE project. They developed specialized communications equipment and devised a special line **discipline** called ALC, for *a*irlines *l*ine *c*ontrol, still in use though it has evolved in order to adapt to improved communications technology.

ALC allows simultaneous communications to take place in both directions on a line (called **full-duplex working**). It also synchronizes the sender and receiver of any message before allowing the transmission of that message between them. It is necessary for both sender and receiver to be synchronized in this way in order that the receiver does not 'misinterpret' the incoming message or miss parts of it. This is called **synchronous transmission** capability.

The message router mentioned above is a prerequisite for the more advanced *s*ystems *n*etwork *a*rchitecture (SNA) — described later — which is now in general use in IBM installations. It routes messages in several senses, as shown in the following examples.

First, it can be used to allow parts of the application environment to receive and process messages when other parts are not available. For instance, when the airline must change its schedules the flight reservation function cannot be active, since the changes mean major alterations to information about future flights; however, the airline will still need its departure control function to be active in order to assign seats and board passengers on departing flights. In such a case, the message router

---

*If excessive errors occur on a line the CCP activates a process to perform fallback or diagnostic procedures in an attempt to restart a failed line or terminal.

can allow departure-related messages through but can intercept reservation-related messages.

Secondly, in a multiprocessor environment, if the target application is not in the processor which receives the message, the message router can forward the message to the appropriate processor.

Lastly, an incoming message may not relate to *any* TPF/II function at all, as when, for instance, a maintenance supervisor at a remote station is working on an aircraft and uses the airline's communication network to update a database held on the backup computer system which is running MVS. In such a case the message router reformats the message to the appropriate discipline (say, synchronous data link control) and routes the message to the MVS system.

Communications lines used in the ACP system are **dedicated**; that is, they are used *solely* for the purpose of communications between the central processor and peripheral devices.

In ALC these lines connect to terminal control units which collect incoming messages and are polled by the central system using one of two possible polling methods. Polling also occurs between the terminal control units and the terminals themselves; this is how the control unit gathers messages from the terminals. In any physical arrangement whereby many devices are connected to one which has sufficient 'intelligence' to conduct polling, this can be the method used to gather incoming data. Thus, polling can take place at several levels in a network. I shall discuss polling in terms of the central site polling remote controllers, but bear in mind that the principle and the techniques apply at any level in the network meeting the two criteria above: a one-to-many relationship between higher and lower levels in the network and sufficient 'intelligence' in the higher level (see Figure 11.4).

In the first of the polling methods, called **roll call polling**, the central site sends a polling message to each controller in a round-robin turn. If any controller has a message, it sends it to the central site upon receipt of the polling message, otherwise it responds with a negative message. This method of polling thus requires a constant exchange of control messages between controller and terminal. It is efficient only if the round trip propagation delay (time it takes the messages to travel out and back) is small, if the overhead due to polling messages is low, and the user population is not a large 'bursty' (i.e. irregular) one. As a controller polls more terminals (has an increased population of users), the performance of this form of polling degrades significantly.

The second polling method is called **hub** or **hub go-ahead polling**. In this method, the central site sends a polling message to the first controller at the beginning of each polling cycle. If this device has messages to send to the central site, it does so when it receives the polling message. Whether or not it has a message, however, it sends a polling

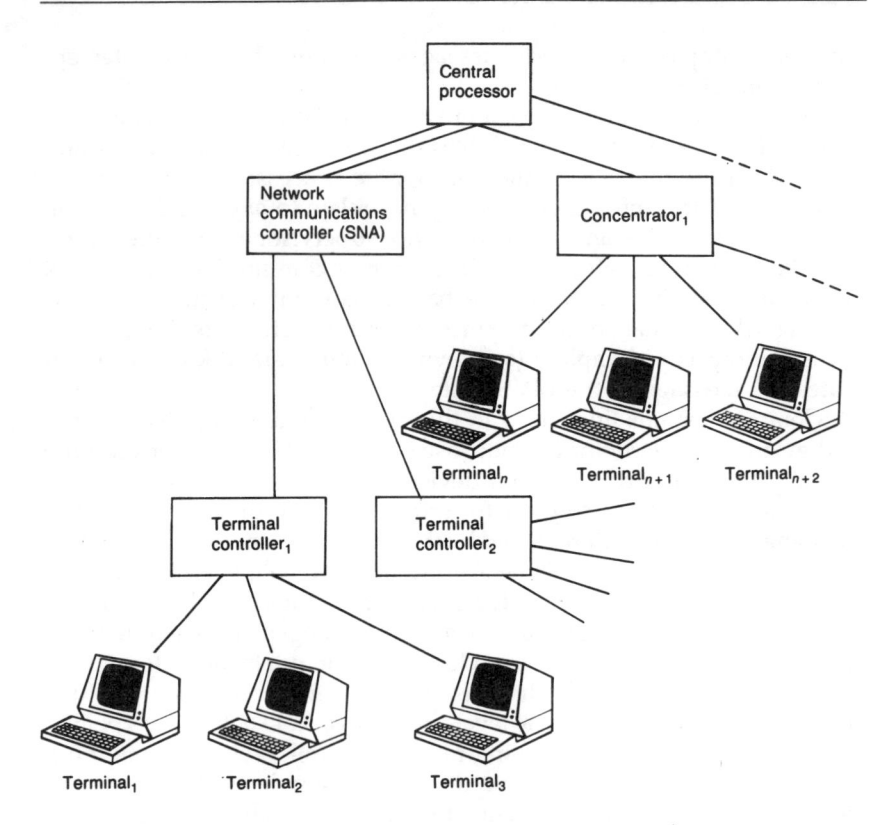

Figure 11.4 The hierarchical arrangement of a network in a TPF/II environment, with intelligence for polling 'spread out' towards the periphery of the hierarchy

message to the next controller. This second controller acts on the polling message in the same way as the first, responding to the central site if it has messages to send and passing the polling message to the next controller in the rota. This continues from controller to controller until all have been polled; only the final controller in the rota sends a response to the central site, whether or not it has any message to send. The central site can then begin polling again.

Round-robin-style roll call polling, then, requires an exchange of messages between the central site and each remote device in turn. A polling message travels outward from the central site, and either a message or a negative response to the polling message travels back from the remote device. The advantage of this method is that the central site can use this method to check the integrity of the transmission circuit between itself and each remote device; no response to the polling message means that communications have been interrupted.

However, the transmission overheads of round-robin are considerable compared to hub polling, where one polling message travels outwards and is passed to n remote devices before a single response returns to the central site (should there be no messages). This is more economic where great distances are involved and delays in transmission are accordingly greater. (Remember it is not only the central site which polls; devices called **concentrators** connected to several terminals poll those terminals if they have sufficient intelligence built into them. This 'distributed polling' reduces the overhead which would occur should the central site have to poll each of the thousands of terminals it serves.)

Each message which a remote terminal sends is prefixed by two special characters used to synchronize the sender and receiver. Following the synchronization characters comes the text of the message. This is followed by a validity check character. Each character comprises six bits.

ALC was a pioneer development in data communications, and many important techniques appeared out of it. It remains in use, evolving slowly. For example, the early display control unit was replaced by a minicomputer which *concentrates* traffic from several, possibly dissimilar terminals, translates codes received (eight-bit, including parity) into the six-bit transmission code required by ALC, interleaves messages from different terminals for transmission (multiplexing), and so on. A more advanced, programmable **network communications controller**, which is a dedicated minicomputer, can be attached to the central processor — programs for it are loaded from within TPF/II, and when necessary 'dumped' back to the central processor through TPF/II.

ALC has, in the most recent versions of TPF/II, been replaced by IBM's *s*ystems *n*etwork *a*rchitecture, or SNA. SNA was developed by IBM quite independently of TPF/II in order to provide a unified structure for linking terminals and host processors.

In this arrangement, TPF/II has an SNA module within it. The central site processor has attached to it a communications controller running a *n*etwork *c*ontrol *p*rogram (NCP). This in turn communicates with a *remote* communications controller, or with 'dumb' terminals as well, using a transmission discipline called *s*ynchronous *d*ata *l*ink *c*ontrol, or SDLC.

SDLC establishes synchrony between sender and user by structuring messages into what are called *frames*, with each frame separated from the adjacent frame by two special characters called *flags*. The receiver checks the incoming data stream for flags, which it uses to establish and adjust synchrony. The remote communications controller, which provides additional 'intelligence' to the periphery of the network, is then linked by a loop to the terminals. This arrangement allows great flexibility, more terminal independence from the central site, and greater integrity.

Further, these changes mean that TPF/II can support the specialized equipment of IBM's Financial Communications System, making it suitable for real-time financial applications.

One last aspect of data communications remains to be discussed: one airline may want to sell seats on another airline and needs to 'talk' to that other airline. For example, you may want to fly to Spokane on United Airlines and then fly on to a more remote airport not served by United but served by Canadian Pacific. United may want to oblige you by providing you with ticketing for this onward service in order to have your business for the Chicago to Spokane part of your journey.

This type of service predates computers — teletypes were used. This function was automated, but the teletype remains the means of communication with small airlines which cannot afford or do not need a higher degree of automation.

The National (US) and the International Air Transport Associations have specified requirements for host-to-host airline-to-airline message switching. The response to those requirements is called *synchronous link control* (SLC). SLC requires the use of private transmission lines (leased from *common carriers* like the Bell System) which are capable of carrying voice transmissions (i.e. telephone lines). These are operated in full-duplex mode (allowing simultaneous communications in both directions) and require the synchronization of sender and receiver. Each link between hosts contains up to seven lines, and a message may use all seven. There is no polling; the recipient processor listens continually and dummy messages are sent when there is no actual message so that the integrity of the connection can be monitored.

In the US, the airlines jointly own a subsidiary called ARINC (Aeronautical Radio Incorporated) which acts as a store-and-forward message switching center for an inter-airline network. It operates using a different discipline from the above, called Asynchronous Data Link, which uses full-duplex low-speed lines in which each character is sent separately, prefaced by a start signal and ending with a stop signal. This method is referred to as **start—stop** or **asynchronous transmission**, though sender and receiver must still synchronize for the receiver to interpret the incoming character correctly.

Internationally, the Société Internationale de Télécommunications et Aéronautique (SITA) carries out a function analogous to ARINC, but across national borders.

The use of low-speed lines and asynchronous transmission permits message traffic to pass between computer system and teletype where necessary. (The replacement of teletype lines is, however, under way.) As I mentioned above, teletypes are required to enable communications to unautomated airlines. It is necessary to apply artificial constraints to teletype traffic to prevent it from swamping the processor. Messages from this source are queued separately from other messages and then are processed on a time-available basis. The cpu loop program has a time-available supervisor which processes work in this queue during any time

TPF/II: A High-performance System

not required for higher-priority processing. Thus this traffic has the lowest priority on the cpu loop.

If one airline reserves a seat on another, it keeps a record of this for itself and uses the appropriate agency (ARINC, SITA or direct SLC link where one exists) to send a reservation message. The commonest use of an SLC link is to link an airline's system to the SITA high-level network. For example, an airline may have a remote station with low traffic; it would be far too expensive to install direct communications.

For instance, for British Airways (BA) to install direct communications (such as a leased, dedicated line) to Rio de Janeiro to support its few flights is far too expensive. Instead BA can use an SLC link to interconnect to SITA and send the message from London to New York as a type B (teletype) message; this is then re-transmitted from New York to Rio as a type A message (ALC). In Rio, a satellite processor polls the ALC lines and receives the message. Hence, costs of such communication are kept low by sharing them, through SITA, among many users.

The incoming message is used to adjust the inventory and record the existence of the intending passenger just as though it had come from one of the recipient airline's own agents. To avoid problems, airlines agree a lower limit of available seats below which other airlines will not make a reservation, e.g. when only four seats remain available on Canadian Pacific's flight, United Airlines will not make a reservation for them.

Questions for review

(i) Describe the differences between the two modes of polling.
(ii) What roles are played in inter- and intra-airline communications by:
   (a) SITA and ARINC?
   (b) SLC links?
(iii) Compare the overheads of synchronous and asynchronous transmission. Which is used with SDLC?

Questions for discussion

(i) Can you think of any circumstances in a system like TPF/II that might warrant allowing a terminal with a message to send to interrupt its controller rather than wait to be polled?
(ii) Can you think of reasons why a system like MP/M should not use polling?

11.4 WHAT ABOUT SUPPORT FUNCTIONS?

TPF/II needs to have certain functions performed in order to ensure that the airline (or other business concern) can carry on its operations. For example, it is necessary to 'capture' the database periodically so that, should a catastrophic failure occur, the organization can return to some time in the *very recent past* whence it is possible to restore the database. (Remember, an airline has no paper-flow to back up its electronic data-flow.)

In non-real-time systems a system is normally halted, or the disk to be backed up is made unavailable for access, and then the data are copied to another disk or magnetic tape. In a 24-hour real-time environment this is clearly not possible. In TPF/II this 'data capture' constitutes a major subsystem which runs online, in real-time, whenever invoked by the computer operator. It takes complex **checkpoints**, which are points to which the system can return to start again in the event of catastrophic failure. Checkpoints must be taken without unduly interfering with the message processing functions of the system even while it runs in parallel with those functions.

Because TPF/II requires a rigid discipline be adhered to by all programs in the system (no program segment can exceed a length of 1055 bytes, for example, and in order to achieve its high performance, all code must be re-entrant), it must exclude all programs which do not or cannot conform to this discipline. Untested programs, of course, fall into this excluded category, as do the bigger, messier programs required for such functions as sorting and combining data to reduce their volume (**data reduction**) and programs which help programmers to develop programs.

Data reduction runs offline on the standby computer, under the control of another operating system (MVS) about which I shall write in Chapter 13. One function of data reduction is to manipulate data gathered as a result of the data collection function in order to provide daily monitoring of system performance and thus allow the system to be 'tuned' to achieve optimum performance. Such information also allows one to discern long-term trends and thus predict growth in the system load — an important function in a system which, because of its rather rigid structure, is difficult to change dynamically. However, it is important to note that such data are inadequate to measure and predict fully all aspects of system behavior. Also, judgements based on an inadequate volume of data can cause real problems: if data collection were only run, say, between 1:00 and 2:30 in the morning when loading is low, any judgement based on these data would not apply to peak periods at all.

Adequate testing is essential in a situation where every program can be considered vital to the correction functioning of the system. There is little protection within the TPF/II system against programs which break chains, do not answer messages, over-write the wrong pool blocks, cause unplanned outages, and so on. This means that final testing (at least) must simulate real-life system operation as closely as possible. TPF/II thus

TPF/II: A High-performance System 271

provides a realistic but controlled test environment. However, as additional protection to the live system, even final testing is normally carried out using a simulated TPF/II environment *dis*connected from the real network and run on the backup processor, perhaps under the operating system I discuss in the next chapter, on VM/SP.

Program development, which in a modern environment requires interactive terminals suitable for text entry and processing and the presence of software tools such as editors, assemblers and perhaps preliminary test beds for early testing, also takes place well away from the live system.

Finally, there are the many other support functions which an airline, as a business, must carry out: the keeping of personnel data, scheduling of personnel (cockpit and cabin crew), payroll, scheduling of aircraft maintenance, accounting, spares and consumables inventory maintenance, purchasing paperwork, and quite probably also some scientific functions such as modelling aircraft or air crew scheduling (money can be saved, for example, by having an aircraft's last flight before maintenance terminate at a station where that maintenance can be performed), modelling aircraft performance in relation to the latest weather forecast to achieve the optimum flight path for existing conditions, and so on. These also will take place well away from the live TPF/II system.

Question for review

Give two reasons why non-critical functions should run on a backup computer system rather than on the primary system.

11.5 COHABITATION AND THE HYPERVISOR

In fact, a TPF/II system will probably not run at its peak operating rate 24 hours per day; yet the system must have the capacity available to respond to short periods of peak loading. And most TPF/II systems, designed for a life of six to eight years, begin service responding to loads (even peak ones) well below the maximum planned (called the *end-of-life requirement*) for the later years of the system's lifetime. Beginning late in 1973 ACP systems were made available which contained a feature to help users take advantage of this otherwise idle computing capacity.

A *hypervisor*, software which allows a second operating system to *cohabit* the central processor with ACP (as it then was), was introduced. This software had to meet stringent requirements: the amount of processing overhead on ACP it would create had to be less than five per cent, it had to ensure that this caused *no impact* on the overall system's reliability, and it had to be totally invisible to ACP and its applications and to the second operating system (OS/VS) and its applications.

The hypervisor was added to ACP through the medium of its interrupt handlers. These contain logic capable of recognizing whether any interrupt belonged to ACP or not; thus it was relatively straightforward to modify these to process OS/VS interrupts.

OS/VS2 (MVS) is the only system other than a TPF/II test system that the hypervisor will host; this simplifies the problem of providing a 'virtual machine', a problem which would be much more complicated if a number of different operating systems could be 'guests'.

The guest system runs in problem mode — that is, in user mode. If guest code is in control of the processor and solicits an interrupt, the *native* TPF/II can seize control of the processor, but the reverse is not true. If the guest system is not in control of the processor when one of its requests results in an interrupt, the interrupt is queued until the guest is once again given control of the processor by the hypervisor. Certain instructions in OS/VS, called **privileged instructions**, are simulated by the hypervisor to prevent OS/VS from obtaining, even accidentally, control over its own status and excluding the native TPF/II system. This simulation also prevents any compromise to TPF/II's reliability due to faults occurring in the OS/VS domain, but it can degrade the perceived performance of OS/VS.

In the next two chapters I shall discuss VM, a virtual machine facility which allows the cohabitation of many operating systems within a single machine (and thus can be used to provide a test and an offline environment for auxiliary TPF/II functions), and OS/VS2 (more commonly called MVS), the operating system which provides the support environment for TPF/II. At the end of these three chapters, you should have a clear picture of a complex, large-mainframe environment and be able to see what possibilities such an environment offers at what relative cost. At the end of this chapter, you should have a clear picture of a special-purpose high-performance operating system.

Question for review

Why was the medium of the interrupt handler used as a means of allowing a second operating system to cohabit the system?

Question for discussion

What means other than the interrupt mechanisms could be used in similar situations? How would these work?

11.6 CASE STUDY CONCLUSIONS

Not all computing needs can be met by a truly general-purpose system. Even though such systems differ and thus offer a varying number and degree of benefits and drawbacks, their very nature means that, while performance may be adequate for most applications which are not stringently time-dependent, they will not provide adequate performance for some applications.

In this and the next two chapters, you will see three operating systems which all run on the same underlying host architectures. Thus, one architecture can, through the medium of the operating system, be adapted in different ways to different applications. This means, of course, that the end user of each of these systems will perceive a different *model* of computer system from the end users of the others. The airline reservation agent will perceive a system which is geared to accept only special, very terse messages of a nature limited by whatever the applications are; he or she won't see something which allows, for example, verbose electronic mail facilities, though, in the case of both TPF/II and other more general-purpose systems, messages can be passed from terminal to terminal.

TPF/II also demonstrates that, in an environment designed to meet such stringent needs, the synergy between the hardware and software is of vital importance to peak performance. Thus, the designer of a TPF/II-like system architecture will need to configure that system's hardware in such a way as always to minimize delay. An example of this is having the terminal concentrators poll the individual terminals rather than leaving the task to the central processor.

On the border between software and hardware, the distribution of the database across all available disks in such a way as to avoid bottlenecks in disk I/O traffic is another such example. Such a technique is applicable to any database system allowing random interactive enquiries large enough to warrant it.

The third lesson which TPF/II affords is that function can be sacrificed to performance, and vice versa. Performance at the expense of flexibility will, probably, have to be compensated for in some way if the computer's users also require the flexibility. Furthermore, the performance/function trade off works well in a uniprocessor environment, but becomes a problem in a multiprocessor environment. By imposing structure and strict discipline on the applications it is possible to achieve remarkable performance and reliability. Reliability is partly a function of simplicity of structure; the more complex and amorphous a system or an application, the more likely it is to contain errors likely to compromise its own reliability.

Finally, the methods and techniques which constitute TPF/II are not confined to it.

IBM learned a great deal about data communications when it designed SABRE in conjunction with American Airlines. Special equipment was designed; these designs were later the basis for designs of similar, more general equipment used to carry out similar functions. High availability is a desirable characteristic for most systems; TPF/II's techniques for achieving this can usefully be adapted. The notion of providing a fundamental, simple auxiliary storage access subsystem has usefully been applied to systems otherwise very dissimilar to TPF. The concept of 'trivial computation' transactions is fundamental to any system involved in dialogue either with a user or with another computer system.

TPF/II is not 'locked' into the problem-solving modes of its past. To meet the same requirements in future using newer architectures it may be possible to look at different architectures with an eye to adding more function and flexibility to such a system without sacrificing its performance. Swissair has already designed and implemented some database management 'middleware' to allow a 'database manager' to handle database processing formerly done by individual applications.

Another possible direction forward is to explore the distribution of processing around the geographical network. This is no simple matter; though some functions would seem to lend themselves to distribution others, such as seat inventory, do not. (An inquiry in New York may result in the sale of a seat from Calgary to Anchorage, though for boarding that flight the passenger must be in Calgary.)

Functions will also undoubtedly evolve. For example, in managing an inventory, it is necessary to know only whether an item (e.g. a seat on a flight) is available for sale or not. However, from a marketing point of view it is becoming more important to consider 'yield' – to whom can the airline sell that seat and for what advantage (which may not be the same as simple income!).

REFERENCES

[1] Siwiec, J.E. (1977) 'A high-performance DB/DC system', *IBM Systems Journal*, **16**(2), 169–95.
[2] Gifford, D. and Spector, A. (1984) 'The TWA reservation system', *Communications of the ACM*, **27**(7) (July), 649–65.
[3] Lorin, H. (1972) *Parallelism in Hardware and Software: real and apparent concurrency*, Prentice-Hall, Englewood Cliffs, New Jersey, pp. 255–6.

GENERAL REFERENCES

Anon. (1979) *ACP/Transaction Processing Facility Concepts and Architecture*, IBM, White Plains, New York, order number GH20-2157-0.

Anon. (May 1985) *Systems Network Architecture: Technical Overview*, IBM, Research Triangle Park, North Carolina, order number GC30-3073-1.

Hellerman, H. and Conroy, T.F. (1972) *Computer System Performance*, McGraw-Hill, New York.

FURTHER READING

Gotlieb, C.C. (1985) *The Economics of Computers: costs, benefits, policies and strategies*, Prentice-Hall, Englewood Cliffs, New Jersey. Sections 8.3 and 8.4 (pp. 210–24) discusses the breakthroughs and economics of data communications, communications standards and the integration of computers and data communications.

Lorin, H. and Deitel, H.M. (1981) *Operating Systems*, Addison-Wesley, Reading, Massachussetts, Section 3.7.2 (pp. 91–2) and Section 3.9 (pp. 94–6) address transaction processing systems and networking and distribution.

CHAPTER
12
Virtual Machine/SP: an operating system

... Are these classifications 'real'? Of course they are, and *the effect that each of them has upon what* [one] *may and may not do constitutes their 'reality'.*

S.I. Hayakawa in *Language in Thought and Action*

Virtual can mean to make one thing have the appearance of and to function as another thing. It can also mean to make one thing to appear as and to function as many things simultaneously.

The actual appearance of a virtual machine can be as an existing real computer or can be as an ideal machine such as the UCSD p-machine discussed in Chapter 9.

12.1 REQUIREMENTS

In the preceding chapter I described IBM's TPF/II operating system and noted that a severe limitation placed on it was a limitation of function — no software development or testing, no non-critical ancillary functions take place on such a system (except under control of another operating system — OS/VS2 MVS — hosted by the hypervisor). An auxiliary system is required to fulfil these functions, and such a system must, obviously, use a common instruction set.

Since this auxiliary system also exists in order to provide hardware redundancy for the prime system as insurance against system failure and to allow necessary maintenance procedures to take place, such an auxiliary system must be: (i) very compatible to the prime TPF/II system at the hardware level (to the degree that no significant variance in the behaviors of the two systems can be observed when the two run identical software), and (ii) the secondary storage of the prime system (running the online TPF/II system) must be fully switchable to the auxiliary system almost instantaneously.

The auxiliary, or secondary, system can take on the other organizational functions which are necessary to support the TPF/II system:

- providing a suitable environment for program development;
- program testing;
- processing allied applications such as aircraft maintenance scheduling and modelling;
- running offline support applications such as data reduction;
- running other business applications: payroll, accounting, etc.

The first of these items requires a means of entering text, organizing it into the appropriate type of file and providing compilers and assemblers. Much PARS programming is done using assembler language in order to gain the performance objectives required.

Testing in a real-time environment presents certain difficulties for the programmer in that watching the actions of a real-time program which takes a matter of milliseconds to execute may not tell a programmer about what is actually occurring. Therefore it is useful to have two testing modes: a step-by-step mode which allows the programmer instruction-by-instruction control of the execution of the program in a controlled, wholly artificial environment (a **test bed**), and a real-time environment which closely simulates reality but in which the program can do no real harm should errors appear.

The final items on the above list are closely allied: they also require program development and testing facilities which may be very similar to those needed for TPF/II PARS program development or may differ due to the different natures of the applications, and access to secondary storage facilities which are *totally* separate from the prime TPF/II system and are separated as well from those devoted to the real-time test system.

Historical data generated by any of these applications systems may require storage media such as magnetic tape which are inappropriate to the live TPF/II environment.

Users will also require different terminals and have different communications needs from those of the airline's reservations and ticket counter agents or their analogs, such as bank tellers, in other applications of TPF/II.

To summarize, the organization needs (i) a very high degree of hardware redundancy, complex and reliable, (ii) easy-to-use switching equipment to switch the primary system's communications and secondary storage subsystems, (iii) dissimilar program development and testing environments and (iv) another communications network with characteristics and a user community very dissimilar to that of the primary TPF/II system.

Any real-time test system, as well as any online TPF/II system resources, must be kept wholly separate from the possibility of interference from other applications. Thus, it would be ideal if the TPF/II test environment could coexist with a general-purpose operating system which addressed the needs of program development, TPF/II offline support and non-TPF/II applications processing.

TPF/II's support system is called MVS, and I shall discuss that system in the next chapter. In this chapter I shall discuss IBM's VM (*Virtual Machine*) Facility/SP (*System Product*), to give it its full name, and show how this operating system is used to provide a program development and test-bed environment for TPF/II applications programs, host a test TPF/II system, and host the support operating system, MVS, which in turn hosts TPF/II offline support programs, non-TPF/II scientific and commercial applications, and program development and test environments for non-TPF/II program development and testing, thus providing a very flexible working environment for a wide range of applications in such a way that the environment *appears* to consist of several different computer systems.

VM also exists as a powerful mainframe operating system in its own right as it provides a wide range of facilities for its users.

12.2 OVERVIEW OF VM/SP

The Virtual Machine Facility/SP runs on the IBM System/370 and other, subsequent descendants of the System/360 such as the 303x, 308x and 3090 series of mainframes and on the so-called PCMs (plug-compatible mainframes) such as the Amdahl/470. It is a system control program consisting of four major components which manages the resources of its host mainframe in such a way that its many *users have a functionally separate computing system at their exclusive disposal*. This is accomplished by simulating each functionally separate computing system – providing a virtual machine for each user (or group of users) which that user or group can create and adapt to his or her own requirements.

Components

There are four components of a VM/SP system.

VM/SP consists of a **control program** (referred to as the CP). It is this which executes in a real machine and controls the real resources available to that computer system. It is the vehicle which creates the concurrent virtual machines.

Operating systems which can execute in CP-created virtual machines are IBM's batch or single-user interactive systems: DOS/VSE (*Disk Operating System*), OS/PCP, OS/MFT, OS/MVT (all mentioned in

Virtual Machine/SP: An Operating System 279

Chapter 3 of Part I), OS/VS1 (a virtual storage system with one virtual space shared among many users), OS/VS2 (a virtual storage system with each user having his or her own virtual space — also called MVS), OS-ASP, TPF/II and RSCS (see below). Multiple-access systems which can be run are VM/SP (it is possible to nest virtual machines!) and the *Time-Sharing Option* (TSO) portions of any of the OS operating systems. VM/SP also provides a conversational operating system called CMS (for *Conversational Monitor System*). With the exception of OS/PCP, all are multiprogramming systems.

Single-user, in this case, means that one user can execute any of the systems listed either in batch or in interactive mode or both. CMS is also single-user, but it differs from the others in that it now has no existence independent of VM/SP though it originally appeared as a stand-alone system. *Multiple-access* means that one virtual system (VM or the TSO option) executes and serves directly many interactive terminals. The user can have the choice of declaring whether he or she would prefer a single-user or multiple-access system by indicating this at the time the link between the terminal and the chosen virtual machine is established.

VM/SP contains the Conversational Monitor System (CMS) just mentioned. It is a single-user operating system designed to operate under VM/SP and it provides a very wide range of general-purpose interactive functions. The user can create, update and manipulate files of data and programs, and can execute programs (whether to test them or to execute them in production mode doesn't matter). The command language of CMS is highly flexible and very powerful, and can be tailored either by the systems programmers or by the users themselves. It allows truncation of commands, the creation of synonyms, and the creation of new commands which are combinations of existing commands.

In addition to its other components, VM/SP contains a *Remote Spooling Communications Subsystem* (RSCS, listed above) which is a single-user operating system running under the CP. RSCS can execute in one or more of the virtual machines and can transfer data between virtual machines and remote users. Thus, it provides telecommunications support for the transfer of files and messages between (i) virtual machines and remote stations, (ii) remote stations to other remote stations, (iii) virtual machines to remote job entry (batch) systems and (iv) remote stations to a CMS batch virtual machine.

Finally, VM/SP consists of an *Interactive Problem Control System* (IPCS) — a group of commands and controls that execute under CMS to provide system problem analysis and management facilities. This standardizes the process of reporting problems with the system and identifies recurring problems. It also provides a tool for looking at and analyzing memory (primary storage) **dumps** (listings of the contents of storage) occurring due to abnormal failure in the control program (CP).

Questions for review

(i) Which portion of VM/SP controls real resources?
(ii) Differentiate between the needs of single-user and multiple-access interactive computing.
(iii) What role does the Remote Spooling Communications Subsystem (RSCS) play in VM, and why do you think it occupies a virtual machine of its own?

12.3 THE VIRTUAL MACHINE

A virtual machine, again, is functionally equivalent to a real system. It consists of *simulated* hardware and software which operate in a real computer system under the control and management of VM's CP. Each virtual machine under VM's control (including any 'nested' VM/SP system) is described in a *directory*; this description includes a description of that virtual machine's simulated storage, I/O devices and console. Figure 12.1 shows a real system executing three different virtual machines under VM/SP control.

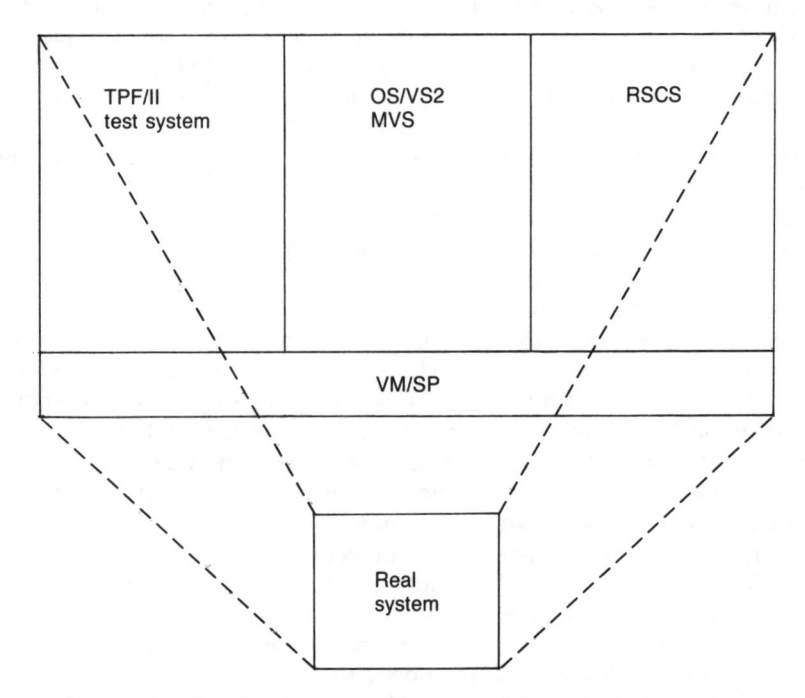

Figure 12.1 A real system executing three different virtual machines under VM/SP

Virtual Machine/SP: An Operating System

One of the advantages of an operating system like VM/SP is that it becomes possible to *test new or modified operating systems* without the need to devote an entire real system to such tests, which are often time consuming. This is one reason why one might want to nest a VM/SP system within the master system: to test a new release of VM/SP without the need to have exclusive use of a real system. The same can be said of testing new releases of any of the other operating systems which VM/SP can host. This reduces the amount of hands-on (exclusive-use) testing time necessary for a newly modified operating system. Such hands-on testing otherwise requires that the testers work rather unsocial hours when other demands for the system are very low. At the same time, it allows the tester the use of a virtual console exactly as though he or she had exclusive access to the real systems console.

Use of VM/SP in a testing mode is not limited to operating systems modifications. Using CMS, an applications programmer can create source programs and data files with the fully screen-oriented edit function, can obtain and maintain previously written source programs and data files, can test and debug a program interactively under the control of the application's target operating system and can design programs whose storage needs exceed real storage limitations. The editor commands are fully programmable: the user can set the place where the command line appears, program his or her own menus, set the font of the displayed characters and the use of colors and can program macros for the function keys. The editor is used by other commands and thus can be used to manipulate output from other commands without exiting from them. The entire command reference manual is also available online.

It is also possible to define virtual devices in order to design and test larger system configurations before purchasing and installing the hardware. With the aid of an appropriate software package, document preparation can be carried out. Computer operators can be trained on virtual machines, where any mistakes they make, no matter how catastrophic, are confined to a virtual machine and do not affect the real computer system and all its other users. Production ('live') work can be run concurrently with testing. Figure 12.2 shows a hypothetical configuration for a VM/SP system.

When an operating system runs under VM/SP, it is given a virtual machine to run in and is dispatched by VM's CP to run in a problem (user) state. Since an operating system often issues privileged instructions which affect its own status, these instructions must not be allowed to execute directly. They are captured by VM/SP through the mechanism of program interrupts; VM/SP then simulates the instructions. The guest operating system thus does not leave the problem state. Since it does not leave the problem state to enter the system state, this can actually *reduce* the overhead inherent in context (state) switching.

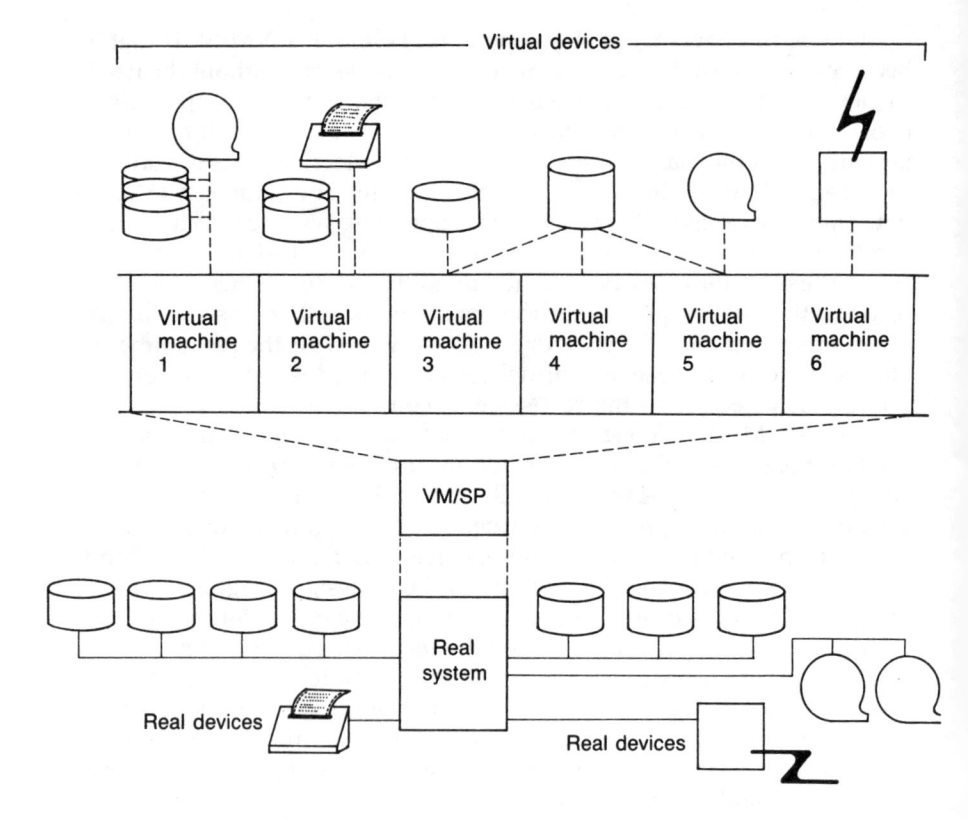

Figure 12.2 A hypothetical configuration of a VM/SP system

Since several operating systems can be guests simultaneously, it must be necessary in the interests of providing a balanced service to users and giving priority where needed that any one virtual machine can be designated as more important than the others. This is called *favored execution*; it is a mechanism which provides an assured percentage of the real processor's time to a particular virtual machine.

Every virtual machine has its own virtual address space. This virtual address space is accessed through the dynamic address translation hardware on the real system, but each virtual machine uses a unique set of segment and page-translation tables. The use of such unique tables isolates the virtual machine in such a way as to minimize the effects of software failure within the virtual machine, whether it is the operating system or applications code. Address space isolation has an additional benefit: it provides some security through isolation. [1]

Questions for review

(i) Why would the capture and simulation of a guest system's privileged instructions *reduce* overheads?
(ii) What further benefits does this method of hosting an operating system provide?

Questions for discussion

(i) Why do you think an operating system hosted by VM/SP is made to run in a problem state?
(ii) List two advantages and two disadvantages of the virtual machine concept.
(iii) What is a virtual machine?

12.4 MANAGING VIRTUAL RESOURCES

Time

Although it appears to users as though 'their' virtual machine is executing instructions, it is, of course, the real processor which actually executes them. CP divides the real processor's time such that it appears to be multiple virtual processors. Thus a virtual machine gains a time quantum or slice during which it has access to the real processor.

A series of low-level scheduler queues exist; the more time one uses the further 'down' the series of queues one's virtual machine advances — that is, its priority decreases.

CP also examines each virtual system's terminal interrupts (interrupts initiated by the terminal user pressing, for example, the RETURN key on his or her terminal). If the rate at which such interrupts occur is high, the virtual machine for that user is defined as a conversational virtual machine. A conversational virtual machine is assigned smaller time-slices. If there are few terminal interrupts, the virtual machine is designated as non-conversational and is assigned larger time-slices. CP then gives conversational virtual machines more frequent access to the real processor for short time-slices, while non-conversational users receiver larger time-slices but at less frequent intervals. The effect of this is to reduce average response time to users.

CP also ensures that a virtual machine can gain access to the real processor only if it is *not* waiting for a resource or the completion of an activity. Thus, if a virtual machine is waiting for a page of virtual storage to be loaded from auxiliary to real storage or is waiting for an I/O operation or for a CP command it has requested to complete, it will not be given access to the real processor.

Questions for review

(i) What is accomplished by progressively reducing the priority of tasks which are heavy users of processor time?
(ii) How does the progressive reduction of priority for heavy users of processor time correspond with the division of tasks into conversational and non-conversational groups?

Questions for discussion

(i) What inference do you think the designers of VM/SP made about the nature of tasks on a virtual machine with few terminal interrupts?
(ii) What objective do you think is met by the low-level scheduler?

Primary storage

In VM's directory each virtual machine has defined for it the amount of storage it is allowed. The directory's entry for a virtual machine contains two values: one is the normal size of storage, which must be at least 8192 bytes, and the other is the maximum size, which cannot exceed 16 megabytes.* Both sizes must be stated in multiples of 4 kilobytes (page size). When a user starts a virtual machine by logging on, the storage that user's virtual machine receives is the normal size. The user can, however, temporarily redefine the size of the virtual machine's storage, up to any multiple of 4 kilobytes which does not exceed the maximum size stated in the directory.

Each virtual machine's storage is actually created, and controlled by the CP, as virtual storage. Thus, a virtual machine's storage can exceed the size of the real system's storage.

Storage in a virtual machine is logically divided into 65 536-byte (64 kilobyte) segments. These are further divided into 4-kilobyte pages. For each virtual machine, the CP creates and updates a set of segment and page tables to describe the virtual machine's storage and to map virtual addresses to page frames in real storage using dynamic address translation. This technique was described in Part I, Chapter 4.

Segments of virtual storage can be *shared* among several virtual machines, but the data or re-entrant program modules in such shared segments must be designated as *read-only*. The shared information *must*

---

*The XA (extended) architecture which became available in 1981 accommodates an extended addressing structure of 2 gigabytes, but the application must be altered to take into account the extended addressing structure before it can take advantage of this. The 'old' addressing structure allowed 24 bits for an address — 16 megabytes. The 'new' structure allows 31 bits plus one bit to indicate whether the old or new addressing structure is in use. The architecture is described further in Chapter 13.

Virtual Machine/SP: An Operating System 285

be part of a monitor or operating system that has been recorded on a CP-owned volume of secondary storage. (More about secondary storage management will be discussed below.) The CMS nucleus is, in fact, shared among CMS users and exists in discontiguous shared segments outside any one virtual machine.

Whether or not such a shared segment is a protected one is specified when the VM/SP system is generated. If a shared segment is protected, any attempt by a user to alter a page will cause that user to receive a message that he or she has violated system integrity and his or her terminal will be placed in a special operating mode. If a shared segment is not protected, any attempt to alter it will result in the user who made the attempt being 'unshared' from the segment but given a private copy of it, including the altered page.

Questions for discussion

(i) Why should a user attempting to alter a non-protected shared segment be given a private but altered copy of it?
(ii) Can you think of reasons why each user is not given a copy of such a segment rather than having to share it?

Virtual storage

In discussing VM/SP, it becomes useful to talk about *levels* of storage. I wish to introduce this concept here so that it becomes simpler to discuss how a virtual storage operating system can run in a virtual machine which is itself created from and managed as virtual storage by the CP of VM/SP.

The *first level* of *storage* corresponds to real storage.

Second-level storage, then, is the virtual storage created by VM's CP to contain a virtual machine.

The operating systems which control virtual machines may themselves be virtual storage operating systems. This means that they can create and control their own virtual storage, which is termed *third-level storage*. VM/SP running as a guest system can, in fact, create several third-level virtual storages at once.

(Note that second-level storage is *not the same as secondary storage* as described in Part I, though first-level storage corresponds to real primary storage.)

An operating system such as OS/MFT which is not a virtual storage system would appear to present few problems, since it does not create its own virtual (third-level) storage. Instead, it executes as though its virtual machine had only real storage, and the CP of VM/SP pages that storage in a way that is invisible to the guest operating system.

The timing delays suffered by a real-storage operating system when its virtual machine storage is paged can be considerable. This may cancel any advantage gained from running such an operating system under VM/SP if the work it executes was *designed* to run in a real storage environment and has strict timing dependencies. To solve this difficulty, a virtual machine may be 'tacked down' to real storage by running in a *virtual equals real* mode. This of course removes a considerable portion of real storage from availability for other virtual machines.

A virtual storage operating system creates and updates a set of page and segment tables that relate to the third-level virtual storage within the virtual machine. When such an operating system is executing, pages containing instructions and data from third-level storage must be available to the processor; that is, they must be present in first-level storage. But the page and segment tables created by the guest operating system cannot be used by the processor, since they refer only to where the guest system 'thinks' individual pages are within a virtual machine. Neither can the processor use the segment and page tables managed by CP, since they do not correspond with the guest system's virtual addresses.

The real computer system must have a set of page and segment tables that relate third-level storage to first-level storage. CP dynamically constructs such tables, called *shadow tables*, and updates them. CP maintains a single set of shadow tables for any one virtual machine. A single set of shadow tables is all that is necessary for those operating systems (OS/VS1, OS/VS2 MVS and DOS/VSE) which create and control virtual storage. With VM/SP as a guest, however, which creates multiple virtual machines each with its own virtual storage, the guest shadow tables are invalidated whenever control passes from one virtual machine to another.

When operating systems like DOS/VSE and OS/VS run under VM/SP they are subjected to two levels of paging: that initiated by a virtual machine, and that initiated by VM's CP. Paging initiated by a virtual machine is handled by CP as a normal input and output operation. Paging initiated by CP is invisible to the virtual machine.

However, performance in such a situation is of great importance. It is always a concern in virtual storage systems, but it is of greater concern in VM/SP because of the multiple levels of paging. A common view of virtual machines is that they should normally be isolated from the real environment. That is, an operating system running in a virtual machine does not recognize that CP simulates the execution of privileged instructions and handles real interrupts. CP simply *reflects* events back to the virtual machine exactly as if that virtual machine were a real one (with the exception of timing). CP has limited knowledge of what occurs *within* a virtual machine; it does not know, for example, how a guest operating system handles multiprogramming.

In some virtual machines, a technique which allows the virtual machine to cooperate closely with the CP and take advantage of the CP's mechanisms is used. This is termed *handshaking*. This creates a communication path between the CP of VM/SP and OS/VS1 and versions of DOS/VSE which can run under VM. The guest operating system and CP make each other 'aware' of mutual capabilities and requirements.

The guest, which can run on either a real or a virtual machine, will be made to 'know' that it is running on a virtual machine at the time it is initially loaded. If the guest finds that it is in control of a virtual machine, it issues an instruction to the CP to ensure that the CP will provide handshaking support. The guest then goes on to activate handshaking. Thus the handshake is two sided and both sides cooperate.

Once handshaking is established, it is also possible to lock an individual page into real storage. Provided sufficient virtual storage is defined, a system such as VS1 can mark all virtual pages as *fixed*. It then disables demand paging, does not open an external page storage file and reduces its use of instructions which control paging. In effect, the guest turns the handling of demand paging over to the CP, thus eliminating double paging overheads.

A second technique available is *pseudo page-fault handling*. When a page fault occurs in a guest, the CP will ordinarily place the entire virtual machine in a *page wait* status and dispatch another virtual machine. If the console operator of the virtual machine so desires, the CP can be made to reflect a special page fault back to the guest, even if the latter is not controlling paging. The guest system then uses this information to put the *process* requesting the page fault into a page wait status. The guest is then free to dispatch another process *without* having to relinquish control of the processor. When the CP completes the real paging operation, it reflects this to the guest, which can then awaken the blocked process.

Handshaking is a software approach to enhancing performance and operational effectiveness. It aids virtual machine execution and reduces CP execution time by reducing the number of privileged instructions and virtual machine paging I/O.

The performance improvement that can result from handshaking is indicated by a benchmark conducted by IBM. A series of jobs were run on an OS/VS1 operating system running in an 'ordinary' virtual machine. The same series were rerun with handshaking between CP and OS/VS1. Relative batch throughput increased 35 per cent while total processor time decreased 29 per cent. With the virtual equals real option, the same benchmark improved relative batch throughput by 14 per cent and decreased processor time 20 per cent. A benchmark of pseudo page-fault handling did not show any effect on performance, but it did favorably affect the level of multiprogramming. [2]

Question for review

Briefly describe the differences between handshaking, running in *virtual equals real* mode and pseudo page-fault handling.

Question for discussion

Why might pseudo page-faulting improve the level of multiprogramming without affecting overall performance?

Processor management

Multiprocessor systems and those with an attached processor (a master processor with a tightly-coupled slave where both processors access the same primary storage but only the master has access to peripheral devices) have different characteristics from uniprocessor systems.

For example, preemption mechanisms for a uniprocessor will not provide the necessary level of control in a multiple processor environment. This requires either more communications among processors or more intricate scheduling and dispatching algorithms to compensate.

In fact, on the attached processor preemption does not apply to the user process; an I/O request will result in suspension of a process on the AP. Since ready work of higher priority does not preempt processes on the AP, processes there will tend to run longer between suspensions; the AP thus tends to give lower-priority work which has little I/O (is relatively computation-bound and not interactive) a great deal of processor time, while the main processor tends to give higher-priority work preference and must, by the nature of the configuration, handle I/O, especially when I/O rates are high, as they are in interactive use. [3, pp. 377-8]

In another example, VM's early versions ran on uniprocessor systems and therefore did not require the means to lock out a second processor from shared resources. When VM/SP was expanded to support attached and multiprocessor systems, it became necessary to provide a means of 'single-threading' access to shared resources; this was done by providing a lock mechanism and lock management to prevent simultaneous update (locks are unnecessary for simultaneous reading).

The designers of VM/SP drew on experience from MVS (described in the next chapter) and provided two types of lock: *spin* and *suspend*. If a particular process needs a resource which is locked and it is possible to delay that process until the resource is available, the process can be *suspended*; that is, it can be blocked and then can await the freeing of the resource in a blocked state. This is termed a *suspend lock*. If the process cannot be suspended, it can be placed in a *loop*. That is, it can remain

Virtual Machine/SP: An Operating System

active but doing nothing other than constantly checking the status of the lock — a *spin lock*. It is important to assure that the holder of a spin lock does not spin too long without gaining access to the resource.

The term *lock* may be a slight misnomer, though it is a mechanism which serves to exclude or lock out; in fact, a *lock* in this sense is more like a *token* or *key* which allows the holder of the lock access to the resource so long as the process continues to hold the lock.

Another form of lock is the *system lock*, a general lock for any activity requiring a lock which does not have a more specific (e.g. a spin or suspend) lock. The time a process is delayed waiting for a lock will increase linearly with the multiprogramming level of the system. [3, p. 376]

Questions for review

(i) Which kind of lock, spin or suspend, will guarantee a faster response? Why?
(ii) In an attached processor system, the more computation-bound tasks tend to run in the slave processor and this work is not preemptable by higher priority tasks. What do you think the effect will be on tasks which have high rates of I/O?

Question for discussion

Why is the time a process is delayed waiting for a lock so strongly influenced by the system's multiprogramming level?

Secondary storage

A virtual machine can support the same devices as the real computer system it simulates. It is the virtual machine which controls these devices, not VM. In discussing secondary storage, however, I shall focus on disks.

The user can, through the directory for his or her virtual machine, define the configuration of the virtual machine in terms of all its peripheral devices. He or she can assign different addresses to these virtual devices or use those of the real devices; VM/SP allows the same virtual address to be used by multiple virtual machines and performs any necessary address translations. The user can also meet additional requirements dynamically through CP commands. Thus VM/SP provides several facilities, for example: virtual-to-real mapping for each virtual machine (with duplications possible between virtual machines) and real addressing to real devices.

VM also supports dedicated devices: one (or more) real device(s) is (are) assigned permanently to and solely for the use of one virtual machine. When a device is dedicated to a virtual machine, it is wholly under the control of that virtual machine. Magnetic tape drives are always dedicated. (They are, of course, impossible to share!) Disks can also be dedicated; this is especially useful as a means of improving performance in certain circumstances. Dedicated devices can be assigned dynamically by CP commands or assigned at 'log on' time by control statements pertinent to the directory entry for that virtual machine.

Sharing disks is more common. Access permission to a shared disk may be of the read-only type or may permit read/write access. In sharing, a real disk is divided into virtual disks, also called *minidisks*.

Each real disk consists of a number of vertical concentric cylinders. For example, an IBM 3350 direct access storage (a non-demountable disk pack-drive combination) consists of 555 cylinders (plus five alternatives used to replace defective cylinders). Each 3350 cylinder consists of 30 tracks; there are 30 vertically arranged rings which make up a cylinder. Each track has a capacity of 19 069 bytes. A virtual disk consists of some number of adjacent cylinders within the real disk. The first two cylinders of the real disk (numbered zero and one) are reserved for use by VM/SP to aid virtual-to-real mapping. Other than that, all other cylinders can be assigned to virtual disks. For example, a real 3350 volume called VOL095 will have its own VTOC (see Section 2.4) on the first two cylinders. Then cylinders 2−15 could be defined as a virtual disk called USER1.VIR001, cylinders 16−86 could be defined as a virtual disk called USER1.VIR002, cylinders 87−198 could become a virtual disk called USERX.XQW666, and so on. See Figure 12.3.

The guest operating system whose configuration includes, for example, USER1.VIR001 and USER1.VIR002 above, will build all the necessary controls and directories on the first cylinders of the virtual disks and will then manage this virtual disk and its data exactly as though the virtual disk were a real, but small, disk.

Questions for review

(i) Distinguish between the way users share the following resources on a conventional multiprogramming system and the way they share these resources under VM.
  (a) Time in the processor.
  (b) Real storage.
  (c) Virtual storage.
(ii) Distinguish between dedicated and shared devices in VM. Why have dedicated devices?

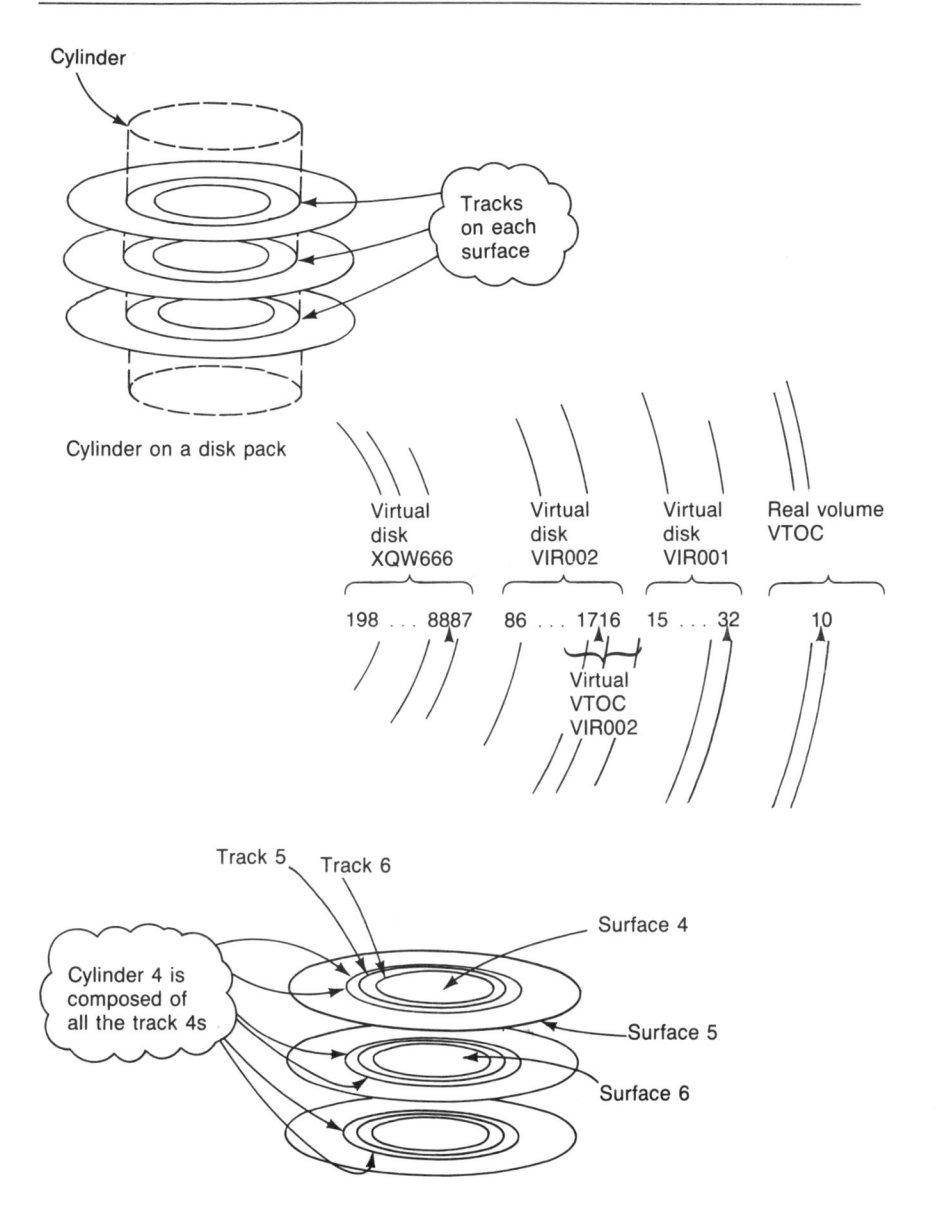

Virtual Machine/SP: An Operating System 291

Figure 12.3 Virtual disks

12.5 MANAGING VIRTUAL I/O

In addition to secondary storage devices, the virtual machine requires an operator's console to facilitate communication between the system and the operator. A **console** is a terminal which receives information about system operation and which accepts commands from the operator; in this sense it is somewhat more specialized than a user terminal.

In microcomputers, one CRT and keyboard actually perform both functions without differentiating them, but in larger multiprogramming systems it is important to give some one person overall operational control of the system, for example to bring devices on- or offline, alter system global information, or change multiprogramming levels or priorities.

When the virtual machine runs a single-user system, such as is the case with CMS, the console and user terminal are identical.

If the virtual machine is running a multiprogramming system with several users, there must be an operator's console and there *may* be users' terminals. In a virtual machine, the console is also virtual; it can be any terminal device designated to be the console whereas in a native system like OS/VS2 it would be a particular terminal dedicated to use as a console and connected to a high-priority channel.

VM also supports virtual unit record devices: card readers, card punches and printing devices. In any multiprogramming system using unit record devices, such devices are rarely constantly busy. Hence VM/SP can map several virtual unit record devices to one such real device.

A technique called *spooling* avoids intermingling input or output from several virtual devices at the real device. *Spooling* refers to the practice of storing data temporarily on an intermediate file in secondary storage (usually on disk) before routing that data to their final destination. (In Section 12.8 I shall return to the use of unit record devices in drawing conclusions from this case study.)

Because virtual machines may need to communicate to other virtual machines or to distant terminal equipment, VM/SP allows a virtual machine configuration to include virtual transmission control units. Indeed, a virtual transmission control unit can be shared by several virtual machines. This makes it possible to design and test the data transmission aspects of any system. Further, the virtual machine can have a virtual channel-to-channel (CTC) adapter or a real, dedicated CTC adapter. The virtual CTC adapter allows a virtual machine to communicate with another virtual machine in the same computing system. The dedicated CTC adapter allows a virtual machine to communicate directly with a real computing system *other than its own real system*.

Further, a virtual machine may be given a *dedicated channel*. If this is so, the virtual machine controls that channel and all its attached devices exclusively for its own use. Thus, CP maps virtual storage locations

Virtual Machine/SP: An Operating System 293

specified in commands to the channel to real storage locations and performs any necessary paging operations, but it does not need to map device addresses for devices on the dedicated channel, because the guest operating system is in full control of these and the virtual and real addresses correspond exactly — one for one. Such an arrangement is virtually necessary when a major multi-user operating system like OS/VS2 is used in a production (non-test) mode. However, a virtual machine may have only virtual channels (which are shared) or may have a mixture of virtual and dedicated channels.

Virtual machine I/O operations are simulated by the CP. When a virtual machine issues a *start I/O* instruction, CP gains control, copies the necessary channel instructions from the virtual machine operating system into its own work area, pages into real storage all virtual storage locations required for the data transfer and fixes those pages in real storage until the I/O request completes, then (if the request is to a virtual disk) adjusts cylinder numbers so that the true location of the request is accessed, maps the virtual device address to the real device address, and schedules the actual I/O operation.

During disk I/O processing, CP inactivates the virtual machine which made the request. Should that virtual machine gain control, CP gives it a code (just as a real computer system would) which indicates the status of the I/O operation. CP also reflects to the virtual machine the interrupts caused by the input/output operation; the system in the virtual machine interprets and processes these. If an error occurs on an I/O operation, CP does not attempt to recover; this is the responsibility of the virtual machine's operating system (except for CMS, see below). CP does, however, record the error.

Input/output operations initiated by the CP for its own purposes are performed directly and bypass all the translation mechanisms described above. CMS uses a different interface to CP in order to request disk I/O. Because of this, CP provides error-recovery operations for standard CMS I/O. However, CMS is not limited to this standard I/O and the knowledgeable CMS user can, if he or she so wishes, bypass the standard interface.

When VM/SP is run on attached processor (AP) systems, the AP does not have access to I/O channels. Any I/O requested by a user process running on the AP must be executed by the main (master) processor. The same is true is system-generated I/O — paging. This requires two levels of interrupt: one of the process on the AP and a second to carry out the I/O request on the main processor.

VM allows the existence of shared pages and these may be modified by a user process. In a uniprocessor, a system subroutine inspects shared pages to determine which have been modified; this occurs each time the low-level scheduler wishes to switch to a different user process. When two processors comprise a system, it is possible that one processor will request a page-in, but the process needing that page will be dispatched to run on the other processor. Since the processors share one primary storage between them but do not note which *processor* is responsible for the change to a shared page, it is reasonable to keep two copies of shared pages (one for each processor), and if a desired page was obtained by the other processor, to do a storage-to-storage copy of that page, thereby avoiding a second paging I/O to fetch the same page.

As I mentioned above, virtual machines may define virtual unit record devices. CP, not the virtual machine, controls the unit record devices designated in the virtual machine's directory entry as spooled. When a virtual machine issues a *start I/O* instruction for such a device, CP intercepts that instruction, modifies it and moves the data into page-sized records on a VM-controlled spooling area on disk.

Input data are data available at a virtual card reader. These data can come from real cards at the real card reader, in which case they must be prefaced by a card stating to which virtual machine they belong. These data can also be created by remote work stations using RSCS (*R*emote *S*pooling *C*ommunications *S*ubsystem) using real cards in a real (but remote) card reader also prefaced by a card stating that they come from the RSCS virtual machine and for which virtual machine they are destined. Alternatively, they can be card images at a virtual card reader. Though RSCS uses the 80-column card image (that is, an 80-character record) to transfer data, this is totally hidden from users.

Output spool space is created on VM's direct access storage when a virtual machine operating system writes to a virtual card punch or printer. CP schedules a real printer or punch or a remote printer or punch to take the output when the user logs off the system or when a CP CLOSE command is issued.

The user may, at his or her option, also spool the virtual machine's console input and output to disk instead of, or in addition to, having it accepted from/displayed to the terminal.

If spooling space becomes exhausted, spooling is halted and the virtual unit record devices are made to appear to their virtual machines in a *not ready* mode. The spooling space can then be enlarged or the largest files can be purged by the VM/SP operator in order to make room for continued spooling.

Spooling can also be used as a means of communication between virtual machines. I discuss this in Section 12.7.

Question for review

A process running under an operating system which is in control of a virtual machine requests I/O. Describe how the guest operating system, the CP and the hardware satisfy this request.

12.6 THE USER'S VIEW

Users' views of their virtual machines vary widely depending upon the operating system their virtual machine runs and the configuration it appears to have. A user may be a CMS user, in which case he or she will see a single-user interactive and personal virtual machine, while users of other operating systems will see computer systems that are largely a function of the operating system with which they interface.

CMS

A CMS virtual machine must have at least 256 kilobytes of virtual storage. The CMS nucleus is shared by several CMS users through the mechanism of one large shared segment. The shared portion is not fixed in real storage, so that a particular page may or may not be resident at any one time. Additional portions of the CMS operating system are shared in discontiguous segments attached to or detached from a virtual machine as required.

The user of CMS is assigned at least two disks: a read-only disk and a read/write disk. The first contains the CMS nucleus, certain CMS commands, and the system library of programs. The second contains the user's permanent and temporary files. A user can have up to 26 virtual disks online (actively attached to his or her CMS session) at any one time – and all 26 can reside on one real disk or can be spread over many.

CMS supports the same direct access devices that are supported by the CP. CMS formats its disks into fixed-length blocks of 1024 bytes, but the file system manages these in such a way that the user *appears to have* fixed- or variable-length records and sequential or direct access to files.

The user's files are identified by three designators: an 8-character file name assigned by the user, a file type which specifies particular file characteristics (e.g. ASSEMBLE indicates that a file consists of assembly-language source-program statements), and a file-mode designator which describes the disk that contains the file and the category (read-only, erase-after-read or read/write) assigned to that file. There is no hierarchical structuring of files, but the user can impose such a structure if he or she finds this desirable.

CMS files consist of 1024-byte blocks or multiples of this. The blocks need not be contiguous on the disk. Blocks are allocated or released automatically by CMS as the file size demands. Each virtual disk has a directory, itself a file, which contains format and size information for each file on the disk together with a 'tree' of pointers to the blocks within the file.

The user is given tools like language processors, standard and personal programming languages, editors, an optional text processor, commands which define system functions and for which the user can create synonyms, debugging facilities and a batch facility which allows the user to execute programs in batch mode by sending jobs from his or her own virtual machine or the real card reader to a virtual machine dedicated to running batch jobs. This last frees the user's virtual machine for continuous interactive use.

In addition to CMS users, systems and operations personnel need to control the real computer system and the VM/SP operating system. Other users may need to control their own virtual machines. A set of CP commands exists which operators and systems programmers can use interactively to exercise control. CMS users can issue CP commands directly from CMS; however, most features offered by CP commands are available directly to the CMS user from CMS itself.

Other users

Each user on a VM/SP system belongs to one or more *privilege classes*; these are indicated in the VM/SP directory entry of the user's virtual machine. The privilege classes define the types of CP commands that a user can issue. Any user can gain access to or relinquish access to the VM/SP system. A *general user* can control the functions associated with his or her own virtual machine. A system programmer, on the other hand, can update certain functions not controlled by any other privileged class users, while the system resource operator can control all the VM/SP real resources except those reserved for the primary system operator or the spooling operator. There are eight classes of user altogether.

Questions for review

(i) Why does the CMS user have at least one read-only disk? What does it contain and why should it be protected from update?
(ii) What is the purpose of the privilege classes in VM?
(iii) What difficulty does the concept of a separate virtual machine for each user impose on the users? Name one method which seeks to remedy this difficulty.
(iv) What function do the user classes serve in the VM/SP system?

12.7 COMMUNICATION BETWEEN VIRTUAL MACHINES

Any requirement for communication between virtual machines can be identical to the requirement for communication between real computer systems. Users of virtual machines may want to exchange data or messages, a CMS user may wish to send the CMS virtual batch computer system a job to be executed, or it may be necessary to send data to or receive data from a remote location. On the other hand, such requirements may be more closely related to the requirements of inter-processor task communication.

CMS users who wish to pass each other data can use spooling. The sender writes the data he or she wishes to send to a virtual output device such as a virtual card punch, and this becomes the virtual card reader of the same or another virtual machine. CP spooling support can make files available to multiple virtual machines. Conversation between users is also possible — avoiding spooling — but this is unsecured.

The *R*emote *S*pooling *C*ommunications *S*ubsystem (RSCS) runs under CP control and provides telecommunications support to transfer files between remote stations and virtual machines. RSCS runs in its own virtual machine, and together with the spool file system of CP provides an environment for the transfer of files from virtual machines to remote RSCS stations, from a virtual machine to a remote job entry batch system, from remote stations to the remote job entry batch system, and from remote stations to a CMS batch virtual machine. An example of a remote job entry batch system is JES, which will be described in Chapter 13.

RSCS consists of a supervisor and line drivers (a device driver for data transmission to remote devices). The supervisor interfaces with the CP spool system and the RSCS line driver, which controls a specific type of remote station. The RSCS network consists of a real processor, transmission control units and telecommunications lines connected to remote stations. The real processor is the one that executes VM/SP. Remote stations are either programmable or non-programmable input/output configurations: minimally a card reader, a printer and a card punch. Programmable remote stations are those which include a computer which can be small, as large as, or larger than the host of RSCS.

Each location in a RSCS network has a location identifier which RSCS uses to establish a path to that location. RSCS need only know the next (possibly intermediate) location on the entire path in order to transmit data to it. The data are stored temporarily at any intermediate points until the next link on the path to the final destination is established. The data are then forwarded to this next link, and so on, until they arrive at the final destination. This is termed a **store-and-forward** system. Once a partial path has been established, messages and files can be transmitted by stages to and from the two ends of the path.

Transferring spool files between virtual machines is an inherent capability in the design of CP. While this method of transfer is desirable for certain classes of data, especially bulk data, it is inefficient for the transfer of a transaction or message. Spooling requires that the data must first be placed on a real spooling device — in secondary storage — before it can be transmitted to another virtual machine. The data must then be read from the spooling device. The advantage of this method is that the data are, in effect, preserved across system failures by being written to a device which records them on a non-volatile medium.

On the other hand, storage-to-storage techniques of transfer are not inherent in the design of CP. These techniques are faster, but could become a problem to manage when large numbers of virtual machines are involved.

Two other means for inter-computer system communication exist. I have already spoken about one but have not named it: the *V*irtual *M*achine *C*ommunications *F*acility (VMCF). This is a software interface which allows one virtual machine to communicate with any other virtual machine operating under the same VM/SP system. It is not an application; it is a facility upon which applications (for example, resource sharing) may be built.

A DIAGNOSE instruction with a special argument list accomplishes this. DIAGNOSE is used to establish handshaking in which a guest operating system learns that it is running on a virtual machine and makes its capabilities known to VM. The connection of one virtual machine to another is a logical process in which two equals (neither is master or slave) are connected for the duration of a single transaction.

Movement is from virtual storage to virtual storage. VMCF fixes one page of the sender's virtual storage and one page of the receiver's virtual storage to real storage (regardless of how much information is to be transferred) for the duration of the transfer so that neither are paged out. As a result, transfer is fast, logically symmetrical and totally asynchronous. VMCF provides a queueing mechanism so that several concurrent transactions can be processed by a single virtual machine. Access to any particular virtual machine is determined by stating whether the virtual machine will accept requests from all other virtual machines so authorized (non-specific) or from one other virtual machine only (specific) [4]. Figure 12.4 shows the possible logical combinations of specific and non-specific authorizations.

The other mechanism for communications is IUCV — *I*nter-*U*ser *C*ommunication *V*ehicle [5]. This enables users to pass any amount of information and allows a program running in a virtual machine to communicate with other virtual machines, a CP system service, and even with itself.

Communication in IUCV takes place between a sender and a recipient over a predefined link called a *path*. Any party to communication can have multiple paths, send multiple messages and receive multiple messages. The path accommodates sending, receiving and multiple messages simultaneously.

Virtual Machine/SP: An Operating System

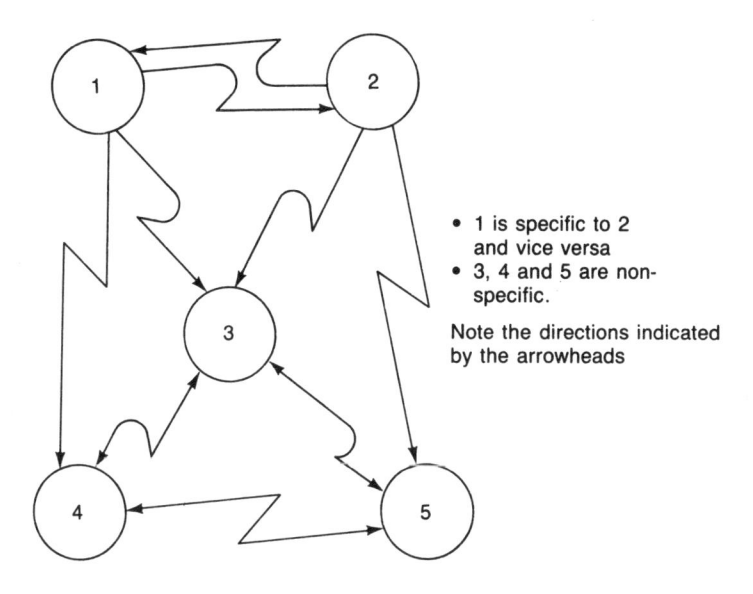

Figure 12.4 Logical combinations of specific and non-specific authorizations

- 1 is specific to 2 and vice versa
- 3, 4 and 5 are non-specific.

Note the directions indicated by the arrowheads

The maximum number of paths possible for one communicator is 65 535. A communicator's maximum number of paths is established in an IUCV directory. If there is no directory entry, the communicator can still have a default of four paths.

The sender, once authorized by IUCV, establishes a connection by invoking a CONNECT function, and the recipient invokes an ACCEPT function. This 'opens' the path and communication can proceed until either sender or receiver invokes a SEVER function (severing the path) or a QUIESCE function (which suspends the path temporarily). A potential receiver who does not want to communicate can also use the SEVER function to prevent the establishment of a path. If a path has been QUIESCEd, it can be reactivated by invoking a RESUME function.

Both the sender and receiver must identify the path to be used in invoking CONNECT and ACCEPT respectively; they do so by naming the path, though the path name each gives is a logical name which is resolved by IUCV — the names are simply two different descriptions of the same path as it is defined in IUCV's directory.

Communications are called *messages* and are created by the sender invoking the SEND function. The recipient invokes the RECEIVE function to accept and acknowledge the message. The recipient also has the ability to request information about messages sent to it and can refuse a message.

If a message is accepted by the recipient, the recipient can respond by invoking a REPLY function.

IUCV maintains queues among which the messages move. They are the send queue, the receive queue and the reply queue. IUCV moves messages from queue to queue in response to a communicator's invocation of one of the functions SEND, RECEIVE, REPLY or TEST COMPLETION (which terminates the communication).

CP checks storage protection for all data moved during an IUCV communication. The method used is the protection key method.

Questions for review

(i) What service does the spool file system of CP provide? What advantage does it have for a user? What disadvantage for the system?
(ii) Describe the Remote Spooling Communications Subsystem's role in communicating with remote devices. What kind of device can RSCS communicate with?
(iii) How does VMCF differ from spooling? What kind of traffic is best suited to VMCF? What kind is best suited to spooling?
(iv) How does IUCV differ from VMCF? What kind of communication is suited to IUCV?

12.8 CASE STUDY CONCLUSIONS

One of the most interesting aspects of VM/SP is the comparison of its costs to the valuable flexibility it provides. The VM/SP operating system obviously has relatively high costs resulting from the imposition of additional layers of software, the problems caused by the requirement to run operating systems in the problem state and the complications of virtual storage management occurring on more than one level. In fact, acceptable performance can be achieved only through additional hardware (microcoded) boosts.

However, VM-hosted systems often run faster than native systems, especially in terms of response time to interactive users. I witnessed a lookup of a name in a series of 133 employee telephone directories containing a total of 329 202 names on a world-wide VM/SP network. This required 3 seconds of processor time − scarcely more than that (5 seconds) in response time − to locate a single name. A lookup of the same name doing a full search of all directories using string-matching took just 17 processor seconds, and only about 20 seconds response time. Note that the definition of acceptable performance rests with the organization which controls the system and with the system's users.

Virtual Machine/SP: An Operating System 301

Performance

Some extra features are available which can boost performance. The Virtual Machine Assist feature performs many of the privileged instruction simulation functions by emulating them in hardware. This feature may be necessary for a production – as opposed to a test – environment to achieve the necessary performance levels.

Extended Control Program Support, in conjunction with Virtual Machine Assist, provides more comprehensive services for virtual machines and extends the assist concept to CP itself.

Lastly, there is VM/SP Attached Processor Support which can be used on systems with an attached processor (AP) or on systems comprising more loosely coupled asymmetric (master and subordinates arrangement) multiprocessor complexes. Two processors simultaneously execute multiple tasks taken from a common queue while sharing a single primary storage. The master controls and performs all I/O. Degraded but continued operation is possible in the event that the attached processor fails. In an asymmetric multiprocessor system, if it is possible to switch channels between processors it is possible to continue to provide a degraded service in the event that the master fails; a subordinate has the channels switched to it and becomes the new master.

The boosts and additional processors improve performance but also have associated costs in initial capital outlay and continuing running expenses. Whether these additional costs result in significant improvements which make the expenses worthwhile remains something which only the owning organization can determine.

Applications

VM comes into its own in two areas: (i) developing and testing major, large-scale software, such as major operating system enhancements, and (ii) providing personal computing facilities – on a scale comparable in speed, space and power to a mainframe – to the CMS user. Further, the possibility of simulating extensive configurations of hardware, including networks, gives a unique opportunity to carry out initial tests without the need to create a real configuration.

As I have also tried to show, VM/SP can be extremely useful in environments like those needed to run systems like TPF/II, where a second computing system is required as backup in the event of primary system failure or planned maintenance, and yet where the support environment for the primary system (TPF/II) has several conflicting requirements: an offline development and initial testing environment, an online but simulated testing environment, and general-purpose facilities for processing allied applications.

On the other hand, it is striking when comparing VM/SP with other operating systems that the design of VM/SP was based on the System/370, which in turn was based on the notion of unit-record equipment. This would seem to be the dead hand of history weighing down the design of an operating system otherwise based on advanced concepts.

VM/SP is not, of course, the only system to demonstrate a continuing, if tenuous, connection to the punched card. Many terminals available on highly advanced systems display an 80-column line; it is possible to fit 80 characters on the screen and any additional characters in a line must either wrap around to the next line, or the terminal operator must scroll right to see the additional characters.

But VM/SP is perhaps unusual in its internal dependence upon the 80-character image. It appears in the VM/SP accounting system, which accumulates accounting records in 80-character card images kept in real storage until they are punched out (on a real card punch) on 80-column cards, though more commonly they are copied to a magnetic medium such as tape. It appears in the use of virtual card readers and card punches (though not limited to 80-character records) on virtual machines and the use of these to send and receive inter-virtual machine communications.

CMS provides a personal computing facility for its users. The user perceives his or her own powerful, but nonetheless virtual, computer system. No doubt this facility will continue to grow in popularity in organizations which already have a considerable investment in large IBM or plug-compatible mainframes and which do a great deal of major software development and modification. However, in smaller environments where this investment has not yet been made it is unlikely that CMS would prove a cost-effective means of providing personal computing.

Instead, it is perhaps more likely that the trend to small but powerful independent personal computers linked together in a network will be more popular, especially since an individual can disconnect a personal computer from the network and take it home (or to another office elsewhere) to work independently.

Questions for review

(i) What are some of the factors affecting performance in a VM/SP system?
(ii) How do the virtual machine assist and the extended control program support help?

REFERENCES

[1] Seawright, L.H. and MacKinnon, R.A. (1979) 'VM/370 — a study of multiplicity and usefulness', *IBM Systems Journal*, **18**(1), 5–17.
[2] MacKinnon, R.A. (1979) 'The changing virtual machine environment: interfaces to real hardware, virtual hardware, and other virtual machines', *IBM Systems Journal*, **18**(1), 18–45.
[3] Tetzlaff, W.H. and Buco, W.M. (1984) 'VM/370, attached processor and multiprocessor performance study', *IBM Systems Journal*, **23**(4), 375–85.
[4] Jensen, R.M. (1979) 'A formal approach for communication between logically isolated virtual machines', *IBM Systems Journal*, **18**(1), 71–92.
[5] Anon. (1986) *VM/SP System Programmer's Guide*, IBM, Poughkeepsie, New York, pp. 141–48.

GENERAL REFERENCES

Anon. (1976) *IBM Reference Summary: VM/370 Commands (Other than General User)*, IBM, Poughkeepsie, New York, order no. GX20-1995-0.
Anon. (1984) *Virtual Machine Facility/370: Introduction*, IBM, Poughkeepsie, New York, order no. GC20-1800-10.
Anon. (1987) *VM/SP System Programmer's Guide*, IBM, Poughkeepsie, New York, order no. SC19-6203.
Attanasio, C.R., Markstein, P.W. and Phillips, R.J. (1976) 'Penetrating an operating system: a study of VM/370 integrity', *IBM Systems Journal*, **15**(1), 102–16.
IBM Systems Journal (1979), **18**(1), issue devoted to papers on VM.

FURTHER READING

Deitel, H.M. (1984) *An Introduction to Operating Systems*, Addison-Wesley, Reading, Massachussetts. Chapter 22 is a case study of VM.
IBM Systems Journal (1979), **18**(1). The entire issue is devoted to papers on VM.
Lorin, H. and Deitel, H.M. (1981) *Operating Systems*, Addison-Wesley, Reading, Massachussetts. Chapter 16 is a general discussion of virtual machines.

CHAPTER
13
OS/VS2 MVS

In this chapter, I shall introduce OS/VS2 MVS (which I shall hereinafter call MVS), the last in the series of three IBM mainframe operating systems discussed in this book.

You will recall that in Chapter 11 I introduced TPF/II, and that program development and certain auxiliary functions such as data reduction had to be carried out on another computing system with another operating system: that companion system is MVS.

MVS is also a general-purpose operating system for large IBM mainframes.* MVS also runs on IBM plug-compatible mainframes such as the Amdahl/470. In fact, MVS usually appears in many, many computing installations which do not use TPF/II. It is usually seen as host to large-scale batch and interactive data-processing commercial applications.

From Part I you may recall that MVS descends from the OS family of operating systems which IBM originally developed for use on the System/360 family of computers in the mid-1960s. To remind you, the progression of development was: OS/PCP, OS/MFT and OS/MVT. Both OS/MFT and OS/MVT gave rise to their own particular descendant operating systems. OS/MFT, which uses fixed partitions, gave rise to OS/VS1. OS/VS1 uses a single virtual storage which it shares among processes; the sum of the sizes of the active processes cannot exceed the size of the single virtual **address space**. (An address space is the range of addresses used by or assigned to a process.) OS/MVT, which uses variable sized regions, gave rise to OS/VS2 MVS (for *M*ultiple *V*irtual *S*torage).

As MVS sprang from the OS family, it was important that compatibility with earlier systems be maintained; yet the changing expectations of what roles large mainframe processors could and should play in an

*What I shall call MVS/370 (versions numbered up to 3.8) runs on the System/370 and its descendant the 303x. MVS/SP1 runs on the 303x. MVS/XA, also called MVS/SP2, takes advantage of the 308x series and the 3090. The various versions and their shifting 'common names' are too complex to describe in detail here. I shall confine my description to MVS/370, calling it MVS, unless I note otherwise.

organization also dictated change. Its predecessor, OS/MVT, already had a number of functions such as an interactive computing facility grafted onto it when designers began planning for an OS/MVT replacement. Thus, these graftings had to be taken into account in designing a successor system. Both history and emerging new requirements would have a strong influence on the design of MVS, as I hope to demonstrate below.

In MVS, each active process *appears* to have a copy of the operating system and its *own* virtual storage address space. In other words, each process (including an apparent copy of the operating system) has a potential 16 (or more, see Section 13.2) megabytes* to work with, the size of the virtual storage address space being determined by the maximum size of the address. I shall use the term *address space* as synonymous with *process* in discussing how MVS manages certain resources, since each process has an address space associated with it. In fact, only one copy of the operating system exists and is shared, but the effective size of an application process remains the same.

Obviously, MVS is quite different from a microcomputer operating system. The sheer size of an MVS system configuration and the variety of functions it must carry out guarantee that it will be large, complex (and complicated), elaborate and richly functional. Since the system was designed to run on a specific family of hosts and their look-alikes, the machine which the users perceive bears a fairly close gross resemblance to the real machine which underpins the system; in fact, the philosophy behind all the OS operating system family has been that the programmer must be a knowledgeable adjunct to the system. The programmer must know something of the system in order to use it effectively; the more he or she knows, the more effective his or her use of the system will be. It is the programmer's job, in the view of OS system design, to provide much of the face of the system that the *end-user* perceives.

Thus, MVS is also quite different in philosophy from the ideal machine inherent in the design of the UCSD p-System. Since MVS does not attempt to make one real computer system behave like a different computer system, it is unlike VM or Unix as well. And of course, its functional specifications and (ultimately) its behavior are entirely unlike that of TPF/II, even though program development and auxiliary applications for TPF/II are carried out on an MVS-controlled system.

*The address of a System/370 is 24 bits or 2^{24}, which is 16 777 216 bytes. The addressing structure of the IBM 3033 with the SE feature was extended to 25 bits. The extended architecture, called XA by IBM, accommodates a 32-bit addressing structure in which the address can be either 31 bits in length (accommodating 2048 megabytes, that is, 2 gigabytes) or 24 bits. The 32nd bit is set to indicate which of the two addressing modes a particular application uses. This allows many older applications taken from the 24-bit addressing structure to run in many cases with little or no alteration in the XA system − providing 'downward' compatibility.

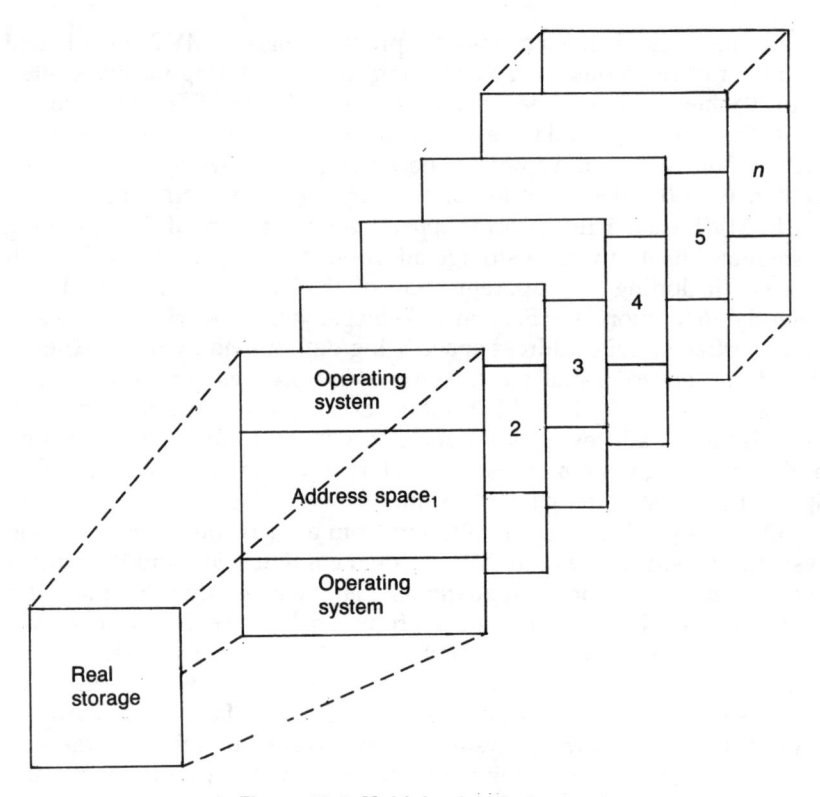

Figure 13.1 Multiple virtual storage

I shall quickly discuss some of the major functional requirements for MVS and then discuss how it manages the resources available to it. I shall also discuss performance, since such a large system requires a goodly share of both real primary storage and processor time. Overheads of such a system can be high: the question remains whether 'the game is worth the candle' to the organization investing in such a system.

13.1 FUNCTIONAL REQUIREMENTS

The functional requirements which dictated the design of MVS are greatly influenced by the histories of the System/360 computer family and OS/360 operating systems family. The System/360 and its OS/360 operating system both appeared in the mid-1960s. Both attracted a large customer base fairly quickly.

One of the initial attractions to the System/360 and OS/360 family was the ease with which users could convert programs to run on these new systems and the ease of migration from one member of the family to another. Thus, pressure to maintain this philosophy of compatibility built up quickly. In this context, compatibility means that the appearance of the system remains the same or closely similar: the job control language grammar, the utility programs and operator commands, the basic apparent philosophy of the system remain the same, while performance and reliability improve and new or extended functions are added. In the evolution of the OS systems there has been a great reluctance to remove some older features; instead, they are either kept but de-emphasized or gradually phased out.

As I said above, OS/MVT had had a number of functions grafted onto it. This was in response to perceived needs in the user community. For example, program development became expensive relative to the cost of the computer. Emphasis was no longer on keeping the cost of development down by off-loading program development to ancillary equipment (for example, card punch machines) and manual methods, but on speeding up the process of program development by saving programmer time. One means is to provide the programmer with interactive computing facilities (a computer terminal and commands to use it in dialog with the central system) and increasingly with tools such as simple-to-use editors for entering program text. TSO (for *Time Sharing Option*) was an optional extra with OS/MVT which was to be fully integrated into the design of MVS. Other examples are the job entry subsystems which relieve the burden of manual scheduling, the software which allows the cooperation of multiple processors, and so on.

Performance was another area which the MVS designers addressed. OS/MVT used real addressing and needed a contiguous allocation of storage to run a process; MVS was to be virtual and to eliminate the need for contiguous storage. But the delay in processing introduced by the overhead of using auxiliary storage as an extension to real storage (see Chapter 4) had to be compensated for in other ways.

A part of user-perceived performance is reliability. The new system would need improved reliability, improved stability. The older systems were subject to a number of known, but difficult to correct, errors which sometimes caused system degradation or outright failure. These had to be addressed in the new system. In addition, the new system would attempt to predict imminent failure by recording transient faults (those which currently existing hardware or software were able to correct) and noting any portion of the system which was subject to repeated transient faults so that corrective action could be taken before outright failure occurred. Further, the new system would attempt *recovery* in the event of failure in a way that the designers of the older systems had not envisaged. The new system with its error detection and warning and its recovery would fail less often and hence offer greater availability than its predecessors.

Otherwise, questions of compatibility and the wide range of uses to which such systems were put dictated that MVS would remain very much a general-purpose operating system for interactive and batch use in a primarily commercial applications area.

Question for discussion

If you were to set out to design an operating system based on the working model provided by an existing operating system, what aspect(s) of the existing system would you adopt in the new system and why?

The extended architecture and MVS/SP2

IBM began development of the extended architecture, XA, in 1976. This was in response to a problem looming on the horizon: in the early to mid-1980s users of large-scale IBM mainframes would run up against the limits of the existing architecture.

A survey made by Robert T. Fertig [1] of large mainframe sites describes the trends underlying this problem. Between 1982 and 1985 the processing power at the average large-scale system site had increased 102%, and primary storage had increased by 101%. The reasons for this were the increase in online database and data-communications applications, greater daily peak loads for all types of applications, the need to run an additional processor as backup support for critical database and data communications applications and, not surprisingly, the increased functions and corresponding processor load from MVS itself, and from its major subsystems.

The shift to transaction- and interactive-mode processing implied in the increased database and data communications applications workload also increased the need to avoid paging in and out for time-sensitive applications code and data: this effectively reduces the remaining real storage available to other processes. The amount of virtual storage addressable and the amount of real storage which could be managed were quickly becoming the key limiting factors.

The resulting System/370 Extended Architecture (S/370-XA) was released in 1981. The architecture was realized in a combination of hardware, software and microcode. It was designed to:

- overcome the limited address space;
- expand the restricting I/O environment;

- overcome the limitation imposed by the maximum of two processors in a tightly coupled multiprocessor arrangement;
- meet increased requirements for high reliability, availability and serviceability;
- improve resource management for large multiprocessing complexes.

The architecture is supported by an enhanced MVS system which is known as MVS/XA.

MVS/XA introduces a 31-bit virtual storage addressing scheme that supports up to 2 gigabytes of virtual storage in each address space. It departs from the common pattern you have seen before of having the system kernel at low address and other system software at high addresses with the area between available for a 'transient' or user process. The storage map of MVS/XA has been restructured from the MVS/370 map and now has a 'line' at 16 megabytes. Immediately below the line are the MVS/370 nucleus and certain common areas. Below these is the private area for all 24-bit addressed applications (which 31-bit addressed applications can use as well). Immediately above the 16-megabyte line sits the extended (XA) nucleus and the extended common areas, with the extended private area for 31-bit applications. In a sense, the operating system sits in the middle of the 2-gigabyte address space, with the applications areas above and below it. The 24-bit applications can access only the lower (non-extended) area of 16 megabytes, but 31-bit applications can access either the upper (extended) area, the lower (non-extended) area, or both.

The extension of virtual storage has some effect even on applications which continue as 24-bit addressed [2]. Before MVS/XA, the S/370 architecture was expanded to provide for up to 32 megabytes of real storage, but I/O from a user application could not access any real storage above 16 megabytes. Hence some I/O caused a storage-to-storage move of data from real storage with an address greater than FFFFFF to real storage with an address lower than FFFFFF before I/O could take place. This resulted in conflict for storage below the 16-megabyte address on 32-megabyte real storage systems.

Later as I describe components of the MVS system I shall decribe how some of these were altered to reduce or eliminate problems which occurred in situations like that which I have just described.

The extended architecture made another major departure from the older S/370 architecture. The rigid data channel subsystem was replaced by a dynamic channel subsystem. This is a microcoded independent processor connected to the processor and memory of the 308x and the 3090 mainframes. The dynamic channel subsystem accommodates a theoretical maximum of 65 356 devices, 256 channel paths, and eight paths per device. MVS/XA implements up to 4080 device addresses (not including

16 used for internal communications) with four paths to each device possible.

The dynamic channel subsystem treats all devices and channels as members of a single logical group regardless of whether there is one processor (as in a 3083), two (3081) or four (3084). This eliminates the need for an algorithm to direct I/O from a specific processor in a multiprocessor arrangement, and any processor in such an arrangement can process an I/O request, regardless of which processor initiated it.

The change from a static to a dynamic channel subsystem required considerable modification to the I/O supervisor, while the expansion of both virtual and real storage necessitated changes in the access methods.

13.2 THE COMPUTER SYSTEM MVS CONTROLS

I have discussed many of the features of the IBM/360 and 370 architectures in Part I, but I have not necessarily identified them as being features of a particular system. Therefore I shall briefly repeat some of them here so that the roles of the various functions of the operating system are quite clear to you.

The IBM/370 family and its descendants are all *interrupt-driven*; that is, interrupts of both the hardware and software varieties are the normal mechanism for context switching. When an interrupt occurs, the Program Status Word (PSW – a special register) is stored as an old PSW. Other information necessary to restart work on the interrupted process is also stored. A new PSW is then loaded into the PSW register. This new PSW contains the address of the interrupt handler routine necessary to process the interrupt. Processing then commences from the address contained in the PSW (i.e. the *new* PSW as placed in the register). The interrupted process may or may not regain control after the interrupt has been processed. If it is *non-preemptive* then it will be redispatched; if not, it will be queued and the highest-priority queued request will be dispatched by the low-level scheduler.

Storage protection

Protection of storage locations is accomplished through the use of three kinds of protection mechanism.

The first is called *key* protection. The hardware provides 16 keys. Data can only be stored in a location if their access key matches that of the storage location; data can only be fetched when the fetch bit of a control register is set to zero (no fetch protection provided) *or* when the keys of the request address and the actual location match.

OS/VS2 MVS

Another of the three types is *low-address* protection; this protects locations 0—511 and is under the control of one of the system's 16 control registers.

The last is *segment* protection; this is controlled by a bit in the segment table entry for a given segment.

Addressing

Dynamic address translation using fixed-length 64-kilobyte segments composed of 4-kilobyte pages (as described in Section 4.3 of Part I) is used by the computer. A cache memory used in dynamic address translation is called the *translation lookaside buffer*; it holds up to 128 addresses and when new addresses are added to it they replace the least recently used of all the addresses currently in it. A virtual address of 16 megabytes is used with a 24-bit address.* About half the 16 megabytes is available for an applications process; the other half is used by the operating system. The operating system itself can, however, address up to 24 megabytes on uniprocessors, and 32 megabytes of multiprocessors.

Addressing is of three types. *Virtual* addresses (addresses within the

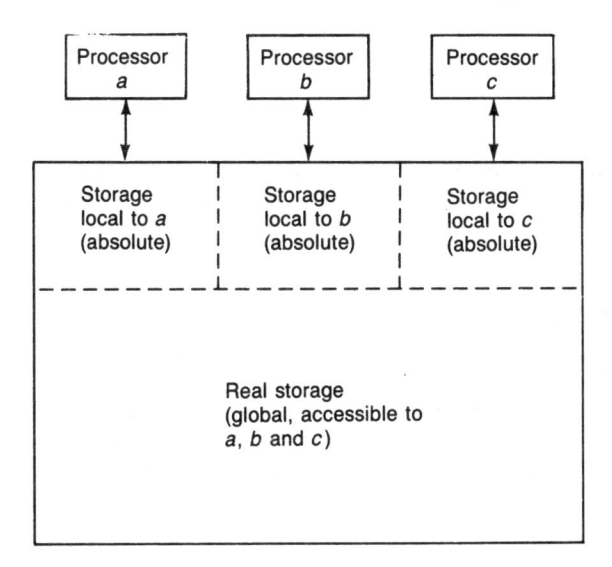

Figure 13.2 Absolute and real storage in a multiprocessor arrangement

*In the XA architecture it is a virtual address of 2048 megabytes with a 31-bit address. In the remaining discussion I shall assume the 24-bit addressing structure unless I indicate otherwise.

virtual address space) are translated to *real* addresses (physical locations in real storage). In addition, a process called *prefixing* converts real addresses to *absolute* addresses.

Absolute and real addresses are usually identical, unless more than one processor accesses a shared primary storage. Then prefixing assigns real addresses 0—4095 to an absolute block of storage. (Note how this affects low-address protection, described above.) When a processor seeks to fetch data from real addresses between 0 and 4095, the real address it seeks is appended to the prefix that is stored in a control register of *that* processor to give an absolute address which points to a 4-kilobyte area local to only that processor. Each processor in a multiprocessor system needs an area to hold data that it *cannot share* with other processors (due to a design decision — see the questions for discussion below), such as the old and new PSWs which apply to it and it alone.

MVS consists of a number of functions with specific roles to play. I shall discuss these below.

Questions for review

(i) How are addresses translated dynamically in this type of system?
(ii) What is the purpose of *prefixing*?

Questions for discussion

(i) Why might a designer wish to prevent one processor from accessing another's stored PSWs in a multiprocessor system?
(ii) Why might a designer find it useful to allow one processor to access another's stored PSWs?

13.3 THE SUPERVISOR

The *supervisor* is the general manager of the MVS system. It provides the controls needed for multiprogramming: scheduling, creating processes, dispatching and provision of mutual-exclusion capabilities to serialize the use of resources. It consists of a number of subfunctions.

System resources manager

The *System Resources Manager (SRM)* is that portion of the supervisor which determines which process will have access to system resources and at what rate a process can use those resources; it is an *intermediate-level*

OS/VS2 MVS

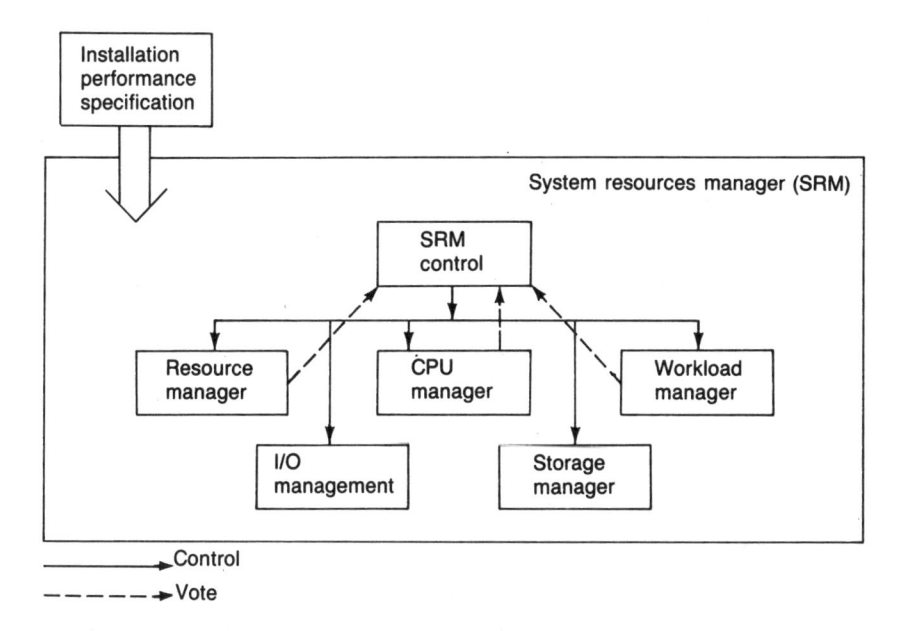

Figure 13.3 System resources manager and components

scheduler. It attempts two things: to distribute resources among competing tasks according to the policy of the organization (set at sysgen time in the *Installation Performance Specification* — *IPS*) and to optimize the use of resources to the greatest degree possible. To rephrase this, it attempts to balance the need to maximize throughput with the particular installation's response-time objectives as stated in the IPS. The SRM's objectives are to keep those virtual memories in real storage which will best use the system's resources and meet the IPS at any instant.

The IPS contains parameters for performance which are set at sysgen time. A unit of activity equivalent to an address space and called a *transaction* is defined. For batch jobs the transaction is the job from beginning to end as defined by the job control language statements created by the user. For interactive users a transaction is the period from when a user's address space becomes *ready* until a terminal wait occurs (as it will, for example, on completing a response to the user).

Each transaction belongs to a type defined by the organization; types are associated with a *performance group* which in turn is assigned a *performance objective*. The objective consists of the minimum amount of *service** which each transaction within that group must receive during

---

*Service is defined as the measure of system resources provided for each transaction serviced: processor time, real storage use and I/O requests.

each processing time interval it is given. *Service* is a linear combination of the amount of the three basic resources used and can be expressed as:

$$s = \frac{t}{k} + c + \frac{(ps * t)}{k}$$

where *s* is service, *t* is processor time, *c* is I/O request count, *ps* is page seconds averaged over the lifetime of the transaction and *k* is a computer-model-dependent adjusting factor.

This minimum must be *exceeded* before the address space becomes a candidate for swapping. The motive for specifying different performance objectives for different types of transaction is to give certain users better performance at the expense of others who (one hopes) don't need it. The relative importance of this depends on the system workload: that is, on how much demand for a resource exceeds (or not) the available supply of that resource.

Work is divided into *domains* which are assigned relative priorities; for example, the lowest domain might be batch jobs, the next lowest domain might be high-priority batch work, then non-trivial interactive use, with the highest domain given to trivial interactive use (*trivial* refers to the resources used, not to the relative importance of a task to the user).

The *S*ystem *R*esources *M*anager (SRM) tries to balance the system's workload on a number of different levels. It may designate an address space as eligible for swapping if it uses excessive processor time, if it uses too much real storage, or if it monopolizes a channel or device. Hence the SRM keeps use-counts on auxiliary devices; then the device with the lowest use-count can be allocated in preference to a similar device with a higher use-count. If real storage becomes a critical resource the SRM can select a process for swapping or can halt the initiation of new processes until the shortage is eased. It can also *steal pages* from other processes in order to satisfy the need for storage on the part of a process starved of real space; it will steal pages on demand only, and then only those least recently used.

In MVS/XA several changes have been made to minimize the effects of the system's increased capacity. The page frame search algorithms have been changed to take into account the longer page frame lists, and some storage allocation locks have been decomposed to smaller locks in order to reduce waiting on locks in multiprocessing systems.

The SRM itself comprises subfunctions. One such is the *workload manager*, which measures resource use by any transaction according to service units a second (called the *service rate*). It maps the service rate to the performance objective to obtain a *workload level* and thus votes in swap decisions. *Workload level* is a function of the current *system* workload, the age of the transaction and the service so far accumulated by that transaction.

The *SRM control* determines what the SRM itself should be doing and calls upon the appropriate subfunction. It solicits votes from the SRM constituents on swap decisions and makes the decision to swap, once votes are counted.

The *resource manager* monitors the system-wide resource usage to determine what resources are under- or over-used, adjusts the multi-programming level and makes recommendations to the SRM control.

The *storage manager* determines when and where page stealing occurs, swaps out heavy users of fixed pages, checks for long waits, monitors auxiliary storage for page slot shortage and halts the initiation of new processes when necessary.

I/O management locates the volume and device (unit) information for a requested file, resolves the relationships between the request for the file and the file itself, assigns the device(s) to the process. If necessary, I/O management requests the operator to mount a volume which it then verifies as being the correct one. If a new file is being created, it will direct the creation of it. It builds the control blocks and chains necessary to carry this out. If any problems occur during this process, I/O management attempts recovery by retrying. If the retry is unsuccessful it requests operator intervention. The operator can then determine whether to cancel the request, cause the requesting job to wait, or assign an alternate device to satisfy the request. Once the process no longer requires a file, I/O management determines what to do with that file based on what the user has requested,* releases the volume if it has been reserved by the process so that it can be demounted or allocated to other users, and erases the control block chains.

The *CPU manager* manages automatic priority groups (priorities automatically assigned when no dispatching priority is indicated by the user), monitors system processor utilization, identifies heavy processor users, seeks to minimize delays due to serialization of a resource and can vote in swap decisions.

Questions for review

(i) What is a possible result of performance objectives where:
 (a) the level of processor time is set very low,
 (b) real storage use values are set very low?
(ii) What, if any, advantage can be gained from the modular design of the SRM?

---

*The user can request that a file can be deleted (removed from the system catalog and VTOC), entered into or removed from the catalog, or that the operating system should free allocated but unused space (the default being to keep such space as a part of the file's extent), and so on.

Real storage manager

The *Real Storage Manager (RSM)* administers real storage. Thus, it *causes* pages to be moved to or from auxiliary storage (but does not carry out the move). It communicates with the SRM, which provides guidance for paging. Only currently used pages remain in real storage and under the full control of RSM; the rest reside on *page data sets* on direct-access devices and are controlled by the *A*uxiliary *S*torage *M*anager (ASM — see below). The RSM invokes the ASM to carry out the paging process.

RSM also maintains a pool of free page frames and assigns frames when needed from the pool. It returns frames to the pool when a process terminates or explicitly frees space, or when an address space is swapped. If a process needs to run in real storage (where the user has specified that *virtual* equals *real* — see Section 13.5) RSM allows this and manages it. RSM also contains page-fault routines (explained in Section 4.3) and controls whether real storage is or is not available to the system (see Section 13.9, 'Error recovery').

(The RSM in MVS/XA is changed from the RSM in MVS/370. It provides a homogeneous view of real storage, eliminating the problem which occurred in the large 32-megabyte real storage systems when I/O routines needed to address data whose address was higher than 16 megabytes.)

Auxiliary storage manager

The *Auxiliary Storage Manager (ASM)* transfers pages between real storage and auxiliary storage page slots. If this occurs on a page-by-page basis it is termed *paging*; if it occurs for an entire process it is termed *swapping* (see Chapters 3 and 4 in Part I). ASM is responsible for maintaining the page data sets: the collections of page slots on high-speed auxiliary storage. These slots contain pages not in active use, copies of pages in active use, and updated copies of changed pages removed from real storage in response to swapping or page-stealing.

When a page is required and not found in real storage, the ASM examines a table called the *external page table* to locate the desired page. This means that the ASM translates a virtual address to a real *auxiliary* storage address. The page can then be copied from its slot on auxiliary storage to a frame in real storage.

When the need arises to move a page from real to auxiliary storage, for example in response to a page-steal, the RSM requests the ASM to locate a free *page slot* on auxiliary storage using the external page table. The ASM then moves the page from real to auxiliary storage and updates the external page table to show the page's virtual address and its page slot address.

OS/VS2 MVS 317

Virtual storage manager

The *Virtual Storage Manager (VSM)* controls the use of virtual storage by each process. The VSM creates the address space (defined above) when the process is being created and subsequently controls the virtual storage within the address space. The VSM tries to satisfy requests for storage by checking control blocks within the address space to see whether virtual storage is available; if so, it updates the control blocks accordingly. It also frees space when requested. It calls upon the real storage manager (RSM) to satisfy any needs for real storage.

Questions for review

Briefly describe the interactions which take place between the storage manager, the real storage manager, the auxiliary storage manager, and the virtual storage manager in the following circumstances:

(i) when a new process is initiated;
(ii) when a page on auxiliary storage is required in real storage;
(iii) when a page-steal occurs.

13.4 THE MASTER SCHEDULER

An MVS system starts up with a process referred to as *IPL* — which stands for *Initial Program Load*. It is the *master scheduler* which carries out the initialization of the system and responds to the operator's commands.

Start-up is accomplished partly by making known to the system the configuration it manages. In other words, the locations and characteristics of all attached devices (defined in tables) and the volumes permanently mounted on them, the locations of the page and swap data sets (files), the master catalog, the program libraries available to all users and the default system storage areas are read from the *IPL volume* (usually a disk) to those areas of storage where the operating system routines will reside while the system runs. (Volumes can be permanently resident or removable, public — accessible by everyone — or private.)

The part of the master scheduler which accepts operator commands, invokes the appropriate routine(s) within the system for execution and responds to the operator is called the *communication task*. Should this task fail, communications with the operator become impossible and the operating system requires a restart.

Operators communicate with the system through system-designated *consoles* which are defined as part of the sysgen process. A *master console* is designated and accepts all commands. It is also possible to designate alternative consoles (which can consist of the card reader and printer) in the event that the master console fails, and to designate secondary consoles which have limited functions. For example, one secondary console could be designated for the control of the magnetic tape drives and thus would receive messages about tape mount and dismount requests and other magnetic tape and tape-drive related messages and could accept commands limited to the use and function of tape drives.

Secondary consoles can be made alternative consoles to each other and to the master console; this guards against the possibility that the failure of any one console will cripple the system. It also proves handy in large installations should the full complement of operators not be available for some reason. One console can double up its functions if necessary to allow one operator to monitor two or more aspects of the system.

It is usual to provide a hard-copy (printed) version of activity at the master console to aid in problem reconstruction when necessary.

Questions for review

(i) What two functions does the master scheduler carry out?
(ii) List two advantages of alternative consoles.

13.5 DATA MANAGEMENT

The *data management* portion of the operating system controls access to files.* The services provides by data management include the establishing and use of buffers, the scheduling of I/O operations, performing the I/O and supporting the many file organizations and access methods which MVS offers: sequential, indexed sequential (in both sequential and direct modes), direct access, virtual storage (all as described in Part I, Section 2.5) and **partitioned data sets** which consist of multiple subfiles contained within one physical file with a subdirectory with entries for each subfile (called a *member*). These last are commonly used to store collections of source or object code programs (i.e. libraries).

---

*In IBM terminology files are called *data sets* as well as *files*, the latter term usually being limited to the physical entity and the former to the conceptual or logical entity.

OS/VS2 MVS

Access methods

Access methods (i) build the necessary control blocks and *channel programs* to carry out the I/O request made by a user program or command, (ii) issue the instruction which invokes the necessary system components and (iii) wait for the operation to complete.

These access methods can be *basic*, which means that the access method allows any record to be accessed at the time the request is made, that no deblocking or buffering is carried out, and that control is returned to the requesting process *before* the I/O operation is complete (the process must verify for itself that the request has been successfully satisfied). Or an access method can be *queued*, which means that records are grouped automatically in anticipation of future requests and control is not returned to the requesting process until the current request has been satisfied.

(Access methods in MVS/XA have been modified so that real storage above the former 16-megabyte maximum can be used for I/O buffers. This removes what had been an artificial constraint on the very large real-storage systems prior to MVS/XA.)

Telecommunications is an aspect of data management which controls communications with local and remote users. It does so by making available *access methods* to do so, just as data management provides *access methods* to access records on files. The methods most commonly in use are the *B*asic *T*elecommunications *A*ccess *M*ethod (BTAM) which supports simple telecommunications applications, *T*ele*C*ommunications *A*ccess *M*ethod (TCAM) which is used almost exclusively by the interactive computing facility (TSO, discussed later) and is a queued method, and *V*irtual *T*elecommunications *A*ccess *M*ethod (VTAM) which shifts many functions performed by the host processor in BTAM and TCAM to an attached communications controller.

Question for review

What is the major distinction between the basic and queued methods?

Questions for discussion

(i) What purpose is served by an access method?
(ii) Contrast the practice of providing several different access methods for different purposes (as MVS does) with the Unix philosophy of hiding these details from users and providing a simple access method. In what cases might one be preferable to the other?
(iii) What is the advantage to be gained from an access method like VTAM?

13.6 INTERACTIVE SYSTEM USE – TSO

In the earlier IBM operating system OS/MFT the emerging need for interactive computing was met by providing add-on software to supply this facility; it was called *Time-Sharing Option* or TSO. In other words, OS/MFT (and later, OS/MVT) was a batch-oriented system with an interactive facility grafted onto it.

MVS, on the other hand, is *fundamentally based* on the philosophy and techniques of interactive use and also accepts batch work. The portion of MVS which allows interactive computing is still called, and is compatible from the user's point of view with, TSO as it originally appeared. However, it is fully integral to MVS and the only option about it is whether or not full use is made of it. By *fully integral* I mean that MVS schedules and services individual TSO users as individual address spaces, rather than scheduling and servicing one address space with TSO which happens to contain one or more TSO users, and the TSO driver (see below) is the system's low-level scheduler.

TSO provides a text editor for the entering and changing of data. It also provides a number of commands which allow a user to create, copy, move and delete files and send messages to other users. As well as the commands, the TSO user can build commands up in such a way as to run an otherwise batch-type program interactively; these commands duplicate the functions provided by the (batch) job control language (JCL).

It is also possible to develop a program interactively and then to wrap that program in JCL statements and submit it as a batch job, thereby freeing the user's terminal for continuing interactive work. For example, a user (programmer in this case) can use the text editor interactively to create a source program, and can then wrap the source program in the necessary job control language statements to submit it to the compiler to run in batch mode. While the program is compiling in the batch mode (**background processing**), the user can carry on with other interactive work (**foreground processing**).

It is common to find that an installation has provided additional software which runs under TSO and offers enhanced interactive facilities: menu-driven full-screen editors, word-processing facilities, split screen (creating windows on different tasks and providing the user the ability to switch back and forth between them), interactive program test tools and so on.

TSO consists of a number of components. The *message control program* provided by the access method (TCAM or VTAM) interfaces with remote terminals. The *time-sharing control task* responds to the system operator's command to start TSO, obtains storage and builds control blocks, manages

OS/VS2 MVS

space within the TSO control region and swaps active TSO users in and out.

The *LOGON scheduler* processes LOGON messages from users. The LOGON procedure interfaces the user to the system by examining a user profile which is unique to each user and which delineates which resources the user should be able to call upon.

The *command processors* and associated service routines provide the functions invoked by TSO commands: the EDIT command invoking the editor, the DELETE command invoking a service routine to delete a file and so on.

The *system driver* allocates system service to time-sharing users and thus determines processor and storage use for each user. In MVS the driver is effectively the low-level scheduling mechanism for the system as a whole.

Questions for review

(i) What elements constitute an interactive computing system?
(ii) What part is played in TSO by the command processor? The system driver?

13.7 MISCELLANEOUS SYSTEM ELEMENTS

Continuing IBM's policy of providing *utility programs* to carry out general functions, MVS also has a large collection of general-purpose utility programs which developed from the earlier utility programs. Some of the functions they provide are: the facility to update individual records in a file or subfile (add, change or delete and renumber), the facility to create, catalog (make an entry in the system catalog), rename, copy, uncatalog (remove an entry) or delete a file, the facility to move a file (a copy operation which subsequently deletes the original), the facility to compress a partitioned data set to recover fragmented space, the facility to load data into an indexed sequential or virtual storage file. There are also utility programs available for restricted use by systems programmers or operators: to verify the integrity of the surface of a disk, to change individual *bits* in a file, and so on.

System support programs are those which provide compilers and assemblers, linkage editors (linking separately compiled program units — or modules — together to create one program) and loaders.

Service aids provide the ability to format dumps (hard-copy) of virtual or real storage, to trace execution in aid of problem investigation and other facilities of use to the systems programmer.

Accounting

System accounting in such a large and complex system environment takes on an importance greatly exceeding its importance in smaller, less complex systems.

The system gathers information about itself and the users and users' processes it hosts by two means: the System Management Facility (SMF) and the System Activity Measurement Facility (called MF/1). SMF is a data collection program which builds accounting records, collects file activity records for each file, volume-use records for each volume, system- and subsystem-use records (more about subsystems later), and allows the system programmer to write special routines to trap additional information and to analyze data and format reports.

In order to avoid losing information when an SMF data collection file is closed in order to process the data, there are two files, called SYS1.MANX and SYS1.MANY. One receives data while the other is available for report formatting and maintenance. A number of events cause data to be recorded. For example, step termination (in a batch job) generates a record type 4 recording the elapsed and processor times, I/O count and virtual and real storage use for that step to be written to the active SMF file, in other words, to record its use of resources. The records are variable in length and start with a word giving the length of the record in bytes. Also included are the identity of the system (set by the systems programmer), the type of record, a time-and-date stamp, the processor's identity and a variable information field.

MF/1 also records vital statistics on the MANX or MANY files, but its recording is specific to the activity of the operating system itself. It records processor, paging, workload, channel, device, page/swap data set and trace activity.

The information gathered can be used to charge users for services, to analyze present performance, to set performance objectives, to locate bottlenecks in the system (for example, an overly busy channel can be identified and its load redistributed among less busy channels) and to help predict computing and storage capacity for the future.

Questions for review

A great deal of effort is expended in capturing data about the state and use of the system.

(i) List two purposes for which such data are used.
(ii) In your opinion, why do smaller systems (e.g. Unix, MS-DOS and CP/M) not capture such data?

13.8 JOB ENTRY

With OS/MVT, two job entry subsystems, each meeting somewhat different requirements, had been created. One or the other would be grafted onto the base system to meet installation scheduling needs or to allow attached and multiprocessor support; the operating system could, however, be run without them, using *manual scheduling*.

Under MVS, one or the other subsystem must be present as the system is otherwise virtually crippled. Strictly speaking, these subsystems are more properly called system services, since they do not provide a conceptual entity which is a complete environment for use of the system for a specialized set of users; however, this is the designation IBM has given them.

The volume and dynamic nature of work commonly run on even single large mainframe systems in large organizations means that it is virtually impossible to provide sufficient manual scheduling services to keep the system fully occupied. Hence MVS incorporates a *Job Entry Subsystem (JES)* which acts as a high-level scheduler. JES works by accepting jobs (user-defined units of batch work) from local or remote card readers or interactive terminals, or jobs which are generated by a program. JES scans all requests for syntactical correctness (in other words, errors in syntax in the job control statements are rejected at this point) and places the work on an appropriate queue.

Placement on a queue is by assigned *class* and priority; the organization designates what the classes are, what the designations mean and who is allowed what priority. CLASS = A may mean jobs requiring less than 30 seconds' processor time and no operator intervention on one system and jobs requiring more than two hours' processor time and more than five interventions on a different system, depending upon what the organization controlling the system wants.

A *converter* converts job control statements, TSO LOGON procedures or a started task (a task which the operator can start with a command from the console) to a form which is readable by the operating system and provides additional correctness checking facilities at this point, with errors being rejected. Next, jobs are sent to the operating system in response to resources being available to execute them.

From this point the operating system takes over, and JES has no role to play until the operating system completes execution of the job, when JES is notified. JES will generate some final messages to the user and, if printed or punched output is part of the job, it is spooled for the appropriate output device. Finally JES purges the job from the system. JES offers aging − the longer a job waits for execution, the higher its priority becomes.

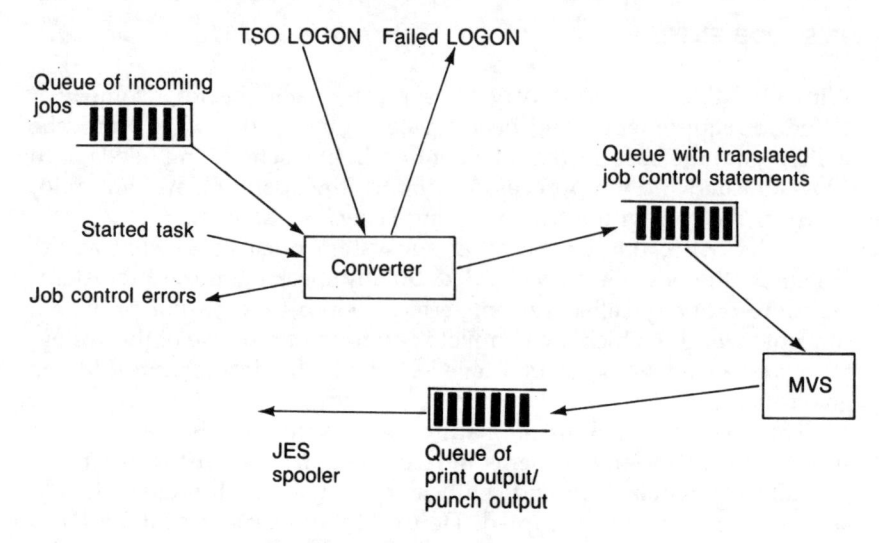

Figure 13.4 The role of JES

Two types of JES are available: JES2 and JES3. Both provide essentially the same basic functions, but JES3 provides additional functions such as scheduling based on the job's requirements for tape and disk and deadline scheduling (completion of a job by a given time).

JES2

JES2 is configured by the systems programmer. It controls a number of teleprocessing lines (in support of remote stations), a number of remote job entry stations, and local devices. It also has a checkpoint file which must be on a direct access volume and which stores a copy of the JES2 queue and other information needed in the event some failure requires a restart of the system (called a warm start − some or all of the system routines are already resident in primary storage and do not require loading from disk). The queue is kept in primary storage, with the copy on disk. JES2 periodically updates this copy by copying the primary storage version to the disk − thus protecting job and data integrity.

If more than one processor has access to the JES2 subsystem, the checkpoint file is kept on a disk shared by all the systems in the configuration. To update the checkpoint file, JES2 must prevent access to that file by other systems for the duration of the update; it does so by issuing a RESERVE macro-instruction and subsequently issuing a RELEASE macro-instruction when the update completes. Checkpoint files can be duplexed; that is, an identical copy of the checkpoint file can be created on a separate volume and also updated, though less frequently than the primary copy.

If an error causes the failure of JES2 or damage to the job queue, JES2 rebuilds the job output and input queues from the checkpoint file under the control of the computer operator. Once the queues are rebuilt, the jobs within them can be re-queued or cancelled at the operator's discretion.

Jobs are queued according to priority sequence and, when they are ready for execution, by priority within individual classes. The queue is built within the JES2 address space in primary storage and contains entries for each job consisting of the job name, priority, a flag to indicate whether it is *held* (prevented from executing except by express command of the operator), pointers to control blocks and to the JES process (conversion, output processing, purging, etc.) for which the job is next eligible. A *held job* is not purged from the queue but is not eligible to be selected for any JES2 processing. The operator must explicitly release held jobs in order for them to be scheduled for execution.

There are 38 classes, with two reserved for system use (one for started tasks — those invoked by command of the computer operator — and one for any TSO user logging on) and the other 36 available for batch users. The job class is specified in the JOB statement of the job control language or if not specified is assigned according to how it entered the system. Generally, jobs of similar characteristics should be assigned to the same class. Priority can be assigned on the JOB statement of the job control language or can be assigned automatically based on the class or accounting information supplied by the user.

Execution of jobs is controlled by *initiators*. An initiator is a form of gate which permits one job at a time through itself into the system. There is a logical initiator in JES2 for each initiator in the system(s) interfacing with JES2. The maximum number of logical initiators is set during JES2 initialization, but the operator controls the number (up to the maximum) actually available.

Each initiator is associated with one or more classes, which it will allow through its gate. The initiator, when it has no work to do, selects any job which is not held and which is first in priority order for its class(es). The classes themselves are ordered for each initiator. For example, *initiator$_1$* might allow classes A, B and C, and would select the highest-priority class A job first, unless there were *no* class A jobs waiting, when it would select the highest-priority class B job, while *initiator$_2$* might allow classes B, C and X and would select the highest-priority class B job first.

A job can be monitored according to three criteria: elapsed time (wall-clock time), processor time, or by amount of output in terms of lines printed or cards punched or both.

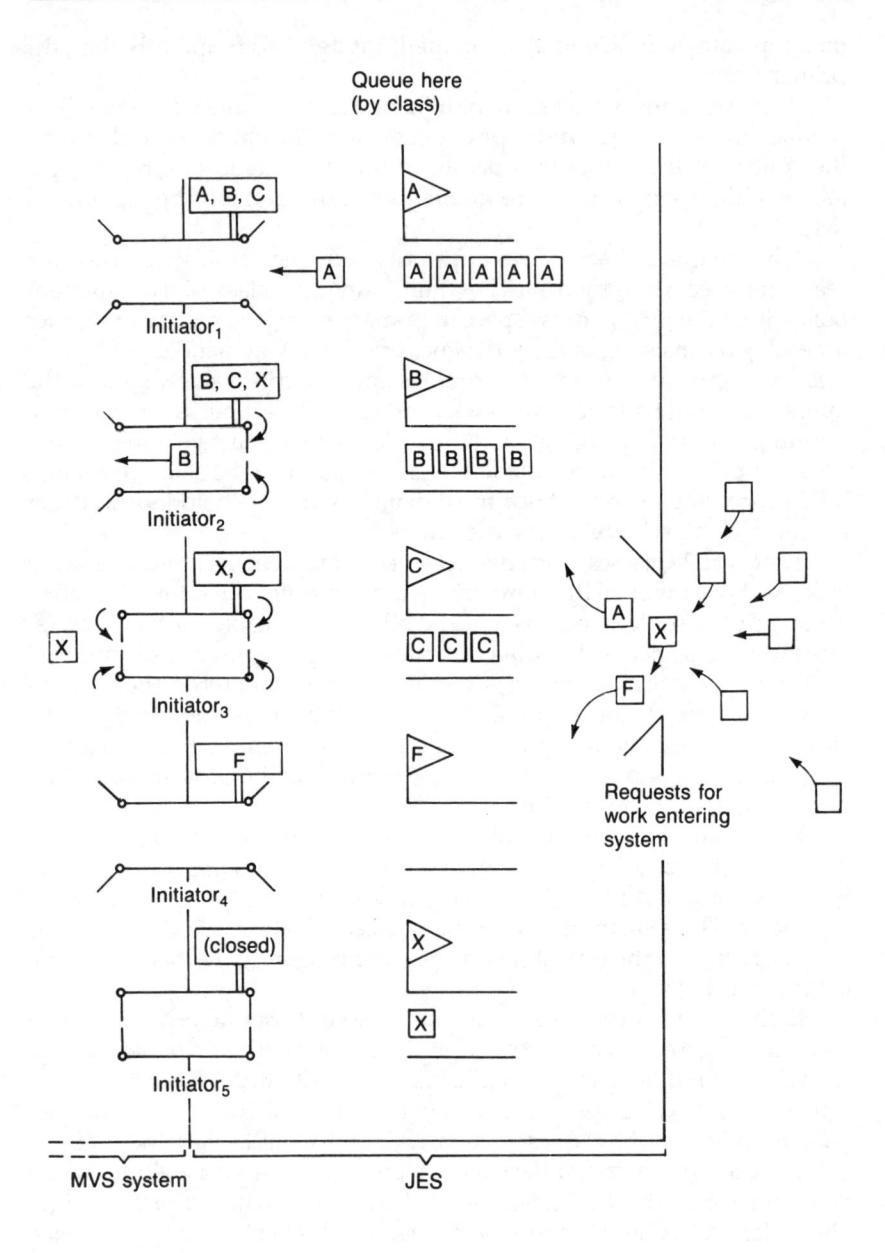

Figure 13.5 Initiators in JES and the MVS system

For output, JES2 queues each unit of work according to a priority based on the volume of output represented by that unit. The user or operator has the ability to specify various aspects of output management such as forms to be used, print-chain (font) or options and features pertaining to non-impact printing subsystems (impact printers use hammers to strike characters on a chain). A print or punch processor selects work from the print or punch output queue with preference given to shorter and older jobs. The user can also route output to a specific local or remote device, to a remote job entry station, or to a pool of remote job entry stations.

JES3

In describing JES3 I shall concentrate on those areas where it differs from JES2.

JES3 provides distribution of *batch* work among several processors which share a spool file and which are loosely coupled together using channel-to-channel adapters. The loosely coupled multiple processors maintain a single image for computer operations, job scheduling and resource management.

One processor, called the *global processor*, provides the functions of input and output, resource management, job scheduling and operator interface for the whole system of interconnected processors. The other processors are termed *local processors*; they provide the communications interface to the global processor and process I/O requests to the shared pool for jobs which they are executing.

Any processor in the system may have its own locally managed devices or may jointly manage devices with JES3 (on the global processor). Some devices are managed *only* by JES3 on the global processor: those which have no permanently mounted volume, for example, magnetic tape drives. Thus, centralized job scheduling, resource allocation and job selection are provided by one processor (the global) on behalf of all the processors in the system.

A JES3 facility called the main device scheduler provides volume fetching. It determines a job's requirements for *mountable* volumes (whether tape or disk) and issues messages to the operator and to a library requesting that the required volumes be fetched. Then it can either make the job immediately eligible for data resource allocation (see below) or wait for the operator to indicate that the requested volumes are available.

Data resource allocation facilities consist of: (i) selection of a job relative to other jobs competing for resources, (ii) selection of an eligible processor (in a multiprocessor environment) on which to attempt allocation, and (iii) assignment of devices, volumes and files to the selected job. *The first job that can acquire these resources on an eligible processor will be granted those resources.*

The main device scheduler, having selected a job for data resource allocation, next chooses a setup processor eligible to run the job. The choice of this processor does not limit that job to run only on that processor. The main device scheduler gives preference in allocation to those devices shared by other processors also eligible to execute that job. If two or more processors share all the devices allocated to a job, they all remain eligible to run that job.

Once the main device scheduler has assigned all the required resources to a job, it issues the necessary mount message requesting the operator to mount on a specific device the first of any mountable volumes required by the job. It then verifies that the correct volume has been mounted. Once all the volumes needed have been mounted, the job is passed to the generalized main scheduler for execution process selection.

When a job releases any resources either by completing, by releasing at the end of any step any device not required for a subsequent step, or by dynamically releasing any device as soon as the connection with it can be severed, the main device scheduler is notified and returns the freed resources to the available pool of resources for assignment to other jobs.

The generalized main scheduling facility of JES3 selects jobs for execution. JES3 initialization parameters define the characteristics of each processor, each class of job and the job-selection criteria to be used. Jobs are assigned priority according to class and priority statements on the JOB statement of the job control language, but processor priority is determined dynamically based on load.

Most data-processing organizations will have a group of jobs which must be completed by a certain time in order to meet schedules. An example might be the overnight update of a bank's master files of checking and deposit accounts, which must take place before the opening of business on the following working day. *Deadline scheduling* in JES3 provides algorithms that increase the probability of a designated job being scheduled to execute by a specific time. The selection priority for that job may be dynamically increased as the job approaches its deadline for beginning execution.

Dependent job control is a feature of JES3 which allows the user to specify a chain or network of jobs to be executed in a specific order. This may be required because some groups of jobs will have data dependencies — the output of one job is the input for another. Dependent job control may also be useful to improve device utilization.

Questions for review

(i) JES fills what role in MVS systems?

(ii) Describe briefly the function of an initiator in JES.
(iii) What are the major functional differences between JES2 and JES3?

13.9 ERROR RECOVERY

One of the most important objectives in the MVS design was increased reliability, which was partly to be achieved through error recovery.

The four major types of errors — soft, intermediate, hard, terminating — are itemized in the following four paragraphs.

Soft errors

Soft or temporary (also called transient) errors are those which can be recovered from by the hardware or which are irrelevant to mainline processing. Soft errors include correctable storage errors, system-corrected errors, external damage and simple system degradation. Such errors are recorded in a special file called SYS1.LOGREC. Recovery routines carry out the recovery and log the error; they also note whether an error threshold has been reached and if so issue a message to the operator and enter a quiet mode for that error type. The interrupted process is resumed.

Intermediate errors

Intermediate errors are restricted to the various system clocks, require software repair but are irrelevant to mainline processing. Intermediate errors involve damage to one of the system clocks (time-of-day, comparator, processor and interval timers). Again, the error is logged in SYS1.LOGREC. If this is the first error, the system tries to reset the clock. If the reset fails, the system marks the clock as bad, masks off interrupts from that clock and resumes the interrupted process. If two or more processors are linked in the system (multiprocessor or attached processor) timing will be carried out on the processor with the good clock. If no good clock exists, the system becomes severely degraded and abnormal ends to tasks requesting clocking functions occur.

Hard errors

Hard or permanent errors are those which cannot be corrected and cause the current instruction to fail; however, the system can continue to function. Hard errors include uncorrected storage error, uncorrected storage protection key error (if either type were corrected they would be classed as soft), invalid register or PSW, or instruction processing damage. The error is recorded, an operator message is sent, storage is removed from use if it is a storage error, the storage protection key is set if it is a key error. *Recovery Task Management (RTM)* is invoked to notify the process of the error.

Terminating errors

Terminating errors are the most serious; these involve the loss of the processor. They include system damage, invalid logout, an error in the machine check (machine failure) recovery software, or occurrence of a second machine check while processing the first. The error is logged. The system stops the processor if it is a uni- or an attached processor. If it is one of a multiprocessor system, the system will issue an emergency signal to the other processor(s) and stop the processor suffering the error. The most serious of all are hardware-detected terminating errors: the system red light comes on, the hardware issues a malfunction alert (and invokes alternative processor recovery software if there are other processors in the system), and stops the stricken processor; the alternative processor then enters alternative processor recovery.

Channel errors

Other types of error affect channels; again, the system records the error and sends the operator a message. If possible, the channel is cleared and the request that resulted in the detection of the error is restarted from the beginning. Otherwise, control is passed to an error-reporting program.

Missing interrupts

An expected interrupt can also 'go missing'. This means that an I/O request was made and *no* reply has been detected. If this occurs, the system conducts a periodic scan (for example, once every three minutes) on all the unit control blocks in the system. (The unit control block defines the device to the system.) It sets a bit in any unit control block it finds which has an I/O request outstanding. The bit is reset when the I/O completes. If the bit is still on when the missing interrupt handler next scans that unit control block, the missing interrupt handler analyzes whether the problem is the channel, the device, the need to mount a volume or the fact that the process has been swapped. It then issues a message to the operator and invokes an I/O restart if the problem was the channel or device.

Resource for reliability improvement

SYS1.LOGREC thus provides a fruitful mine of information for the systems programmer intent on improving system reliability. It has been observed that any unit showing a number of soft failures over a period of time is more likely to fail in a hard way than a unit which does not show such soft failures. Thus any unit consistently appearing in SYS1.LOGREC can be investigated, serviced or replaced *before* it fails. The software and hardware error recovery routines also serve to continue to provide a service to the users in the event of all but terminal failures; even terminal failures may not result in complete loss of service if the processor lost is one of a multiple processor system.

Questions for review

Describe briefly the system-wide effects of:

(i) a soft error,
(ii) a hard error,
(iii) a terminating error in the attached processor of an attached processor system,
(iv) a terminating error in a multiple processor configuration.

Question for discussion

What is the value of setting different levels of error? What are the costs of doing so?

13.10 SYSTEM INTEGRITY

The data any organization owns is valuable, as is the ability to process it. In addition, the privacy of individuals identified in data is socially valuable. These points have been recognized by the recent spate of data privacy statutes in many countries.

Integrity is a concern of the entire system: the ability of the system to protect itself against corruption. It may mean preventing the ordinary user from having access to parts of the system which are 'none of his or her business': operating-systems code, store and fetch protection, password data sets, privileged modes of operation and execution of privileged instructions.

Security means the denial of any access to the system at all for unauthorized people or agencies, for example by making it exceedingly difficult to log on to the system without first being authorized. (It is generally conceded that it is impossible to prevent absolutely all unauthorized access attempts from succeeding.)

Within a system *privacy* must be assured by allowing the owners of data to classify it in a way suitable to their uses and to control access to it.

Potential integrity problems fall into several categories. One is that system resources *must be uniquely identifiable*; if this is not the case, one user may gain access to a resource which he or she should not have or does not want access to because its identifier duplicates that of a resource which that user *can* legitimately access. One cross-check possible, then, is for the system to assure that no two resources share a single identifier. (Note that it is possible to have two removable disks with the same identifier, for example.)

Another potential problem is concurrent use of resources which should be serial. MVS provides a hierarchy of locks, some of which are accessible to users and some of which only the system itself can access. Spin locks, for example, have a greater urgency than suspend locks (both are described in Chapter 5 under 'Processor management'). The RESERVE and RELEASE macro-instructions used by JES in updating its checkpoint file in a multiprocessor environment is an example of such a lock active across systems; ENQ (for enqueue) and DEQ (for dequeue) are the comparable macro-instructions within a single processor system. All such locks serve to serialize resources when required (for example, to prevent concurrent update taking place).

System data appearing in a user-accessible area of the user's address space also presents an integrity compromise; segregation of system and user storage areas must be strict. User storage areas must be segregated from each other in order to preserve privacy. A problem may occur if user-accessible identifiers are given to important system control structures; if the user can pinpoint a system control structure he or she may then be able to alter it — whether intentionally or not is unimportant to the effect the alteration may have. As I have mentioned, the IBM large mainframe family uses hardware storage protection keys to prevent the system itself (since it is so complex) from violating storage protection. This prevents system data appearing in a user-accessible area. A system-enforced convention for the naming of system control structures also acts to prevent user access to vital portions of the system.

MVS also offers an additional option — Authorized Program Facility (APF) — which allows the system manager to identify restricted services and test the authorization of any users for that service, to identify 'trustworthy' programs (for example, systems software programs not actually a part of the operating system), and to authorize certain libraries of programs to act in a certain manner.

Finally, MVS supports a number of different password or passkey levels. All VSAM (*Virtual Storage Access Method*) files can be protected at the file or lower levels. They can be protected from any access by certain classes of user, and can admit others for specified purposes: read (with or without supplying a password, at the organization's discretion), update, control (delete). The system's master and secondary catalogs (the master catalog controls access to the system files and to secondary catalogs; the latter contain user files) are VSAM files and can be thus protected. TSO LOGON is controlled by password access. Batch jobs are generally expected to be checked by staff, but it is possible to add a password capability.

Questions for review

(i) Differentiate between *integrity* and *security*.
(ii) How does MVS address the serialization of a resource
    (a) in a single-processor system,
    (b) in a multiple-processor system?

REFERENCES

[1] Fertig, R.T. (1983) 'XA the view from the trenches', *Datamation*, **29**(5) (May), 125–36.
[2] Bond, R.L. (1983) 'XA the view from White Plains', *Datamation*, **29**(5) (May), 139–52.

GENERAL REFERENCES

Anon. (1978) *Introduction to JES3* (release 3), IBM, Poughkeepsie, New York, order number GC28-0607.
Anon. (1976) *OS/VS2 Catalog Management Logic* (release 3.7), IBM, Palo Alto, California, order number SY26-3826.
Anon. (1979) *OS/VS2 MVS System Programming Library: JES2* (release 4.1), IBM, Poughkeepsie, New York, order number GC23-0002.
Anon. Notes from IBM course H3764 (1978), *MVS Installation and Maintenance*, drawn from various IBM publications not listed separately above.
Lorin, H. (1986) 'Systems architecture in transition – an overview', *IBM Systems Journal*, **25**(3/4), 256–73.
Matick, R.E. (1986) 'Impact of memory systems on computer architecture and system organization', *IBM Systems Journal*, **25**(3/4), 274–305.

Tucker, S.G. (1986) 'The IBM 3090 system: an overview', *IBM Systems Journal*, **25**(1), 4–19.

FURTHER READING

Deitel, H.M. (1984) *Operating Systems*, Addison-Wesley, Reading, Massachussetts. Chapter 21 is a case study of MVS.

CHAPTER

14
General conclusions

A number of conclusions about operating systems can be drawn from a perusal of the operating systems presented in this book. I shall discuss these below. You, of course, should feel free to agree or disagree with the conclusions I shall draw, based on your own experience and your own reading of this and other material.

Computers were developed because of a need to carry out massive amounts of simple arithmetic computation to solve certain classes of problems. The storing of prewritten program instructions helped make the necessary computation speeds possible and created a group of computer users, programmers, who themselves needed to draw on the power and speed of computers to make their own task of programming easier and quicker. It is also a necessary, but complex, task to manage computer resources effectively.

Early computer and software development was driven by a relatively small community of users, some with highly specialized needs.

Software, especially operating systems, developed and then continued to evolve in order to make ever more effective use of the expensive resources of the computer system and the increasingly valuable time of programmers and users.

Advances in hardware were aimed at making computers and their peripheral equipment increasingly reliable, faster, cheaper to run (for example by reducing power consumption − either direct consumption or consumption by cooling systems) and with larger capacities for data and program storage while using less physical space. And, of course, advances were aimed at reducing the costs of manufacture and subsequent maintenance. Increasing speed and reliability also means that such systems become ever more suitable for real-time work even in potentially critical situations: air traffic control, defence systems, nuclear power control systems, chemical process control. Reduced size and cost has placed digital systems in standard consumer durable goods such as televisions and washing machines.

The need to respond to the expansion of digital systems can be met in a variety of ways: by providing mass-produced chips with little or no flexibility (as in consumer durable goods), by providing flexible and easily changed software in the form of general-purpose systems and by every means between.

Yet a large investment in, say, software of a certain type — for example large-scale accounting, personnel, payroll and inventory control systems in a large organization — may mean that there is a reluctance to innovate (at least on the surface); the reluctance increases with the size of the investment. This is one reason why programming languages developed in 1960 (such as COBOL and FORTRAN) remain in common use despite efforts to introduce new, better languages. Thus many fourth-generation operating systems maintain much of the exterior appearance and characteristics of their third-generation antecedents.

However, often radical changes have occurred beneath the visible shell of a system: the program code which makes up the system may have been redesigned from the ground up using the third-generation system as a working model while the supporting machine has changed radically and the operating system's underlying code has been carefully engineered, modularized and optimized, using new techniques. New features and enhancements have been added, and so on.

The architectures which underpin the operating systems have also changed radically in various ways: constantly expanding primary storage, new secondary storage devices and techniques like virtual storage for hiding the distinction between the two; attached, multiple and dyadic processor arrangements; the explosive expansion of networking and data communications.

Operating systems development can be thought of as being driven by three not always cooperating forces: (i) the need to preserve a working face consistent with the requirements of the users and compatible with software developed on and for older systems, (ii) the need to respond to changes in the underlying architecture which make the system as a whole cheaper to buy and operate, more reliable, more secure, smaller and faster; (iii) the users of computer systems have also changed their perceptions of what kinds of service the computer can and should provide and the means by which it should provide those services. The need to preserve a known face and at the same time respond to innovation in support mechanisms and to changes in users' perceptions and needs means that operating systems tend to evolve rather than to innovate with a complete break from past practice except where wholly new needs have arisen.

Yet, according to Peter C. Patton [1], the development of novel systems can have a high payoff for the developer. On the other hand, the attendant risks, say from the failure in the marketplace of immature technology or techniques, are correspondingly high. Users resist the high cost of migration to radically novel forms unless they can see that the benefits to them outweigh the expense, trouble and risk.

Systems which evolve from current conventional systems have a lower payoff for the developer, since competition is likely to be greater. However, the attendant risks are lower; the technology and the techniques are 'tried and true' if a little tired. It will probably be a simpler matter to convince users to migrate since the migration costs will be lower and less risky.

REFERENCES

[1] Patton, P.C. (1985) 'Multiprocessors: architecture and applications', *Computer*, **18**(6) (June), 29–40. Published by IEEE, Los Alamitos, California.

GENERAL REFERENCES

Lorin, H. (1986) 'Systems architecture in transition – an overview', *IBM Systems Journal*, **25**(3/4), 256–73.

Matick, R.E. (1986) 'Impact of memory systems on computer architecture and system organization', *IBM Systems Journal*, **25**(3/4), 274–305.

FURTHER READING

The *IBM Systems Journal*, **25**(3/4) contains several interesting papers looking into the future of large mainframes. These papers, two of which are listed above, also contain some interesting insights into past developments as a guide to the future.

Iliffe, J.K. (1982) *Advanced Computer Design*, Prentice Hall, Hemel Hempstead, UK. This book looks at advanced computer design and many of its presently available (1987) manifestations. The book is quite detailed in its presentation, but contains interesting discussion on the influence of applications (e.g. image enhancement) on computer design.

Glossary

access Generally, to locate an item of code or data in storage and use it in processing. Access may mean a transfer from secondary storage.
access method The type of physical access being performed (e.g. read, write) or the method of file access (e.g. direct, sequential).
access mode *See* **access method**.
address space The range of addresses, whether virtual, real or absolute, used by or assigned to a program.
agent process A process which facilitates transparency in network systems such that the user will be unaware of which processor or computer is actually doing the work.
anticipatory fetch A page fetch in which the page is actually fetched *before* specific reference is made to it in order to improve paging performance at the cost of an occasional mis-fetch. See **demand fetch**.
archiving Storing data maintained for historical use but seldom accessed; copying and storing vital data in a secured facility to prevent tampering and establish a position from which recovery of loss of data through fire, etc. is possible, usually by means of storing magnetic tapes containing copies of key files.
argument An argument is a parameter, such as a file name, appended to a command in order to make the command's action more specific.
arithmetic operation An operation with numeric inputs and outputs, e.g. addition, subtraction. *See* **logical operation**.
artificial contiguity The *appearance* that all parts of a program are contiguous in storage to other parts of the program, as occurs in **virtual storage** systems.
assembler A program which produces a machine-language version of a program whose source is written in low-level (i.e. assembly) language.
associative memory A memory device in which all parts of the memory are searched in parallel. Also called **content-addressable memory**.
asynchronous I/O Input or output operations which make use of buffering in order to transfer data between devices using independent timing in such a way that the process need not wait on each logical I/O operation before continuing to execute.
asynchronous transmission A method of data transmission in which a message is transmitted one character at a time with variable intervals between characters. Thus the sender and receiver must establish synchrony for each character. Also called *start–stop*.

Glossary

authority Software permission to access data or programs.

auxiliary storage Any storage in a computer system other than primary storage. This term often includes not only 'true' secondary storage such as disk and tape, but also certain types of internal storage such as 'bulk', slave or cache storage *not directly addressable* in machine code.

availability A measure of computer system reliability, usually stated as a percentage of the total time the system is required or scheduled for use.

average load The average level of work that is being performed, usually expressed as a percentage of maximum capacity of the system. *See also* **peak load**.

background command A program that can run unattended while allowing the user to initiate and interact with other programs.

background processing A term for processing low-priority work performed when computer resources are not otherwise needed. *See* **foreground processing**.

base address The lowest-numbered location of an area of storage, to which is added a displacement (relative address) to produce an absolute address.

base register A register used to contain the starting address of a portion of code or data so that parts of that portion can be located by adding a displacement value to the contents of the register.

basic direct access method Direct access method for records in a file where a request for I/O in a program causes an immediate transfer of data rather than a delayed, **queued** transfer.

basic sequential access method Sequential access method for a sequential file in which each request for I/O causes an immediate transfer of data, and in which the application process determines whether the transferred data are equivalent to a logical record or not.

batch-processing system A mode of processing where a program and its complete collection of data is processed individually before the next program is started, typically used in data processing for producing periodic reports, payroll, etc.

bdevsw table A table in Unix used to connect the I/O routines for block devices (e.g. disks) to the kernel.

best-fit A placement strategy which involved searching a list or table of all available space to find that which provides the closest possible fit. *See* **first-fit**, **worst-fit**.

binary file A term for files consisting of codes that have no corresponding printable characters, e.g. compiled programs.

binding time The instant at which a process is tied directly to any physical devices it uses.

bit map *See* **bit matrix**.

bit matrix A two-dimensional table in which each bit represents an object (location, record, etc.) with the bit set or not to indicate the status of the object.

block (1) In most systems, a standard unit of storage allocation and transfer on disk or other magnetic storage device. (2) A group of records treated as an entity for purposes of access. (3) To halt a process because of an interrupt.

boot A short form of **bootstrap**.

booting procedures Programs used to load the operating system initially.

bootstrap Any sequence of instructions (usually contained in a read-only memory) used to load other instructions. In an operating system, a common technique is to use a few ROM instructions which load a few instructions from disk, which in turn load more instructions, and so on, until the entire unit is loaded.

bounds register A means of preventing a process from accessing storage outside its assigned area: lowest and highest addresses available to a process are stored in bounds registers and any addresses generated during execution of the process are checked against these registers.

bucket In file structures allowing direct access, the address at which a record resides; in most systems this is synonymous with **sector**.

buffer An area of primary storage (or a small memory in a device such as a printer) where data are held temporarily to facilitate transfer between devices operating on different time cycles or at different speeds.

byte-sex In a computer word, the byte-sex determines whether the address of the least or most significant byte of the word is the address of that word.

catalog A directory recognized by the operating system which holds pointers to most or all files held on a computer system.

cdevsw table In Unix the table used to connect the I/O routines for character-oriented devices to the kernel.

checkpoint (1) *noun* A point in the execution of a program where a *checkpoint routine* is invoked to copy the contents of key locations and register to non-volatile (permanent) storage such as disk so that, should a failure occur, a position from which restart can occur has been made. (2) *noun* The data which constitutes a restart position. (3) *verb* The operation of writing such data.

cold start Starting a computer system by loading all the system software into primary storage as a first step. *See* **bootstrap**.

command file A file that contains a sequence of commands.

command language A **job-control language**, or more usually, its interactive equivalent.

command language interpreter An operating-system routine which recognizes and acts on a limited range of commands from a terminal in order to change the program or terminal status.

communications processor An intelligent device that performs interface functions between one or more computer systems and the **communications subsystem**.

communications subsystem That part of a computer system's hardware and software which deals with communications.

compact To move data in primary storage or on disk so that they occupy contiguous locations, leaving a contiguous area of free storage.

compiler A language processor that translates source coding in a particular high-level language into object (machine) code that can be executed on a particular make (and sometimes model) of a computer.

computation bound *See* **CPU bound**.

computer system The collection of interconnected hardware, its operating system, systems software and often its applications software and its community of users, considered as a whole.

Glossary

concentrator A unit of hardware which gathers in or disperses communications, usually from and to (respectively) terminals that share a single communications line. Concentrators commonly provide buffering, change of transmission speeds, etc.

concurrency (1) Happening at the same time. (2) The condition of multiprogramming: a processor apparently simultaneously executing several processes. (3) The use of multiple processors to execute non-dependent code simultaneously.

configuration A group of interconnected functional units that together form a computer, a subsystem (as in 'the disk configuration') or a computer system.

connect time The time during which a terminal is actively connected to a computer system in a *session*.

console The operation station of a computer. In single-user systems this is the same as the user's terminal.

content-addressable memory *See* **associative memory**.

context The state of a process or processor at the time a branch occurs within the process, or the processor switches control to another process. In this book, the term is used specifically to mean the state of the processor.

context switching The operation of changing execution from one process or task to another while saving register and primary storage contents where necessary, so that the suspended (**blocked**) process can be resumed at a later time.

control mode *See* **kernel mode**.

control program The kernel of an operating system, especially VM/SP, which uses this to designate its kernel.

control state *See* **kernel mode**.

control unit (1) An *instruction* control unit is that part of the central processor that holds the instruction code of a computer and its related microcode, and performs such functions as fetching instructions and operands, decoding instructions, etc. (2) A *peripheral* control unit is a device for controlling several secondary storage or input/output devices.

CPU bound A process which tends to use the processor until its time is up, as opposed to a process which interrupts itself frequently by issuing I/O requests. Also called **computation bound** or **processor bound**. *See* **I/O bound**.

cpu loop program In TPF/II the 'heart' of the operating system's kernel.

critical region Any code which only one task at a time may execute and which controls or is itself a critical resource and is therefore uninterruptable.

critical section *See* **critical region**.

DAT *See* **dynamic address translation**.

data (1) Facts, concepts, information, directives in a form which can be communicated and interpreted. (2) Inputs to a computer program or routine which are manipulated by arithmetic or logical operations and which determine the results of the processing.

data channel In large computer systems, a functional unit, often a minicomputer, that handles data transfer to peripheral devices, including such tasks as queueing, buffering, conversion, error detection and resolution, and multiplexing.

data coupling The degree to which processors share data concurrently, usually through a common storage.

data-processing system A system designed for the transcription and storing of data and their automated ordering, selection, updating and reproduction.

data reduction The process of sorting and combining data to reduce its volume and make it more suitable for some purpose. In operating systems, *data logging* on the actions of the system provides the input for data reduction, which then produces output used to trace errors, monitor performance, etc.

database An organized pool of data held in a computer system, shared among and manipulated by many applications programs and controlled by a central authority.

database management system (DBMS) The software controlling and accessing the data of a database on behalf of applications programs and enquiries.

database system A computer system designed around a database.

DBMS *See* **database management system**.

deadline scheduling A complex and problematical form of scheduling work on a computer system in which the goal is to complete any given piece of work by a given date and time.

deadlock A situation in which two or more processes are prevented from proceeding because each has allocated to it a resource required by the other. Also called *deadly embrace*.

dedicated Reserved for a particular use, for example using a voice-grade telephone line exclusively for data transmission between specific computer systems, even though the line could be used for normal telephony.

degree of multiprogramming A relative measure of the number of processes running in **concurrency**.

demand fetch A page-fetch strategy requiring that a page be fetched upon specific reference to it, and not before. This method is somewhat slower than **anticipatory fetch**, but more sure.

descriptor An identifier. In MP/M the term refers to a control block identifying a process.

device driver A low-level system routine which performs interfacing functions between the operating system or an applications program and a peripheral device. The term can also refer to a hardware unit which has the same function.

device independence The condition in which the operating system may use a different type of device to service the requirements of a program than that specified by the programmer. (Or the programmer may make only a generic specification, or none at all.) This is accomplished by the use of a logical name or device designation to specify a general class of device without reference to any specific make, model or physical device.

direct access *See* **random access**.

directory A list of names of and other information about files belonging to a particular group which is used to identify and locate those files.

discipline Another term for *protocol* – a set of rules for interchange of data.

disk A magnetic disk. The term may also refer to a **disk pack**.

disk pack An assembly of from two to 20 magnetic disks arranged vertically on a spindle. A disk pack may be removed from a disk drive, or it may be permanently mounted.

Glossary

distributed computation network A network where individual tasks are undertaken concurrently on several host computers, each with resources it requires placed close to that host or the user, but with the applications software and **database** distributed throughout the network.

distributed operating system A single operating system run on all the hosts in a network.

dormant process A process which is suspended or **blocked**.

downtime The time, as a percentage of the total of a period, that a system or component of the system is inoperable.

drum A magnetic drum unit — a direct-access device in which the recording surface is a cylinder.

dump (1) A printed copy of the contents of primary storage used for locating and resolving errors. (2) To copy the contents of primary storage for purposes of **checkpoint** or due to an error.

dynamic address translation (DAT) In a virtual storage system, the conversion of virtual addresses to real addresses, which takes place *as instructions are executed*.

dynamic priority A scheme for queueing work according to an assigned priority which can change dynamically in response to the situation of the process, e.g. by increasing as the process 'ages'.

emulator A program or hardware that performs emulation; specifically, a hardware adaptation and software which allows one computer to emulate the actions of a dissimilar computer. *See also* **simulator**.

entry In TPF/II, a unit of work. The term has other, more common meanings.

executive processor In distributed operating systems, the node which is hosting, at any given instant, the operating system.

fail-safe The design objective in creating a system that will fail only in ways which do not result in a dangerous condition or in any loss. In computer systems, this usually means full redundancy so that backup systems can take over in the event of the failure of the primary system.

fail-soft A design objective intended to create a system which will fail in such a way that some useful function can continue (see **graceful degradation**) and no serious loss of data, for example, will occur.

failure A complete loss of function. *See* **fault**.

failure atomicity To fail in such a way that, if a single part or action fails, the entire thing also fails. This prevents partial change to the system and is of importance in distributed systems.

fallback (1) A change to a different mode of operation as a result of failure encountered in the primary mode. (2) In TPF/II, the switch to running TPF/II on the backup computer system.

fault An abnormal condition resulting in reduced performance or capacity. *See* **failure**.

fault-tolerant A design objective intended to create a system in which faults, for example in the hardware, do not seriously degrade the performance of the system or render it unusable.

fetch strategy (1) The strategy used to determine, in virtual storage systems, which page will be fetched next. (2) The strategy for determining which instruction in primary storage to locate and load into a control unit.

FIFO *See* **first-in–first-out**.

file A named collection of records and, often, access-related control information for that collection.

file descriptor (1) A unique identifier for a file within a system. (2) A non-negative integer which identifies a file to the system in Unix.

file index *See* **volume table of contents**.

filing system The method by which files are organized.

filter A program that reads information from a standard input, transforms it in some way (usually by eliminating extraneous data) and writes it to the standard output (a Unix term).

firmware Hardware, such as a read-only memory, with a microcoded program.

first-fit A placement strategy in which the first space big enough to accommodate the object for which space is being sought is the one actually used. Its benefit is that it is relatively quick. *See also* **best-fit**, **worst-fit**.

first-in–first-out (FIFO) An algorithm used in determining the order of handling or consideration: a method whereby that which has waited longest (been earliest in the queue) is dealt with or considered before other items which arrived later in the same queue.

flag (1) In a Unix command, that part of the command which modifies or defines more precisely what the command is to do. (2) A signal that an event has occurred.

foreground processing Processing a job or task in a multiprogramming system which has higher priority (usually because it is running in interactive mode); a foreground task therefore receives resources reallocated from lower-priority work (**background processing**).

frame In virtual storage schemes, a standard, page-sized area of real primary storage in which a page can reside when required for execution.

front-end processing A term applied to processing communications from the external interface to a system. *Back-end* is the interface between the main computer and other facilities such as data channels.

full-duplex working A communications method whereby transmission can occur in both directions on a link simultaneously. A telephone connection, where the user can hear and talk at the same time, is an example of this.

graceful degradation The state in which a system or part of a system can continue to provide a useful but reduced service in the event that one or more of its components has failed.

hard-coded Said of data imbedded within an instruction and therefore difficult or impossible to modify, probably derived by analogy from *hardwired*, meaning performed by electronic circuitry rather than software.

hard-sectored disk On disks, a method of establishing divisions in a track permanently, at the time of manufacture, for example by incising slots on a disk-pack spindle.

hardware Any tangible element or group of elements in a computer system. In this book, the term generally refers to a computer with all its peripheral

Glossary

and associated equipment, though the term can refer to electronic circuitry alone.

high-level language A programming language which hides the structure and facilities of the computer system in order to concentrate upon the solution to a class of problems which exist in the world external to the computer system.

high-level scheduling The determination of which jobs or requests will have access to the *computer system*. See also **intermediate-** and **low-level scheduling**.

highest-resource-ratio-next scheduling A scheduling algorithm which attempts to eliminate some of the bias in **shortest-job-first scheduling**, developed by Per Brinch-Hansen. The priority of a unit of work is a function of the combination of estimated service time and waiting time.

home directory In a hierarchical filing system, the directory you are placed in when you log onto the system.

host A term denoting any processor running a specific task where more than one processor is available, as in a network.

hub go-ahead polling A polling method in which the central site transmits an invitation to send to the first remote site at the beginning of a polling cycle. The invitation is then passed from one remote site to the next on the rota, with only the last remote site replying if there are no messages to be sent. If any remote site has a message to send, it does so upon receipt of the invitation, but passes the invitation to the next site on the rota.

hub polling *See* **hub go-ahead polling**.

i-list In Unix, the list of **i-nodes** on a **volume**.

i-node In Unix, information about a file such as: the file type, owner, and where the file is located.

i-node table A table used by the system to store the **i-nodes** of open **files**.

i-number The offset of an **i-node** from the start of the **i-list**.

I/O bound A process which engages in a great deal of I/O activity relative to the amount of computation it does. *See also* **CPU bound**.

I/O port An interface by which data enter or leave a device.

I/O processor *See* **data channel**.

indexed sequential A file organization in which two access methods are possible: sequential and direct. This is accomplished by ordering the file sequentially, according to a key field, and creating a separate index which points to the location of records within the file for direct-access purposes.

indexed sequential access method (ISAM) The access method which allows access, either direct or sequential, to an **indexed sequential** file.

indirect block In the method used by Unix for storing large files on disk, an indirect block is used to store pointers to blocks which are themselves index blocks to blocks which contain file data.

initialization The act of setting up the environment necessary for the running of a process: for example, the setting of counters to zero, opening data files, etc.

input device A device such as a terminal keyboard which converts data from one form (e.g. key strokes) to another (e.g. bit patterns which can be written to the electronic storage of a computer system). Devices can be keyboards at a teletype or CRT terminal, punched card or tape readers, optical or magnetic character readers (OCRs and MICRs), analog-to-digital (A/D) converters, and so on.

instruction pointer (IP) *See* **program address counter**.

instruction set The set of bit patterns (or their representation) that control the operation of the computer and thus define which actions a computer can perform.

integrity The freedom from error of data or program instructions.

interactive processing system *See* **time-sharing** system.

inter-block gap On magnetic tape, a gap of approximately 2.5 cm (1 inch) between one block of data and the subsequent block. This gap allows for braking and acceleration of the tape transport without the danger of losing data.

intermediate-level scheduling Scheduling which tasks will have access to the processor. *See also* **high-level** and **low-level scheduling**.

interpreter A language processor which translates and executes one (source or p-code) instruction at a time, usually without retaining the machine code so generated.

interpreting To translate and execute statements in a source or other non-machine code one at a time, in sequence.

interrupt To stop the execution of one sequence of instructions and transfer control to another sequence in response to a signal or an event. Interrupts can be assigned priorities, can be external to the system, and can be generated by hardware, software or the user.

interrupt handler The system software or firmware (microcoded) routine which processes the **interrupt** signal and performs the necessary operations to transfer control (ultimately) back to the suspended process in a **context switch**.

interrupt vector The address of an **interrupt handler**, located in the hardware such that a signal of a particular type will activate a branch to the address contained in the vector. A vector thus indirectly identifies an **interrupt**.

interval timer A routine or internal clock which marks set intervals of time, for example as used in **round-robin** scheduling.

IP *See* **instruction pointer**.

ISAM *See* **indexed sequential access method**.

job One or more related applications programs and their associated data, bundled together for processing. **Job-control language** is used to define the boundaries of the job. The term *task* can also appear in this sense.

job-control language A command language, computer-system-specific, which instructs the operating system about the conditions and order of programs required in order to run a **job**. The language is normally used to describe batch processing systems, while the term **command language** is used to describe interactive commands with analogous functions.

job scheduling *See* **high-level scheduling**.

kernel The essential low-level functions of an operating system which must always be resident in primary storage and which comprise the most basic supervisory aspects of the operating system.

kernel mode (also called **control mode**) The mode of the system when portions of the operating system are in control and executing.

key The field by which records in a file are ordered.

LAN *See* **local area network**.

latency *See* **rotational delay**.

least frequently used A page-replacement strategy in which a use-count is kept for each resident page, and those with low counts become candidates for removal in the event that a page frame is required but no free frames are available.

least recently used A page-replacement strategy in which a time-stamp is associated with the page and updated with each reference. A page which has not been recently used may become a candidate for removal should a page frame be required when none is free.

level of multiprogramming *See* **degree of multiprogramming**.

linked list A list of items in which each item except the last contains a pointer to the next item in the sequence.

loader A systems software routine which fetches executable program modules from secondary storage (or, in the past, from cards) and places them in primary storage prior to commencing execution.

local area network (LAN) A computer network using direct cable links between the nodes and thus one normally limited to a small geographic area (e.g. a building, a campus). Networks which involve the passage of communications through public carriers or which change transmission media (e.g. cable to microwave to satellite) are not included in this definition.

lock mechanism A means of serializing key resources in a multiprogramming environment by allowing one process to 'lock out' others from a resource until the process holding the resource no longer requires it.

lockout The situation where one process has exclusive use of a resource until it completes processing, thereby preventing other processes from using that resource.

logged in Said of a user who has identified him- or herself to the system and whom the system has accepted so that he or she may begin to use the system interactively.

logical operation Also *logic operation*. Any operation in which one or more inputs are compared or evaluated in accordance with a rule; the output of the operation indicates the result of the operation. For example IF A = B compares A and B and the result will be expressed in terms of TRUE or FALSE. *See also* **arithmetic operation**.

logical record A record considered with regard to its data content rather than its actual physical form on a storage medium.

look-ahead processing Also termed **pipelining**. In an instruction control unit, a sequence of registers with buffers allowing several instructions to be in different stages of execution at any instant.

loosely coupled multiprocessing An arrangement of two or more processors or computers in which the degree of interdependence of the elements in the arrangement is weak, and the elements are semi-independent of each other and can be dynamically configured to run entirely independently of each other.

low-level scheduling The level at which *ready* processes compete for the processor itself. Note that **intermediate-level scheduling** determines which programs will *become* processes, that is, which will be created and then passed to the low-level scheduler.

machine code *See* **machine language**.
machine language The bit patterns capable of controlling the operation of a particular make (and often, model) of computer.
macro-instruction In a programming language, usually assembler, an operator that, when used in an instruction, causes the assembler to generate a *sequence* of one or more machine instructions.
magnetic tape A common secondary storage medium consisting of a plastic strip substratum with a magnetizable surface on which recording takes place.
mailbox A system of interprocess communication in which a designated area of primary storage or a designated register (the *mailbox*) is reserved for 'messages' left there by one process for another. The sender does not signal the recipient in any way, but the recipient must check the mailbox periodically.
main memory *See* **primary storage**.
main storage *See* **primary storage**.
mask A pattern of bits or characters which are to be combined with input and included in output. Some **PSWs** include mask bits which a particular instruction or instructions can set so as to influence instructions which follow in the program's sequence.
mean time between failures (MTBF) A measure of system or component reliability. It is usually expressed as the number of hours of continuous operation divided by the number of failures occurring within the period under observation.
memory *See* **storage**.
message-driven A system whose actions are prompted by the arrival of messages from remote terminals or other systems.
microcode Bit patterns held in a control unit which are read as pulses and control the operation of logical gates and registers, and especially control the transfer of data between or within registers.
MIMD Multiple-instruction stream, multiple-data stream: a designation in Flynn's classification for an arrangement of parallel processors which are essentially individual computers with facilities for work sharing. Other designations are **SIMD**, **SISD** and **MISD**.
MISD Multiple-instruction stream, single-data stream: a designation in Flynn's classification. Since it appears that the data stream must be multiplied as well, this category is not in general use.
modem The unit of equipment which alters a digital signal to suit the medium in which it will be transmitted and which alters a signal received from the medium back to a digital signal. The telephone alters sound waves to electrical signals at the mouthpiece (modulation) and at the other end translates electrical signals back to sound waves (demodulates). *Modem* is a contraction of *mo*dulate-*dem*odulate.
multicomputer system A system of individual computers coupled so as to allow communication and work sharing.

multiprocessor system A system in which two or more processors share communications or memory or both.

multiprogramming A method of computer operation in which two or more processes are executed apparently simultaneously by interleaving allocation of a single set of resources.

multiserver Any system in which two or more identical, independent resources exist to serve a queue of waiting work.

mutual exclusion The practice of allowing one process to exclude all similar processes from a resource for a finite period; thus, a method for providing serialization where concurrency is possible.

NCP *See* **network control program**.

network A data network consisting of transmission equipment, at least one transmission medium and control procedures which provide data communications services between computers or between users and a computer or a group of computers.

network communications controller A unit of equipment capable of controlling the communications over a data **network**, usually a minicomputer dedicated to this task.

network control program (NCP) A program run by the **network communications controller** with the objective of controlling communications in a data **network**.

network operating system An operating system which controls a network by means of a communications subsystem which exists under the control of an operating system.

non-stop computing A computing system design with sufficient redundancy built in to guarantee that the system is capable of performing its function fully on a non-stop basis.

not used recently A page-replacement strategy similar to **least recently used** in which the entry in the page table is modified each time a page is referred to and also each time a page is modified. Choices about removing a page from a frame are made on the basis of both reference and modification.

nucleus *See* **kernel**.

object program A machine-language program, said of any program which was originally written in **assembler** or a **high-level language** and has been translated to machine-language form.

operating system The software which manages the resources of the computer system on behalf of its user(s) and which provides an interface to those users.

organization (of a file) The way in which records in a file are stored physically, as opposed to **access mode**.

output device A device providing a means of transferring data out of the computer system, usually to a human (reader), though such devices include output to electrical and electromechanical devices and to data transmission media.

overlay (1) To write over. (2) To use the space allocated for one purpose for a different purpose, thereby erasing whatever was in that space.

PAC *See* **program address counter**.

page A standard-sized unit of storage (usually 2 or 4 kilobytes). In primary storage, the page-unit is called a **frame**. In paged virtual storage systems, a program is divided into virtual pages which fit into the frames when required for execution.

parallel A term meaning **concurrent**.

PC *See* **program counter**.

PCB *See* **program control block**.

peak load The maximum workload envisaged in planning a computing system.

per process data area (PPDA) In Unix the structure which contains the information about a process that must be available to the **kernel** when the process is executing. It is also called the *user table* or *user structure*.

peripheral In a computer system, a device which makes or receives (or both) data transfers at the request and possibly under the control of the central processor.

peripheral controller A functional unit in a computer system which handles data transfer between primary storage and **peripheral** units.

peripheral processor *See* **data channel**.

physical record *See* **block** (1) and (2).

pipe In Unix, a connection made between the standard output of one program and the standard input of another program.

pipelining *See* **look-ahead processing**.

placement strategy The method for determining where in primary storage a process will fit.

polling A means by which a main processor determines whether any of its peripheral devices require its attention; it signals each in turn at discrete intervals.

pool In TPF/II, a group of fixed-size free blocks of primary storage.

PPDA *See* **per process data area**.

preemption The ability to interrupt work of a lower priority to seize any resources necessary for execution of a higher-priority task.

primary storage Also called **main storage**, **main memory**, **memory**, or *core*. The main internal storage of a computer.

primitive A basic or very fundamental step in processing, often consisting of moving or altering one or more bits.

priority An assigned rank within a queue, indicating the precedence of elements in the queue.

privileged instruction An instruction which implements some system function; for example, one which alters one of a computer's control registers.

problem programming language *See* **high-level language**.

procedure call The technique of passing control from one program or process to another, with the expectation that control will return to the caller when the called procedure completes.

process A program during its execution; a running program.

process identity The unique identifier assigned to a process as it is created.

process table A table where the kernel keeps information about processes. The **process control blocks** kept in tabular form, as it is in Unix. There is one entry in the table for each process, and the entry is analogous to the control block.

processor (1) The 'intelligent' unit of a computer or similar device. (2) A central processor in systems with central—peripheral processor arrangements (e.g. central processor and data channels). (3) The main or only intelligent unit in a computer system.

processor bound *See* **CPU bound.**

program A sequence of ordered, related instructions designed and coded to accomplish a specific task.

program address counter (PAC) Also **program counter.** A current instruction address register, a simpler form of **PSW.**

program control block (PCB) A data structure containing operational information about a **process.**

program counter (PC) *See* **program address counter.**

program status word (PSW) Especially in larger multiprogramming systems, a word or special register used by the operating system in effecting a context switch. The current **PSW** is the register holding the address of the next instruction to be executed together with the condition codes and mask (possibly) modified by the currently executing instruction. The old PSW holds the same information for a suspended task and the new PSW for a task about to begin or for an **interrupt handler.**

property of locality A term describing the strong tendency of computer programs to execute one section of code for some period of time (*temporal locality*) or, when moving from one datum to another, to move to an adjacent datum (*spatial locality*).

PSW *See* **program status word.**

pure code *See* **re-entrant code.**

pure text Shared **read-only code** such as an editor or compiler.

quantum *Plural* quanta. *See* **time-slice.**

queue A data structure that is inherently *first-in—first-out*, containing items awaiting service or attention. A new entry to a queue is called an *arrival* and that which supplies service or attention a *server*.

queued sequential access method An access method for blocked sequentially organized files. This method allows the transfer of a block of logical records in a physical entity (the **block**), but the applications program is only 'aware' of receiving/writing one logical record at a time.

random access Also **direct access.** The ability to obtain any datum, either in primary storage or in secondary storage, directly rather than by serial access to all data that precede it. It is more proper to speak of **direct access** to a record on secondary storage and **random access** to a datum in primary storage.

read-only code Program code which cannot be modified by a user because it is protected against writing.

real storage Also **primary storage, main storage, main memory.** In a more specific sense used in this text, it refers to the coordinate-addressable storage of a **virtual storage** system. The term is intended to clarify its difference from virtual storage and the virtual storage extension of **auxiliary storage.**

real-time (1) A system in which the response to any event (for example an interrupt) follows that event without delay, to the extent feasible. Such systems are commonly monitoring and control systems for complex plant such as chemical and nuclear reactors, power plant, air traffic control and many military applications. (2) A data network in which response to operators at terminals is achieved so quickly that the operators can work with no sensed interruption to their thought processes. (3) Generally, systems with a **response time** of less than three seconds can be called 'real-time' and appear widely in airline reservation and credit checking applications.

record (1) A group of related data items (normally related because they refer to a single entity — for example, one employee) which is considered a unit for processing purposes (e.g. an employee record in processing a payroll). (2) The term can also mean data considered as a unit for access and transfer, as in the term **physical record**.

re-entrant code Also called **pure code**. A sequence of instructions which contains no values that are changed during the execution of that code, or that must be reset prior to any subsequent execution, and which can therefore be executed simultaneously by different activities.

relative addressing A common technique in computing whereby a **base address** or point is established at a known address so that subsequent points can be located by a displacement value which is added to the base address. Relative addresses are expressed as base address plus displacement. Resolution of the actual address takes place when the sequence of code involved is loaded, often by placing the base address in a register and computing displacements as additions (or subtractions in some cases) to this **base register**.

relative file A file in which a record can be accessed directly by its relative number from the start of the file.

release Of an operating system (or virtually any software package) a particular (numbered) version. While no standards exist, it is common that minor changes are incorporated in releases whose decimal fraction changes (there would be minor differences, say, between OS/VS2 MVS release 3.7 and 3.8, for example) and major changes such as an extension of function are signalled by a change in the integer part of the release number (as, for example, a change from release I.5 to II.0).

relocatable program An object or machine-language program which is designed to facilitate loading at different primary storage locations at different times. Resolution of actual addresses takes place at loading time, and a common technique for this is the use of **relative addressing**.

remote communications network The simplest and cheapest of networks, this type exploits batch-processing capabilities by allowing *remote job entry* and remote printing of results, but does not include the interactive use of the network.

replacement at random A replacement strategy for virtual systems in which, when a page is required but none is free, a frame is selected at random for replacement.

replacement strategy The algorithms used to select page frames for replacement in a virtual storage system.

resource-sharing network A network in which any of the resources of any **host** in the network are made available for use and access by any other host.

response time A measure of system speed and efficiency, and usually of user satisfaction as well, which applies to interactive systems. It is the mean period

Glossary

that elapses between a user at a remote terminal sending a message (by pressing the 'send', 'return' or 'enter' key) and the receipt of the first character of the response from the host.

roll call polling A polling method wherein the central site invites a remote device to transmit and the remote device transmits either a message or a negative reply, whereupon the central site then polls the next remote device in the rota.

rotational delay The mean time taken by a sector to rotate under the read/write head in a disk. (*See also* **seek time**). Also called **latency**.

round-robin A scheduling algorithm in which each activity receives attention for a given amount of time, in rotation, with all other activities waiting.

scheduler That part of the operating system responsible for supervising the allocation of resources to tasks (especially time) and which determines the order or priority of requests for service.

scheduling The allocation of resources to tasks, especially time in the system and time in the processor.

secondary storage Magnetic storage media which are not directly addressable (by coordinates) but which are accessed by the I/O ports. Also termed **auxiliary storage**, backing stor(ag)e or file store.

sector In most disk systems, the smallest unit which can be accessed directly. Normally this means a division of a track, with all tracks being divided evenly in such a way that the division of the surface of a disk can be pictured as wedge-shaped. Some disks have variable numbers of sectors on their tracks, with more sectors in the outermost tracks than in the innermost.

seek The movement of a disk read/write head to the appropriate track. Such a movement is either extension from or withdrawal to a rest position.

seek time The mean time required for a seek to any track on a disk. The amount of seek time can be controlled by file design and is a factor in the speed with which direct access takes place.

segment (1) In **virtual storage** systems a large unit of code or data that is the standard unit of transfer in and out of **real storage**. (2) In Pascal, a unit of executable code.

semaphore A 'flag', a bit or combination of bits which signal that a particular event has occurred during processing. In some systems, semaphores can be realized in the hardware. In others they are software constructs. In multi-programming systems, semaphores are a means of passing minimal information between concurrently executing processes. In multiprocessor systems, a semaphore or semaphores indicate(s) the status of any one processor to the others.

separate executives In data networks, an arrangement whereby each host has its own operating system and data communications are effected by a communications subsystem.

sequential access method (1) A system routine for serial access to a file. (2) The presentation (in ordered files) of records to a process by order of their key values. (3) The writing to a storage medium of records in order by their key values.

shell A term adapted from the Unix operating system and now widely used to indicate the high-level commands available to a system's user. This term now seems to be supplanting the older **command language**.

shortest-job-first scheduling A high- or intermediate-level scheduling algorithm which depends upon a user's estimate of the time required to run a job and which seems to process first those with the lowest estimated execution times. The effect, where an installation processes many short jobs, is to provide a high level of throughput at the expense of longer jobs waiting. This mechanism is often paired with a 'guillotine' mechanism which terminates jobs that exceed their estimate by more than a given percentage.

shortest-remaining-time scheduling An intermediate-level scheduling algorithm which, like **shortest-job-first** scheduling, depends upon a user's estimate of time required to run a job. It uses a decrementing time-stamp and awards priority to tasks which are closest to completion. (It also often uses a 'guillotine'.)

SIMD An acronym of *S*ingle *I*nstruction *M*ultiple *D*ata stream, one of Flynn's designations used to denote a computer with multiple memories and an arithmetic–logic unit for each memory, but with a single processor. *See also* **MIMD, MISD** and **SISD**.

simulator Software designed to allow one type of computer to simulate the actions of a dissimilar computer and thus to execute programs intended for a different machine without requiring changes in the program. Simulators are slower but cheaper than **emulators**.

single server A system in which one resource exists to serve one or more **queues** of waiting items.

SISD Single-instruction stream, single-data stream. A category in Flynn's classification. All true **von Neumann architectures** are SISD. *See also* **MIMD, MISD** and **SIMD**.

slot In virtual storage systems, the term for the page-sized units of space on secondary storage, where parts of a virtual address space are stored when not actively required.

soft-sectored disk A disk whose sectoring is established at the time the disk is initialized for use, rather than during the manufacturing process (i.e. a **hard-sectored disk**).

source program A program written in a programming language other than machine language. Such a program must undergo a process of translation (assembly, compilation or interpretation) before it is executable.

spooler The program which carries out **spooling**.

spooling An acronym for *s*imultaneous *p*eripheral *o*peration *online*, this refers to the practice of using a fast storage device, such as a magnetic disk, as a buffer for data being transferred between primary storage and a slower device such as a printer.

stable storage A storage medium which guarantees the integrity of data in the event of failure, used in **non-stop** and in many distributed systems. The medium may be a non-volatile form of primary storage or, to protect against disk failure, a second disk on another port or channel which is a perfect mirror of the first disk.

stack A data structure in which items can be added or removed from one end only, as opposed to, for example, **queue**. A *heap* (as in the p-System) is a

Glossary

stack which 'grows' in the opposite direction (in terms of addresses taken to add to it).

start–stop *See* **asynchronous transmission**.

standard input In Unix and its look-alikes, the standard method of input – usually a terminal keyboard.

standard output In Unix and its look-alikes, the standard output device – usually a CRT screen or printing device.

state *See* **context**.

state switching *See* **context switching**.

static priority A scheduling priority which, once assigned, does not change.

storage The collective term for *all* storage considered as a whole: primary and secondary. Also called **memory** or **store**.

storage protection key A method of protecting storage locations in a multiprogramming system by assigning a value, called the key, to each task and allowing the task to access only storage with the same assigned value.

store *See* **storage**.

store-and-forward A method of sending data over a network in which one or more intermediate nodes receive data from senders and reroute them to onward stations, storing the data until successful onward transmission is confirmed.

swap area An area on secondary storage reserved for processes which are **swapped out**.

swapped in Said of a process, page or segment resident in primary storage in systems where inactive processes, pages or segments are kept in secondary storage (**swapping systems** or **virtual storage systems**).

swapped out Said of a process, page or segment which resides in secondary storage because it is inactive (as in **swapping systems** or **virtual storage systems**).

swapper The portion of the operating system responsible for making decisions about swapping processes.

swapping system Any system in which inactive processes are kept on secondary storage devices in order to make room in primary storage for active processes.

symmetric independent multicomputer system An arrangement in which two or more *identical and anonymous* computer systems, which do *not* have any communications links, are all equally capable of performing exactly the same work, and in which a human agent schedules which jobs will run on which system.

symmetrical multiprocessing A multiprocessing arrangement in which two or more *identical* processors are linked by data communications. A single operating system controls all such linked processors and 'floats' between them. *See* **executive processor**.

synchronous transmission The capability to transmit a group of characters (e.g. whole messages or significant parts of messages) with fixed or no intervals between characters, with special characters 'framing' the transmission group in such a way as to identify it as such, and to identify its sender and receiver(s).

sysgen *See* **system generation**.

system configuration A term describing a computer system in terms of its components and connections.

system file table In Unix, the table which contains pointers to **i-nodes** in the **i-node table**.

system generation The process of tailoring the operating system to fit the **system configuration** it is to manage, and to set certain variables to attune the system to an installation's particular workload and policies, for example, to set scheduling **quanta**.

systems software (1) Those programs or routines in a computer system which are available to perform processing tasks that are not specific to the needs of a particular user. (2) Such routines (e.g. compilers, editors), but exempting those which are considered a part of the operating system.

table-driven Said of software when the state of elements within an array initiates action in the software.

tape (1) *See* **magnetic tape**. (2) Punched paper strip.

tape drive (1) The motor, capstans and related devices which move magnetic tape through a magnetic tape unit. (2) A magnetic tape unit.

test-bed Special routines and data written to facilitate testing a program.

throughput A measure of work done by a system: usually expressed as some unit of work done per some unit of time, for example instructions per second or transactions per minute. In some references this is spelled *thruput*.

tightly coupled multiprocessing In multiprocessing systems, those systems with a structure in which the links between processors (such as a shared memory) are close and where any failure in the shared resource will probably cripple the system.

time-sharing A system in which a number of simultaneous users are each given trivial amounts of time (a **quantum** or **time-slice**) in which to process interactively or conversationally.

time-slice (1) A small unit or **quantum** or time during which a resource is allocated to an activity and where many activities will each receive such a quantum in turn, as in **time-sharing** systems. (2) The use of small units of time as a low-level scheduling device in an operating system.

track A very thin path on any magnetizable medium (tape, disk or drum) on which data can be written. In magnetic tape, tracks run parallel to the long edges of the tape and each byte is recorded on nine (sometimes seven) parallel tracks. In disks, the track is a concentric ring on the surface of a disk platter.

transmit by reference To exchange a message by supplying the recipient with the location of (reference to) the message.

transmit by value To exchange a message by sending the text of the message to the recipient.

turn-around time A measure of a system's efficiency and especially of user satisfaction (usually in a batch-processing environment). It is the mean time between the submission of jobs for processing and the receipt of the results of those jobs.

uniprocessor A computer system in which only one processor capable of executing program instructions is present. Others may be present to handle specialized tasks, e.g. data-channel processors, network controllers. Used to distinguish such systems from true multiprocessing systems where the coupling is so tight that the system appears to have only one processor.

user directory In many operating systems, each interactive user's private directory containing information about all his or her files.

user mode When a user process is executing and user application code is in control of the processor. Also called *problem mode*. See **kernel mode**.

user structure *See* **per process data area**.

utility program A system software routine which performs some standard, often required function in the course of processing, for example, to make a copy of a file.

virtual Making one thing appear as or behave as another, different thing.

virtual address In virtual storage systems, the untranslated addresses in a source or, especially, an object program as they appear before the translation process.

virtual storage Also called *apparent storage*. (1) A system in which the addresses in a program bear no direct relation to locations in **real storage** but must undergo a translation process to determine true location, whether in real storage or auxiliary storage. (2) The total amount of storage apparently available in a virtual storage system, dictated by the addressing structure. (3) The whole range of addresses available to a program in a virtual storage system.

virtual storage access method (VSAM) An access method related functionally to **indexed sequential access method**. Records are maintained in key order, allowing sequential access, but are also indexed to allow direct access. Whenever a location full of records is selected for storing a new record, the records are divided between the old location and a new one, and the index is updated to reflect this. Thus, there is never an overflow, and records are always preserved in key sequence, though at the cost of occasional movement of records.

volatile A storage which requires continuous electrical input in order to retain stored data. Data are lost if the power is interrupted.

volume A physical unit of magnetic storage such as a reel of **magnetic tape** or **disk**. The word tends to be used in a sense analogous to the *volumes of a printed work*. An example is a multi-volume payroll file which occupies more than one reel of magnetic tape due to its size.

volume identification label An external, human-readable label on a reel of tape or a disk pack or diskette cover.

volume label An internal, magnetically encoded, computer-readable label on a reel of tape, a disk pack or diskette which corresponds (one hopes!) to the external **volume identification label**.

volume table of contents (VTOC) Also called a *file index*. An area on a disk or disk pack which describes the contents and locations of the files and free space on that volume.

von Neumann architecture Any computer constructed according to the principles laid down by John von Neumann and his colleagues in von Neumann, J., Goldstine, H.H. and Burks, A.W. (1946), *Preliminary discussion of the logical* *design of an electronic computing instrument*, part I, Vol. 1. This architecture is characterized by the concept of stored program instructions, separation of program instruction and data, automatic ordering of instructions and provision for modifying instructions during execution. The instructions are executed serially (i.e. there is no parallelism).

VSAM *See* **virtual storage access method**.

VTOC *See* **volume table of contents**.

warm start Starting a computer system in which many or all of the system routines are already resident in primary storage. The other form of start is called a **cold start**, that is, starting from a point where no system software is presumed to be loaded. *See also* **bootstrap**.

work station A visual display terminal at which a certain type of business-related work (e.g. order-entry) is performed. In this book, the term refers as well to microcomputers as nodes in a network.

working set The set of **pages** in a **process** which are most heavily accessed and therefore tend to become fixed in **real storage**.

worst-fit A placement algorithm in which all available space is looked at to locate the largest possible area of free space (provided it is large enough to contain the process). The purpose of using such an algorithm is to allocate space to a process and at the same time leave an area free which is as large as possible.

Index

ACL, 264, 265, 267, 269
ACP (Airline Control Program), 51, 249,
    see also TPF/II
ACP/TPE II, see TPF/II
AMD 2900, 209
AMD 2901, 209
APF (Authorized Program Facility),
    332–3
APL, 132
ARINC, 268
AT&T, see Bell Laboratories
access, 20
    direct (in Unix), 224
    to executable programs, 78
    to files (in p-System), 187
    to permissions, 290
    to real storage (in MVS), 309
access methods, 44, 310, 318, 319
    basic, 319
    basic direct (BDAM), 45
    basic sequential (BSAM), 44
    basic telecommunications (BTAM), 319
    direct, 44, 224, 319
    indexed sequential (ISAM), 45
    queued sequential (QSAM), 44
    random, see direct above
    sequential, 44
    telecommunications (TCAM), 319, 321
    virtual storage (VSAM), 45–6, 333
    virtual telecommunications (VTAM),
        319, 321
access mode, see access method
accounting, 81, 91–3, 147, 322–3
Ada, 150
address, 13, 21, 89, 100, 101, 173, 259
    absolute, 14, 82, 312
    base, 101, 102, 262
    dissociation of addresses, 100, 102
    frame, 106–7
    of a device, 29–30, 82–3, 309
    of a message, 72
    of a virtual device, 289
    real, 103, 312
    virtual, 102, 103–4, 111–2, 311–2
address space, 282, 304, 305, 313, 315,
    320, 325

address translation, dynamic, 103–15,
    282, 284, 311
addressing, 200, 309
    cursor, 202
    relative, 83, 101
agent process, see process, agent
algorithm
    banker's algorithm, 75–6
    placement, see placement algorithms
    scheduling, see scheduling algorithms
allocation
    of data resources (in MVS/JES3), 328
    of primary storage, 59–64
        in CP/M, 159–61
        in TPF/II, 264
        in Unix, 236, 241
    partial allocation and deadlock, 73–5
    strategy, 133
    unit (AU), see sector
Amdahl 470, 211, 278, 304
anticipatory fetch, see fetch, anticipatory
apparent storage, see storage, virtual
architecture, 14, 24–5, 31, 34, 142, 178,
    179, 186, 203, 263, 273, 274, 336
    extended (IBM large mainframe), 305,
        308–10
    von Neumann, 10–11, 126
archiving, 78, 90
argument, 212, 227, 262
arithmetic operation, see operation,
    arithmetic
Arpanet, 143
artificial contiguity, 102
assembler, 14, 321
assembly language, see language,
    assembly
associative memory, see memory,
    associative
asynchronous I/O, see I/O, asynchronous
asynchronous transfer, see transfer,
    asynchronous
asynchronous transmission, see
    transmission, asynchronous
Atlas, 98
atomicity, failure, see failure, atomicity
auxiliary storage, see storage, auxiliary

359

Index

availability, 18, 247, 274, 309
  of TPF/II, 250–1
average load, *see* load, average

BASIC, 209
bdevsw table, *see* control blocks and tables
BDOS (Basic Disk Operating System)
  of CP/M, 157, 159, 162–4
  of MS-DOS/PC-DOS, 172
BIOS (basic input/output system)
  of CP/M, 157, 159, 208
  of MS-DOS/PC-DOS, 172
  of p-System, 197–8, 203, 208
BOS (early IBM operating system), 51
BSD, *see* Unix, BSD
background processing, *see* processing, background
base address, *see* address, base
base register, *see* register, base
basic direct access method, *see* access method, basic direct
basic sequential access method, *see* access method, basic sequential
batch processing system, **56**, 80, 87, 122
Bell Laboratories, 211, 243
best-fit, *see* placement algorithms, best-fit
binary file, *see* file, binary
binding time, **82–3**
bit map, *see* bit matrix
bit matrix, 162–3, 262
block
  devices, *see* devices, block-structured *and also* sector
  files, 159, 220–1, 225
    indirect block in Unix, 220–2
  processes, 166, 232, 234, 288
block map table, *see* page table
boot time, 200
booting procedure(s), 220
bootstrap, 171, 172, 187, 208, 252
  in MVS, 317
bounds register, *see* register, bounds
Bowles, Ken, 179
Brinch-Hansen, Per, 87
bucket, *see* sector
buffer, 25, **33**, **40–1**, 54, 55–6, **71–2**, 214, 225, 257, 318–9
  cost of a buffer, 72
  size of a buffer, 72
  translation lookaside, *see* memory, cache
Burks, A.W., 9–10
Burroughs, 50, 98
byte-sex, 195, **196**, 205

C, 211, 288, 239–40
CCP (console command processor – CP/M), 157–9
cdevsw table, *see* control blocks and tables
CMS, 259, 285, 293, **295–6**, 302

COBOL, 18, 40, 336
CP (Control Program of VM), *see* VM, CP
CP/M, 59, **157–69**, 170, 198, 208, *see also* MP/M
CP/M-80, 157, 159, 171
CP/M-86, 157, 159–61, 170
CP/Net, 164, 167–9
CPU bound, 54, 137, 198, 235, 288
cpu loop program (TPF/II), 254–5
cache memory, *see* memory, cache
call
  procedure call, 145
  remote procedure call, **144–5**
  supervisor call, 255
  system call, 166, 224, 232
    exec, 233, 236
    exit, 234, 237
    fork, 233, 236
    wait, 234
    wakeup, 238
capacity, 125, 142, 147, 150, 254, 322
catalog, 77
channel
  data, 25, 29–32, 33, 54, 133, 249, 292–3, 309–10, 314, 322
  dedicated, 292–3
  program, *see* program, channel
checkpoint, **270**, 324–5
circular waiting, 74
client/server network model, 203
cluster, *see* sector
code, *see* program
code generators, 180
code pool, in p-System, 191, 192, 196, 199, 201, 202
cold start, *see* bootstrap
command
  built-in (CP/M), 157–8
  command-driven interface, *see* interface, command-driven
  command file, 213–4
  external and internal (MS/PC-DOS), 171
  in MVS/TSO, 320
  in the p-System, 182–6
  in Unix, 212–5
  in VM/CMS, 296
command language, in Unix, 212–5
  command language interpreter, 226
  command processor (in MVS/TSO), 321
communication task (in MVS), 317
communications, 143–6, 263
  access methods, *see* access methods
  data communications, 274, 308, 319
  interprocess (IPC), **72**, **144–5**
    in Unix, 237–8, 239, 242
  interprocessor, 288, 297
  inter-system communications in VM, 287, **296–300**
  inter-user, 206
communications control program (CCP) in TPF/II, 263–4
communications controller, 319

Index

communications processor, **144**
communications subsystem, **144**
compact files on disk, 187
compact processes in primary storage, **62–3**
compatibility, 49, 50, 178, 276, 304, 307, 308, 320
compiler, 19, 191, 321
  optimizing compiler, 93
  quick-and-dirty compiler, 93
  vectorizing compiler, 133
compress (space in a file), *see* compact files
computation bound, *see* CPU bound
computer, 123–4, 130, 133
  satellite, 18, 25–6
  sharing a, **54–6**
  system, **3–4**, 20, 119–20, 132
concentrator, 248, 252, 267, 273
concurrency, 53, 67–9, 79, 83, 94, 133, 141, 145, 150, 180, 191
  and security, 332
configuration, 165, 199, **251**, 252, 292, 301, 305, 317, 325
conflict, 81–2, 139, 309
  conflict resolution, 81, 138–9
console, 280, 292, 317
content-addressable memory, *see* memory, associative
contention, 139, 140
context, **34**
  kernel context or mode, *see* system *below*
  problem context
    in Unix, 232–3, 237
    in VM, 281
  system context, 232–3
    in Unix, 237–8
    in VM, 281
  user context or mode, *see* problem *above*
context switching, **34–5**, 55–6, 199, 232, 234–5
  in VM, 293–4
contiguity, artificial, *see* artificial contiguity
control blocks and tables, **36**, 69, 257, 314, 319, 321
  bdevsw, in Unix, **224**, 225–6
  cdevsw, in Unix, **224**, 226
  ECB (entry control block), in TPF/II, 253, 259
  FAT (file allocation table), in MS-DOS/PC-DOS, 175–6
  FCB (file control block), in CP/M, 161–4
  i-node table, in Unix, 223
  I/O control block, in TPF/II, 260
  per process data area, in Unix, *see* PPDA
  PPDA, in Unix, 223, **229**
  process control block (PCB), **35–6**, 166, 229
  process descriptor, in MP/M, 166–7

control blocks and tables (*cont'd*)
  process table, in Unix, 229, 238
  routing control parameter list, in TPF/II, 253
  shadow tables (VM), 286
  system file table, in Unix, 222–3
  task I/O table (TIOT), 35
  text table, in Unix, 230–1
  unit control block (UCB), 35
  user structure, in Unix, *see* PPDA *above*
control program, *see* VM, CP
control unit, 265
  transmission control, 292, 297
controller, peripheral, 29
costs
  of a computer system, 91–2, 178, 307
  of hardware, 96, 150
  of I/O, 39
  of program development, 307
  of software, 96–7, 300
coupling
  data, **126**, 127, 137
  loose, 127
  tight, 127
Cray-1, 29
critical region, **65–6**, 70–1
critical section, *see* critical region

DAT, *see* address translation, dynamic
DBMS, *see* database management system
DOS/360, 51
DOS/VSE, 278, 286, 287
data, 3, 18, 38–9, 76–8, 118–9, 126, 173, 230, 250, 260, 261, 331
  in distributed systems, 138
  in early systems, 19–22
  global data in Pascal, 191–2
  integrity of data, *see* integrity
  in multiprocessing systems, 135–6, 143
  in multiprogramming systems, 76–8, 79–80
  read-only data, 284
  in Unix, 227
data channel, *see* channel, data
data communications, *see* communications
data coupling, *see* coupling, data
data fetch, *see* fetch, data
Data General Eclipse, 29
data management, in MVS, 318–9
data protection, 136
data reduction, 270
data sharing, 124
data-processing system, 22
database, 78, 100, **118–9**, 168, 202, 206, 239, 240, 250–1, 253, 260, 261, 263, 265, 270, 273, 274, 308
database management system (DBMS), **118–9**, 202, 206, 207
database system, **118–9**
dataset
  for files, *see* file
  for transmission equipment, *see* modem

deadline scheduling, *see* scheduling, deadline
deadlock, **66–7**, 70, **73–6**
   deadlock prevention, 74, 136, 137
deadly embrace, *see* deadlock
DEC system-20, 208
dedicated
   channel, *see* channel, dedicated
   transmission line, *see* transmission, dedicated line
degradation, graceful, **139**
degree of multiprogramming, *see* multiprogramming, degree of
Deltamatic, 248
demand fetch, *see* fetch, demand
descriptor of a process, in MP/M, *see* control blocks and tables
device
   activity, 322
   address, *see* address, of a device
   block-structured, in p-System, 186
   dedicated, 289
   independence, **82**
   I/O, 21, 57, 138, 224, 239, 280
   interactive, 186
   logical, in CP/M, 164–5
   management, 228, 327
   in MVS, 314
   output, 3, 16, 17, 21, 144
   in the p-System, 201–2
   peripheral, 29, 165, 168, 197, 224
   virtual, 281
   write-only, 186
device driver, *see* driver, device
Digital Research, 157, 165
Dijkstra, E., 75
direct access, *see* access methods, direct
directory
   in CP/M, 159, 163
   home, **215**
   in MS-DOS/PC-DOS, 175
   in p-System, 186–7
   root, **215**
   in Unix, 215–6, 217–8, 220
   user, **78**, 215–7
   in VM, 289, 295
discipline, **264**
disk, 20, **38**, 42–3, 93, 98, 104, 119, 159, 161–4, 165, 174, 290, 295
   drive, 224
   hard-sectored, **38–9**
   pack, **38**, 261, 262
   RAM, 199–200
   soft-sectored, **39**
dispatcher, in MP/M, 166
distributed computation network, *see* network, distributed computation
distributed operating system, *see* operating system, distributed
distributed systems, 124
downtime, **250**

driver
   device, **46**, 159, 165, 224–5, 241
   line, 297
drum, 20, 98, 104
dump, 279, 322, *see also* checkpoint
dynamic address translation (DAT), *see* address translation, dynamic
dynamic priority, *see* priority, dynamic

ENIAC, 17
emulator, **50**, 178, 301
   p-machine emulator, *see* p-machine emulator
end-of-life requirement, 271
entry, in TPF/II, **253**, 254–5
error detection, 308
error recovery, 247, 293, 307, 314, 329–31
Ethernet, 203
exclusion, mutual, **64–5**, **69–71**, 74, 91, 138, 312
exec, *see* call, system
executive processor, *see* processor, executive
exit, *see* call, system

FAT (file allocation table), *see* control blocks and tables
FDOS (functional disk operating system – CP/M), 159
FIFO, *see* placement algorithms
fail-safe, **134–5**
fail-soft, **135**
failure, 133, **134–5**, 270, 276, 282, 298, 307, 324, 325, 329–31, *see also* fault
   atomicity, **135**, 138
fairness, 81
fallback, **247**, 252
fault, **134**, 307, *see also* failure
   handler, 193, 201
   in p-System, 192–3
fault-tolerant, **135**, 152
fetch
   anticipatory, 116
   data, 29
   demand, **115–6**
   page, 107
   strategy, **115–6**
fetch–execute cycle, **17–18**, 34, 67–8, 126
file, 20, 21, 39, 76–8, 119, 138, 158, 159, 161–4, 213
   efficiency considerations, 92–3
   representation in catalog or directory, 78
file allocation table (FAT), *see* control blocks and tables
file binary, in Unix, **218**
file control block (FCB), *see* control blocks and tables
file descriptor, 222, 223
file index, *see* volume table of contents
file management, 41, **42–6**, 77–8, 89–90, 94

Index

file organization
  in CP/M, 161–4
  in MS-DOS/PC-DOS, 174–6
  in MVS, 318–9
  in p-System, 186–90
  in TPF/II, 260–2
  in Unix, 215–9, 240
  in VM/CMS, 295
file protection, in Unix, 218–9
file sharing, in Unix, 218–9
file system, *see* file organization
file special, in Unix, **218**, 219, 224
filter, 215–6, 227
firmware, 150
flag, *see* argument
Flynn, Michael J., classification of multiprocessors, 126–7
Focus Computer (Germany), 208–9
foreground processing, *see* processing, foreground
fork, *see* call, system
FORTRAN, 18, 132, 133, 209, 336
fragmentation
  of primary storage, **62**, 97
  of secondary storage, 187, 222
frame, page, **98**, 103, 104, 106–7, 116, 315
full-duplex working, **264**, 268

GEORGE3, 242
Goldstine, H.H., 9–10, 17

handshaking, 287, 298
hard-coded parameters, 165
hard-sectored disk, *see* disk, hard-sectored
hardware, 4–5, 8, 17, 18, 67, 112, 113, 136, 139, 143, 149, 165, 264, 280, 308, 335
  cost of hardware, *see* costs
hardware interrupts, *see* interrupts
hardware redundancy, 123, **133**–5, 276, 277
high-level language, *see* language, high-level
high-level scheduling, *see* scheduling, high-level
highest-resource-ratio-next scheduling, *see* scheduling algorithms
home directory, *see* directory, home
host, **144**, 145, 146
hub go-head polling, *see* polling, hub
hub polling, *see* polling, hub
hypervisor, in TPF/II, 271–2, 276

i-list, **220**
i-node, **220**, 225
i-number, **220**
I/O, 40
  asynchronous, **54**
  block-structured, 225
  buffered, concurrent, 53
  character, 225–6
  communications, 263

I/O (*cont'd*)
  cost of, *see* costs
  management, in MVS, 314–5, 318–9
  virtual, 292–4
I/O bound, 198, 235
I/O port, 20
I/O processor, *see* channel, data
iAPX86, *see* Intel
iAPX88, *see* Intel
IBM, 118, 170, 248, 249, 274, 308, 321, 323
  influence on computer and software design, 48–52
IBM PC, 170, 244
IBM 360/370, *see* System/360, System/370
IBM 303X, (3031, 3032, 3033), 278, 305
IBM 308X, 249, 278, 309, 310
IBM 3090 Vector Facility, 127, 249, 278, 309
IBM 3350 disk drive, 251, 290
ICL DAP, 127
IP (instruction pointer), *see* registers, special-purpose
IPL (initial program load), *see* bootstrap
IPL volume (MVS), 317
IPCS (interactive problem control system), *see* VM, IPCS
ISAM (indexed sequential access method), *see* access method, indexed sequential
indexed sequential access method, *see* access method, indexed sequential
indirect block, *see* block, files
initialization, 16
initiators, in MVS, 325–7
input
  device, *see* device, input
  standard input, in Unix, 213, 214
instruction
  privileged, **272**, 281, 286, 301, 332
  separation from data of, 79, 126, 230
  sequence, 132
  sharing, 124
instruction pointer (IP), *see* registers, special-purpose
instruction set, 13, 14, 49, 276
integrity, **88**–**91**, 94, 118, 285
  of circuits and polling, 263, 266
  of data, 90–1, 324
  of systems, 331–3
  of work, 324
Intel
  8046, 211
  8080, 157, 170, 180, 208
  8085, 170
  8086, 159
  iAPX86, 172
  iAPX88, 172
interactive processing system, *see* time-sharing system
inter-block gap, *see* tape, magnetic
interface
  command-driven, 171

interface (cont'd)
  menu-driven, 181–6
  user, 202
  in Unix, 241–2
intermediate-level scheduling, see
  scheduling, intermediate-level
interpreter, 180, 196
  command language, 118
interpreting, 180
interprocess communication (IPC), see
  communication, interprocess
interrupts, 26, **31**, **33–5**, 54, 87, 130, 137,
  138, 166, 237, 255, 272, 286, 293
  clock, 232
  driven system, 31, 32, 310
  handler, **34–5**, 56, 172, 255
  hardware, 31, 310
  missing, 330–1
  program, 281
  software, 31, 310
  terminal, 283
  vector, **35**, 172
interval timer, see timer, interval

JES (Job Entry Subsystem), 138, 139, 297,
  307, 323–8
JES2, 324–7
JES3, 324, 327–9
job, 18, 323
job-control language, see language,
  job-control
job scheduling, see scheduling, high-level
Job Entry Subsystem, see JES

kernel, 153, 201, 224, 225, 226, 228–35,
  253–5, 285, 295, 309
  in MVS, 312–6
key
  for ordering data, 43–4
  for storage protection, see storage
    protection key

LAN (local area network), see network,
  local area
LISP, 18, 150
LSI-11, 180
label
  volume, **42**, 174
  volume identification, **42**
language
  assembly, 101, 165, 211, 228, 277
  command, **118**, 226–8, 279
  high-level, 18–19
  job control, 18, 138, 307, 320
  machine, 11–16, 19, 21, 180, 198
  programming, 132
latency, see rotational delay
least frequently used, see replacement
  strategies
least recently used, see replacement
  strategies

level of multiprogramming, see
  multiprogramming, level
Liaison (extension of the UCSD
  p-System), 202–7
linkage editor, 321
linked list, **192**, 222
load, 270
  average, **122**, 123
  balancing, 136, 138
  peak, **122**, 123, 125, 126, 271, 308
  work, **80**, 93, 122, 126, 137, 153, 308
    313–4, 322
loader, 15, 321
loading, of programs, 82
local area network (LAN), see network,
  local area
locality, property of, see property of
  locality
locality, spatial, see property of locality
locality, temporal, see property of locality
locks, 91, 288, 332
  file, in Unix, 240
  spin, 288–9
  storage allocation, 314
  suspend, 288, 289
  system, 289
lockout, **139**
log in/on, 215, 321, 325, 333
logic operation, see operation, logic
logical operation, see operation, logic
logical record, see record, logical
look-ahead processing, see pipelining
loosely coupled multiprocessing, see
  multiprocessing, loosely coupled
low-level scheduling, see scheduling,
  low-level

MASCOT, 150
MERT, 239
MIMD, **127**
Minix, 244
MISD, **127**
MP/M, 165–7, see also CP/M
MP/M-86, 165–7, 168
MS-DOS, **170–7**, 185, 208
MVS, see OS
machine code, see language, machine
machine language, see language, machine
magnetic disk, see disk
magnetic media, see disk *and* tape
magnetic tape, see tape, magnetic
mailbox, 28, 31–2
main memory, see storage, primary
main storage, see storage, primary
mask, **34**
meantime between failures (MTBF), see
  reliability
memory, see storage
memory, associative, **107–9**, 112, 114
memory, cache, 25, 222, 311
memory, content addressable, see
  memory, associative

Index

memory, read-only (ROM), 49
message-driven system, 246, 252
microcode, 49–50, 150, 308
Microcomputer Applications Associates, 157
microinstruction, 51
Microsoft, 170
mode, *see* context
modem, 248
Modula-2, 209
Motorola 68000, 211
multicomputer systems, 122–47
Multics, 211, 242
multiple instruction multiple data, *see* MIMD
multiple instruction single data, *see* MISD
multiprocessing, 122–47, 288
  loosely coupled, 127–8, 327
  symmetric independent, 124–6
  symmetrical, 139–40
  systems, 122–47
  tightly coupled, 128–9
multiprocessor system, 126
multiprocessors
  in MVS, 309, 310, 312
  in TPF/II, 265, 273
  in VM/SP, 301
multiprogramming, 79, 97, 119, 286, 312
  degree of, *see* level *below*
  level, 252, 287, 289, 292, 314
  systems, 48–94, 114, 133, 136, 137, 166, 229, 292
multiservers, 133, 142
multitasking, in MP/M, 167
mutual exclusion, *see* exclusion, mutual

NCI of Vancouver, 208
NCP (network control program), *see* network control program
networks and networking, 143–4, 146, 152, 164, 168, 267, 274, 277
  applications, 145–6
  distributed computation, 145–6
  in CP/M (CP/NET), 164, 167–9, 302
  in the p-System (Liaison), 202–7
  local area (LAN), 127, 146
  remote-communications, 145, 297
  resource-sharing, 145, 169
network communications controller, 267
network control program (NCP), 267
network operating system, *see* operating system, network
networked systems, 124
nodes, 144, 168
non-stop computing, 134
not used recently, *see* replacement strategies
nucleus, *see* kernel

OS (IBM's mainframe operating system) family, 118, 304, 306–7
OS/360, 50–1

OS (*cont'd*)
OS-ASP, 279
OS/MFT, 60, 279, 285, 304, 320
OS/MVT, 62, 63, 279, 304, 305, 307, 320, 323
OS/PCP, 59, 279, 304
OS/VS, 272
OS/VS1, 286, 287, 304
OS/VS2, 138, 276, 279, 286, 292, 304–33
MVS, 22, 41, 118, 265, 270, 278, 279, 288
MVS/XA, 304, 314, 315–6
MVS/370, 304, 309, 315
object program, *see* program, object
occam, 132, 150
Omninet, 203
Open University, The, 208
operating system, 4–5, 25, 36, 96, 133, 137, 138, 146, 149–50, 152–4, 172, 178, 191, 201, 232, 273, 278, 282, 285, 295, 322, 336
  distributed, 138, 146
  multiprocessing, 136–9
  network, 146, 167–9
operation
  arithmetic, 6
  logic, 6–7
organization, of a file, 20, 45–6
output
  device, *see* device, output
  standard output, in Unix, 213, 214
overhead
  of communications, 147
  of context-switching, 199
  of forecasting, 116
  of input-output operations, 58
  of paging, 287, 307
  of polling, 265, 267
  of preemptive scheduling, 74
  of processing, 271
  of routing, 141
  of space, 222
  of space re-allocation, 62–3
  of software, 96–7, 119, 138, 139, 147, 150, 306
  of swapping, 100
  of transmission, 267
overlay, 159, 198, 233
preplanned, 100

p-code, 178, 179, 191, 193, 196, 198–9, 203
  execution of a p-code program, 193–6
p-machine, 178, 209, 276
p-machine architecture, 190–3
p-machine emulator, 178, 179, 190–3, 196–8
p-System, 178–210, 305
p-world, 209
PAC (program address counter), *see* registers, special-purpose
PARS (programmed airline reservation system), 248, 249, 277

Index

PC (program counter), *see* registers, special-purpose
PCB (program control block), *see* control blocks and tables
PC-DOS, **170–7**
PCM (plug-compatible mainframe), 52
PDP-7, 211
PDP-11, 180, 211
PL/M, 157, 165
PME, *see* p-machine emulator
PPDA, *see* control blocks and tables
PROLOG, 150, 209
PSW (program status word), *see* registers, special-purpose
page, paging, **98–9**, 104, 105–17, 283, 285, 311, 322
  data sets, in MVS, 315
  fault, 107, 287, 315
page replacement, *see* replacement strategies
page table, 106, 108, 111–12
Panamac, 248
parallel algorithm, 132
parallelism, 132–2, 133, 136, 150, *see also* concurrency
parameter, *see* argument
parity, 90
partition, fixed, 59–60
partitioned data set (file), 318, 321
Pascal, 179, 180–1, 190–1, 200
  compiler, 180, 191
  concurrent, 150
password, 90
peak load, *see* load, peak
per process data area (PPDA), *see* control blocks and tables
performance, 17, 22, 24–5, 91–3, 122, 124, 125, 300, 306, 307, 322
  and fetch strategy in virtual storage systems, 116
  in multiprocessing systems, 140–3, 147
  in the p-System, 178, 198, 199
  and price, **97**
  in TPF/II, 265, 273, 274
  in VM, 286, 287, 300–1
performance measures
  monitoring, **91–3**
  response time, **81**, 283, 300, 313
  throughput, **81**, 124, 125, 136, 142, 198, 287, 313
  transactions per second, 251
  turn-around time, **81**
peripherals, *see* device, peripheral
peripheral controller, *see* controller, peripheral
peripheral processor, *see* channel, data
Petri net, 151
physical record, *see* record, physical *and* block, files
pipe, **145**, 214–5, 227
  remote pipe and procedure, **145**
pipelining, **17–18**, **24–5**

placement algorithms or strategies, **63–4**, 104, 111, 116
  best-fit, **64**, 111
  first-fit, **64**, 111, 236
  worst-fit, **64**, 111, 187
polling, **26–8**, **31**, 252, 253, 254, 263, 265–7, 268, 273
  hub go-ahead, **265–7**
  hub polling, *see* hub go-ahead *above*
  roll call, **265**
  round-robin, 265, 266
pool, code, in p-System, *see* code pool
pool records (TPF/II), *see* record, pool
portability
  in CP/M, 165
  in MS-DOS/PC-DOS, 177
  in p-System, 178, 196, 197, 200–1, 209–10
  in Unix, 240
preemption, **55**, 134, 288, 310
primary storage, *see* storage, primary
priority, **69**, 81, 85–6, 166, 232, 235, 255, 282, 283, 292, 313, 315, 325
  dynamic, **86**
  rule, 71
  static, **86**
privileged instruction, *see* instruction, privileged
problem programming language, *see* language, high-level
problem state, *see* context, problem
procedure call, *see* call, procedure
process, **3**, 4, 21, 34–5, **36–7**, 87, 98, 100, 102, 104, 119, 141, 203, 223, 229, 254
  agent, 146
  behavior in time, 68–9
  binding
    to an address, 102–3
    to a device, 83
  creation of, in Unix, 233–4
  in Pascal, 191
  interface to data, 38–40
  in swapping time-sharing, 57–8
process identifier or identity (pid), 233
process management
  in CP/M, 166–7
  in MVS, 305
  in TPF/II, 254
  in Unix, 228, 229–31, 234–5
process switching, *see* context switching
process control block (PCB), *see* control blocks and tables
process identity, *see* control blocks and tables
process table, *see* control blocks and tables
processing
  background, **236–7**, 320
  foreground, **320**
  power, increase in, 308
processor, **3**, 8, 16, 122, 123, 124, 126,

Index

processor (cont'd)
  129, 130, 131, 132, 133, 138, 139, 140, 168, 283, 293, 322
  attached processor (AP), see System/370
  distributed array, 127
  executive, **139**
  global, in MVS/JES3, 327
  local, in MVS/JES3, 327
  optimum use of, 81
  peripheral, see channel, data redundancy, 247
  temporal sharing of, 54–5, 232
processor bound, see CPU bound
program, **3**, **4**, **18**, **19**, **20**, **29**, **36**, 88, 99–100, 101, 105, 116, 117, 173, 196, 201, 223, 229
  channel program, **31**, 319
  consistency requirement in, 69
  distributed program, 302
  efficiency of, 92–3
  I/O program, 29, 30, **31**
  machine-language program, see object below
  object program, **14**, 82, 93, 102
  protection of, 89
  re-entrant program, 82, **83–4**, **102**, 137, 139, 229–30, 253, 260, 284
  relocatable program, **82**, 101, 253
  representation in catalog/directory, 78
  source program, **14**, 82–3
  utility program, **50**, 158, 187, 201, 228, 241, 242, 263, 307, 321
program development, 271
program address counter (PAC), see registers, special-purpose
program control block (PCB), see control blocks and tables
program counter (PC), see registers, special-purpose
program status word (PSW), see registers, special-purpose
propagation delay, 265
property of locality, **101**
  spatial, **101**
  temporal, **101**
protection, of a system, **88–91**, 94, see also integrity
protocol, see discipline

quantum, see time-slice
queue, 60–1, 66, 142, 167, 225–6, 253, 254, 259, 264, 300, 323, 324
  device queue, 260
queued sequential access method, see access method, queued sequential

RAM disk, see disk, RAM
RJE, see remote job entry
RSCS (remote spooling and communications supervisor), see VM, RSCS
RSP, see run-time support package

random access, see access, direct and access method, direct
reader (process), 78
real storage, see storage, real
real-time, environment, 20, 22, 87, 123, 165, 239, 246, 252, 267, 270, 277
record, 20, 21, **38–40**, 119, 162, 249, 261–3
  file header, 43
  logical, **40**, 161
  physical, **40**, 161
  pool, in TPF/II, **258–9**, 262–3
recovery, see error recovery
region, variable, 62–3
registers, 13, 16, 102, 191, 193
  base, **101–2**
  bounds, **89**
  special-purpose, **34**
    IP, **34**
    PAC, **34**
    page table origin register, 113–4
    PC, **34**, 67, 232–3
    PSW, **34**, 37, 310
    STOR, 113–4
relative addressing, see addressing, relative
release, of software, **252**, 281
reliability, 17, 123, **134–5**, 136, 138, 147, 178, 272, 273, 277, 307, 309
  mean time between failures (MTBF), a measure of, 16
relocatable program, see program, relocatable
remote communications network, see network, remote communications
remote job entry (RJE), **145**
replacement at random, see replacement strategies
replacement strategies, **116–7**, 314
  least frequently used, **116**
  least recently used, **116**
  not used recently, **116–7**
  replacement at random, **116**
resources, 131, 133, 153, 169, 306, 312, 313–4
  allocation of, 136
  and concurrency, 69–71
  data as a resource, 79
  data storage as a resource, 43
  and deadlock, 73–4
  and mutual exclusion, 65, 70–1
  virtual resource, 283–90
resource network, see network, resource-sharing
resource requirements, 124
resource sharing, 54, 59, 125, 129, 144, 202, 242, 288
resource-sharing network, see network, resource-sharing
response time, see performance measures
Ritchie, Dennis, 211
roll call polling, see polling, roll call

rotational delay, 45
round-robin, *see* scheduling algorithms
run-time support package (RSP in p-System), 196–7, 198

SABER, SABRE, 248, 264, 274
SDLC (synchronous data link control), 267
SIMD (single instruction multiple data), *see* single instruction multiple data
SISD, *see* single instruction single data
SITA, 268, 269
SLC (synchronous link control), 268, 269
SNA, 264, 267
SNOBOL, 209
SVC (supervisor service call), *see* call, supervisor
safety, property of, 75
satellite computer, *see* computer, satellite
scheduler/scheduling, 5, 80–1, 85–8, 94, 137, 214, 234, 307
   deadline scheduling, 86, 328
   generalized main scheduling (MVS/JES3), 328
   high-level scheduling, **85**, 87, 323
   intermediate-level scheduling, **86**, 87
   in MVS, *see* system resources manager
   job scheduling, *see* high-level *above*
   log on scheduling in TSO, 321
   in MP/M, 166–7
   in MVS, 312–5, 324–9
   main device scheduling, in MVS/JES3, 327–8
   master scheduling in MVS, 317
   non-preemptive scheduling, 87
   and deadlock, 74
   preemptive scheduling, 74, 84
   in TPF/II, 255
scheduling algorithms, 85, 137, 288
   FIFO, **86**
   highest-resource-ratio next, 87
   round-robin, 56, **86**
   shortest-job-first, **86–7**
   shortest-remaining-time, 87
scratch pad, 84
secondary storage, *see* storage, secondary
sector (as an exact storage location for a record), 45, 162–3, 175–6, 186, 200
   hard sector, *see* disk, hard-sectored
   soft sector, *see* disk, soft-sectored
security, 332
   of data, 79–80, 118, 282
   in Unix, 238, 241
seek, **45**, 224
seek time, **45**, 200
segment
   combined with paging, **111–14**, 284
   in Pascal, 191, 193–4, 196, 200–1
   in virtual storage systems, **109–14**, 115, 116, 284, 295, 311
   segment table, 110–1, 286, 311

segment table origin register (STOR), *see* registers, special-purpose
semaphore, 65–**6**, 72–**3**, 191
   Boolean, 73
   counting, 73
separate executives, **138–9**
sequential access method, *see* access method, sequential
server, 168, 203
   disk, 204–5
   print, 204, 205–6
   semaphore, 204, 205
   single, **131**, 142
shell, 117–8, 120
   in Unix, 212–5, 223
shell programming, in Unix, 226–8
Shore, J.E., classification of multiprocessors, 127
shortest-job-first scheduling, *see* scheduling algorithms
shortest-remaining-time scheduling, *see* scheduling algorithms
signal, in Unix, 237
simulator, **50**, 178, 301
single server, *see* server, single
single instruction multiple data (SIMD), **126–7**
single instruction single data (SISD), **126**
slots (page), **98–9**, 103, 104, 106–7
soft-sectored disk, *see* sector, soft
software, 127, 139, 143, 150, 280, 308, 335, 336
   applications, 51, 89, 96–7
   costs of, *see* costs
   engineering, 52, 152
   interrupts, *see* interrupts
   quality, 51–2
   tools, 242–3
   systems software, 14–16, 18, 25, 89
   writing software, for Liaison network, 206–7
source program, *see* program, source
special file, *see* file, special
spooling, **167**, 205–6, 292, 297, 324
   area, 294
   file, 327
stable storage, *see* storage, stable
stack, **191**, 196, 199, 258–9
standard input (Unix), *see* input, standard
standard output (Unix), *see* output, standard
start
   cold, *see* bootstrap
   warm, **159**, 324
start–stop, *see* transmission, asynchronous
state, *see* context
state switching, *see* context switching
static priority, *see* priority, static
storage, 3, 13, 16, 18, 94, 122, 123, 124, 130, 168
   allocation, *see* allocation

Index   369

storage (cont'd)
  auxiliary, 21, 104, 117, 274, 315
    managing auxiliary storage, 41–2
      in MVS, 316
    direct access, 294
    global, 126, 129
    local, 126, 129
    main, see primary below
    management, in Unix, 240–1
  primary, 21, 59–64, 82, 98, 100, 101,
    115, 129, 135, 157, 158, 159, 162,
    168, 171, 172, 181, 191, 192, 198,
    199, 200, 224, 236–7, 239, 257–9,
    264, 284–5, 301, 308
    protection, 310–1, see also storage
      protection key
  real, 97–8, 103, 104, 105, 106–7, 111,
    116, 149, 285, 286, 287, 293, 295,
    298, 309, 314
    managing real storage, in MVS,
      315–6
  secondary, 21, 98–9, 118, 129, 135, 137,
    143–4, 181, 198, 220–2, 241, 276,
    289–90
  simulated, in VM, 280
  stable, 135
  virtual, 96–120, 284, 285–7, 293, 298,
    305, 309
    managing virtual storage, in MVS,
      316
  volatile, 200
storage protection key, 34, 89, 300, 332
store, see storage
store-and-forward, 297
Strachey, Christopher, 57
superblock, in Unix, 220
supervisor (MVS kernel), see kernel
swap
  area, 236, 322
  decision, 315
swapped in, 57, 191
swapped out, 57
swapper, 235
swapping, 97, 100, 199, 200, 236, 313–4,
  321
symmetric independent-multicomputer
  system, see multiprocessing systems
synchronous data link control (SDLC),
  see SDLC
synchronous link control (SLC), see SLC
synchronous transmission, see
  transmission, synchronous
synchrony, 69, 214, 267, see also time
System/360, 48–50, 248, 249, 304, 306–7,
  310
System/370, 111, 130, 211, 249, 278, 302,
  309, 310
  attached processor, 130, 288, 293, 301
  extended architecture, see architecture,
    extended
system, see system generation
system call, see call, system

system configuration, see configuration
system file table, Unix, see control blocks
  and tables
system generation, 252, 255, 313
system resources manager, in MVS,
  312–5
systems network architecture (SNA), see
  SNA
systems software, see software, systems

TOPS-20, 208
TOS (early IBM operating system), 51
TPF/II, 246–74, 276–8, 279, 301, 304, 305
TSO, 118, 279, 307, 320–1
table-driven system, 165
Tanenbaum, Andrew, 244
tape, 20
  magnetic, 20, 38, 39, 42–3, 92, 277
  inter-block gap on, 39
tape drive, 39, 92, 224, 290
telecommunications, see communications
test-bed, 277
testing operating systems, 281
Thompson, Ken, 211
throughput, see performance measures
tightly coupled multiprocessing, see
  multiprocessing, tightly coupled
time, 68–9, 133, 282, 283
  time-dependent behavior, 68, 87, 131–2
  time-independent behavior, 69, 132, 133
  time-sensitive applications, 308
  time-sharing (interactive) systems, 56–8,
    80, 86, 87, 94, 97, 100, 117, 118,
    119, 122, 235, 288, 305, 307, 320–1
  time-slice, 53, 56, 57, 86, 166, 232, 234,
    255, 283
timer
  interrupt, 31, 32, 55
  interval, 87
timing, 286
  delays, 286
transaction, 246, 274, 297, 298
  in MVS, 313, 314
  concurrent transaction, 298
transactions per second (measure of
  performance), 251
transfer, asynchronous, 298
transient program area (TPA), 157
transistor, 17
translation lookaside buffer, see memory,
  cache
transmission
  asynchronous, 268
  dedicated line, 265
  synchronous, 264
transmit by reference, 72
transmit by value, 72
turn-around time, see performance
  measures

UCSD p-System, see p-System
'unbundling', effects of, 51–2

uniprocessor, *see* processor
unit, in Pascal, 200–1, 203
University of California at Berkeley, 244
University of California at San Diego (UCSD), 179–80
Unix, 41, 62, 118, 145, 152, 171, 185, 208–9, **211–44**, 305
  BSD Unix, 232, 244
  Unix files, 21
user directory, *see* directory, user
user structure, Unix, *see* control blocks and tables
utility program, *see* program, utility
utilization, 38–43, 96, 122, 139, 315
  in critical systems, 123
  in multiprocessing systems, 141

VAX VMS, 208
VM or VM/SP, 152, 189, 271, 272, **276–302**, 305
  CMS, *see* CMS
  CP, 278, 279, 280, 283–7, 289, 290, 292–3, 294, 295, 297, 300
  IUCV, **298–300**
  IPCS (interactive problem control system), 279
  RSCS, 279, 293, **297**
  VMCF, **298**
VOS, 209
VSAM, *see* access method, virtual storage
VTOC, *see* volume table of contents
Versal (Sweden), 209
virtual, **97**
  address, *see* address, virtual
  computers, 153, 228
  machine, **280–2**
  storage, *see* storage, virtual
  storage access method (VSAM), *see* access method, virtual storage

volatile storage, *see* storage, volatile
Volition Systems, 209
volume, **38**, 39, 41–3, 77, 186, 187, 188–9, 200, 204–5, 207, 208, 219, 220
volume identification label, *see* label, volume identification
volume label, *see* label, volume
volume table of contents (VTOC), **42–3**, 78, 174–5, 290
von Neumann, John, 9–10, 17
von Neumann architecture, *see* architecture, von Neumann

wait, *see* call, system
wakeup, *see* call, system
warm start, *see* start, warm
Western Digital, 180, 209
  Pascal Microengine, 180, 209
work load, *see* load, work
work station, **203**
working set, **98–9**
worst-fit, *see* placement algorithm
writer (process), 78

Zilog Z80, 170, 180, 198, 208

70XX IBM series of computers, 49, 50
7074, 248
7080, 248
7090, 248
8080, *see* Intel

1400 IBM series of computers, 49, 50
360, *see* System/360
370, *see* System/370
303X, *see* IBM 303X
308X, *see* IBM 308X
3090, *see* IBM 3090